OUR INHERITANCE

THE FATHER'S GOOD PLEASURE

Dory Robertson

OUR INHERITANCE

THE FATHER'S GOOD PLEASURE

REDEMPTION
AT ITS SOURCE.

1. God created our world

2. Then He created man Because He wants a family.

3. To walk and talk with Him - To be our Father.

4. He gave us His Word so we could know Him

5. And learn to worship Him

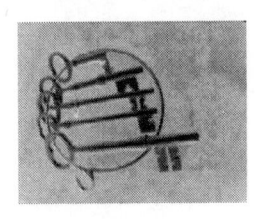

6. He gives us the keys to His kingdom.

7. That we may live with Him forever
❤❤❤

And God said, *Let us make man in our image, after our likeness. For you are the temple of the living God; as God has said, I will dwell in them, and walk in them; and I will be their God and they shall be my people.*

For as we have many members in one body, and all members have not the same function, so we, being many, are one body in Christ, and every one members one of another".

Dedicated to The Body of Christ
That Living Organism
Though Whom Jesus
Shows Forth His Love
to The World.

God has brought us out of darkness into the Kingdom of His dear Son. The battles we fight are prevalent in the Body of Christ.

"*No temptation has overtaken you except such as is common to man*".

To you, the Lord would say:
"*Ye shall not need to fight in this battle; set yourselves, stand ye still, [stand in the position of faith] and see the salvation of the Lord with you. Be not afraid nor dismayed by reason of this great multitude; for the battle is not yours but God's*".
[2 Chronicles 20:15&17].

So teach and instruct one another with the Psalms and with festive praises, and with prophetic songs given to you spontaneously by the Spirit, so sing to God with all your hearts!
Col 4.16   The Passion Translation by Dr. Brian Simmons.

❤

Scriptures are taken from
The King James Version, Public Domain
The New King James version,
copyright 1982, Thomas Nelson Inc.,

The Amplified Bible, Old Testament Copyright 1987,
by the Zondervan Corporation.
The Amplified New Testament Copyright 1958, 1967
by the Lockman Foundation.
The Passion Translation [TPT] by Brian Simmons

Also I refer to 'The Restoration of Original Sacred Name Bible' [herein known as ROSNB]. Any other version is identified.

All Scripture used by permission. All emphasis is by the author except in the Amplified Bible verses.

OUR INHERITANCE - THE FATHER'S GOOD PLEASURE
Written in 1987   Just now being published in 2022
Dory Robertson, Ocala, Florida

Poetry in this book, taken from my book 'Songs of My Life, Poetry and Prose' from the heart of God, Image on Page 126 is from my dear friend Marybeth Karsteadt. She is now dancing with the Lord of her life.

Praise the Lord! For it is good
to sing praises to our God   [Ps 147:1]

These poems were written over the course of many years as I learned to listen to God's voice. He spoke of His love and grace, and showed me the true meaning of what He did for us. In this book 'Poetry and Prose' He not only expresses how He feels about His chosen ones, but also gives me opportunity to express how much I love Him.
   1 Jn 4.19   *We love Him because He first loved us.*
Please remember most of this book was written in 1987.
I was healed and delivered of what I wrote here, and it continues. Thank You Jesus. And as I am revising it, I am adding some things I learned since then. Of course I have written 21 other books since then also listed in the back.
   And all the glory for them goes to my Lord, Jesus.

CONTENTS	PAGE
Our Inheritance	2
Love of Jesus-The Beginning	3
His Love Overcomes Our Enemies	26
His Love and Ours	50
My Foundation	71
His Foundation	90
Gift of Life	114
Fear of Man	138
Fear of Men	164
Fear of Losing Control	186
Victory over Fear	204
Man of Sin	223
Two Witnesses	242
Who is the 144,000	244
Trusting in God	248
Trust Scripture	274
Your Destiny	277
Hope, Expectations, Disappointments	279
Deceitful heart	304
Offenses	308
The Spirit and the Soul	339
Law to Grace	354
Obedience and The Will of God	373
Perfect Law of Liberty	392
What Happened at the Cross	398
Greatest Offence	403
Jesus The Son of Man	405
Bride of Christ	408
Our House/ Our Home	421
Research	422
Those in Christ	425
Epilogue	430

These chapters all have a study guide
and Scripture references.

❤

Dory Robertson
is an Ordained Minister
of Pastoral Counseling
And Author of 22 Books.

Jesus went back with me through time, and I saw the truth. Even though I was starved to receive His life, I was incapable of bringing this truth about myself, out into the light. I was a throw-away; of no value to anyone. No one was really interested in what I had to say or what was happening to me. The best I could invent for myself was wishing I was someone else. I was a phony, a counterfeit, and I did not belong. Oh God, my whole life has been living on the edge of inconsistency. How can it possibly be any different.

But when God opened my eyes to understand Chapter two of Ephesians; that I was no longer a stranger and a wanderer, the door of the kingdom exploded off its hinges and I ran through.

> I knew then that I belonged.

I am aware that there are many others who have gone through similar experiences, but know that God loves you so much He sent His Son to the Cross to change all that. When we commit our lives to God, He is committed and covenanted to bring to wholeness that which has been broken and devastated in our former life, B.C., or before Christ comes into our life. He is looking for responding trust to a passionate love poured out from the Father's heart.

Redemption is not only for eternity - God wants to redeem each and every area of our life, now. He wants to heal our brokenness, to bind up our wounds, heal our broken heart; change us, our motives, attitudes, our ways of thinking and doing, into the image of Christ. Changed - transformed - metamorphosis - like a caterpillar into a gorgeous butterfly. Changed and Becoming -

Embarking on the adventure of a lifetime,
Discovering the riches of the kingdom of God,
Getting to know the Creator of the universe,
Because His desire is to be known,
And knowing who you are in Christ ❤

OUR INHERITANCE

1John 3.1 Behold what manner of love the Father has bestowed on us, that we should be called children of God! Therefore the world does not know us, because it did not know Him. Beloved, now we are children of God; and it has not yet been revealed what we shall be, but we know that when He is revealed, we shall be like Him, for we shall see Him as He is. And everyone who has this hope in Him purifies himself, just as He is pure.

But the anointing which you have received from Him abides in you, and you do not need that anyone teach you; but as the same anointing teaches you concerning all things, and is true, and is not a lie, and just as it has taught you, you will abide in Him. By this you know the Spirit of God, Every spirit that confesses that Jesus Christ has come in the flesh is of God.

1 John 4.2 1 John 4.10 In this is love, not that we loved God, but that He loved us and sent His Son to be the propitiation for our sins. Whoever confesses that Jesus is the Son of God, God abides in him, and he in God. We must know that God created man to be His temple.

1 John 5.20 We know that the Son of God has come and has given us an understanding, that we may know Him who is true; and we are in Him who is true, in His Son Jesus Christ. This is the true God and eternal life. That which we have seen and heard we declare to you, that you also may have fellowship with us; and truly our fellowship is with the Father and His Son Jesus Christ. And these things we write to you that your joy may be full.

For whatever is born of God overcomes the world. And this is the victory that has overcome the world — our faith. Who is he who overcomes the world, but he who believes that Jesus is the Son of God. Love has been perfected among us in this that we may have boldness in the day of judgment; because as He is, so are we in this world.

John 14:23 If anyone loves Me, he will keep My word; and My Father will love him, and We will come to him and make Our home with him [Eph 2.22].

SO WHY AND HOW DID THIS ALL COME ABOUT?

❤

THE LOVE OF JESUS   The Beginning.

"And God said, Let us make man in our own image, after our likeness; so God created man, in the image of God created He him, male and female, and God blessed them".
Genesis, the Book of Beginnings, tells us what God did and how He did it: the heavens and the earth teeming with life that was good in God's sight; and with the creation of man,
"Behold, it was very good".
Eden means delight.
"IT IS THE FATHER'S GOOD PLEASURE TO GIVE YOU THE KINGDOM".[1] ❤
Gen 2:7   *And the Lord God formed man of the dust of the ground, and breathed into his nostrils the breath of life; and man became a living soul.*
KJV [the breath of God - Spirit given]
God breathed His own life into the man and placed him in the Garden of His Pleasure to walk and talk face to face.
Then the man sinned. His great love for His creation would not allow them to eat of the Tree of Life which was also in the garden; to live forever, but separated from God by their sin - forever.
"And now, lest he put out his hand and take also of the tree of life, and eat, and live forever".[2]
So with sorrow He drove them out of His presence.
"And he placed at the east of the garden of Eden cherubim, and a flaming sword which turned every way, to keep the way of the tree of life".[3]
Our soul is the seat of our emotions, our mind/will; our character and personality, our heart of hearts; our identity is buried in our soul. It is who we are; and all our earthly experiences dwell within our soul because of our memories. It is how we relate to others. There are so many Scriptures that pertain to the soul as it is a living thing from which we function and expresses who we are [Gen 2.7].

We are a soul, with a spirit, walking around in a body.

All our decisions are decided in our mind that comes from our soul Here are some ...
Lev 26:43 *they will accept their guilt, because they despised My judgments and because their soul abhorred My statutes.*
Deut 4:29 *you will seek the Lord your God, and you will find*

Him if you seek Him with all your heart and all your soul.
Deut 30:6   love the Lord your God with all your heart and with all your soul, that you may live.
Job 7:11   I will speak in the anguish of my spirit; I will complain in the bitterness of my soul.
Job 30:25   Has not my soul grieved for the poor?
Ps 19:7   The law of the Lord is perfect, converting the soul;
Ps 33:20   my soul waits for the Lord; He is my help and shield.
Ps 42:1-2   So pants my soul for You, O God. My soul thirsts for God, for the living God.
Matt 10:28   And do not fear those who kill the body but cannot kill the soul.
Matt 10:28   But rather fear Him who is able to destroy both soul and body in hell.
John 12:27   Now My soul is troubled, and what shall I say?
Ezek 18:4   Behold, all souls are Mine; The soul of the father As well as the soul of the son is Mine; The soul who sins shall die. [But God's compassion sent His Son Jesus to redeem those who would receive it [John 1.12]

Your soul, yes it is your life.

Prov 4:23   *Keep your heart with all diligence, For out of it spring the issues of life.* [guard, what comes in or goes out]. Yes, your heart is attached to your soul. Emotions, heartbreak, joy...all are a result of what's going on in your soul, issues of life.

All these verses show us that we are a soul. Our identity, character and personality, emotions and desires, our free will and imaginations are bound up in our soul. The thoughts of our mind come from what is buried in our soul and this is that to which we react/respond. Most of our actions are responses to memories stored in our soul. We are a soul with a spirit and walk around in a body. 'Keep your heart'? Why? Think about it. A heart beat keeps us alive and experiences life.

Spirit given so man could communicate-fellowship with God Who is Spirit.
We Are the Focus of His Desire.

So, getting back to Adam...
God did speak and share with Adam, many wonderful heavenly things; and also the wonders of the earth in which he lived. With God's wisdom, he named all the animals. God

gave Adam satisfaction and fulfillment in his spirit, then He gave this first man what it would take to complete his physical life; a mate comparable to his soulish needs. This was done in the beginning - to show us how important it is to seek God first and He will take care of all our cares.

But curiosity got the best of them and approaching that tree gave satan the opportunity to speak his enticing words. His goal was to steal their identity that was created in the image and likeness of God. Now we know satan was always after the glory; so his intention was to have this man covered by the glory, to worship *him* in this garden of paradise.

So now they were no longer sure of who they were - fear and intimidation is always satan's bag of tricks. Covered by God's glory they were drawn to give that glory to another. Adam was tempted to make his own decision of 'whatever'. We know where he got the idea that he could be his own god. And here was the sin-nature born. His mind no longer focused on the spirit realm, now from a carnal view...

He lost his spirit perception and passed it down to us.
But it is obvious Adam must have made Eve an idol in his life. Did fear go through his mind as he saw the possibility of losing his mate because of what she had done; as God had warned? Now they were seeing each other without the cover of glory light, and were astonished. Now naked, they believed Gen 2:16-17 *You will surely die*; so they hid themselves.

We know Adam lived for 930 years; so what died? His spirit died, cloaked in darkness, he could no longer fellowship with a Holy God, His Creator. He lost spirit perception; now only a carnal mind.

Mistrust and fear had opened a door to deception and wrong choices. Praise God - Genesis 12 & 22 reveals the next man He chose made the right decision and placed his idol on the altar.

There were two animals slain to cover Adam and Eve. Obviously, one would have not been large enough to cover two people. Later on at the time of the Exodus from Egypt, there would be one lamb for a family. In the Temple, the priests offered one lamb, every year, for a nation. Centuries later One Precious Lamb, the Ultimate Sacrifice, was lifted up once, for all the world.

There can be seen as early as Genesis the shadow of the Lamb slain before the foundation of the world [Gen 3:15

& Rev 13:8], for the sin of the world. The love of Jesus is here in the beginning, revealed to His creation! Since Adam gave the animals their names he could have known many of them in the same way that we relate to our pets. Is it possible they conversed with them, for Eve does not seem surprised to hear the serpent speak. Just as God confused language at Babel, He could have done it here first when sin entered the world, and gave the animals their own way of communication that now, we cannot understand.

It must have been quite a shock for them to see those beautiful creatures slain. But the full knowledge and violent impact of what their rebellion towards God would really cost, was still in their future. Nine centuries passed as Adam watched his iniquity bear fruit beginning with Cain's murder of his brother Abel.

The law of sowing and reaping was graphically in place!

His beautiful Eve stood there before him and Adam saw her for the first time - Her glory covering gone - Oh, will she die as Father said? She was deceived by the snake's craftiness; but he made the decision to eat the forbidden. He was tempted to be like God, but he forgot he already was like God. This liar stole their identity and as a result the 'sin nature' was borne in mankind to be passed down through the generations. Adam's mind became carnal and his spirit witness was buried in darkness. They so quickly hid themselves with fig leaves thinking God won't find them out.

I guess we can figure it out that they were standing next to the fig tree they had just eaten of the fruit; and because of his disobedience, betrayal of relationship, blasphemy to be his own god, he lost it all. Adam handed over to satan, his God-given authority over the earth and everything in it.

They lost their glory light and stood naked before each other. It must have been quite a shock. They'd never really seen each other before, only God's glory, for He was their covering.

But now for Adam and his wife, God made coats of skins to cover their nakedness.[4] They were no longer wrapped in God's light and glory. They were no longer innocent. They must have been terrified when they realized the consequence of their sin was immediately manifested in their sight. Remembering what God said - the fear of death has now entered the human race.[5]

When Adam partook of the tree of the knowledge of good and evil his mind became carnal. Trying to decide for himself how to deal with his sin factor, he grabbed something from his natural environment with which to hide from God. They were standing next to the fig tree they had just eaten of; and so they grabbed some fig leaves to cover their nakedness [Gen 3.7].

[FYI] Fig leaves are shaped like a man's hand and are very much bigger.

But God's supernatural response to our sin defies our carnal mind and wants to hide us in Christ, under His Blood.

Even as Adam was receiving God's judgment - he was also seeing God's grace and mercy as the animals were slain in his place and they were covered by the blood. In a world wrought with harsh toiling there was still a way to please God. Chapter four of Genesis indicates that Adam built an altar and taught his sons about this blood sacrifice, as he learned it from the Lord. His sons Cain and Abel, sacrificed to the Lord. The Bible declares:

1 John 1:9-10 *If we confess our sins, He is faithful and just to forgive us our sins and to cleanse us from all unrighteousness.* And...*Without the shedding of blood there is no remission of sin.*[6] [In the temple or on the cross].

Cain inherited his father's rebellion
and did it his own way.

We can see in Genesis 3:18 that, not until after Noah's flood did man eat of the flesh of animals [Gen 9.3]. Of course they used the wool for clothing. It is obvious they must have been vegetarians until then. Genesis four tells us Abel kept flocks and brought fat portions of some of the first born as a sacrifice to the Lord.

Since they did not eat the meat, does this tell us the whole focus of Abel's life was to be a sacrifice, holy and pleasing unto his God? Maybe this is what really riled Cain?

If we may assume Adam constructed an altar and used it; perhaps we may also presume he built it close to the entrance of the garden he had been driven from. We may have here a pattern in view, similar to another.

As we search the Scriptures and study them so we can know the heart of God revealed in His Word, we may observe certain principles carried from Genesis through Revelation.

In the Old Testament there is revealed types and shadows. In the New Testament we find fulfillment and reality. Example: The animal slain on the altar for a blood sacrifice in the Old Testament was the type and shadow. Jesus on the cross was the fulfillment, the reality.

Here at the gate into Paradise, the Garden of God's Pleasure; man's fellowship with his Creator was cut off by cherubim and a flaming sword. What stood in their way was judgment, the law of sin and death.

Hebrews four tells us the Word is like a two-edged sword. The flaming sword of judgment was analogous of the law placed within the Ark of the Covenant. God's people were judged by this law.

Adam had no more access to the Tree Of Life and the presence of his Creator. No longer could they walk and talk with their God in the cool of the day. Man's covering of glory and light was lifted and they were indeed naked and vulnerable to the elements of a cursed earth. Their lives were dry and barren as they toiled for their sustenance.[7]

We now know that even if Adam built his altar toward the entrance to the garden of Eden, he could not go back in. He had to wait for Jesus,

The mediator of a better covenant,
established on better promises.[8]

So here we have in the beginning, the altar of sacrifice, the gate, and the Word of judgment, that stood between man and the Tree of Life - the presence of God.

Centuries later Adams' imagery became more substantial as God gave Moses instructions to build a visual aid for His plan of salvation. It was called the Tabernacle of the Congregation. It was a mobile temple of worship.

The reason for this Tabernacle was that God may dwell in the presence of His people.[9] This has always been His good pleasure and is His median purpose for creation.[10]

Many chapters of the Bible are given over to describe the Tabernacle. Every aspect of this Tabernacle was symbolic of Jesus and His ministry of redemption. As these Scriptures are researched there comes revelation of God's wonderful ways with His people. God is trying to show us something.

Moses was admonished of God when he was about
to make the tabernacle, See, saith He,
that you make it according to the pattern
shown to you in the mount.

It was precisely the image of our entry into the Kingdom of God. When Moses was given the pattern[11] to build this Tabernacle, God began with the Ark, the Mercy Seat, the nucleus of all. God must be central to our lives.
In all things He [must] have the preeminence.[12]
For my purpose however, we'll begin at the other end for we may visualize here, our journey back to the Father. The Tabernacle was surrounded by a fence too high for one to see over.

*Except a man be born again,
he cannot see the kingdom of God.*[13]

The supporting pillars were banded with silver [redemption] and placed into sockets of brass]judgment]. This fence enclosed an area 150 feet long and 75 feet wide.

One could not just wander onto the premises because there was only one gate.[14] This gate was of blue [heavenly], scarlet [the Blood], and purple [royalty] fine twined linen [righteousness]. Jesus tells us the way to life is through a narrow gate.[15] There is only one way, one opening into the kingdom, that is through Jesus.

I am the way. [16]

Now we know at that time, only the priest could enter the tabernacle to perform the sacrifices, and they did this for all the sin of all of Israel; a ritual that lasted for thousands of years.

As the priest stepped through the gate [of repentance] they were confronted with the altar of bloody sacrifice of bulls and goats. As they put their faith in the blood sacrifice of the animal to cover Israel's sin, so must we receive the Blood sacrifice of Jesus, *That taketh away the sin of the world,*[17] in order to come into the kingdom.

1 John 1:9 *If we confess our sins, He is faithful and just to forgive us our sins and to cleanse us from all unrighteousness.* And - *Except a man be born again he cannot enter the kingdom of God* [Jn 3.16].

The kingdom of God is here represented by the entire enclosure. Studying Hebrews 9-10 and Exodus 25-40, will give a good understanding of the correlation here explained. When the Tabernacle furniture was set up according to God's schematic, the twelve tribes were assigned their place surrounding the tabernacle- and seen from above, it was in the form of a cross!

It is not so strange that in the center of Exodus

chapters 25-40 describing the building of the Tabernacle, there comes the specifications for the priesthood. In chapter 30:17-33, the Word declares who may enter into the presence of our Holy God to worship; with a comparison between the Old and the New Testament. Ezra 3:8-11 tells us who was overseer to restore the Temple. The consecrated Priest[18] Redeemed, Cleansed, Anointed;
1. Redeemed by the Blood, Sin Forgiven.
2. Cleansed by the washing of water by the Word,[19]
3. Filled with the Holy Spirit, the anointing.[20]

Again we look at the shadow and the fulfillment. The privilege of a priest is access to God. The priest and his functions were minutely detailed in the middle of the instructions for the Tabernacle and Building because only a priest of God can partake of God's plans and building of the kingdom of God.

Keeping our eyes fixed on Jesus the Author and Finisher of our faith, He will lead us on the strait path. Revelation 5:9-10 tells us He has made His people to be priests and kings unto our God. See also 1Peter 2:9 *God has made us to be a kingdom of priests.*

The Tabernacle was constructed of the materials the Israelites had in their possession, of which they had gotten from the Egyptians;[21] wages for 430 years of slavery. Some population experts claim there could have been over a million people that left Egypt in the Exodus. These riches they willingly gave back to the Lord.[22]

Directly behind the altar of sacrifice was the laver, the place where the priest washed.[23] The laver was lined with highly polished brass.[24] The women of those days used brass for the same purpose we use mirrors today.

Genesis 38 tells us in verse 8 the women put to death their vanity to honor the Lord. I would venture to say they afterward showed forth an inner beauty as the adorning of a meek and quiet spirit which is in the sight of God of great price.[25]

I am definitely not against makeup and jewelry, but there is excess of anything that can lead to lust and idolatry. We can repent of the sin of vanity and ask God to develop and bring forth the inner beauty of our spirit in subjection to Lord Jesus.

As the priest washed, he had to see his reflection. James 1:22 tells us that as a hearer of the Word we can see ourselves as in a mirror. We get washed by the Word. That priest in the Tabernacle had to be a doer of the law or he did not dare go into the presence of God.[26]   **I am the Truth.**

We can look into the perfect law of liberty and continue in it. Hebrews 10:19 affirms that because of God's grace we may with boldness, enter in by the Blood of Jesus. Past the laver we go through the outer veil and into the Holy Place.

In this room we find the candlestick or golden lampstand, one beaten work of pure gold. It had one shaft and six branches making it appear as a tree [the Tree of Life].[27] It speaks of Christ wounded for our transgressions and bruised for our iniquities and by his stripes we are healed [Isaiah 53:5]. It did not burn candles. Beaten olive oil was used for fuel. It burned constantly.[28]

Jesus, the Light of the world.[29]

Across the room was the table of shewbread. One loaf for each of the 12 tribes of Israel, and there was sprinkled frankincense and myrrh on each loaf.

And Jesus is the Bread of Life.[30]

The Holy Place had a second veil. Before this veil separating the Holy Place from the Holy of Holies, was the altar of incense. The coals on this altar were kept burning always, and incense was placed on it every day; a double portion on the Day of Atonement. Represented here were the prayers of Israel, of God's people.[31] The incense was composed of sweet spices holy unto the Lord, never used for pleasure to the natural man.

How many times Moses stood there and interceded for stubborn rebellious Israel is not recorded. But Jesus, our unchangeable High Priest ever lives to make petition to God, to intercede with Him and intervene for us. The horns on the corners of the altar speak of the power of prayer.

Exodus 30:6&36 tells us the altar of incense was the place where God met with Moses. It was just before the inner veil that led into the Holy of Holies, which contained the Ark of the Covenant and the mercy seat upon which the blood sacrifice was smeared.

Within the Ark was soon to be hidden the stone tablets on which were engraved the laws of God. They would be inscribed in the heart of God's people [Heb 8:6-13]. The law - the Word of God - as a two edged sword, judges and divides between the holy and the profane [Heb 4:12]. And so the flaming sword, the judgment of the law that separates us

from God, is satisfied in the shed Blood of Jesus. He died in our place and opened again the gate into the presence of God.
I am the way, the truth, and the life.
Into the presence of the Shekinah glory of God, the Holiest of all; one had to pass through the Holy Place - Jesus. This inner veil was the door [Jn 10:9].
No man cometh to the Father but by me.[32]
I Am The Door [John 7.9; 10.9].
Now we know that all this was the pattern, in image form, of our redemption bought by the Blood of Jesus. We are given all this understanding now because God always begins at the beginning to show us His manifold wisdom in bring His creation back to Himself.

The temple standing in Jesus' day was a replica of Solomon's magnificent edifice. Built by Herod, it was to placate the people so they wouldn't rebel against Roman rule. It was also a matter of great pride and lust for Herod; but the Ark was missing.

After Nebuchadnezzar destroyed Solomon's temple and took Israel captive to Babylon in 600 B.C. there is no more mention of the Ark of the Covenant being in the Holy of Holies. There was no Ark in Zerubabel's temple. In Herod's temple there was no Ark. Only an empty room - separated by a veil, was there to remind Israel of their loss.

It took a very long time for the enemy to break through the wall, and so the priests had time to hide the Ark. Old Nebbie never did have possession of the Ark; that's why it was missing. Strange that in now times, it has been rumored that the Ark has been found but left in its hiding place.

In Solomon's temple, this was no flimsy curtain but a work of enormous size, hung upon four pillars of acacia wood that were overlaid with gold.[33] This curtain was said to be four inches thick. It was embroidered with massive figures of angels and heavenly scenery. This is the veil that was rent in two at the crucifixion of Jesus.[34]

1Kings 6:23 tells us in Solomon's temple the veil was more than 15 feet high, and it could have been at least that, in the temple standing in Jesus' day. Perhaps Israel built it so; in anticipation of the return of their Ark. They never realized it would come in a different form.

Jesus died at the time of the evening sacrifice.[35] The

priest was standing at the veil before which was the altar of incense, because there was always a sacrifice of prayers and incense offered to God at the time of the evening sacrifice. The ninth hour; the evening sacrifice was three o'clock in the afternoon. What a sweet savor unto the Father was His Beloved Son.

Now picture this. A ritual was being carried out according to Jewish law.[36] This was Passover. The lamb was slain for Israel's sins. The priest was standing before that curtain with the blood; standing before the Holy of Holies which once contained the Ark of the Covenant. But the Ark was gone!

Where was it? He was hanging on a Roman cross up on Golgotha gasping out,

Forgive them Father, they know not what they do.

Israel's offering - slain on the altar in the Temple.

And on the Hill Was God's Offering.

It is finished!

For Sin - the Final Sacrifice of Blood.

At this exact moment an earthquake rocked Jerusalem. That massive veil ripped from top to bottom. An astonished priest was thrown into the Holy of Holies on his face, yet he comprehended not what he had chosen to deny.

Was this Caiaphas? - the one who had just condemned to death the Lord of Glory - the fulfillment of all that Israel therefore was created! Caiaphas is recorded to be high priest from the beginning of Jesus' ministry [Lk 3] up to the time of the crucifixion [Jn 18]. He was high priest by Herod's appointment, not an Aaronic descendant, from whom the priesthood was passed down; and Caiaphas is not a Hebrew name. It's of Chaldean origin! A short time after the resurrection, he's been removed from that office never again to enter the Presence [after Acts 4 he is gone].

Going back to the time of the Exodus and the beginnings of God fulfilling His covenant promises to Abraham and his Seed we read; *Moses finished the work. Then a cloud covered the tent of the congregation and the glory of the Lord filled the tabernacle.*[37]

And so the Most Holy One dwelt with his people.

The primary reason for the tabernacle was so that God would have a place to stand on the earth to reveal Himself to a people called out of the world unto Himself. A Holy God cannot dwell just anywhere. The Word declares that *The earth is the Lord's and the fullness thereof*. But the earth had been put under a curse. Man would toil amid thorns and thistles. But God...

In the Old Testament God had a special place set aside that His Holiness could be manifested. It was quite small - a box that was carried around wherever His people journeyed. To think the Creator of the universe would abide in a little box is beyond my capacity. How our God loves us. His desire to dwell with His people is so great, and He showed us the way back into His presence.

He was willing to do that as another type and shadow - of Jesus dwelling in our hearts. He sets us apart from the world, delivers us from the curses and will manifest His holiness through us as we become His tabernacle - His dwelling place. God has been working since Adam to get us back into His presence; back into His Garden of Pleasure.

Many similar elements are here in the beginning with Adam. God established a model; ie.; the altar, the blood sacrifice, the cherubim and sword, the judgment gate, the tree of life and the presence of God. This pattern was followed through, expanded in the Tabernacle, and then brought to reality.

Jesus is reality. He is anything and everything we need for all time; and He fulfilled it all.

As we accept His Blood sacrifice for the forgiveness of our sin we come into right relationship with Jesus and through Him we are reconciled with the Father.[38]

The Song of Solomon is thought by some to be an allegory of Jesus and His Bride. There are several verses that speak of the bride and bridegroom coming into the garden. Is Jesus waiting in His garden for us to walk with Him? Or as the fourth chapter of the Song of Solomon, verse 12 suggests, are WE His garden?

A garden enclosed is...my spouse....
If Jesus dwells within you, and it is
   the Father's good pleasure to give you the Kingdom
may He not build His garden within you?...that He might walk and talk with you,
In the cool of the day?

Hebrews 10:19 challenges us with boldness - to enter in.
The love of Jesus did not have its beginnings in the garden of

Eden. When Adam sinned God did not say OOPS! - find Himself in a dilemma, ponder what we might call makeshift plans, list all the options; then choose the lesser of two evils. We were,
Predestined to the adoption of sons by Christ Jesus according to the good pleasure of His will ...He chose us in Him before the foundation of the world that we should be holy and without blame before Him in love.[39]

IT'S THE WHOLE REASON FOR OUR EXISTENCE. ♥

The Old Covenant made provision for the animal blood sacrifice to cover man's sin just as the animals' skin covered Adam and Eve. This was another type and shadow. When Jesus died on the cross in our place He forever broke the power of sin over us, and the righteousness of God in Christ was imputed to us,[40] as we come into right standing with God.

Adam and Eve were naked and not ashamed in the garden.
Thou art clothed with honor and majesty: who covers thyself with light as with a garment.[41]
They were covered by the righteousness, holiness and glorious light of the presence of God, a gift from their loving Father. He extended His glorious covering over them even as He does us, the children of His Kingdom.

Adam was made in the very image and likeness of God. Man was always meant to be covered, protected and clothed with His presence. He extended His glorious garment of light over them. [That's why we have no fur nor feathers].

When they sinned, He withdrew His light and they saw their nakedness. Now ashamed, they hid themselves from God. In Jesus we are covered by His Blood and as we confess our sins we are made righteous in Him [1Jn 1:9].

Jesus took our shame upon Him as He hung there, naked before the world. Oh no, those Roman soldiers certainly had no regard for modesty. Sometimes our theology is founded on wrong propositions. Though this point will not negate our salvation, we should come to terms with certain facts.

The crucifixion of Jesus was not like that nice holy image we may have in our head, or hanging around our neck. Understand that Jesus was Himself sinless, innocent. He actually BECAME our sin! This is from where comes the real power to set us free. All the filth of our gross iniquity was laid on Him. Perverse lust, greed, murder, rebellion, self-centeredness, pride, bitterness, raging hatred, a deceitful betraying heart, yes, and all OUR goodness - and much more. And still He loved us.

Remember the two goats sacrificed for the sin of Israel? One was slain and the blood placed on the mercy seat. The other had the sins of Israel laid on its head and taken outside the city into the wilderness. Jesus was taken outside the city and He was the Blood sacrifice. He became the naked outcast. Oh yes, those Roman soldiers wanted to humiliate those criminals as much as possible.

Our shame of nakedness before God was one more thing from which we had to be redeemed. Oh yes, an unbeliever stands naked in his sin before a Holy God. But now a believer in Christ stands covered by the Blood sacrifice of Jesus on the cross.
[Gal 3:27 and 2Cor 5.10]
For as many of you as were baptized into Christ have put on [clothed yourself with] Christ.
He took our nakedness to the cross and clothed us with Himself -
So we will not be found naked.[42]
The skins with which Adam and Eve were clothed, represent what Christ did here. Matthew 22 tells us what happens if we try to bypass God's provision.

He took on our identity; a sinner separated from God. He became our sin so that we could become like Him. He was never concerned with His own dilemma. Not for one instant did He cease from loving us with a heart full of compassion and mercy.

Forgive them Father. Choose them instead of Me.
And the very heart of our precious Savior burst with grief over our lost condition. Some have had visions of Jesus on the cross and report that He looked somewhat like something passed through a meat grinder. When those Roman whips got through with Him He didn't even look human [Isaiah 53:2].

He was indeed the sacrificial victim, torn by dogs and the beasts of Bashan. Satan had his way for a moment. And then 1John 3:8. He came to destroy the works of the devil; and so,
*He [God] hath made him who knew no sin;
to be sin for us, that we might be made
the righteousness of God in him.*[43]

We are not just covered by His righteousness, it is something we become. It all means we become the righteousness of God as God is righteous. It's another gift from our gracious Father; a trade in. Our sin for His righteousness [2Cor 5.21]
....➜

> When Jesus died on the cross He became the ultimate sacrifice.

The Great Exchange.
His desire is to bring us back to the image that He originally planned for us.

For whom he did foreknow, he also did predestinate to be conformed to the image of his Son.[44]

When He died on the cross He did away with the altar of sacrifice to bring us to the altar of incense. Beginning with Exodus chapter 25, God instructed Moses in the minutest detail of how to construct the Tabernacle. He was to have certain furniture within those walls that were demonstrative of God's unique purposes in the restoration of His creation.

The Tabernacle is representative of Jesus and His plan of salvation. Of furniture, there were 6 pieces. Six is the scriptural number of man; and this structure also describes our way back to God.

1. The fence being made of fine twined linen speaks of the righteousness of the saints in Christ [Rev 19:8].
2. The altar of sacrifice is fulfilled in us through Romans 3:25 & 12:1&2.
3. The laver - made of brass - *the washing of the water of the Word* [Eph 5.26] the mirror is the Word. As we apply the truth of the Word to our lives, we are transformed into His image; then people should see Jesus mirrored in us.
4. The candlestick - the light of the world [Jn 9:5]
5. The altar of incense is analogous of the interceding Christian. As we come to this altar to seek His face, we are invited to come through the veil into
6. The Holy of Holies, the presence of Jesus in our heart.

Jesus fulfilled all, that we may become the fulfillment of His purpose ♥

Moses built the Tabernacle according to the pattern he saw. Where was the real thing? Revelation 8:3-4 tells us what Moses replicated on the earth. He saw our Great High Priest Jesus, our Intercessor, standing at the altar of incense, before the throne of God. Moses saw first in the heavenlies what he built on the earth [Heb 8:1-2]. God shows His prophets what He wants to do before He does it, so that through man's cooperation, God may accomplish His perfect will on the earth.[45] 1Chronicles 28:9-19 reveals David was also given, *The pattern by the Spirit.*

David was the man God chose through whom to reveal to His people a glorious channel of communication and fellowship. He was quite possibly borne on the wings of praise and worship into the heavenlies to see how it was done before the very throne of God [Rev 5:11-12]. He recorded his intimate moments with God, in the many Psalms he wrote.

David was shown the true purpose of the priesthood as the pattern was laid out before him. He translated those instructions to his son Solomon, who was also to duplicate this heavenly temple.

Listen carefully, for the Lord has chosen you
to build a house for His sanctuary.
Build it according to the pattern.

Chr 28 & 29 David could not build the Temple because he had man's blood on his hands. The only blood that may enter the Temple of the living God, was the blood of the sacrificial lamb.

As we research what David was shown we may receive revelation into the meaning and significance of the pattern. Strong's Concordance is a most helpful root resource when one does not speak the language. David was given the graphic example for:

1. The porch - to tie fast the mouth, put to silence.
2. The courts - surround and separate.
3. The chambers - something lofty [the heavenlies?]
4. The parlors - to enter a private chamber.

Revelation Chapter 7 finds us before the throne of God. Chapter 8:1 says there is silence in heaven. Habakkuk 2:20 also tells us,

The Lord is in his holy temple;
let all the earth keep silence before him.

The porch is the entrance to a house. This refers to the entrance of our house which is our mouth. When we come before the Lord we ought to keep silent. Hear what He has to say, even if it means to put our hand over our mouth.

The court that surrounds and separates is the hedge [Job 1:10, Zec 2], protection God puts around His people and separates them from the world [Jn 17:9-26, Eph 2:6].

The chambers: He brings us into the heavenlies by His Spirit as we commune with Him through praise and worship.

The parlor is that secret place of the Most High in which is the most coveted, to abide under the shadow of His wings [Ps 91].

We now can further see how the plans of the Tabernacle are fulfilled in His people. David received the revelation of a true worshiper coming into the Holy of Holies, the presence of God; for he also saw the Heavenly Mercy Seat.

The author of the book of Hebrews is questionable to some Theologians. Others believe it to be Paul. The book is replete with heavenly schemes; filled with passages pertaining to the Priesthood of Jesus, especially His office as Melchizedek, the High Priest of Genesis who had no recorded beginning of days nor end of life. Each time a priest is introduced in Scripture, you will find a list of his genealogy, his father, grandfather, etc. You don't find that for Melchizedek.

Heb 4:14-17 *Seeing then that we have a great High Priest who has passed through the heavens, Jesus the Son of God, let us hold fast our confession. For it is evident that our Lord arose from Judah, of which tribe Moses spoke nothing concerning priesthood. And it is yet far more evident if, in the likeness of Melchizedek, there arises another priest who has come, not according to the law of a fleshly commandment, but according to the power of an endless life. For He testifies:*

You are a priest forever

According to the order of Melchizedek.

Of all the writers of the New Testament, none is more qualified than Paul to grasp the reality and revelation of the priesthood and its purposes revealed in the true pattern, Jesus. The chapters in Hebrews relating to the tabernacle must have been written by one who was there; on the earth - and in the heavenlies.

Paul, as a Pharisee among Pharisees understood in the flesh the workings of the Temple. But also 2Corinthians 12 reveals a man taken into the heavenlies to see first hand the, *Great High Priest Who is seated on the right hand of the throne of the Majesty in the heavens, a minister of the sanctuary and of the true tabernacle, which the Lord pitched, and not man.*[46]

Paul knew the significance of the priesthood even more than Moses because Paul understood that,

Better covenant established on better promises.
What does all this mean to us, the Lord's new covenant worshipers? We may come freely into His glorious presence because of the Blood sacrifice of the appointed and anointed unique precious Lamb of God. The office of priesthood is no longer delegated to the chosen few. The New Covenant priesthood is given to every believer.[47] It has always been the plan of God to bring us into His presence, See Ps 99:9-100:5; Ex 19:6.

After the chapters in Hebrews of Paul clearly explaining the Priesthood of the true Pattern - he tells us now
Having therefore, brethren, boldness to enter
into the holiest by the Blood of Jesus,
let us [also] draw near [to God].
We may go in because Jesus opened the door. He is there waiting for us. Read Hebrews 10. When we come to do His will because we are sanctified by the Blood of Jesus, our guilty conscience and our flesh are cleansed. We have been made worthy to stand before Him,
Through the offering of
the body of Jesus Christ once for all.
We also, may stand before the throne of His holiness, because we have been reconciled in the body of His flesh through death, to present us holy and unblamable and unreprovable in His sight [Col 1:21-22]. Now, in the beginning of His ministry He declares ... Matt 4:15 *The land of Zebulun and the land of Naphtali, By the way of the sea, beyond the Jordan, Galilee of the Gentiles: The people who sat in darkness have seen a great light,*
Not only did He come for His chosen people,
but for all of us.
Read Hebrews 9:14; 10:22; and 1John 3:20-21, especially in the Amplified Bible if you can. Because Jesus offered Himself as an unblemished sacrifice to God - we can have our conscience cleansed from dead works and vain imaginations to serve the living God. As we come before Him, we offer the sacrifice of our love, obedience; our bodies, to do His will.[48]

And even as guilt and condemnation would rise up against us to make us back away, 1Jn 3 tells us...
For He is above and greater than our conscience [our hearts] and He knows]perceives and understands] everything.

[Nothing is hidden from Him].
And we receive from Him whatever we ask....
It is here in His presence we may have the motives and attitudes of our heart changed and purified. It is here that we may find the awesome love of God is continuously shed abroad in our heart that we may run boldly into the presence of our Father.

IT IS HIS GOOD PLEASURE ❤

Moses saw the altar of incense before the throne of God and the prayers of all the saints from the beginning of time, [Rev 8:3-4] offered as a sacrifice of praise and worship. Abel's first born of his flock, slain on the altar of sacrifice, a sweet smelling savor pleasing and acceptable to God. He saw by the Spirit, Abraham's obedience to offer his only son Isaac; Sarah's submission. Joseph's humility and obedience; others too numerous to mention here.

Moses had to have seen it! No wonder His face was so lit up with the glory of God that none could look at him. He saw the final sacrifice of the Lamb of God. He understood! So he built on the earth what he saw in the heavenlies according to the exact pattern. He knew what it all represented so he surrounded it with a fence and reconfirmed the reality every time he stood before the altar of incense. This was the vision Abraham had on Mt Moriah. As he prepared to offer his son, Isaac, he saw - The True Final Sacrifice!

Moses' desire to be in God's presence above all else, placed him constantly at that earthly altar, as he saw in the Spirit, the incense rising before the Throne of His Holiness.

Because this pleased God, He would stay His hand of judgment and extend His hand of mercy to an oftentimes rebellious people. Exodus 33:11 tells us Joshua did not depart from the Tabernacle. He became the second greatest leader of all Israel. We too may come as often as we please and stay as long as we want.

As the Body of Christ on the earth, we are the light, the salt, the bread as we feed hungry ones with the good news. We become the channel of water springing up unto everlasting life; not only for ourselves but for thirsty ones God will send along our path.

Christ in you, the hope of Glory

We become the holy place, the presence of Jesus abides in us. It has nothing to do with how holy we may or may not feel [1Pet 1:15-16]. Jesus has chosen to dwell in our hearts by His Spirit. In John 14, He explains this fact very clearly. The Holy Place in the Tabernacle was analogous to Jesus' presence in us. Remember this altar of incense was just before the veil that led into the Holy of Holies; *Where I will meet with you.*[49]

Moses was in the presence of God as a type and shadow of the worshipers of the New Covenant.

And the smoke of the incense with the prayers of the saints ascended up before God.[50]

John the Apostle was brought into the heavenlies. He saw Jesus, the embodiment of the entire promise of God in the plan of redemption. John walked with Jesus our glorious Savior, Lord and King, as High Priest and Bridegroom, searching for the overcomer, His priest/bride, in the midst of His church body [Rev 2&3]. Many are called, but who will answer?

John also saw the Ark of The Covenant in heaven,[51] and he saw the Tree of Life.[52] Here again we see Jesus, our Ark of safety Who fulfills the law in us, and we receive His abundant life,[53] as we obey His Word. In giving ourselves over to praise and worship,

God inhabits the praises of His people.[54]

We may come into His presence at the altar of incense:

There I will meet with you.

Let my prayer be set forth before thee as incense; and the lifting up of my hands as the evening sacrifice.[55]

Remember when the veil before the Holy of Holies split in two? Was it to let God out or to let us in? Whatever it was, one thing was accomplished. Now God could dwell in the temple HE built for His presence.

Out of an unregenerate heart and mind we know nothing of praise and worship to our God. Walking in the Kingdom of God is unlike anything we have ever experienced in our natural life. Our mind must be renewed so as to be able to know the things of God. *The fear of God is the beginning of wisdom.*

Ps 111:10 *If any man lack wisdom ask it of God Who gives liberally of Himself* [James 1:5]. As a created being, it is beyond our capacity to understand the Creator, but He graciously allows us to know Him. The meaning of Psalm 91:14 is a call to intimacy.

Every step we take, every choice we make concerning our life in God is causing us to grow and mature and be socialized in His Kingdom. It was all planned out in the beginning before the foundation of the earth. God gave us a great analogy as we see our babies grow and mature in our family. We must learn to worship. We must learn to worship our Lord and King. It's a growing into day by day, and we never arrive. It just keeps getting better as we step into our heavenly inheritance.

Some time ago I was in a church service praising and worshiping God. There was in a vision before me, a meadow of beautiful lilies. God said, *When My people put on the garment of praise, they are clothed more majestically than King Solomon.*[56] The temple priest was the only one allowed to burn the incense. Now we may freely come; as our Great High Priest Jesus stands before the Throne calling us into the Holy of Holies.[57] He opened the door,

INTO THE PRESENCE OF THE FATHER.

♫ As I come into your presence
Before your holy throne
I offer the sacrifice of love -
And to You I sing your praises
To worship You my Lord ♫
May my life be always lived before You
In the shelter of Your wings
In the secret place on high
And covered by the Fatherhood of God

♥

STUDY GUIDE

1. When did God decide that He would make His creation a people of His own; that would inherit His Kingdom? Eph 1:36
2. When man failed his first test did God give up on us? Rom 5:17
3. What is God's greatest pleasure? Luke 12:32
4. When did God begin to restore that which was lost? Gen 3:15
5. Year by century, God patiently worked out His magnificent plan, literally showing man what He would do, and how He

would do it. Who paid the penalty for man's first rebellious uprising? Gen 3:21

6. What universal law came into effect immediately? Gal 6:7

7. Of all the types and shadows set forth in the Old Testament and fulfilled in the New, which one is the most pertinent? Heb 10:11-12 The Tabernacle of the Congregation was also known as the Tent of Meeting. It was here the Most High God, Creator of all that is - condescended to fellowship once more with the man He created.

8. Jesus willingly shed His Blood. How did the Father respond? Heb 10:12-17

9. What is meant by the great exchange? 2Cor 5:21

10. Can we do anything to earn so great a salvation? Eph 2:8-9

11. What can our response be to so great a sacrifice? Ps 116:12-

12. Did Jesus suddenly burst into our world or was His birth and death a part of some kind of plan. How do we know? Rev 13:8, 1Pet 1:20, Heb 8:5, Eph 1, 1Cor 10:1-15, 1Jn 3:8.

13. What is God's ultimate purpose for man? Jn 14:23, Rev 21:17

14. I'd like to add a P.S. In the Scriptures that refer to The sons of God, I think it is important to at least have this basic revelation. The word 'sons' comes from the Greek word meaning children, offspring of either sex, male or female.

Gal 3:26-29 tells us we are all children of God because of our faith in Christ Jesus. There is neither male nor female, we are all one. If we belong to Christ we are Abraham's seed and heirs according to the promise. Just because some translations use the word sons, it by no means leaves out females. 2 Cor 6:18 tells us, *I will be a Father unto you and ye shall be my sons and daughters, saith the Lord Almighty.*

So now we know that we know that us females are also,
'sons of the Most High God'.

And remember that Men Are a part of the Bride.
PRAYER: Thank you God that You've already made provision for me. I receive it from your hand.

❤

Oh how He loves you and me
He died to save us
What more could He do?
♥

SCRIPTURES

1. Lk 12:32
2. Ge 3:22
3. Ge 3:24
4. Ge 3:21
5. Ge 2:17
6. He 9:22
7. Ge 3: 17-19
And Heb 2:15
8. Heb 8:6
9. Ex 40:3
10. Re 21:
11. Ex 25:
12. Co 1:18
13. Jn 3:3
14. Ex 27:16-17
15. Mt 7:13-14
16. Jn 14:6
17. Jn 1:29
18. 1Pe 2:9
19. Ep 5:26
20. Jn 14:16-17
21. Ex 12:35-36
22. Ex 35:29
23. Ex 30:18-21
24. Ex 38:8
25. 1Pe 3:35
26. Ex 28:43
27. Ex 25:31-40
28. Ex 27:20
29. Jn 9:5

30. Jn 6:35
31. Ps 141:12
32. Jn 14:6
33. Ex 26:31-32
34. Mt 27:51
35. Mt 27:45-51
36. Ex 30:7-8
37. Ex 40:33-35
38. 2Co 5:18
39. Ep 1:45
40. Ro 4:68
41. Ps 104:2
42. 2Co 5:23
43. 2Co 5:21
44. Ro 8:29
45. Am 3:7
46. He 8:1
47. 1Pe 2:5
48. Ro 12:1
49. Ex 30:6
50. Rev 8:34
51. Rev 11:19
52. Rev 22:2
53. Ro 8:24
54. Ps 22:3
55. Ps 141:2
56. Lk 12:27
57. Heb 8:1
* Rev 5:9

THE LOVE OF JESUS TEACHES US TO LOVE OUR ENEMIES.

Come unto me all ye who labor and are heavy laden and I will give you rest. Take my yoke upon you and learn of me; for I am meek and lowly of heart, and ye shall find rest unto your souls. For my yoke is easy and my burden is light.[1]

For some of us, relationships can be the heaviest burden we ever bear. If we are bullied about, taken advantage of, demeaned or deeply offended in our childhood; we can for years carry hidden within us resentment, anger and hatred.

There can also be the anguish of rejection and the fear of abandonment that produces a lonely empty heart. We may become self-centered and demand to be taken care of. Too often there develops no responsibility or submission to authority.

As the years roll by acquaintances perhaps drift away without any real explanation. We want to grab and hold on to anyone that seems to care. Because as much as we sometimes resent the intrusion, the reality is we can not survive without community. Such a dichotomy!

Even when we believed we had found our Prince or Princess Charming pretty soon the honeymoon is over and the battle for recognition comes on stage again. Ever yearning, never gaining; striving to please yet never appeased. All the time going further and deeper into our fantasy world.

We believe at once that no one really cares, but it doesn't matter; I can get along without them! Self pity and isolation settles down in the midst of our camp. There seems to be none out there who would stand still long enough to want to listen to our inner cry.

As defiant as we become to push back the tide of fear, in the loneliness of midnight hours our grieving soul takes over to remind us we really do need other people.

Our hostility may become an invisible barrier that blinds us to those who would reach out to us. The fear of more rejection that would certainly verify our insignificance has shored up the wall. We have not yet discovered there is an even greater eternal need. But the Spirit of God still hovers over His creation seeking to bring His light into the empty darkness of our soul.

Ah, but one day we discover the truth so far beyond our wildest dream. There is Someone Who cares! There is Someone Who is already pleased with us. We don't have to strive. We can't earn His love. He knew us as we were being formed in our mother's womb. He said, Look Father, another precious one for us to love and receive into our family, Here is Psalm 139.16.

> *You have formed my inward parts;*
> *you have covered me in my mother's womb.*
> *I will praise you for I am wonderfully made.*
> *My frame was not hidden from you*
> *when I was made in secret.*
> *Your eyes saw my substance,*
> *being yet unformed.*
> *In your book they all were written,*
> *the days fashioned for me,*
> *when as yet there were none of them.*
> *How precious also*
> *are your thoughts to me, Oh God!*
> *How great is the sum of them!*
> *If I should count them,*
> *they would be more in number*
> *than the sand.*[2]

This revelation came to me with overwhelming rejoicing and fear. One minute my heart was racing with great celebration and the next I was in a pit of despair and terror knowing this was too good to be true. As yet I had no concept of family ties or relationships.

It took time for the salve of His love to soften the outer barrier of the heart I had protected for so many years. But with His patience and mercy I was able to think in my mind that perhaps He does love me. I continued to spend many hours digging deep into the Word of God for here was my path to life - out of the dread darkness I had oniy known as my portion.

And so, as I received that small spark of life, He was able to expand it a little at a time that I could realize more and more of the healing Balm that was bringing me to wholeness.

As I searched His Word for my very life, I found Scripture that God wrote just for me.
*I love the Lord, because he hath heard
my voice and my supplications.
Because he hath inclined His ear unto me,
therefore will I call upon him as long as I live.* [3]
Jesus was God bending down His ear to hearken to the voice of my cry. One day I was thinking about Jesus dying on the cross and was doodling. I drew a very primitive cross and put Jesus on it, I guess to contemplate what it was really all about. Jesus spoke to me and said,

'I did that because I knew
you would need My love'.

♥

God touched me so deeply that day
and wrapped me in a warm blanket of
His presence. Though there were many times I thought He would leave me if I didn't measure up; slowly but surely, day by day He ministered to me through His Word, the life He implanted in His Word. I began to see I didn't have to leave or hide from Him.

The Lord promised His people He would not leave nor forsake them. This promise is a Kingdom principle.
*For he himself has said,
I will never leave you nor forsake you.* [4]
God knows exactly what we need to hear. How I rejoiced!

A very long time ago I had a vision. It was of Jesus lifting me up to the Father; but it was strange because I was very small, and wrapped up like a mummy. I didn't understand at the time, but it was me, so bound up by fears and a heart broken by so many painful things of my past, I wondered why-how I even survived. Now, so many years later [50!], I see myself before His throne, worshiping with a heart free to see Him as my Father, and I as His daughter.

The written Word becomes our Living Word as the Holy Spirit imparts the light and life of each passage into our souls. This is one way our character and identity becomes established and we are transformed into His image.

The first time the Lord led me through the letter Paul wrote to the Ephesians, He introduced me to His glorious inheritance. Not only did He want to make me a part of His family but I realized He'd had His eye on me from the foundation of the world. This was an awesome thought but deep inside I was not able to relate to it entirely because of my fractured family experiences.

I had felt rejected and unfit all my life. This stuff was really great, but I would have to remain on the outside looking in. I could never really partake of it. I did not understand the tenacity of the One called Redeemer.

Though I had read His letter to the Ephesians it was several years later that Chapter 2, vss 19-22 was engraved on my heart.

Eph 2:19-20   *Now, therefore, you are no longer strangers and foreigners, but fellow citizens with the saints and members of the household of God...*

I am actually a part of a family. The love of God has made a home in my broken heart and gathered all the pieces into His heart. I never have to leave. But remember this is all a part of growing in the Lord. The knowledge of this has to be buried in our heart and soul - it doesn't happen overnight.

Through the years and never relenting, my Lord and Savior moved with patience and caring on the heart I had closed to all outsiders. He worked from within chipping away the cold hard stone and gave me a heart of flesh.

Growing in God's precious unconditional love is the greatest adventure of a lifetime. New feelings were opening to me. The Creator God was touching a place of creativity within me. I had been shut down for so long it was difficult for me to reach beyond my stingy perimeters.

One day, as a sister in the Lord was praying for me, she saw [in a vision] an egg shell around me. The hand of God was putting a crack in it. When a baby chick comes out of its shell it does ever so slowly and cautiously. Too quickly and the tiny spark of life will fail. My loving Savior totally aware of this principle allowed me to slowly and cautiously come out of my own shell.

For those first years my living mountains and valleys were very sharply curved and I was on its roller coaster. One day I'd feel so great that Jesus was mine and I had the world whipped. The next day the depression was more than I could handle.

God was trying to show me that the love He was depositing in me was not a savings account. Try as I could to make it just Him and me, He was working just as hard to show me my attitudes toward other people.

The criticism and judgment of others, that I had always tried to keep inside was of a sudden getting very obvious to my heart. God was showing me something I had to deal with. If I wanted to be a part of the body, the church, the family of God, then I had to love my neighbor. And I had to start acting like it.

I spent day and night hours as usual in my imagination, judging condemning and handing out life sentences to those of whom were offensive to me. Actually people that don't meet our expectations are grist for our judgment mill.

The standards we think we are living by are the standards with which we judge others. Except our righteous criteria is usually in our head not in our heart. I had always been guilty of criticizing and judging others. Who ever has not may cast the first stone. When I came into the Kingdom of God I had to change the docket. I had a lot to learn.

One day God was finally able to get through to show me that it was not individuals I had a problem with. It was virtually the whole human race. It was a matter of me vs them. I had always thought of myself as worthless and unlovable.

In my self-pity and rejection, fear of being hurt again and anger; I had succeeded in turning off the world. I rejected them before they could reject me. And I did it with a vengeance. I had much anger to deal with.

When one truly believes they are worthless there is no foundation on which to build relationships. It is therefore totally illogical to believe that someone they can't see could possibly have any thought or care about them or could make a difference in their life. In order for God to get through to me there had to be a massive rearrangement of attitudes and emotions; major healing of brokenness; and deliverance from hatred of myself and others.

I swore I would never cry again and my heart began to turn cold. But God's love is stronger than anything in the universe. He is not called The Hound of Heaven for nothing. In Matthew 15 Jesus calls deliverance
The Children's Bread.

The word bread used in this context is the same word used in the verse, *Give us this day our daily bread.* Proverbs 30 says, *Feed me with food convenient for me.* God has prepared for us a total menu that will bring us into the healing, deliverance and restoration we each need to be conformed into His image; to allow us to take hold of our Kingdom inheritance. It is His workmanship in us. If we want it, we seek, knock and ask and keep on; and we yield ourselves into His loving care [Phil 2.13].

The Lord taught me many things in those days as I learned to forgive. My shredded emotions were being healed and responding to His Life. I was experiencing peace as I never did before. The tight knot in my stomach I had always lived with, I thought was a natural part of life. It wasn't. The more I let go of my anger and bitterness the more it let go. The more I forgave the more I was being established in His love. His Word says unless we forgive, we cannot know the Father's forgiveness.[5]

Always being an emotional person I reacted quickly and mostly negatively. When I did not feel the Lord's presence I just knew He had left me. I had since my new birth, a desire to eat His Word and so in my spirit this feeling was not confirmed. The conflict came when other's were being visibly blessed and feeling the presence of God; and I was not.

I was given to jealousy and more self-pity. It was difficult to deal with. Learning to take one day at a time has to be a choice. Slow down inside and let the Lord grow you up in His time and in His way. One day, in 1975, the Lord told me He was leading me through a desert place. I was to keep my eyes on Him!

1. Jesus was led by the Holy Spirit into the desert.
2. Joseph was in a desert place in Egypt, in jail for many years.
3. Jacob was in a desert place with his Uncle Laban, twenty years running from his brother.
4. David was in a desert place running from Saul for many years.
5. Moses was in the desert for forty years - twice!
6. Elijah declared there would be no rain for 3 ½ years.
Jezebel was furious and swore to kill him.

God told him to go to the brook Cherith - [means to cut as in covenant]. The Brook Cherith was a tributary of the river Jordan.

Jordan stands for death to self-life. Then he was told to go live at Zarephath with a widow, for that time of drought. Zarephath means to refine. God sent him there for three years.

Both Moses and Elijah were brought to a place called Horeb, meaning desolate - but also called the Mount of God. There, each one met the God of the universe, the Lord of the whole earth. And each one was taught of God how to deal with the enemy.

If we are to take the Old Testament as our example, then what seems to be abandonment by God, is truly a time of preparation.

In Galatians 1, Paul tells us when God called him into the Kingdom he did not confer with flesh and blood. He went by the Spirit into Arabia, that God would,
Reveal His Son in me.
Revelation 12:6 introduces the woman who flees into the wilderness where she has a place prepared by God.

The wilderness prepared for us by God is not a place of destruction and abandonment. As we examine the lives of these men we may clearly see the hand of God on each - they were provided for. What I see is they came out of that place knowing Who was their God. And they had clear direction for their lives.

Elijah was taken apart with God. This mighty Kingdom warrior still had the weakness of his flesh and said, 'Oh God, get me out of here'! But God had further plans for His prophet.

As God began to manifest His presence, Elijah saw His awesome power in consuming fire; able to dry up the heavens, cause fierce winds and earthquakes and now - God reveals Himself in a still small voice.

So often we look for the great miracles of God - His supernatural power to cast out demons, and heal; and His answers to life and death situations. God also wants us familiar with His still small voice, His voice of fellowship and intimacy.

For this we must come apart, and be still.
The devil's desert place is a coliseum of rending and tearing down to kill, steal and destroy. In His merciful love, God

brought me through His own desert place to purge and refine, and to listen for His voice. And in His mercy, He gently grew me up and brought me into a deeper relationship with Himself. I complained and murmured and had to repent many times as God brought me to a place of trusting in Him even though I did not feel His presence.

In my cycle of friendship, rejection, resentment; friendship, rejection, resentment; I was more like a racquet ball being pounded and coming back for more. But I was determined that life would recognize it had a contender.

In all my life before Jesus, my feelings were fine tuned to rejection. When I would detect the smallest breach in a relationship I would reject that person first so that I could walk away unscathed.

It never really happened that way though. I would soon experience the loneliness, isolation and pain all over again. I am not advocating a relationship with the Lord on feelings. We must walk by faith. What I'm sharing is that I lived in my feelings and God was in the process of changing that. One cannot walk in faith and feelings. They are opposed to each other. Now I can confess with John the Apostle,
I know that I know Him.[6]
And I'm still learning. And we must be careful of that to which we heed. The roaring lion is ever on the prowl.

It is imperative that we continue to study and meditate on the Word of God. It is our Well of Salvation for spirit, soul and body. We grow in the Kingdom according to the level of our faith. Maturity comes by hearing, and hearing;

And hearing the Word of faith reinforced in one's life.

Living a life of faith is a continual day by day trusting in God, as He delivers us from those things which would devour our very life. God impressed me with Deuteronomy 8:2&3, but in His great mercy did not tell me how long. The faith and trust my Father has built in me, He knew could come no other way. [see Prov 3.5-7].

And just now I am able to put into words and understand what it was He brought me through. I never before asked for an explanation, I was just glad for the victories. There was much stress and depression in my life, and if God had not intervened, I would have ended it all.

Please remember my adult life reaped what had been sown in my childhood. Great fear, anxiety mistrust, insecurity, rejection, fear of abandonment; much more.

Looking back I can realize my desert place was being married to a man who was committing adultery on me - for many years. And for all that time there was such a lack of communication. If it had not been for God, I would not have made it. I was really in denial and did not allow my conscious mind to state it as fact. My life seemed like a vacuum.

Adultery destroys one's capability to love. Read Pr 5-7. That precious thing that is stolen is the capacity for family relationships, intimacy, fulfillment; and in the end, the destruction of a man's soul. Our relationship reaped the consequences and in the end I knew it had been true all that time. Not only did I deny what was happening but also refused to admit to myself, any emotional response. Please know I really loved this man and wanted a family with him; but I had to bury these emotions because - please understand - I had never learned how to have real communication /relationship with anyone. Now this may be hard to understand, but a child learns how to communicate in the family they grow up in.

It only added to my zombie-like existence. I really thought I was protecting my heart from being broken. And I continued to submit my grieving to the Lord. I know my own responses also added to the problem, but strange as it may seem to one who has never experienced this, I seemed almost paralyzed to do anything about it. I could not handle one more family breakup!

I thought if I ignored it - it would go away, and I put my head in the sand. The pain was too hard to acknowledge, and the fear of rejection and abandonment took it's toll on my mind. Confrontation was not acceptable. The stress this caused my physical well-being became evident as years went by and I looked like an old woman before my time.

I prayed constantly for God to heal our marriage. For almost 20 years all I had was my God and His Word. I kept expecting Him to change things. Now God certainly did not bring about these circumstances. He is omniscient, all knowing, and He knew what it would take to bring me through those years that He knew were coming. He already had my provision in hand. He taught me how to be an overcomer in the midst of rejection for here again came the edict of no value. I don't know why we could never have good talks.

Rejection had tried to kill me - now it would try to erode and destroy. There were times I could have drowned in self-pity and self-hatred. Too often I allowed circumstances to distract me and I lost sight of my real goal in life -

To know God; to know Him at

the depth of intimacy for which I was created.

Time after time He would pull me into His loving arms and show me His faithfulness in the face of my despair. Day after day I walked it out though not always in victory, for my greatest fear was abandonment. My greatest enemy was betrayal of my trust, for too often I'd had the rug pulled out from under me.

In the end I did confront, with a Scripture God gave me, verses that told Mike God surely knew what he was doing. And in the following years after Mike left, God has continued to show me how much He loves me and that He would never leave me, and has proved it time after time. After Mike left, He gave me specific instructions of where to go and what to do. No bag-lady for me.

Mike married the 'one' and he died a few years later. Ex 15:13 *You in Your mercy have led forth The people whom You have redeemed; You have guided them in Your strength To Your holy habitation.*

God told me He gave us emotions that we could experience life. He did not intend they be ground into hamburger by other people. My emotions were always either dead or on fire. God helped me resolve these inconsistencies, as I gave up my right to be resentful and bitter. Please understand I had a long history of bitterness, from childhood and two previous husbands.

During those 20 years Mike was in the Air Force and so we moved many times. We lived in a variety of places and the Lord always brought me into a fellowship somewhere in the city that would help me grow in Him, as I continued to learn how to trust God. Those special times of refreshing from the Lord's presence sustained and encouraged me to continue no matter how often I fell down and skinned my knees.

What my problem was: there dwelt a deep dissatisfaction within; a sense of never being fulfilled; an emptiness that seemed to devour me. As many of us do, I was looking to other people to make me happy. Now isn't that some kind of enigma. I hated people yet still pulled on them for relationship, trying to make them meet my needs.

One must understand the anxiety that rejection spawns; and then the despair, when that hunger is not satisfied. Actually, when a heart is devastated and surrounded by walls of protection, it is impossible for love to break through. The fear of betrayal is ever there to defend. So unless God heals - we remain impenetrable. But healing and restoration is God's priority, and

He's the only One Who is capable of performing that good work.

So we don't have a right to put that kind of demand on people. I had to realize only God can meet the real need of my heart. God wanted to be the focus of my attention. Though I did not comprehend at the time, I now know that God was doing a work in me that would go on through eternity. God does not just give a slice of bread to the hungry, He gives them a wheat field.

When we turn our face toward God He will satisfy our hunger and thirst for life. He was doing that in me. I had to decide if I wanted to fill that place with God or with people. With people the disappointments kept coming. We cannot have our real needs met by people. When I turned to God, I found the joy of His presence and His healing power. People can't restore brokenness or heal our fractured past, although they can love us with God's love.

In every disaster area of our lives God wants to build up the old waste places; raise up the foundations, repair the breach and restore our paths.[7] We are in a hurry to banish the pain but

God sees a deeper work to be done and He only can bring it to fruition.

Through these trials and tribulations we can develop patience and learning to wait on God as He digs ever deeper to the source of the pain. It had become a part of my personality to be a victim so that many of my life experiences victimized me! I always came out the loser no matter what the contest. To truly believe my life could change was beyond my imagination.

My need for the Lord was at a point of being frantic. I had finally found someone that loved me in spite of who I was

or how I performed. But it could never be just me and Him. The deeper work was,
You shall love the Lord your God with all your heart, with all your soul, with all your mind, and with all your strength. This is the first commandment. And the second, like it, is this: you shall love your neighbor as yourself. There is no greater commandment than these.[8] Jesus spoke these words and tells us, all the others are herein fulfilled.
If someone says, I love God, and hates his brother, he is a liar; for he who does not love his brother whom he has seen, how can he love God whom he has not seen. And this commandment we have from Him: that he who loves God must love his brother also.[9]

It's hard to explain the paradox of love/hate unless you've lived in the world of rejection/abandonment. It is fantasy conjured up that never takes real form in the real world. You dream of intimate experiences but they dissolve before your eyes, because fear that grips your heart tells you this can never be. And so - it never is! But God continued to deliver me and heal me. One day in the middle of one of my pity parties, the Lord told me I WAS receiving His love, but I was not looking in the right direction. His love was being manifested to me

THROUGH THEM - THEM - THE OTHER PEOPLE

that I had seen as my enemy for so long; my healing was coming through His people, the body of Christ. He was trying to help me receive love in the physical realm. I had to understand that now I was a part of the family of God.

My heart had been thoroughly stomped by people. There was a time when my light almost went out because of people. I'd been emotionally victimized and abused by people, mostly by rejection.

I really did not know how to have friends. But now things are different; I now live in another world. God in His infinite wisdom used people to put their arms around me, tell me they loved me, remembered my name at the next meeting and invited me to be a part of them.

He caused my lamp to be lighted and to shine [Ps 18:28]. Looking back I can remember there was always someone wanting to hug me, to just say hello. I'd been to hundreds of gatherings of the saints, but there were few that I was really able to relate to because of the fear of rejection. But at one of His most opportune moments, God touched me deeply.

At the closing prayer I began to weep uncontrollably. Many came to pray with me and touch me with their love. I found myself confessing my hatred for people and asking their forgiveness. Many of these I never knew before, but God was there to bring His healing. God - through His wonderful people, persevered.

And remember no matter what you see on the outside of a person, you can't always know what's happening in their heart or in their home. And God doesn't always tell. Sometimes He says,

Never mind what's wrong, just love them.

So I say to the Body of Christ, Please keep loving me; the wounded, the rejected, the hurting. Even if we reject your love at first and don't know how to handle it - please keep loving us. You are bringing healing just by being you; by allowing the love of Christ, the Balm of Gilead, to flow through you to bind up our broken heart.

In those years I learned to understand the frailty of the human spirit. I came to know you can't draw water from a rock [unless God is in it]. A person can only give what they have. If there is a woundedness within the heart there can be no supply of love or caring forthcoming.

There are many good people in the world, but their patience with a person that keeps turning on them, is very limited. They can be offended beyond the capacity to repair when they know not the Lord of Love. People in the world do not have that Lifeline coming down from so gracious a Father. They do not have the resources to fulfill our many needs.

We must realize that people react to pain and offenses in many different ways. Sometimes with anger or arrogance. Sometimes it is with despair and withdrawal. Psalm 29 tells us,

The voice of the Lord breaks the cedars, yes the Lord splinters the cedars of Lebanon.
- Lebanon - heart;
- Cedars firm, break, burst, tenacity.

So much insight when you know what the words mean.

A wounded heart is shut up like a fortress. Stubbornness is a trait of an angry man; an anger that arises from always having to prove you have a right to live. Only God's unconditional love will minister life to the broken heart. There will be a different kind of breaking that the life of God may pour forth out of that pain.

If one does not have God's unconditional, unlimited love, one cannot give it out. If we begin with emptiness and a heart filled with hurt and despair, God has to heal so that He may deposit His kind of love therein. Love is a living viable commodity. It must flow at all times. If it gets dammed up it stagnates and is in danger of dying. The world cultivates human emotions that operate on a base of performance. It can never work any other way because of our nature. Love with God's love - caring for the sinner not the sin.

Rom 2:4 *the goodness of God leads you to repentance?*

We must renounce any good thing we think can come out of our human love and ask God to exchange it for His. Human love is selfish and demanding, conditional and limited. Though it will serve until something better comes along; here God is offering that something better, His best. Won't you receive His kind of love and share with others? It's the unconditional kind.

There is an abundance available through the heart of God.

Please know that even God's love that is unconditional, does not love the sin we seem to get wrapped up in - but He will always love the sinner, the person; and this is what I mean to love people - but we don't have to spend time with them.

Some of us grew up never able to please our parents. We become conscious of inadequacy and inferiority and strive to be O.K. We become performance oriented which produces a man pleaser which produces the fear of man.

This is not the game of finding someone to blame and putting life on hold because they did it to me. We can seek out the root cause of the pain and with God's help, throw it into the sea of forgetfulness. Ask Him, He knows.

Beginning with the healing power of forgiveness, we can choose to cast it out of our life because of the Blood of Jesus, shed for our redemption. As we comprehend the wickedness of our own heart,[10] we can learn to be compassionate in understanding others. We don't have to stay the way we are - because of Jesus. We can trade our human inheritance for His inheritance in us.[11] In realizing these things therefore, we neither accuse nor excuse; there can be rather, an understanding. The Word tells us we must take responsibility for how we act and react.

Our insight into why people do what they do helps us to respond in more positive ways. God knows the pain that is oftentimes our focus................➜

> He is in the business of restoring our souls.

Sometimes there has been a physical battering. In these last generations the womb has not always been a safe place to be either; and some family environments have been downright hazardous to life expectancy.

For some there may have been a battering in our emotions, a tearing down of our personhood, a disdain of our humanity. This may also cause a hardness of heart, a critical spirit, a breaking down of relationships that seem too far gone for even a sovereign God to mend. But know that God is able! [2Co 9].

At some point in our walk with the Lord we may come to a stopping place of either wonderment or outrage, to deal with certain questions. Someone said, 'Our growing up in God will never go past our questions'. These must be answered for those to whom it applies.

Where was God when I was being beaten, abused, raped, left hungry, rejected, abandoned? When I needed arms around me; when I was helpless, hopeless? Where was He? [I was not abused like this. I speak for those who were].

If God created me for Himself, where was He? The years of my childhood were harsh and no one protected me. Where was He? No one showed me how to call on Him. No one told me of His love. Where was He?

Where was God? He was in the same place that He was in that day when men were mocking, beating and spitting on His Beloved Son, Jesus. That same place when they tore open His flesh with a Roman whip laced with sharp pieces of metal.

God was in the same place as in the day He watched as they drove those thorns into Jesus' brow. He watched them hammer spikes through His Son's hands and feet.

He was in the same place as in that day when Jesus implored His Father to forgive them, they know not what they do. The Father watched with aching compassion as He declared throughout the universe...

This is My Provision !!

Now we can place these questions into the wounds of His hands and feet. We can lay our outrage into the heart that broke for love of His people. We can come to the cross of Jesus and forgive. We can come to the place of going on with God as He brings us through step by step, healing and restoration for the lost years of our life.

So rejoice in the Lord forever more *for He hath done great things and He is greatly to be praised.* The Lord wants us to receive His unconditional love because that's what heals the pain within. As we are being healed we can also respond to others unconditionally. That is, love them no matter what they do or don't do. If they don't respond - well, you have obeyed Mt 6:14. That is not to say we barge into people's lives to the point of offense. *A bruised reed he will not break, a smoking flax he will not quench.*[12]

We can respond to them with patience and caring. He wants to heal and restore - turn our lamp up to burn strong. We can learn from Jesus how to have this same sensitivity.

Inasmuch as ye have done it unto the least of these my brethren, ye have done it unto me. Right now God wants to loose the power of His forgiveness into your life! When we come to the cross our sins are forgiven - we are reconciled to God. When we forgive others we are reconciled to them. The ministry of reconciliation[14] is given to bring forth life into relationships. Here is where the healing begins to flow.

Our dealings with our fellow man is on God's priority list. What He has to say about it can be seen in Mt 5:21-26. But it's not just a lesson we learn like ABC's. It is what we are becoming; a channel of His love and reconciliation. Be sure to know we must first be reconciled to God.

For some of us there are so many we must forgive. The long list seems overwhelming. Allow the Spirit of God to help you sort it out. If you are here at this crossroads wanting this healing from God be sure that it is forthcoming. The Amplified Bible explains in Matthew 6:14

For if you forgive people their trespasses, [their reckless and willful sins, leaving them, letting them go, and giving up resentment], your heavenly Father will also forgive you.

Your Lord and Savior, your Healer and Deliverer is ever present to reach out and touch you. As the Holy Spirit brings to your mind people and experiences just say, 'Lord I forgive, Lord I forgive'. And somewhere in there be sure to say, 'Lord,

I forgive myself'. We can beat ourselves up with condemnation and guilt. The Word says
There is therefore now no condemnation to them which are in Christ Jesus.[15]

Even as you are forgiving, God is flooding you with the reality and assurance of His forgiveness. Perhaps you have been angry at God for allowing these things. Would you permit God to be sovereign over the whole matter of your life and use it for His glory? Jn 9:3 So the works of God may be made manifest.

For those who were raised in a dysfunctional home, [and listen, this dysfunctional is real! We just don't have to stay there!] and/or were separated from their birth family by foster care or adoption because of abuse; I think it is safe to say there is always anger and most often it is entrenched in the very marrow of our bones. Look up in the Concordance for Scripture references of what happens to our bones because of anger. Then ask God to forgive, heal and restore. And lift these people up to God, you letting go.

Over a long period of time I was trying to deal with my anger, in the Lord. No sooner would I assuage my irate emotions when it would again rear it's ugly head. It was eating me for dinner and I continued to seek God for deliverance.

One day God told me, You do not have anger, you are an angry person. It was buried in my character, my emotions, the intentions of my heart; not only anger but a deep rage. And then one day God showed me also, outrage!

But for my blessed Savior, my Redeemer, the lover of my soul - I would not be writing this. I would not have kept my sanity. Anger and rage is a devourer.

I had several attacks of spastic colon to attest to its avaricious appetite; bursitis and other infirmities, and raw emotions that looked for the tiniest spark to ignite, caused a fire in my bones.
But still I kept it all inside. Though a few times I exploded at the person that was hurting me, most of my anger caused a raging storm in the pit of my stomach. Bitterness and resentment don't really effect the other person. It plays havoc with us.

And yet child of God, for this also Christ died.
The Spirit is able to pierce and divide asunder the joints and marrow as we humble ourselves before the Lord [Heb 4:12].

You can lay down the right to get even, or to justify yourself; and forgive. Your merciful and gracious God will move in your behalf. He yearns for you to come into His peace and rest. He saved it for you [Heb 4:9].

For we have a High Priest who is touched with the feelings of our infirmities. Let us therefore come boldly unto the throne of grace that we may obtain mercy and find grace to help in time of need.[16]

You may ask, How can Jesus know what I'm feeling? Heb 4:15 tells us He was in all points [in whatsoever] tempted/tested as we are. He experienced every aspect of the human condition. Read John 8:41 and see what they called Him. In their carnal mind - He was. He took the stigma of illegitimacy to the cross and poured out His Blood for this curse [Read Dt 23.2; and they thought He was].

And His ancestry in the flesh was something to behold, if we claim our problems came down the line. Jesus was born of the lineage of Judah. 1Chr 2 tells us Judah's first born son was so evil that God slew him.

Judah had two illegitimate sons, and from Judah also came Achan who took a spoil of accursed and devoted things [Jos 6:9 Amp] from Jericho and caused men to be killed in battle. There is murder, adultery and idolatry - and evil kings coming from David's loins of whom came Mary, the mother of Jesus. And all was dealt the blow of death on the cross with our Redeemer.

So no matter what has been your portion in life, when you come to the cross - the Blood has paid the price. Through the Blood of Jesus we are given the liberty to walk in our new inheritance as a child of the Kingdom; brand new, born again from above, adopted into God's family.

All this is not a fairy tale. It is real. It is a gift from God to set us free from the things that held us captive. There are thousands of gifts and promises revealed in the Word for us to partake of each as needed. It is God's medication for our pain and wounds. God is faithful. One of His greatest gifts to me is peace in my mind. We can release anger and bitterness to the Lord. Ask God to help redirect your emotions into positive responses.

We can be so self-centered and self-important and involved in doing OUR THING, [on the phone, cooking, watching TV] that no one including our kids can interrupt even for a second.

We can ask [our patient] God to take our irritability and un-interruptible-ness and give us in its place, the peace that passes understanding so that the fruit of the Spirit can begin to bud and bloom in our heart and mind; patience, etc.

Many times in forgiving people we find the same old memories popping up again and again. The enemy has us believing that we did not forgive to begin with. It makes us heavy of heart and keeps us on a merry-go-round. Actually the cause can be bitterness, the emotional pain, the broken heart, the down deep wounded spirit, the hurt that the Lord needs to touch.

The offenses we've experienced need forgiving and sometimes we must go to the person in private and deal with the issue. But we must also go to the Lord for healing and cleansing to remove that bitterness and the offense from our system; our soul, our heart. You see, we are personally responsible for our own actions and reactions. I have found in forgiving, that each memory of a specific offence needs forgiveness. Yes, clean the slate!

In Christ, we always have a choice of what we'll do in any circumstance. The more we give in to unforgiveness and resentments the more we give place to the devil and our flesh gets pulled into the trap [James 4:6-12; Eph 4:21-32].

Perhaps these attitudes were established BC. There may be some legitimate reasons why we are the way we are. But it cannot be repeated enough times that in Christ we are appointed the freedom to choose - our way or His. His way calls for change. There really is liberty and freedom in Christ [Gal 5:1]. You can be delivered and set free to renew your mind and heart as you put on that New Man and submit yourself to God [James 4:6-10].

Being then, made free from sin, ye became the servant of righteousness, so now yield your members servants to righteousness, unto holiness.[17]

If you will turn in your Bible to 1John 1:9 and do what it says - God showed me a bottomless pit directly under that verse of Scripture. It is awaiting all your pain, all your sin, all your anguish and fears. Begin now to dump these things God shows you, as He responds to your repentant heart.

You may use this bottomless pit as often as necessary down through the years of growing and walking in your Father's Kingdom. As we do this and rid ourselves of the old issues we can ask God to bring us to 1Thessalonians 5:23,

May The God of Peace sanctify you wholly spirit, soul and body.
He will fill that place with His unconditional love. It is the Blood of Jesus that prevails for sin and for healing. God has shown me repeatedly the effects of my past and how they were capable of producing recurring emotional pain and bitterness, resentment and frustration, etc. He taught me day by day to lay it all out before Him - to receive His forgiveness for my sin response in any issue and be cleansed from all unrighteousness by the Blood of Jesus.

Not only was I released from condemnation and guilt but also was I healed emotionally and progressively, physical healing came as a result. At one time He reminded me that the Blood of Jesus prevails when we acknowledge our sin - not if we justify our actions or are looking for revenge.

And now Father in your mercy and grace bring forth a healing of the emotions to all who would come to You in these matters. Let Your Balm of Gilead, Your healing ointment bring blessed rest to these memories that have tormented your children for so long. Thank You Lord.

Jesus told the woman at Samaria, the Water He would give her would be a Well of Water springing up into everlasting life. By her responses to Him, she revealed her hunger for God. See how she ran to spread the Good News.

We too may receive this Water of Life for ourselves in looking to Jesus for our restoration. As we grow in the Lord we can receive a greater portion, to flow through us and out to others who are just as needy.[18]

Paul shares with us an especially beautiful prayer in Ephesians 3:16-21 *That you being rooted and grounded in love, may be able to comprehend with all the saints what is the width and length and depth and height - to know the love of Christ which passes knowledge; that you may be filled with all the fullness of God.* PRAISE THE LORD!

Just on the basis of living out our days there is a dissatisfaction and hunger for something more than what we have, because of desires and frustrations. But other people were never meant to meet our needs just as we cannot meet theirs. This kind of thing brings control, demands, judgment, criticism.

We are called to love people and to trust God.
We must consider that relationships will happen all our lives whether of positive or negative kind. Even though we may

think we've dealt with our prejudices - there will come suddenly another arena in which to fight our lions.

Personalities unlike ours will grind and scrape and mutilate all our ideals and bore into our very soul and heart attitudes we never thought existed. But God - well!
Search me oh God, and know my heart; try me and know my thoughts; and see if there be any wicked way in me, and lead me in the way everlasting. A way not predicated by performance. My friends, isn't that what we ourselves need, as well? It is self-will that gets us into a lot of skirmishes, But...

God is a present help in time of need.
That time of need may well be the moment that our emotions exploding with anger. This will be decision time. It worked for me. God showed up! As we open our heart to God He can fill those empty places with all His fullness - the love and peace - and we can pass it on to others.

The Midrash, a Jewish exegetical treatise on the Old Testament, dating from the 4th to the 12th century, in Shir Hashirim]Song of Songs] has God proclaim,
Open your hearts for me, even as slightly as a pinpoint, and I will open for you gates wide enough for chariots to enter. But the opening must extend through the entire heart, said the Kotzker Rebbe. However minute the opening, it must pierce the entire heart. [Excerpt from Rabbi Herbert Rose, Temple Beth Shalom, Ocala, Fla., article in the Star-Banner, Sept. 1996].

God made us in His image because He wants us for Himself to share His eternal life and blessings with; *His riches in glory.*[19] He created us with a special place that can only be filled with Himself. He created us for Himself.
Being the world's friend is being God's enemy. Whoever chooses to be a friend of the world takes his stand as an enemy of God.[20]

As the Father watched Adam betray their relationship, He knew the heartache that man would suffer in future generations. How He grieved as He watched Cain murder his brother Abel, and saw the river of innocent blood that would overflow its banks, running down through the centuries. We must remember that God gave us a free will. He could not stop Adam nor could He stop Cain. And we must decide for ourselves Who we will worship. God does not want Robots.

Yet this God Whose name is Love created man for Himself. He is a jealous God. He pulls on us through that love to restore us into His presence. [Romans 5] *For while we were yet sinners,* He poured out His innocent Blood,
While we were yet His enemies we were reconciled to God through the death of His Son.[21]
In researching some of the words in Psalm 139:14-16, we may conclude certain principles laid down in the genesis of our life.

We were wonderfully made and set apart for God, to be bound together with Him. Not destined for destruction, He covered us in that secret place and formed us deliberately in such a way that eventually we could receive His life into our spirit and be conformed back into His image.

All this was done for the purpose of reconciliation. Even as that egg and sperm came together [in no matter what sort of circumstances or human failure], God responded to that spark of life and began to orchestrate what would eventually be His sons and daughters, capable of bearing His light and glory; ruling and reigning with Him for all eternity [Is 60:1-2; Jn 17:22; Rev 5:10].

God wants to fulfill us in Him; to make us perfect and whole, healthy in spirit, soul and body, balanced in all things and finally without spot or wrinkle. I praise God for all the people in the world that God has used and will use in the future as His hot iron - on all my wrinkles.

And may I share here, God sent me to College - for a degree in Sociology - but the lesson was to understand that people are people, every one different and they have the right to be who they are whether we like them or not.

Just a note - I always thought I was stupid - [Final Grade 3.78] but God said - see - you're not!

♫ I'm Standing Here Before You Lord
To Enter in Your Holy Presence
I Lift My Hands and Heart
To Worship You, For You Are Lord
You Are Lord
You Are Lord ♫

STUDY GUIDE

1. When did God find out about you? Ps 139
2. But even further back than this? Eph 1:4-5
3. What are some of His plans for restoration? Isa 58:12
4. Is it possible to really know God? 1Jn 2:3
5. Could He possibly care about your relationships with other people? Mk 12:30-31.
6. How high on God's priority list is your dealings with your brothers and sisters? Mt 5:21-26
7. How important is it to forgive others for offending us? Mt 6:16
8. Did people get offended at Jesus? Mk 6:3   Lk 7:23
9. Have you ever been angry at God?
0. Maybe you are right now. He may have disappointed you. Not done what you expected. Made you wait too long.
See Isaiah 59:1
11. God wants to draw you back. Will you let Him?
12. Use John 1.12-13 and 1John 1:9.
13. God hasn't gone anywhere. It's you that turned your face from Him. Read Rom 5:6-11. God has such great purpose for you.

Turn around - He's right there.

14. The next move is yours. Read Heb 12. That great cloud of witnesses, that innumerable company of angels and saints gone before us, are cheering us on. We are not alone - we just have to choose that we want to continue. The enemy of your soul has been vanquished - defeated at the cross. If you are feeling alone, find other believers for encouragement and fellowship.

One more scenario I must transcribe. Many years ago, on my mother's 75th birthday, my family got together and gave her a humongous birthday party. All the children, grands, nieces, nephews and dear friends were there; a lot of people. I was living in Alaska at that time.

But somehow they forgot to invite me.

PRAYER: Lord, teach my heart to love as You love
and to forgive others
as You have forgiven me.

♪ Jesus loves me this I know
For the Bible Tells me so...   ❤

SCRIPTURES

1. Mt 11:2830
2. Ps 139:1318
3. Ps 116:12
4. Dt 31:6
5. Mk 11:26
6. 1Jn 2:3 He 13:6
  And Rom 2:1
7. Isaiah 58:12
8. Mk 12:3031
9. 1Jn 4:2021
10. Jer 17:9
11. Eph 1:14
12. Mt 12:20
13. Mt 25:40
  and Heb 9:15
14. 2Co 5:1821
15. Rom 8:1
16. Heb 4:15-16
17. Ro 6:1819
18. Jn 4:14
19. Ph 4:19
20. Js 4:4 Amp.
21. Rom 5:10

You are an original,
I made you like you are
I set aside all others,
And made for you a start
The beginning of a perfect you,
So we could become one
I birthed you and re-birthed you,
So you would never be alone
Each and every one of you,
fills a place in my heart
And I will never leave you,
We'll never be apart
I made each one individual,
Never like another
But I brought you all together,
So you could be brothers
Your spirit, soul and body are different in time
And when I gather all of you together -
You will be mine
So remember I made you
Exactly as you are
And you will share in My glory
For as long as I Am your God.
♥

HIS LOVE AND OURS

*Love not the world neither the things
that are in the world.
If any man love the world,
the love of the Father is not in him.*[1]
*Behold what manner of love the Father
hath bestowed upon us, that we should be called
the sons of God; therefore the world knows us not
because it knew him not.*[2]

As we become further involved in the Kingdom of God, deeper revelation comes to us from the Word. We begin to know and experience the unique love of the Father. Our 'School of Hard Knocks' education that taught us how to live in the world must be laid aside as we learn to walk in the Spirit.[3]

The Father's unconditional love is unlike anything we've ever known. First of all it is total commitment with nothing asked nor taken from the recipient.
But God commended his love towards us, in that, while we were yet sinners, Christ died for us..when we were enemies, we were reconciled to God by the death of his Son.[4]

Why? Because true to His nature, God is love. If this sounds too simplistic, we must remember the Gospel, [Good News] *is published abroad to the foolish, the weak, the base and the are nots of the world; the ignoble, the common people. And it confounds the wise!*[5]

When men covenant with men they agree on the terms, make oaths, draw up papers, shake hands, etc. Common in Abram's era also was blood sacrifice to bind covenant between men. In those days, both parties to a covenant walked through the blood sacrifice and sealed covenant that could not be broken, oftentimes under pain of death.

The covenant between Abram and God was not different, only unique in that God swore by Himself - for there was none greater. God does His mighty works when man steps out of the way. God cut the covenant with Abram as a deep sleep came upon him in the midst of blood sacrifice, from a heifer to a young pigeon, symbolic of the rich and the poor. **The LORD is a God of Covenant.**

The Lord Jehovah walked through that blood sacrifice alone, and He alone confirmed the covenant so that He alone will receive all the glory. A smoking furnace and a burning lamp passed through those bloody remnants, affirming God's judgment and mercy on a people yet to be born.

Because man is incapable of keeping faithful to his part of the covenant in his flesh, God caused Abram to sleep [a type of death to his flesh] and Jehovah, the God of Covenant, walked through that blood sacrifice alone; a type and shadow of his death, alone on that cross. He paid the death penalty in our place, because man broke the covenant.

For when God made promise to Abraham, because he could swear by no greater, he sware by himself, for men verily swear by the greater, and an oath for confirmation is to them an end of all strife. Wherein God, willing more abundantly to show unto the heirs of promise the immutability [the permanent character of his word] of his counsel, confirmed it by an oath; that by two immutable [unchangeable] things, in which it was impossible for God to lie, we might have a strong consolation, who have fled for refuge to lay hold upon the hope set before us.[8]

His covenant and His oath to keep it, is backed by His integrity and character in which there is no shadow of turning.[9] We have a covenant with God because of His faithfulness, not ours; *and This I recall to my mind, therefore I have hope. It is because of the Lord's mercies that we are not consumed, because his compassions fail not. They are new every morning; great is thy faithfulness.*[10]

God does not use up leftovers from the day before. The manna in the desert became foul if saved for the next day.[11] He desires to give us of His sweet anointing a fresh portion each and every day. We only need to receive. We do this by yielding ourselves to Him.

The covenant God made with Abram is passed down to us through the Seed Who is Christ. The covenant promises came before the law was given [430 years later]. Apart from the law, we inherit these promises by faith.[7] [Jeremiah 31.31-33].

In Exodus 19:18, here again, the smoke of a furnace pertained to God's presence, on the mountain with Moses; and indeed would His presence be with Abraham's progeny from that moment on because of His covenant. Engraved on tablets of stone, they would learn how to worship and obey the God they didn't know, Who had just brought them out of bondage.

His righteous judgments would chastise and rebuke, protect and deliver His beloved nation as they were led through the desert with Moses.

2Peter 1:4 tells us there are exceedingly great and precious promises by which we may become partakers of His divine nature. There are so many promises in the Word of God. Forgiveness, mercy, grace, hope, healing and restoration, to name a few.

And the best of all is His resurrection life.

Herein is love, not that we loved God, but that he loved us, and sent his Son to be the propitiation for our sins...
And He Himself is the propitiation for our sins and not for ours only but also for the whole world.[13]

Note: The Greek word for propitiation is the same root word the Bible uses for mercy seat. Remember the Ark of the Covenant in the Holy of Holies of the Tabernacle of the Congregation, and finally in the Temple, the Ark had the mercy seat[14] on which the High Priest smeared the blood of sacrifice on the Day of Atonement.

The word propitiation means atone, expiate; appease or extinguish the guilt incurred. The mercy seat, the lid of the Ark was the expiatory place or thing; that is, the atoning victim. Jesus was - He is our mercy seat. He Himself is our propitiation.

The soul that sins it shall die.[15] *The wages of sin is death.*[16]

The shedding of blood was the only vehicle used to satisfy the law of sin and death. The Old Testament sacrifice for sin was an animal substitute.

Now, once at the end of the ages, He hath appeared to put away sin by the sacrifice of Himself.[17]

From this we see that Jesus was the means and the end of all atonement for all the sin of all the world.

Isaiah 53:10 tells us the soul of the Redeemer was made an offering for sin; and 1Pet 1:18-19 confirms our redemption with the precious Blood of Jesus. He paid the price - He set us free from the penalty. He also reconciled us with God. The fact is that the Father turned His back on Jesus when He became our sin on the cross,[18]

My God, my God, why hast thou forsaken me?

He graphically portrayed the separation between God and sinful man. Because it took the mightiest force of sacrificial love to redeem us from the law; it is love that fulfills the law. Remember as you read these next verses; Eph 2:10, and Ph 2:13,

We are his workmanship, created in Christ Jesus unto good works.. For it is God who works in you, to will and to do of his good pleasure.

So when Mt 5:48 tells us what we must do, know that it is God Who works it out. He asks us to yield our life to His agenda. *Be ye therefore perfect as your Father who is in heaven is perfect.*

Col 3:14 tells us, *Put on love, which is the bond of perfectness.* A bond is a uniting principle, a joint, a tie, like a ligament. Romans 13:8-10 explains:

He that loves another hath fulfilled the law.

Vs 9 reiterates the law and then tells us since love works no evil to its neighbor, *therefore love is the fulfilling of the law.* Then Gal 5:7 *All the law is fulfilled in one word, thou shalt love thy neighbor as thyself.* So if love is the fulfilling of the law, then love is the key to perfection. And if that's not enough, even our faith avails us nothing except that it is,

Activated and energized and expressed and working through love.[19]

But only the unconditional kind - all else brings judgment. Faith works through love. If we have not God's unconditional love, totally free from judgment and criticism in any given situation or for any given person, then we need not pray because,

Rom 14.23 *Whatever is not of faith is sin.*

There is much strife among men. Without Christ there is discord. Without Christ we would not know our God nor our brother. The way is blocked by our ego. Christ opened the way to God and to our brother. We can become vulnerable because He did it first. We can live with one another in peace. We can love and serve one another, and come into one accord.

When we have the Father's unconditional love abiding in us - it transcends all the negative emotions and feelings in which we learned to operate from, in the world system. Only the first four commandments have to do with serving God. The last six have to do with our fellow man; but we can't do it without God's love..

It's easy to say, I love God, when you can't see Him and, He lives in heaven anyway. But the man who lives and

works beside you - you can see. We have to relate to people every day in every way. This brings us home to the true meaning of God's love - the kindness and mercy shown to someone we don't know or don't want to know. Not to get something from them, but just to serve them perhaps in incidental ways, or even with something significant to their survival; without expecting a reward or recognition.
Or just to say 'Hi, have a good day.'

This is God's love, unconditional, unlimited; released through God's people to a world that knows not the Father. Jesus prayed to the Father on our behalf, that we all may be one as the Father and the Son are one.

That they also may be one in us. And the glory [of being a son] which you gave me I have given them that they may be one even as we are one. For what purpose? *That the world may believe that thou has sent me.*

In reading John 17, we can see that the glory Jesus had with the Father before the world, was laid down as He took upon Himself the flesh of humanity. This is clear in verse five. Did He give it up so intensely that He had to ask Father to give it back to Him?

Read Phil 2:7 to understand the enormity of what Jesus did. Can any of us let go of Self, so intensely that it is no longer a part of our makeup. This will make way for the glory of a son, that the Father freely gives His children [Isaiah 60:1-2].

The graphic display of unlimited selfless love demonstrated through the body of Christ is what God is using to be the witness of His love to the world.[21] The power of the Holy Spirit within us gives us the power to love as He does. The goal of our life must be to gain confidence in His love. All else will follow.

Dietrick Bonhoffer once said... Where human love can no longer expect its desire to be fulfilled, it stops short and turns to hatred, contempt and slander.

Perhaps the greatest expose' of this observation is marital discord and divorce. On the other hand what better place to practice sacrificial love but in our own homes, in our own families, on a daily basis.[22] He knows our frame. He'll help us do this if we will turn to Him. For some of us this is not an easy decision. The power of the Holy Spirit gives us the power to yield and choose to love as He does. It is by definition, God's grace which is sufficient, to be applied to any and all circumstances in our daily lives.

It is only by His grace that we accomplish anything in His Kingdom. Because of our selfish nature, God had to plan, initiate, and Himself carry out the method of reconciliation. But we must yield to Him the hardness of our heart.

Really the only kind of love we can generate, borders on how another person relates to us. *But he that dwells in love dwells in God and God in him.* This is God's provision. We yield, He makes it happen. The result is;

By this shall all men know that ye are my disciples, that ye love one another.[23]

One day God led me to pray, Lord, I give to You the human kind of love that dwells in my heart. It is so inferior to what Your love represents. I ask for and receive Your kind of unconditional love that I may share with others.

If you pray this, expect God to begin causing you to change attitudes and habit patterns. We must decrease, that He may increase; line upon line; precept by precept; here a little, there a little.[24] This is the kind of love I had for Mike when he was not the husband I had expected when I married him.

Jesus is our peace. He has broken down every wall. Even the most loving one here in the flesh cannot match the merciful, gracious love God has shed abroad in our hearts. When we partake of that love, it seems we cannot say thank you, enough. And when it comes to our neighbor, we don't have to fall short.

It is only this infinite force of reconciliation loosed on the earth that can turn the world upside down - or rather right side up. Our community with another consists solely in what Christ has done in both of us. We cannot produce life by our own words and deeds, but only by that word and deed which really binds us together - the forgiveness of our sins wrought by His priceless gift of love. As we forgive people we release God to forgive their sins and show them His love. This is where our faith is energized and expressed.

No wonder we are called to love our enemies and pray for them that despitefully use us. What weapon could be more powerful to pierce the hardest heart; to bring peace to an explosive situation. It is God's love shed abroad in our hearts that we may be taught of God to love one another. Paul begins many of his letters to the churches with, *Grace and peace to you from God our Father and the Lord Jesus*

Christ. Grace and peace can only be a blessing from a loving Father's heart Who sees our desperate need.

The manifold resources of many people of God diligently researching the Word of God over many years has been brought together to produce the Amplified Bible. Within each verse there is contained the wealth of word studies to produce the fullest meaning.

The following portion of Scripture is taken from this source to bring out the richness of His plan. Digging into Ephesians 3:14-19 reveals the total concord between the Godhead: Father, Son and Holy Spirit; here revealed in awesome profundity in what is His final purpose, to reproduce His love in us.

For this reason [seeing the greatness of this plan by which you are built together in Christ] I bow my knees before the Father of our Lord Jesus Christ, for whom every family in heaven and on earth is named, [that Father from whom all fatherhood takes its title and derives its name]. May He grant you out of the rich treasury of His glory to be strengthened and reinforced with mighty power in the inner man by the [Holy] Spirit, [Himself indwelling your innermost being and personality].

May Christ through your faith [actually dwell, settle down, abide, make His permanent home] in your hearts! May you be rooted deep in love and founded securely on love. That you may have the power and be strong to apprehend and grasp with all the saints, [God's devoted people, the experience of that love] what is the breadth and length and height and depth [of it].

That you may really come] to know [practically through experience for yourselves] the love of Christ, which surpasses mere knowledge [without experience]; that you may be filled [through all your being] unto all the fullness of God [may have the richest measure of the divine Presence, and become a body wholly filled and flooded with God Himself].

In the gospels Jesus shows forth the Father's love so graphically as in Luke 15 with the parable of the Prodigal Son. A certain man had two sons and the younger wanted his portion of legacy, now! Soon the young man left home and went to a far country where he wasted all he had on riotous living.

The word prodigal means addicted to wasteful expenditure - time, money; habits wrought over a long period of time. Perhaps the father tried to bring correction, discipline - but the son would not listen. He realized the only way to get through to him was to let the son go. Unconditional love sets another free to make their own decisions and choices, and also allows them to reap the consequences.

After a short time he found himself starving and got a job feeding swine. While trying to fill his empty belly with pig food, he remembered that even his father's servants ate better than what he had. His decision to go home was based on the realization that not only did he sin against his father but also against God. He would arise and go home, and beg his father to allow him to be a servant/bond slave.

The parable also speaks of a father who knew each son had to decide for himself what to make of his life and on which road each would travel. In giving the son his share and letting him go, the father placed that responsibility on the young man's shoulder. We each must come to ourselves. We each have a decision to make for our life's direction.

Was this young man so involved in doing his own thing that he was totally unaware of his father's love? Jesus was telling us of God the Father's love in this parable. What is your Father saying to you? And are we so blinded by the cares of this world that we can't come into that place of

Casting all your cares upon him for he cares for you.[25]
The father constantly watched and patiently waited for his son's return. The Bible declares,
When he was a great way off the father saw him, and had compassion, and ran, and fell on his neck, and kissed him.

Moving down to verses 28-31 we see a different attitude. We find another young man not even wanting to recognize it is his own brother who has returned. He calls him, *This son of yours...;*

All too often a fallen brother is kicked out of the family!

With anger and resentment of the other's frivolity and spend-thrift ways; there was not demanded a time of restitution, nor an earning again of his position in the family.

He must have thought, How easy to just say, 'I'm sorry'. He goes on comparing and measuring what he has done and what his brother has or hasn't done, making sure his father is doubly aware of the unworthiness of this wayward dolt.

Criticism, pride and self-righteousness was hidden within his heart. He was quick to point out his brothers graphic sins, but could not recognize his own. It's clear to see this other young man needed correction also, but the father in his wisdom, does not even address this point.

Our Father God has bestowed on mankind a unique gift called a 'free will'. Since He will not violate our right to use our free will, we must be sure to recognize the only way God will move in our behalf is by faith which pleases Him,[26] and by yielding our agendas to His plan for our life.

Jesus had to yield His free will. Yes, if He was human at all, [and He was] He constantly had to make choices, as we do. Because of His consistent submission to His Father, He quickly yielded His life, and His hope was in His Father.

If we are to receive our inheritance as joint-heirs with Christ,[27] can we do less? And if God gives us freedom of choices, we also must allow others their liberty. We have no right to criticize another for what they do or don't do [1Cor 4:7].

This is one of the virtues of unconditional love. That's right. As we receive it from God - so may we share it with others. Every time we say yes to God - it gets easier. His awesome grace will be sufficient.

With tender mercy and unrelenting love, the father passes over these grievances because the word prodigal means addicted to wasteful expenditure - time, money; habits wrought over a long period of time. Think about it - Father 'wasted ' his resources on a frivolous child, probably spent much time with his children as a loving father; and was in the habit of giving them what thy wanted.

And so he replies to the brother, *It is meet that we should be merry and glad, for this thy brother was dead and is alive again, and was lost and is found.*

In verse 15 the son also considered himself unworthy. The father deemed him unprofitable. He was glad to restore his son to the family. He was received again to the place from which he left. With these words of the father, restoration begins. His place in the family had been saved for him.

True Forgiveness Is Trusting That Person Again in the Place Where They Failed.

Father God receives us again as we come back to the place we left. God understands our humanity; our fears and apprehension of what might happen if we 'let go'. His love and forgiveness exceeds our expectations.

Some may have a problem with this concept, but is this the way of fully trusting in God and having expectations only in Him? [Ps 62.5] And does not God trust us again in the place where we failed Him? We cannot change people. We can only love them and forgive them seventy times seven. However this trusting does not apply to two year olds. We still must watch them carefully.

Yet because we may have been hurt in the past, we continue to keep records of debtors. We keep the pain current by evaluating our present status in accordance with our past. If we will release this burden to the Lord He can bring into our life the same measure of peace He had in the garden of Gethsemane, when He knew He was about to be crucified.

My peace I give unto you.

God doesn't always move in one person's life as He does another. He may remove one from a situation - and offer the other, grace to abide. I say offer because God does not force His will on us. We must be sure to search out God's purpose in every situation and then trust and obey. On the other hand we may choose to do things our own way. We'll usually find a dead end on that road. Prov 30:5 in the Amplified Bible declares,

Every word of God is tried and purified. He is a shield to those who trust and take refuge in him.

Are you willing to turn around? Either God's Word is real or it's not. If it's not then let's all party for tomorrow we die. There is nothing else of any value. Eccl 4:4 tells us,

Then I saw that all painful effort in labor and all skill in work comes from man's rivalry with his neighbor. This is also vanity, a vain striving after the wind and a feeding on it.

Or we may base our life on the ways of God; put all our eggs into that trustworthy basket and find peace and safety under the shadow of the Most High Magnificent Almighty God, Who is aware when even a tiny, blind, naked sparrow falls out of its nest and dies, a few feet from food and nurturing [Mt 10].

Each of us is written in the Book of Life as an individual. There is no group cut-rate, half-price fare ticket here. Jesus has become the personal Savior of each one. There was no collective 'yes Lord', so that maybe the short one in the back of the room kind of gets lost in the shuffle and is just carried along with the throng.

NO - CHRIST HAS SEPARATED US UNTO HIMSELF.
God deals with us individually because we are individual, special and unique in His family. Even though the nature of mankind makes us very much alike, we are each a precious stone joined with others,
> For a holy temple in the Lord...built together
> for a habitation of God through the Spirit.[28]

How often do we in the body of Christ keep a list of measures and comparisons. Do we scrutinize the blessings others seem to receive. Do we judge or criticize their worthiness in any issue? With whom do we compare others? Ourselves of course. Oftentimes, we measure others by our own standards. Let me quote Paul speaking of judging from outward appearances.

> Just as [you] are Christ's, even so we are Christ's ...we dare not class ourselves or compare ourselves with those who commend themselves. But they, measuring themselves by themselves, and comparing themselves among themselves are not wise. We however will not boast beyond measure, but within the limits of the sphere which God appointed us... But he who glories let him glory in the Lord. For not he who commends himself is approved, but whom the Lord commends.[29] [Also examine 1 Samuel 16:7]

Perhaps God wants to use a person in that position for His purposes. We must be careful to discern the Father's will apart from our own. God is speaking these days about loving-kindness toward our brothers and sisters; to consider one another, to exhort and provoke unto love and good works.

God is telling His body of believers we must be patient and long suffering of each other. We are to accept our brothers and sisters with all their soulish warts and wrinkles and let the Spirit of God work out His good pleasure in each of them in His own good time.

Often an intolerant and critical attitude toward another stems from our own insecurity; our fear of criticism; a knowing that we are unacceptable, perhaps because we grew up in a conditional love atmosphere. Living under a cloak of criticism tends to make us critical of others. Or could it be the guilt of some secret sin that we believe will destroy us if discovered. In our fear we become critical of others, believing if we are in a position of being able to criticize then surely our own behavior is beyond reproach. These are some of the defense mechanisms we learn in the world. It can also come from a self-righteous spirit ruling in our heart. Give it up! Put it under the Blood. Humble yourself before God.

The truth of unconditional love means that God does not love you any more after you're saved than He did when you walked in darkness. He does not love you any more as a mature Christian than He did when you were first born again. He does not love you any more on this day as a born again believer, than He does the vilest sinner. Not the sin but the sinner.

While we were yet sinners, Christ died for us. Why? Love!
But God who is rich in mercy...,[32] *By this perceive we the love of God, because he laid down his life for us.*[33]
He did this 2000 years before we were born so what terms could we have met? None were possible. This is the power of unconditional love. It never changes. Right here you can take the pain of a love you had to earn and could not, which has kept you in fear and bondage, and give it to your Savior, Redeemer, Deliverer and Healer.

Forgive all - Forgive all.
Release all into your Fathers hands.

Perhaps you've not realized this gift of God's love was His good pleasure sent forth in your behalf. Receive this truth and release to God all your concerns of this matter for He cares for you. Cast this burden on the Lord. Let the healing hand of your Father touch the pain of never being good enough and bring you to wholeness.

We really are unworthy. We cannot earn it nor attain it. Our worth comes from God. Let His covenant love flood your aching heart. Lay down all your efforts to please Him with your striving to gain His approval, because ....➔

> The truth of unconditional love is that it is not predicated on behavior.

No matter what we've done or will do cannot change God's attitude toward us. When God touches us with the riches of His goodness and love, it leads us to repentance [Rom 2:4]. Yet unbelief, most often based in fear, cannot annul His love. We will have a harder time receiving it [Rom 3:3-4].

Fear can produce unbelief. Give it all to God. Unbelief will keep us from His presence, but does not change His love factor. Unbelief cannot annul His faithfulness.

God is true and every man a liar.
Jesus came into a world that was made by Him, yet they knew Him not.[34] He came to His people, yet they received Him not.

Malachi was the last prophet to speak the Word of the Lord to Israel - then 400 years of silence. Ten generations passed in which the people of the Most High God had reduced the law of Moses to controversial ritualistic hypocrisy. The resurrection of Lazarus was analogous to what God wanted to do for His beloved Israel. Jesus wept at the cold funereal stance of a nation that should have been drawing the world back to its Creator.

The nation to whom were committed
the oracles of God, lost sight of their mission
and had become a travesty. [35]

Malachi speaks of how they rejected God's love; of priests that had caused His people to stumble and had corrupted His Covenant. The first four commandments speak of relationship to God, the last six speak in relation to our fellow man. Can we understand why God calls them His 'chosen people'?

Romans 3.2 *Most important, God distinguished the Jews from all other people by entrusting them with the revelation of his prophetic promises.* [taken from The Passion Translation]

He had to have a definite place in which to reveal Himself. He couldn't just appear anywhere. He gave them His Word and the revelation of 'a Holy God' that would redeem them from a sinful lifestyle and make them a 'holy people' if they would follow Him. He gave this revelation to their ancestor Abraham, the father of their nation. But they lost sight of Who God was, even though they still cried out for Him [for four hundred years].

Now comes Moses with the good news; the revelation of Who their God is, and ... well read the Bible; *'In the beginning'*.

So from a paltry few to a powerful nation, He brought them out so He could bring them in. Bring them in - to what?

Bring them into His kingdom; that they would know where they belong and receive the blessings of belonging to the God Who created them. Reading the first five books of the Bible will bring revelation of what He did to reveal His identity.

Deut 4:37-38   *And because He loved your fathers, therefore He chose their descendants after them; and He brought you out of Egypt with His Presence, with His mighty power,*

They were chosen to reveal to the world, the Redeemer of mankind. He would set us all free from slavery to a vicious master, one cloaked in darkness so we couldn't know who it was that tormented us. The whole world dwelt in darkness and His chosen people, Israel, was chosen to reveal our Savior. They still did it in spite of their rejection of this reality and rejected Him as a nation.

Because Israel became callous to the love of God, every man also, dealt treacherously with their brother. Family problems ran rampant, wives and children were no longer considered of value. There came the abomination of sacrifice without obedience. [1Sam 15]. The warning to turn back to God and hook into His Covenant fell on deaf ears. BUT...

God made sure that His purpose came to fruition, for many of this chosen people brought His love and promise to the world; and some paid with their lives from an ignorant people who chose their sin instead of His holiness.

Praise God, He has always had a remnant to not bow the knee to Baal; a people who know God to be their only Source of Life. These hungry ones are a simple folk. Ones who will continually hunger and thirst for God himself. These are for whom the angels burst through the veil and into our world. With joy they shouted the arrival of *Immanuel, God is with us.* To Simeon and Anna was revealed the Consolation of Israel. The blind wanted to see God. The deaf desired to hear His Word. Mary, seated at the feet of her Master, chose the better way.

But there was another Mary with whom God is not so pleased. Read Jeremiah 7.18-19 and 44.15-27. The imposter.

So contended Malachi to show his people who they were - and what was their heritage. The Father - the source of life in the Spirit and the flesh. As they let go of one - they had no respect for the other. We may readily see the correlation to the society of our century. Read in context, Mt 2.10.

Have we not all one Father?

They believed they were OK no matter what they did. But lest we judge them for their darkened heart we must ever examine our own; desperately wicked and deceived but for

God's grace and mercy; always wanting us to know how much He loves us.
This is life eternal, that they might know thee, the only true God, and Jesus Christ whom thou hast sent.[36]
And so Jesus comes to a people who knew not the Father. They never understood what He was all about.
Neither knoweth any man the Father, except the Son, and he to whomsoever the Son will reveal him.[37] *No man cometh unto the Father but by me.*[38] *I and the Father are one.*[39] *I am in the Father and the Father is in me.*[40] *As the living Father hath sent me, and I live by the Father, so he that eateth [become one with] me, even he shall live by me.*[41] *Philip saith unto him,*
Lord show us the Father...and Jesus saith unto him, he that hath seen me has seen the Father.[42]
Jesus came to reveal the Fatherhood of God, the Originator, the Source of Life; with a love that does not look at what we have done or haven't done, in order to receive us into His Kingdom. Unconditional love has no limitation nor restriction. It is absolute covenant Father faithfulness. This true Source of Life does not cause inception only to end in abandonment. He wants our response.

In reading Dennis Burke's July `94 Newsletter I saw he also was writing about God's love. It's wonderful how God shares His revelations among His people, giving each of us a taste of His glory. As we learn to come together and unite as a body we may receive from each other. Chapter four of Ephesians is displayed each time we partake of this unity. And so Pastor Burke reveals one of God's gourmet dishes:

God Loves Without Needing Any Response,
but He Expects His Love to Create a Response.

Malachi tells us,
Behold, I will send you Elijah the prophet before the coming of the great and terrible day of the Lord.
The great and terrible day of the Lord is the day of His vengeance [Isa 61:2]. Yes, Jesus told us John the Baptist had Elijah's fiery spirit. But most Bible prophecy has a twofold meaning. Let's see how this prophecy is fulfilled by Jesus Himself.

The name Elijah means, God of Jehovah. Jehovah is translated Jesus, in the Greek. Who was the God of Jesus? Hebrews 1:5 declares,
Thou art my Son, this day have I begotten thee.

Hebrews one transcribes the Father's strategy concerning Jesus. He laid aside His heavenly throne and became a man, born into the human race for the purpose of reconciling creation back to the Father. The Living Bible words it this way,
> But God said about Jesus, I am his Father and he is my Son...And so God, even your God has poured out more gladness upon you than anyone else.

Our Lord Jesus was equal with God but made Himself in the likeness of men [Phil 2:6-8]. Our Lord Jesus submitted Himself in flesh as a son, so that God became His Father. Jesus brought to a devastated world - the ministry of the Father's heart. Though He was God, He became 'the Son bonded to the Father' revealing to the world at once, responding covenant to trusting faith. *I have not spoken of myself, but the Father Who sent me.*

Jesus so totally identified with His creation - we cannot fathom the sacrifice our most precious Lord became. So completely an example for us to follow - He pulled all the plugs. Jesus showed us how, and then made it possible for US to become sons of the Father;
And I have declared unto them [the true meaning of] thy name, and I will declare it, that the love with which thou hast loved me may be in them, and I in them.[43]

The Father's heart is again revealed to His creation, in Jesus. In covenant love the *Sun of Righteousness* [Mal 4.2] now comes to dwell within His people to heal and restore the heart of the fathers to the children, and the heart of the children to their fathers. And isn't that exactly what this world desperately needs at this particular time? The spirit of Elijah! Elijah was the prophet of fire. John the Baptist, who had that same Spirit of fire burning in his bosom declared...
> *I baptize you with water but there comes one who will baptize you with the Holy Spirit and with fire.*

There will come a time and is even now being prepared, that God's prophets will call down fire from heaven, to walk in the Elijah spirit in the end time, to destroy the hordes of hell and bring deliverance to the captive; bring God's people back to Hm. The Word of God will cause a fire in the hearts of those hungry to know where they belong.

Realizing the Old Testament was given as an example, we can understand that the New Testament only reiterates by the Spirit of grace; those principles set forth for the people of

God by which to be governed. 2 Chronicles 7:12 tells us that as we humble ourselves and pray and seek his face - listen - 2Chron 7.15 *Now mine eyes shall be open and ears attentive.*

As a people drawn into covenant relationship, we have the attention of the Most High God. He provides, He guides, He protects, He disciplines.

The eyes of the Lord run to and fro throughout the whole earth to show himself strong in behalf of them whose heart is [turned] towards him[44]Yes, there may be offenses, pain, grieving - but

It is The Father's Good Pleasure To Give You the Kingdom.

Our Father God has created within Himself
A place called home
It is an ever expanding place
of acceptance, warmth and love.
It was deliberately formed
in the center of His Being,
Surrounded by His arms of love,
So that all His children would fit,
And be forever safe.

What love is this cannot be ignored
It penetrates the heart and soul
No question as to where it comes
But needs our all in all
It's only Him - the One Who died for me
His name is Jesus - only Jesus
Whose love can penetrate
The heart and soul - Oh how He loves.

This one I copied from a magazine some years ago.
Lord, With My Empty Cup I Crawled To You
Across The Desert Barrenness, Uncertain In Asking
Any Small Drop Of Refreshment.
If I Had Only Known You Better,
I'd Have Come
Running With a Bucket !!

♥

Remember Luke 6:46-48   *But why do you call Me 'Lord, Lord,' and not do the things which I say? Whoever comes to Me, and hears My sayings and does them, I will show you whom he is like: He is like a man building a house, who dug deep and laid the foundation on the rock. And when the flood arose, the stream beat vehemently against that house, and could not shake it, for it was founded on the rock.*

1 Cor 10:1   *For they drank of that spiritual Rock that followed them, and that Rock was Christ.*

1 Cor 10:6-7   *Now these things became our examples, to the intent that we should not lust after evil things as they also lusted. And do not become idolaters as were some of them.*

Our God is a jealous God -

Isa 42:8   *I am the Lord, that is My name; and My glory I will not give to another, or My praise to carved images.*

Isa 48:11 *Or how should My name be profaned? And I will not give My glory to another.*

God's people were covered by His glory and yet they were worshiping idols. Giving their glory to another.

They were no different than our society of today.

And what does our sin nature cause us to worship today? Money, sex, famous people, self ego, position, the list goes on....

STUDY GUIDE

1. How is God's love any different than ours? Rom 5:8-10
   Why is it unconditional?
2. What makes God's covenant any different than man's? He 6:13
3. How can we receive the covenant promises God made with someone 4,000 years ago?   Rom 4:13-25
4. What good thing is available to us because of God's faithfulness?
5. Can we just love God and ignore everyone else? 1Jn 4:7-21
6. What does God's unconditional love allow us to do with our free will?   Lk 15:11-32
7. We are unique and special. For what purpose does God call us His precious stones? Ep 2:19-22, 1Jn 1:3,7

8. For some, there is much pain in our lives. But we don't have to keep it. Mt 11:27-30. Give this burden to your Lord. He'll take it.
9. Can God take care of your cares better than you? 1Pe 5:7
10. How can we know God's love is unconditional? 1Jn 4:9-19
11. If God really truly forgives us totally, then Romans 8:1 is true and we can forgive ourselves.
12. John 17 tells of the glory Jesus had with the Father before the world was. Then in V 22, Jesus had a glory given to Him by the Father, of which He has given to believers. He walked among us as the perfect Son to show us how to do it.

    He gave us His best and His highest; equipped us to walk in Holy Spirit anointing and power as He did. Romans 8 tells us of a glory which shall be revealed in us.

    1Peter 5:1, we will be partaker of that glory. Hallelujah! Isaiah 60 tells us His glory shall be seen upon us!

PRAYER: Thank you God, that you love me in spite of my failures. Thank you for the love of Christ which surpasses any other kind of love, and that you'll never leave me nor forsake me.

How do I love thee Lord -
Oh - so many ways
Thank You for Your love and grace
That stirs Your life and love within me.

We are the city of God
Brought forth
by His glorious Word
Joined together by the Blood of Christ
Cause we have made Him Lord
Our love for one another
Is because we are brothers
And we'll never come to an end
For Jesus has come to touch our hearts
And says He is our friend
So we come together in unity
To worship and praise our King
That glorious One - That holy One
It is to Him we sing.

We are not of this world
We belong in heavenly places
For this is what God intended
So we could learn
To walk in His graces
A school to test our trust
Will we abandon God
If things get too rough
Or will we abandon our own agenda
And lean on God -
To His cause surrender

♫ So Cover Me Lord With
Your Fatherhood
Cover Me Over With Righteousness
Heal Me Now
In The Depths of My Soul
And Cover Me over with Love ♫

Shut in with God
in a secret place
Being with Him face to face
Sharing your heart,
your soul, your mind
With only Him you will abide
There in the darkness
of the night
Where only He will be
the light
These precious moments
one on one
You'll never forget
until you're done

♥

Love came looking for me
When I didn't know how to reach out
The barrier of pain kept me hostage
With a heart full of doubt
But love was determined to capture me
Enfold me in His arms
And cause my heart to open
To the love that came looking for me.
You opened the gate for me to come in
You gave Your precious Son
To pay for my sin
Now Your glory and Your righteousness
Covers my soul
Because You gave without regret
I give You my all
♥

SCRIPTURES

1. 1Jn 2:15
2. 1Jn 3:1
3. Ro 8
4. Ro 5:8,10
5. 1Co 1:26-28
6. Ge 15:718
7. Ro 4:13-14
8. He 6:1318
9. Jam 1:17
10. Lam 3:2123
11. Ex 16:1920
12. 1Jn 4:10
13. 1Jn 2:2
14. Ex 25:21-22
15. Ez 18:4
16. Rom 6:23
17. Heb 9:26
18. 1Co 5:2
19. Ga 5:6 Amp
20. Jn 17:21-22
21. Ac 1:8
22. Ep 5: 21-28
23. Jn 13:35
24. Isa 28:10
25. 1Pe 5:7
26. Heb 11:6
27. Ro 8:17
28. Ep 2:21-22
29. 2Co 10:7-18
30. Mt 6:14 Amp
31. 1Jn 4:10
32. Fp 2:4
33. 1Jn 3:16
34. Jn 1:10
35. Ro 3:2
36. Jn 17:3
37. Lk 10:22
38. Jn 14:6
39. Jn 10:30
40. Jn 14:11
41. Jn 6:57
42. Jn 14:8-9
43. Jn 17:26
44. 2Ch 16:9

MY FOUNDATION

> *Them that dwell in houses of clay,*
> *whose foundation is in the dust..* Job 4

I was born in February 1932. Our country was still struggling to rise above its depression and jobless era. Most men were scrambling to find ways to feed their families, but from the few stories I heard of my father he was not one of them. He had been in the army for a while and married my mother five years his junior. Mother was seventeen at the time and before she was twenty-five, we were a family of seven.

There was much quarreling and turmoil in our household with my father coming and going. Mostly going and not working resulted in more arguments. I'm sure there was more to the problem than I was aware. My mother would lock him out of the house which made him even more angry. He would force his way in, no matter what was done to stop him.

One day at the age of three I climbed on a chair and opened the latch to see what the 'milk man' wanted. It was my father who shoved me and the chair down the hallway of our tenement and stepped over me. In a rage he pulled my mother into a bedroom and raped her.

My mother never cried out for fear of the neighbors knowing what was happening. She could not handle the embarrassment. She only held hatred in her heart for he did this every time he got into the house. That day she vowed it would be the last. The court system forced a separation. We never saw him again.

I paid dearly for my mistaken identity for on that day my mother turned me off emotionally and only clothed and fed me for many years after that. She screamed at me that I was never to dare do that again!

Since I did not have the mental capacity to understand what I had done, the terror of the moment had me paralyzed in fear. Rejection and the fear of abandonment gripped my heart as I saw my older sisters also turn away from me.

I was never able to get things together in my mind that it was okay to finish a project I had started. For many years into adulthood there was the inordinate fear within me that always asked the question, Is this what I was never to dare do again? I can only guess how many times I have sabotaged my own plans and goals.

Only with the presence of the Lord Jesus and His loving arms around me was I able to pry into my subconscious emotions. I was barely a year old in the Lord, when I began to wonder why I kept seeing a vision in my head, of a little girl on the floor with a chair on top of her. He revealed these things to me for healing and restoration and so I began to overcome my wasted childhood.

I discovered two things on that day. Men were to be hated and feared; and I was without value. As the years passed by I also learned to despise and reject with a vengeance, the little girl that I was. As an adult, I unconsciously blamed her for all my problems..........................→

> She was a haunting figure that would never leave.

In the process of healing my emotions God showed me I was the only one that could help her. He revealed to me the most pathetic creature I'd ever imagined. A little girl that nobody loved. A little girl who just barely made it one day to the next. A little girl for whom Jesus died and was moving heaven and earth to show her how much she meant to Him.

Then He filled my heart with so much love ♥

I had to ask her to forgive me for my hatred. I had brought on so much self-destruction because of self-hatred. As I reached out to take that little girl in my arms, it seemed that she again became a part of me, yet there was a peace I'd never had before.

I began to see that because Jesus died for me I had a right to live. Because Jesus loved me I had a right to receive His love. That experience was my first step into being made whole. I never knew why I had always felt fragmented.

I know there are many people who cannot function to their fullest capacity in the Lord because of childhood wounds. I hear voices declare You can't blame your past and those people for what you are going through now as an adult.

We make our own decisions.

I can assure all, that none of what I've written is cause for searching out a Patsy - one I can lay on the blame so I am justified for my bitterness. These things happened. They nearly destroyed me. But Jesus is my healer, He is my peace, and my consolation. I hide myself in Him. I have forgiven all concerned and chose 50 years ago to give it all to Jesus.

Every day since then, I have lived one day at a time for healing and restoration, in the presence of my Savior, Redeemer and Lord; just as Paul said 1 Cor 15:31 *I die daily.*

Please know that Jesus longs to hold you also in His arms and share your sorrows and grieving, to comfort and heal. The Word says He, the Great Physician, took all your dis-eases [mental, physical, emotional and spiritual] to the cross. Today He says to you... Be thou made whole[1]

He became an outcast so that you might come into His Kingdom.[2] Allow Jesus to touch your broken heart and bring you peace. All these memories of my past were buried very deeply in my sub-conscious. Some few things I was told by my siblings, but most of it was revealed by the Spirit of God for the purpose of healing and restoration. If God did this for me, He will surely do it for you as you keep your eyes on Him. The only thing I did to bring this about was to yield myself to God, because I want all He has for me.

There are many of whom had the tragic experience of losing a parent through death or even divorce. But if there is one caretaker who really cares, it can make a tremendous difference in a child's self-evaluation. My mother loved me but never showed it. For me - there was no one. That is really the truth.

At the age of nine I went to visit an Aunt that lived near our house. Because her house was on the way home from Church, and it was on a Sunday, it was probably around 10:00 in the morning. She answered the door, let me in and went back into the bedroom, saying she would be right back.

I sat there alone for so long I was embarrassed to stay, so I just left and went home. The devastation of her rejection stayed with me for a long time, and continued to prove none of my family valued me. At the same time I was experiencing the fourth grade, more of which is shared in another chapter.

At the age of eleven, we moved and a new neighbor woman for whom I babysat, befriended me, and in some ways tried to mother me. But the truth is also this; by that time of age, these things were firmly rooted in my soul.

I was unable - incapable of receiving from her. And so I maintained the same incapacities. I did not understand at the time that God had sent her into my life. I do now, and realize she inserted some stability into those few years.

I am also cognizant that many people who experienced deep rejection in their childhood are seemingly able to overcome and compensate in various ways. I say seemingly because I believe somewhere in time they were able to make the decision and choices to turn away from the enigmatic. Human nature is so intense as to have the capacity to submerge memories. Somewhere at sometime God must show them His redeeming love and bring release. Speaking for myself, my mind was so numbed I didn't realize I ever had choice in any matter. I had become very apathetic about life.

When God told me I had the power to choose, I was astounded and it opened a whole new world to me. As I shared in previous chapters, the Lord performed supernatural surgery on my mind in the early weeks of getting to know Him. I'm so glad He knows exactly what we need and when we need it.

In the days of my youth many families were caught up in the emotional depression of the time and being unable to find work deepened the impact. Later in life while living in several western states I discovered those people overcame much of the problem of poverty because they had land on which to farm vegetables and raise rabbits and chickens, even if it was just a backyard plot.

I was raised in the well known `concrete jungle' and veggies just don't thrive on asphalt or the tar roof of an apartment house. I vividly remember the box of clothing that would show up at my house from time to time. It never had my size in it. Only my older sisters got new clothes. In these years of restoration God has delivered me from being a hand-me-down. He gave me this song.

    Thank You Lord, for Your great love,
    You've brought me to Your rest.
    I'm no longer second hand,
    You've given me your best.

Being the youngest of four girls, I was never paid much attention. There was much strife between the others as they pursued their own interests. My one year younger brother with whom I was close, was sent to boarding school when I was eleven and our relationship was no more.

Until that year we lived with my grandmother. Nana always had her days and nights mixed up and she was the typical night owl. And so, although she was present in the house she lent me little nurturing or mothering. My sister Barbara was her favorite.

Deserted by a father I never knew and left unattended most of the time because of a working mother, much time was spent believing I was unworthy of anyone's caring. My grandmother lived with us but she was a night person and slept most of the day. The root of rejection propagated fear and isolation.

There are few substantial memories of my early years, but it is not uncommon, for most people with troubled lives will confess this. There will be a stunting of emotional growth for these, and a serious identity crisis. Above all there is a torturous mentality of abandonment. Most have had night terrors brought on by dreadful anxieties and the focus is always on negative experiences. As children and adults, That is the only perception we have of reality.

Many children for whom there is a scant supply of love from their caretakers do not do well in school and have an aching lonely heart. They may have already grown to adulthood, married,]several times? [and borne children and still the agony of former years are tormenting. Never sure of themselves or - we're never sure of a husband's or friend's caring; so fearing they will leave we never assert ourselves. Or we may become demanding and controlling to appease our frustrations and our fear of rejection. Oftentimes we lose the relationship anyway. In our heart and mind we are still a castaway.

I was not physically abused by my mother. She did not know how to handle the pain of what was happening to her, so she blamed me; [until God showed me the truth, I thought I was responsible for his leaving]. From that time on and for many years, she emotionally rejected me. Rejection strips one of their identity. This is why, beginning in my childhood, I belonged to nothing and was going nowhere. I was fed and clothed, but shut out from relationship.

Experiences and/or relationships down through the years continued to prove I had no value. I had no place on which to stand and declare ownership. Abandonment and the fears and accompanying trauma is pure devastation to that little heart that has no foundation of trust.

Emotional neglect is a nightmare of pain and loneliness from which life long attitudes are formed. The enemy bombards our mind constantly with the agony that no one cares and works feverishly to prove it time and again, causing offensive situations that plant deep roots of bitterness.

One acquaintance told me [B.C.] that I did not have a personality. At the time I was a heavy drinker. At the time I thought what he said was very funny. I had no idea how to develop a personality or identity. Neither one of us realized the truth of that statement.

Is it possible any one else can understand where I'm coming from in all this? I thank God I'm not in that place anymore.
As the years drag by there never seems to be any solid thing on which to hold. Fear becomes a blanket that smothers and engulfs every attitude about self and others. It becomes easier to not think about tomorrow. We either dwell on yesterday or project ourselves far into a future fantasy.

We have no control of our lives and can hardly subscribe to purpose. We seem to be always defending our right to live but never gain a victory. We carry our grievances around for all to see and hear about, constantly.

Since everything is wrong in our lives we judge and criticize every person and every event in our mind even on into the night when our emotions and bodies are exhausted from the struggles of surviving the day.

Morning arrives and the dread of facing another day keeps us in bed till noon. We become so self centered there is no real sharing in relationships. We have so small a reserve of life that to give anything away would cause bankruptcy. Never realizing we must give in order to receive we become a walled city shutting out all invaders. We are alone and lonely even in a crowd and thrive on self-pity. The sand castle of our lives slowly disintegrates. We have no resources to draw from and unless we get serious competent help - we pass many of these traits down to our children.

And I thank God that I got serious help.
[Please remember this book was written in 1987. I have changed some to bring it up to date, and the healing continues.

In the next chapters you may consider the enormous challenge God faced in restoring me. He had to break the mold in which I was held captive. Do you think He was up to it? God is in the business of restoration, and totally competent. And now this-

I love the Lord because he hath heard my voice and my supplications. Because he hath inclined his ear to me, Therefore I will call on him as long as I live.[3] .

When I read those words more than 20 years ago, [now 50 years ago] I was astounded that a Sovereign God would care that much for people; *especially me.*

The thought that God would bend down and listen to the abandoned child within me, surpassed my understanding; but He heard the cry of my heart.

...And you shall be called sought out, a city not forsaken.[4]

I was forty years old when someone told me Jesus loved me and cared about me. He also gave me a sound mind.

For as a man thinketh in his heart - so is he.[6]

Whatever you believe yourself to be that's what you become. I saw myself as an outcast and had no foundation to my life. From the insecurity of this came a constant turmoil of fears day and night. I was a victim of my own imaginations.

In Healing for the Mind, by William J. Finnegan, Revival Literature, Asheville, NC., he says, It is all together tenable that our minds are subconsciously focusing on lies instead of the truth. We must be deprogrammed from untruth and programmed constantly by the Word of God [Psalm 119:11].

This is very true, as it is now happening to me

And all who call on the Name of Jesus.

Remember, it's a process of healing and restoration.

It is necessary to understand our new birth into the Kingdom does not immediately produce a full grown mature perfect Christian, any more than a baby fresh from the womb can function as a tax paying citizen in our society.

It is sad to realize the world derides as hypocritical those who are struggling to make the Word of God real in their lives. Many give up because of the pressure to produce. Frustration and depression, condemnation and guilt hang heavy in their heart and they begin to believe there is no use trying. But brothers and sisters, God sees your struggle.

For the eyes of the Lord search back and forth across the whole earth, looking for people whose hearts are perfect [turned] toward him, so that he can show his great power in helping them.[7]

This word perfect may intimidate, until we see in Strong's Concordance it means to be friendly, loyal, complete. The Word says we are to be perfect as the Father in heaven is perfect.[8] He would not have said it, were it not possible.

Some times we get hostile toward a God we don't understand. We may believe He puts unreasonable demands on us. But hear what saith the Spirit:

If our heart condemn us, God is greater than our heart and knows all things. Beloved if our heart condemn us not, then we have confidence toward God.[9] *How much more shall the Blood of Christ, who through the eternal Spirit offered himself without spot to God, purge your conscience from dead works to serve the living God.*[10]

Let us draw near with a true heart in full assurance of faith, having our hearts sprinkled from an evil conscience, and our bodies washed with pure water. Let us hold fast to the confession of our hope without wavering, for he is faithful that promised.[11]

We can lift this burden of a guilty conscience and a condemning heart to the Lord [Mt 11:28-30] and be free to walk in the liberty He promised.[12] This is why the statement of Romans 8:1 is so powerful. Do you believe it?

There is, therefore, now no condemnation to those who are in Christ Jesus.

The consistent renewing of our mind will cause us to see that changes in our life are definitely possible and accessible. At the moment of coming into the Kingdom of God, He now has permission to change us. It is God that performs that good work in us. He will perfect us.[13] So pay attention - *The law of the spirit of life in Christ Jesus [makes] us free from the law of sin and death,*[15]

We can throw off the trappings of mistrust and turn our friendly face towards our Father. The tremendous influence of a passive mind can be a major stronghold in the lives of people for whom there has been a scarcity of childhood nurturing. In many ways the decision is made to remain insensible to our environment because of so many disappointments and discouragement.

That which we perceive to be threatening to our status quo tends to be tuned out and turned off. Since we haven't learned the skills to cope with problems, we fine tune our defense mechanisms. We withdraw and maintain our wall of protection so that none may enter. But the incorruptible seed[14] that birthed us, is awaiting the water of the Word and the fertilizer of praise, growing in grace, and walking in the Spirit. Bury yourself in This Word of Life.

This attitude must be dealt with by a decision to grow and mature in the Kingdom of God,[16] because satan will use it to keep us from pursuing God's goal for us. We must yield to God for discipline and correction.

Heb 12:7-9 *As you endure this divine discipline, remember that God is treating you as his own children. Who ever heard of a child who is never disciplined by its father? If God doesn't discipline you as he does all of his children, it means that you are illegitimate and are not really his children at all. Since we respected our earthly fathers who disciplined us, shouldn't we submit even more to the discipline of the Father of our spirits, and live forever?* [Holy Bible, New Living Translation]

A passive mind is not one which is empty of activity. A passive mind is like a railroad tunnel. Trains running through it must be programmed to stop at certain intervals. If there is no program they keep running through the tunnels.

Likewise satan keeps the passive mind very busy; but with mundane issues that have no real value, and no real answers. The Word tells us we must discipline our mind, take our thoughts and imaginations into captivity,[17] bind strongholds,[18] and renew our mind constantly by the Water of the Word of God.[19]

> Everything in the Kingdom of God is ours [20] →

→ But we must appropriate it. First of all we must know about it. We cannot take hold of something of which we haven't heard. Faith comes by hearing, and hearing, and hearing.[21] The devil hates to see us get out our Bible.

Suddenly we begin to remember all the things we should have done yesterday or need to do tomorrow. If he can't bring some kind of disturbance he will surely make us drowsy and too sleepy to concentrate. These are some of the wiles of the devil we must overcome. If he can keep us distracted he can keep us from the Word or from praying.

How ironic the word wiles comes from the root word to travel, accompany, in proximity. The deceiver may align himself along the highway of our personal [unique to the individual] natural tendencies; those we have developed through the years, and he continuously interjects his crafty guile. And to add insult to injury can actually be the author of negative attitudes toward self and God. I say maybe - because we have much flesh and self-will to contend with. So the powers of darkness are ever looking for a door into any situation through which he can bring disaster.

He searches for our weak, unprotected places. For example, if we refuse to forgive people for their offenses, a spirit of unforgiveness will have an open door to drive that unforgiveness deeper into our heart. Then he calls in his buddies; resentment, bitterness, anger, etc.

Pretty soon relationships begin to erode and rejection and loneliness join the club; fear and suspicion of everyone comes to speak in our ears. We are prone to be offended, often. This can be a pretty accurate scenario of what the enemy of our soul sets up to destroy us. There are many other friends invited to the party; Self-pity is a biggie.

Now let's go back some years into the childhood of one coming from a dysfunctional family. There are already these forces of evil active in the home even before this one is born.

A cranky baby is many times responding to the stress and strife in their environment. Since the parent is already stressed out, they may respond to that crying baby with anger and frustration; hence we have a case of child abuse in many different stages.

This opens the door in that child, to fear, mistrust, insecurity, rejection, resentment, hatred of self, anger...I could go on forever. As the years go by, these things get a stronger hold on us. This is one of the reasons new born Christians have such a hard time measuring up! No, one does not get delivered from all their gunk in one day. Wouldn't that be wonderful?

Moses was told they would take the land a little at a time]Dt 7:22]. As they grew stronger and multiplied they could conquer the enemy and then live in that city.

Well, when we conquer the enemy in any given area of our life, we have to grow strong and learn to live in that newness of life. Otherwise the enemy comes back, and he has the key to the door [Lk 11:24]. This is why God brings us through day by day, little by little. We are learning to trust in Him. We are learning He will not abandon us. He is still our friend even if we don't win the battle right away. He'll come back and help us again. Sometimes we just have to pull back and get a second breath.

Hey - watch how our babies grow. it is the best graphic example God could set before our eyes [1Pet 2:2]. Finally we learn how to lock that door with the Blood of Jesus and hang the key on the cross.

God knows the whole layout of our land just as He knew exactly how to lead Joshua. Remember Jericho. God's people had to obey, submit to God's plan, then Who was it that broke down that impenetrable wall? The enemy was exposed, they were defeated.

Satan only has a hold on us through deception. He hides in the very fabric of our being, personality, emotions, mind-set, and very often our physical body. Many diseases are caused by the enemy. Our body was created to basically repair itself.

Take for example a broken bone. The trauma and impact it took to break it; the fear and confusion, the agony of pain, all may invite the enemy to gather round and accentuate the circumstances and then maintain the status quo as long as possible.

I was in an accident many years ago when a huge flat bed truck ran into me on the freeway. He rear-ended me and pushed me into a large open area on the side of the road, meant for emergencies. I was towing another car - Demolished both cars.

After that was terrorized by trucks near me on the freeway; and suffered physical pain for many years afterward.

God is delivering me and healing me as I trust in Him to lead me on the path He has set before me. God is in the business of restoring our souls, giving back all the enemy stole. And allowing us to rest by still waters as He brings us day by day into our inheritance

There are many good books on deliverance in Christian Bookstores. I would encourage prayer and wisdom from God as to which one would help any individual. God knows exactly what you need. Remember-

The Blood of Jesus and the Name of Jesus
are the tools of our trade.

These are the two mightiest weapons against the devil. Humble yourself, draw near to God and the enemy will flee.

You are not responsible for what an adult did to you as a child. You are responsible and must confess your response to all this. You've lived with resentment, anger, bitterness, etc. for long enough. Now you can receive God's forgiveness as you forgive them and be cleansed from all unrighteousness. God did it for me.

This means deliverance from any power the enemy has in this arena. The Spirit of God will reveal your enemy then you tell it to leave in Jesus Name. And - [maybe a new concept]

Forgive yourself for all your failures and mistakes. Be released, in Jesus Name.

A revelation from God caused me see through his plans in my life issues. Much of the time there is in any given area of our life - a fear. This is what the devil hones in on. In the place where trust in God has not yet been established, the enemy will bombard with his lies and torment.

Fear renders us powerless - But...
God has not given us a spirit of fear
but of power, love and a sound mind.[22]

We can be suspicious of people's motives and our mind is in constant turmoil because of it. Now you have a choice. Which one do you want; fear or the power to overcome.

As we renew our mind *we will know the truth and the truth will make us free.* Since all Scripture is inspired by God,[23] we ought to pray and ask God to give us understanding.

Ephesians 2:17-19 are Spirit borne words that Paul wrote to inspire and encourage us on such a journey as this.
For through him we...have access...to the Father, we are no
more strangers and [wanderers], but fellow citizens with
the saints, and of the household of God

This verse was awesome to me because I had never perceived myself as belonging. I never had roots. Always on the outside with no identity I was doomed to wander, forever looking for the corner to hide in, that I could call my own. A serrated ticket detached from society; no recourse, no entrance open to me. Bur as I'm writing this the Lord brings to mind 2Peter 2:11.

For so an entrance shall be ministered unto you
abundantly into the everlasting Kingdom
of our Lord and Savior, Jesus Christ.

God, how I thank You for Your loving kindness that speaks to my pain and gives me Your peace. It is so wonderful to look back and remember how God ministered that truth to me. No matter how many times we read the Bible we can't possibly apply it all to ourselves, even over months and years. God knows exactly when a certain arrow must strike our heart and deliver His glorious .... ➜

Word of Life.

This testimony may sound absurd to someone who has never experienced true rejection or the feeling of abandonment over a long period of time; feeling that there is no one there for you. All I can say is it loses much in the translation. Those who have lived it - know!   When God opened my eyes to understand Chapter two of Ephesians; that I was no longer a stranger and a wanderer, the door of the Kingdom exploded off its hinges and I ran through! I knew then, that I belonged! Eph 1:17-19 gives us this promise:

That God...give unto you the Spirit of wisdom and revelation in the knowledge of him, the eyes of your understanding would be enlightened. THIS ALSO IS HIS GOOD PLEASURE.

Seeing, entering into and walking in the Kingdom of God is to venture into the unknown. Only as the Holy Spirit accompanies us and enlightens our mind and heart can we assimilate the life of Christ within. Psalm 119 is an amazing testimony to the power of the Word in our lives.

In our own imaginations we cannot know God.

*The entrance of your word gives light,
it gives understanding to the simple..*

[one who is teachable].

*Thy word is a lamp unto my feet and a light unto my path.
For my thoughts are not your thoughts, nor are your ways my ways, saith the Lord. For as high as the heavens are from the earth, so are my ways higher than your ways, and my thoughts than your thoughts.*[24]

So we must beseech the Lord to change our thoughts and our ways to come into line with His.[25] Renewing our mind comes from reading, studying and meditating on the Word, spending time with the Lord in fellowship and worship and,

yielding ourselves to the changes

God is arranging [Romans 12].

As the Word mirrors what we are, it also reveals what we may become. God does it so that He will receive all the glory.

Without Him we can do nothing .

*For it is God who works in you both to will
and to do of his good pleasure.*[26]

A few years before she died, Mother shared some very little of what my father was like. In a matter of a few moments she gave me understanding of some of, [what I was to learn], were my worst fears that plagued my mind.

When you were a baby he grabbed you up out of your crib by your legs and flung you against the wall because you were crying. I thought she was exaggerating because I had been vocalizing my frustrations as to why she would never talk about my father. I was stunned and could hardly believe what she said.

I had my doubts that it was altogether true for afterwards I thought about it several times and prayed God would show me how to deal with it. I did not get any answer for a long time.

I was astounded and not sure I heard it right; but she assured me it was true. I asked God to deliver me from this trauma which I knew had been the foundation of many of my fears and anxieties. He knew exactly when this would happen. God has His own timing for all things. If we want God to move a mountain, we have to wait sometimes for Him to set up the mountain moving equipment. And in His time - it happens. God works in His timing, not ours.

As God's power brought healing, deliverance and restoration from these things, He set me free from the trauma and impact of my father's rage. I realized this is where terror, anxiety and the fear of violence entered my life, and God showed me what had been the repercussions. God continued in the following years, to heal and restore my life.

One day [before this healing] I shared it with a friend who had experienced much physical violence as a small child. This precious lady and I were ministering to each other as the Spirit of God was performing spiritual surgery on our emotions.

[I am now revising and upgrading some of my thoughts since 1987. From that time until the year's end of 2008, I had received more deliverance and restoration from this terrifying experience].

I praise God for His love and the fact that I can edit these pages for a new edition, and experience God's peace about it. The fear of violence will intimidate until relationships erode - or never come to be. You will not interject your opinion lest someone disagrees. You will never confront for fear of retaliation. On the other hand, your self-image may become buried behind a mask of arrogance and anger because you're never allowed to be who you really are.

At the moment my father threw me away I became an outcast and what my mother did, only reinforced it. I've chosen to forgive them both. With our unforgiveness, resentment and bitterness we continue to speak destruction to our present, of which will naturally leak into our future, day by day. As I yielded all these things to God, He gave me His peace.

I chose to quit passing judgment on my mother, and now understand that she did her best with what she had. She worked very hard to raise 5 children by herself. Her childhood was also the pits. Her father walked out on her. How could she possibly give to her children what she did not have. The sins of the fathers, the results of iniquity will be passed down generation ad infinitum until the Blood of Jesus breaks the curses.

When someone in that family gets saved and finds out they have a new inheritance, they can trade in their old one for their Kingdom heritage.[27] Then these consequences can be stopped by prayer and faith in the Blood of Jesus. We don't have to continue to reap what others have sown in our life.

The Lord gave me understanding of the pitiful human nature that is bound by sin. Only Jesus can deliver us. If we don't have Jesus' love in our hearts we can't give it. If we are bound by fear and torment, despair and hopelessness how can we possibly give life and love to those around us.

Growing up in the 30's and 40's in New York City was fun for some. For me it was a gray bleak day - every day. The depression years were a reality in my heart. Though the country was slowly raising itself up by the bootstraps, I was getting buried deeper into my own emotional despair.

Mother worked hard to get us off welfare. Raising five children alone was an enormous task, but she determined to beat the odds. She never knew the pain of loneliness and self-hatred I endured growing up. She told me in later years that she had always loved and trusted in God. But I think the tragedy was she believed she was being punished for her sins.

It is not acceptable in a person's heart to admit they hate their mother. I was shocked when God told me it was true. I knew He was right. In later years there was not those feelings, but I wept bitterly for the empty, hopeless years of my childhood.

I became a victim of circumstances. I became a victim of my mother's unforgiveness for the man she once loved; but my own resentment and bitterness was causing still further destruction. With God's mercy, grace and wonderful love I was able to forgive her.

We were never allowed to talk about our father. We were strictly told if asked, to say he was dead. In school or from inquisitive friends I remember confessing almost ritualistically, 'I don't have a father'.

In complying with this falsehood I was actually destroying any evidence of my relationship with a father figure who is the foundation of the family. Here again I separated myself from the traditional family unit and declared I did not belong. I was different from my peers who always seemed to be a part of a complete family. This scenario dogged my footsteps - until Jesus.

Some of my readers may be scratching their heads, wondering what all this is about. Where are the connecting lines to make such assuming statements? We have to understand that whatever we do in the natural always has spiritual consequences. That's why God keeps telling us to walk by the Spirit and not by our flesh. He knows what happens.

My Father God has given me roots in His Kingdom. Colossians 2:6-7 tells us we shall be rooted and grounded in Christ Jesus. So it matters not where one is located on the earth. God's precious Word that I have come to trust in tells me,

For here we have no continuing city,
but we seek one to come.[28]

We are the planting of the Lord,[29] with fixed roots that go deep in Him. If we are rooted in Him, we can bloom where we are planted. God has delivered me from being a vagabond. A vagabond is always looking for the next place to be, never satisfied with where they are. Always looking for a place of rest.

Someone told me one time that I have roots in God but it's like they're in a glass of water. I was in geological transition then, but God's love and peace has filled that place of instability. I've been able to settle in my heart that I do belong in the place where I'm at. I'll stay here till He comes for me.

I never confronted my mother with these things I share here. The Lord gave me a precious love for her that pulled down the wall of alienation between us. Forgiveness washed my heart so completely, that we were able to be friends for the last 10 years of her life.

She went to be with the Lord in 1989, and in this revision of the book I wrote in 1987, I feel the Lord is saying to share more than I did previously. So this has been a part of the story of how my foundation came to be built on sand. Now let me tell you in the next chapter, how my Lord Jesus Christ became my Cornerstone as He reconstructed my house on solid Rock. He gives strength to overcome, Strength to bear, Strength to go through, Strength to share. I must tell you here that God is a God of mercy and restoration. I asked Him one day, 'Why didn't I die? He told me -

'Because I Caught You'.

Some people may say 'My sin is too great'
But Jesus would say
'MY SACRIFICE WAS GREATER!!'

Some things were never meant to be
We make mistakes in the course of our life
We sometimes pursue a forbidden path
Not knowing the trouble out-of-sight
We try and try to make it work
Blinded by self-satisfaction
We ride along on stress and fear
And never take any action
We live a life of loneliness
As though it will be alright
But in the final course of life
It dissolves into the night.
So Lord Jesus, I give to You,
The life You have given me
For the plans and purpose
You already have
Cause that's what was meant to be
♥

STUDY GUIDE

1. In all my years with the Lord I never strove to bring memories of my past into the here and now. When I found God I found the only treasure I will ever want. Actually it was me who was lost - not God. How are you doing?
2. Keeping my focus on Jesus and wanting to know Him has been my priority since I was born again. What is your focus? What are your priorities? Is it the work of the Lord? Or is it the Lord, Himself?
3. Since He is the Author and Finisher of our faith what can we possibly add?
4. If we will cooperate and yield to His plan for our life, He will bring us safely through each place of opportunity.
All the times of my restoration, healing and deliverance - I assure you emphatically - was initiated by the Holy Spirit to bring me to a deeper place of trust and faith in Him.
5. Contemplating our navel will get us nowhere. Reading and meditating on the Word, spending time with the Lord; these are keys to the Kingdom.
6. When we give up our control and put God in charge He will lead and guide us into the places He has for us. We are free from worry about the past or future and are able to live in the now moment.
7. Ponder these points. See how they line up with what's happening in your life. Any changes to be made can be put safely into your Lord's hand. He will cause restoration in His time.
PRAYER: I yield my life to You Lord. Mold me and make me - adjust my nature to line up with Your will for me. Healing and wholeness is my inheritance in my Father's Kingdom. I receive and thank you Lord.

> The Kingdom of God has come in its power
> Alive and well in this very hour
> By the Sword and His Spirit
> We live by the Word
> Because, sons of God
> We have made Jesus Lord.
> Forever we will conquer
> The enemy of our land.

I pray you will look up these verses I've referred to
in this book and read them in context.♥

1 Cor 3:10-12   *According to the grace of God which was given to me, as a wise master builder I have laid the foundation, and another builds on it. But let each one take heed how he builds on it. 11 For no other foundation can anyone lay than that which is laid, which is Jesus Christ.*

1 John 4:9-11   *In this the love of God was manifested toward us, that God has sent His only begotten Son into the world, that we might live through Him. In this is love, not that we loved God, but that He loved us and sent His Son to be the propitiation for our sins. Beloved, if God so loved us, we also ought to love one another.*

Oh what love the Father
has for us; created in His image
and likeness, so desiring us
to be what He planned
and purposed from the beginning.

♥

SCRIPTURES

1. Mk 5:34
2. He 13:12-14
3. Ps 116:1-2
4. Is 62:1
5. Is 53:4-5
6. Pr 23:7
   Je 30:17
7. 2Ch 16:9LB
8. Mt 5:48
9. 1Jn 3:20
10. He 9:14
11. He 10:22-23
12. Ga 5:1
13. Ph 1:6
14. 1Pe 2:23
15. Ro 8:2
16. Is 54:2
17. 2Co 10:4-5
18. Ep 5:26
19. Ro 12:24
20. Ro 8:32
21. Ro 10:17
22. 2Ti 1:7
23. 2Ti 3:16
24. Is 55:8-9
25. Ps 103:7
26. Ph 2:13
27. Ro 8:16-17
28. He 13:14
29. He 61:3

HIS FOUNDATION

> *Nevertheless, the foundation of God*
> *stands sure, having this seal,*
> *The Lord knows them that are his...*
> [2Tim 2.19]

In recalling the few memories I have of my earlier years, there seems to have been scant opportunity to expand the horizons of my mind. I can't remember really having fun as a youngster; running and playing, exploring my environment, games of make believe, etc. as I see kids doing today. Matter of fact because of my childhood non-experiences I found it difficult to identify with my own children's antics as they were growing up.

In my young years we were not allowed to make any noise or run in the apartment because the man who lived under us worked nights and slept days. I learned this from my sister who spoke to his wife who confessed she never knew any children lived in the apartment above them for all that time. There were five of us. I will leave the implications of this to your imagination.

My mother was a very quiet person, and was aware that people lived under us. We lived in the Bronx, New York, on the fifth floor of an apartment house. We did not have a back yard in which to run and play.

The street on which we lived had a lot of traffic plus an overhead elevated train. Under that, ran a trolley car and automobiles constantly driving past our house. All this defies explanation to those of whom never lived in a really big city. Needless to say we could not just go outside as do many little ones these days who live in private homes with those wonderful fenced-in yards.

My first two years at school were certainly propitious to fill my somewhat empty mind. My grades reflected my enthusiasm. I remember receiving an award and being skipped one half year grade; 2B to 3B. The school system of grading is a little different these days. Now they don't separate into 6 month terms.

In 3B the students are still establishing a groundwork for Mathematics, the foundation from which much is derived. I missed it! As a result I collided with fourth grade arithmetic totally unprepared, and the teacher of that class was vehemently intolerant of my lack of understanding and proceeded to ridicule me at every juncture. Catching up became impossible for me as she derided every stammering wrong answer and consistently saw me as stupid and disobedient. I was 9 years old.

My mind became almost paralyzed with fear as she repeated over again that I could never learn anything and had to stay in class and study' as the others went to auditorium and saw a movie. My other grades were passable and I was very good at spelling. This however, did not dissuade her.

Although I dreamed of sweet release at the end of the year, I was horrified to learn I was left back and had to do fourth grade all over again - with the same teacher. And so I learned that no matter what I did, I was still worthless and there was no help for me. My other grades continued to suffer decline................→

> Remember this.
> When one believes a lie,
> it becomes truth to them.

My anger and hatred for people intensified as yet another classroom of my peers saw me scorned almost daily and related to me as though I were untouchable. And so I never really learned to relate to people, and of course it got worse as I grew older.

This was coupled with the fact that I had very poor eyesight even in the first grade and was belittled as four-eyes. Because of the deficiency of relationships at home I was incapable of sharing these fears and traumas with anyone. I really felt that no one cared anyway.

As the Lord brought me through forgiveness

I began to understand this nun's lack of the resource of real love. Perhaps she even saw a little of herself in me. We tend to despise those things in others that we deny in ourselves.

However the truth for me at the age of nine and ten was, this is how God feels about me; for this teacher was a Nun - supposedly a representative of God Himself. Only as I came to have a personal relationship with Jesus and began to experience His love, grace and mercy did I realize this person represented only her own fears and bitterness.

No matter who you are or what vocation you strive to accomplish if you don't have the love of Jesus in your heart, you cannot reach down into the woundedness of another, with compassion to heal.

I was not yet a year old in the Lord when He opened the door for me to attend a weekend Seminar in of all places, a Catholic retreat house run by the same order of nuns who taught me as a little girl. In that scenario God brought me to face all the bitterness and hurt that filled my heart. These nuns were so gracious and filled with compassion as God redeemed that part of my past.

Our God is Awesome.

After I became a Christian in 1972, it didn't take me long to realize there are many tables to eat from. Hungry for the real source of genuine life I quickly became a part of whatever was available. I was like an insatiable baby bird for I'd been starved for so long. The next months and years were spent going from Bible studies to retreats, meetings, fellowships and to Church. I listened to tapes, read many books and the Bible of course. WoW! I had a lot of stuff up there in my head. My life was very slow to smooth out as I was told it would, though I surely knew a lot about God and His Kingdom.

Hebrews 5:12-6:3 seems to make clear there can be a misunderstanding of the necessity and importance of having a rock foundation under us. Verse three in the Amplified Version says,

If indeed God permits, we will [now] proceed [to advanced teaching].

I am so glad God did not allow me to continue until I was established on the Rock. There are some people who have no idea of what it means to build on established principles of anything.

This is why many of us all through life; read the instructions only as a last resort!

So much of the previous years were involved with God healing my past. The pain of rejection and believing I had no value so permeated the depths of my heart that God in His wisdom and mercy ministered His love and acceptance as the first steps toward restoration.

Please realize that I was forty years old when I was born-again. By this time my heart was imprisoned by walls too massive for me to break through. All these years was this garbage buried in my soul. To believe that it was OK for me to live and not just exist - took a long time to understand. If you don't know who you are or where you belong and afraid to trust anyone; where do you begin?

Just to know God was there, that He would not betray me; and it was OK to enter into the real world was all I could handle for a long time. But then I had to discover reality. How I even despised my name and in 1963, changed it, hating to reveal the other ever again. Yet in 1983, in a vision of extreme love and tenderness I saw Jesus lifting me up to the Father and He said, *I named her 'Gift of God'* -

Oh God, thank You for Your love.

This chapter is based on several months of Journal entries written in the late 70's. God began a deep work of establishing me in His Kingdom through what He taught me in those years of growth. I still keep journal records, but in those early years I wrote in it consistently. Looking back I can see how God was teaching me to stand on His Word. *And most of all to trust in Him.*

As I was writing this chapter and reading all those old journal notes, God was recalling to me the wonderful months and years that followed as He walked with me, laying stone by stone - reminding me of how my relationship with Him had grown and sharing memories of His grace and mercy in each fiery trial.

Looking back I saw how my faith began to take on more positive strength. I realized hope in God was being firmly planted in my heart. I began to see who I was in Christ and was at the threshold of understanding how to partake of the Kingdom of God; His righteousness, peace and joy.

Be mindful these journal entries are the result of being in the Word, in prayer and seeking His will for my life. Also there were other entries on the days between those noted, but they were not related to this subject.

Please note that herein is recorded verbatim what is in my journal and so I give a word of understanding. Sometimes we record our prayers and wait on God to answer, so we can see how He's working in our lives. Most often I'd write what was on my heart. Since I love to write, I have always been able to put my thoughts on paper easier than verbal expression.

There were times that God would speak within my spirit even as I was writing and I knew He was giving me the answers to my questions so I wrote it all down.

He would direct me to specific Scriptures and by the Spirit apply its truth to my heart and bring healing and understanding to the issue I was struggling with. Over the months He was unfolding the Doctrine of Christ as the primary base of my foundation.

When God works to install a principle in us, it does not happen overnight. Be assured I am still in the building stage and I praise God for His love and patience with me. Back in the early 80's, at the time of these particular entries in my journal, I was experiencing confusion and frustration. God has asked me to share my heart in this book. I pray others will benefit.

I was recently reading, The Life of John G. Lake, Published by Kenneth Copeland Ministries, 1994. He wrote, First we see that the Kingdom is based on principles. Principles are greater than doctrines. Principles are the foundation stones upon which all other things rest. Doctrines are the rules, the details by which we endeavor to carry out things that the principles contain; but the principles are the foundation stones upon which all things rest.

Pastor Lake wrote this before 1935. God revealed it to me by His Spirit in 1983. And reading his book confirmed I was on the right path. Please note that all in this chapter is verbatim from my journal during these months.

Please remember this was written in 1987.
And these journal entries are from former years as I was growing in the Lord. I still had and have a long way to go.

JOURNAL ENTRY 6 MARCH [1979]

He's also shown me some of my spirituality is a facade so people won't see I'm not as holy as I would like them to think. I never spend enough time just one-on-one with the Lord. I waste a lot of time that could be productive for His Kingdom. I strive and struggle to bring about the maturity I yearn for and relationships for which I hunger. I was hungry for God but didn't really know how to do it.

These things seem always at the tip of my fingers just beyond my grasp. I find lately that I'm jealous and resentful of others that have found that closeness with the Lord for which I've been searching. God is telling me now that He hasn't brought me further because my foundation is very shaky and He won't let me go on until I take care of this problem.

Oh Lord, show me how to get a solid foundation under me.

I'm tired of the confusion and fear that rules my life. I don't know who I am or where I belong. There is a great deal of unbelief in my life. I feel like the good things that have happened, have been experiences for the other me [though I'm not sure who that is either].

Things have always been that way. To believe the goodness of the Lord is really for me - has been very uncertain. That's why things happen at me. I've not actually partaken of them. They are all displaced and misaligned and a part of me keeps waiting for some experience to happen to the real me. My prayer at the end of this entry was; Lord I release this burden to You and I await Your divine touch.

So God began to show me that I was trying to build the first and second floor of my Christian experience without anything solid under me. No wonder my whole building was in a state of collapse. I'd read the BOOK but didn't understand...

How to wait on God..................➔

| I wanted it all done yesterday. |

I tried to ignore all the fears and problems I had. They did not go away. I kept thinking if I could learn it all then I'd be able to walk away from the garbage of my life. I'd be all God wanted. Well friends, God does not want us to be a walking encyclopedia of the Kingdom of God.
I had truth from the Word, but there was no reality in my heart.

And so much I did not understand. It seems I was feeding on the tree of the knowledge of good and evil. I could tell you what was expected of me, but to perform it I could not. Had I honestly taken a good look at myself I could say that I had become holier than thou and self-righteous in front of God and everybody. Especially my family. I should never have written those letters. It made them so mad. [They were catholic]. God told me in the beginning, if I would remain faithful and trust Him, that He would save my family. For my generation, I am the only one left; ninety-one years old. All the rest are with Him in His heaven. Thank You Jesus.
I know I will see them again.

JOURNAL ENTRY 7 MARCH

I made a decision today to allow God to directly deal with my non-disciplined habits and attitudes. I'm trusting God to do what needs to be done. I've made up my mind to be obedient to whatever He says, in His promise to lead and guide me with His eye. Praise God He delivered me from a defeatist attitude.

As I'm writing this chapter now, God is telling me that to be undisciplined is to be in rebellion. WOW! It is a sin against God. I never realized the enormity of this. Some of us wear non-discipline as a badge, boasting and telling of our latest escapades. Father forgive me. I'm just as guilty. Thank You for the Blood.

I also began to do what I now sometimes see in others. Every sermon I heard, every book I read, every Scripture - I applied to other people and for sure knew that was exactly what they needed to get their life together. My real problem was not becoming established in truth; not allowing the Life of God to flow. I was striving to make it happen; trying to produce that which only God is able.

As a new Christian we begin to experience the wonderful ministry of God to our devastated life, and we think, Now we have it together, now we can make it. We have yet to realize the example of Joshua, taking the promised land one city at a time. God takes us one day at a time, and we'll still be in process up to and including the day we go to be with Jesus. I guess like many of my brothers and sisters out there, I was having a hard time going from law to grace. I had read the letter Paul wrote to the Ephesians previously, but I was not able to assimilate its truth. Proverbs tells us,

Except the Lord build the house, they labor in vain[1]

We must remember *We are his workmanship.*[2]

We can come into His rest,[3] as we lay down the works of our soul. 1Cor 3:11-23 is wonderful news. God will cause the changes so we can get it right. If you see yourself in this mirror talk to God about it. Don't take this as condemnation.

We all produce a lot of junk. Just let God's fire burn it up now so we can receive the reward; and let's do it His way. God brings awareness of any given subject for the purpose of healing and restoration. As we wait on God He is ever gracious to do that which we commit to Him. As we surrender to Him, draw near to Him, He will draw near to us. And so

God began to teach me from the Word what it meant to be built on His foundation.

As I was Journaling, God gave me several Scriptures on being established.

But the God of all grace who hath called us unto his eternal glory by Christ Jesus after that ye have suffered a while, make you perfect, stablish, strengthen, and settle you.[4] To the end he may stablish your hearts unblamable in holiness before God....[5] With whom my hand shall be established; mine arm also shall strengthen him.[6]

My favorite is *Believe in the Lord,
so shall ye be established.[7]*

It's my favorite because God showed me His mighty hand of deliverance for Jehoshaphat as he and all Judah trusted in God and kept their eyes on Him. In trusting God and releasing my control, He has brought me through massive battles. There are about one hundred verses for the word establish in the Bible. I encourage you to study these for yourself.

The word establish means 'to build up, be permanent, prosper, rise up, to station as a pillar, union with, and completeness.'

I wanted to band-aid all those hurtful years so I wouldn't have to be reminded but they kept rearing their ugly heads. Our life experiences plant a large variety of seeds in our heart. Sometimes the crop grows above ground and sometimes like potatoes, carrots and beets, the fruit of what was planted is quite hidden. Then sometimes we look for harvest and find it has been rendered of no good use by underground critters, all buried in our soul.

The Word tells us the human heart is deceitful above all things and desperately wicked. Not all of us wind up behind bars for murder but how often have we harbored hidden resentment and anger, criticism and even hatred.

While our friends see only the smile on our face, the underground critters of offenses and unforgiveness are eating away at our life source and we have a hard time balancing out the emptiness in between.

Sometimes our emotions are shredded.

Now the world's psychiatrists and psychologists will help you sort out and recognize all that ails you. But they don't know about the precious Blood that redeems; they don't have the Water of Life to wash you clean from your sin; the Balm of Gilead; the Oil and the Wine to dress your wounds.

They don't know the Sun of Righteousness Who has healing in His wings. They don't have the hope that is laid up for us. All they can do is pat you on the back and say, Come see me again, next week.

We can come to Jesus with the same problems and the healing and restoration begins. We must be aware of the Great Physician's fee. It is us! He will charge our impatience, our irritability, resentments, bitterness, especially our unforgiveness. We may have to wait on Him even when there's no one ahead of us. We can't tell Him how to do it or what to work on first. We yield to Him. He works patience in us as we wait. Then as His peace covers us,

God sits in the heavens and does what pleases Him.[8]

Since it is His good pleasure to share His Kingdom with us, see what Proverbs 10:22 tells us. In my book <u>Restoring the Temple of God</u>, He showed me how, in researching the names of the builders who restored Israel's temple and the wall, in the 5th century, correlates with how He rebuilds us born-again children of God.

The blessing of the Lord, it makes [truly] rich,
and He adds no sorrow with it.
[neither does toiling increase it] ❤

JOURNAL ENTRY 8 MARCH

Hebrews 6:1-2 reveals the Master's intentions. Leave the principles, go on to perfection, don't stay in the foundation. But it doesn't tell us, Skip over them, they are not important.

This passage shows us what are the foundation stones on which God wants to build. There is only one thing to do with a shaky foundation and that is tear it down and build a new one from scratch. As I was thinking and praying and reading back what I'd written the day before, the Lord asked me to turn to Hebrews six.

He began to teach me about the

First principles of the oracles of God.

They are listed in Eph 6:1-2.

'1. doctrines of Christ
2. repentance from dead works
3. faith toward God
4. doctrine of baptisms

5. laying on of hands
6. resurrection of the dead
7. eternal judgment.

The above numbers 2,4,5 - I had been able to understand because these are things we do. Numbers 6&7 are waiting for the return of our Lord and King. I did not have understanding of numbers one and three. When one puts up a building that is going to last for eternity it must have a good substructure; unless one plans on having the building collapse sometime in the near future. The bedrock must be reliable. What God is saying is this Rom 9:33 *Behold, I lay in Zion a stumbling stone and rock of offense, And whoever believes on Him will not be put to shame.*

Get established in Jesus so you will be imbedded in the Rock.

If we have built on a shaky foundation it is not good sense to shore it up. We must tear down what we might think is sufficient and build a new one based on truth. Whenever a building is restored the unstable portions must be torn down and the rubble removed. In studying the Books of Ezra and Nehemiah we can see a strong spiritual quality as to how God goes about restoring our temple.- Ezra's name means '*God has helped*'.

Nehemiah's name means *Yahweh Comforts*

The Comforter - God's Holy Spirit.

Nehemiah and Ezra are concerned with rebuilding the temple and the wall around Jerusalem. With great detail each chapter reveals how they overcame the enemy and continued to build even as the accuser tried to undermine their efforts with mockery and finally conspiracy.

My new book The Temple of God Restored, describes how the rebuilding of the wall and gates of Jerusalem compares to how God is restoring us, the temple in which He now resides. With great detail God delves into our life; but He first of all surrounds us with His presence and teaches us how to maintain His protection from the enemy, as we build our wall with stones of ....➜

| Faith, Trust, Praise and Worship. |

Because we live in the world before we come to know God, we are vulnerable to hearing and taking into our computers all kinds of religious notions. Some things go in one ear and out the other, but mostly our mind word processor stores ideas from books, TV, our own and others' thoughts, and any resource that is in the world of religion and philosophy.

As a born-again believer we must be aware that whatever may be broadcast about religion - if it does not line up with the Word of God, then it is not even an issue the believer must deal with. This is why we must know the Word, so we won't be deceived.

I've seen Christians become very offended by what cults may say concerning Jesus. But if it's not Bible doctrine, then it's not the real Jesus. Now, is God capable of defending Himself? I have realized in growing in the Lord that the Bible is God's revelation of Himself. It is not man's sometimes depraved notions of the god he would like to serve. That's one reason why we have so many cults in the world. Some people figure out which god seemeth right, then pressurize certain scripture into that mold.

An unredeemed man can read the Bible and see history, war, sex, murder, etc. and even justify his own cruelty towards his fellow man - and never see Jesus. If God does not reveal Himself to us by supernatural revelation we just do not see Him. But God is more than willing to reveal Himself.

You will seek me and find me when you search for me with all your heart.[10] *[I will let you find Me].*

The bulk of religious ideas we bring into the Kingdom at rebirth rarely matches up to His reality and leaves much to be desired. Those perceptions, images and imaginations were stored in an unredeemed mind. This is part of the rubble.

When I realized the conflict I said, 'OK God, I take all this package of religion and I lay it at the foot of the cross. Please show me Who You really are'. I was so glad to see there is clearly explained in Hebrews 5:12-6:2 the importance of laying Kingdom foundations stones that we might come to full age.

Even as I am writing this chapter now, the Lord continues to teach. We receive understanding little by little, precept by precept, line upon line, until we come of full age, and research gives us awesome understanding. In my Journaling He spoke to me of the first foundation stone;

The Doctrine of Christ -
But what is the doctrine of Christ? Researching Strong's Concordance tells us:
3056: Doctrine - LOGOS - fluent, utterance,
something said, including the thought;
a type of discourse, a computation]or reckoning];
The Divine Expression - It is the motive behind it all.
Our construction plans are found in the Maker's Manual otherwise known as the Bible.
#3056 gives reference to
#3004. Let's examine this one
#3004: To lay forth or relate, the systematic or set course.

So God is explaining His design, His motivation; His plan of redemption. This is the Doctrine of Christ; how, why, where, when, who. God brings understanding into the light that we might become skillful in the word of righteousness. For the purposes of what God is showing me, He's drawing my attention to the second chapter of Ephesians.

And you hath he quickened, who were dead in trespasses and sins;...For by grace are ye saved through faith; and that not of yourselves: It is the gift of God: not of works, lest any man should boast. For we are his workmanship, created in Christ Jesus unto good works, which God hath before ordained that we should walk in them...

Phil 2:13 *for it is God who works in you both to will and to do for His good pleasure.*   [This means God does it and we cooperate].

We are made near by the Blood of Christ...He is our peace...That he might reconcile both unto God by one Spirit...Through him we have access by one Spirit unto the Father...Ye are no more strangers or foreigners, but fellow citizens with the saints, and of the household of God...

Built on the foundation of the apostles and prophets, Jesus Christ being the chief cornerstone; together grows unto a holy temple in the Lord... built together for a habitation of God through the Spirit. He gave me life when I was dead in sin. He brought me in. When He told me I was no longer a stranger and a wanderer, my heart leaped for joy! Because of His great love for me He implanted His Kingdom; Himself - within me, to enable me to walk in His love.

As God began to reveal the truth of this Scripture to me, I realized the Kingdom of God is the reality and the world is the fantasy. Romans chapter four reveals a man who knew what were his priorities. He saw the goal, the far country; and set his face toward the prize.

He believed God, Who giveth life to the dead
and called those things which are not, as though they were.

Everything of the world will pass away. I had been receiving a lying world of illusion as a basis for my life. No wonder nothing seemed real. No wonder everything was displaced, always happening to the other me.

Praise the Lord, now the reality of God's Kingdom can operate in my life. Now I can begin to experience the life God has for me. Hallelujah!

The eyes of your understanding being enlightened;
that ye may know the hope of your calling,
and what are the riches of the glory of his
inheritance in the saints.[11]

What does all this mean to someone who is just coming into Kingdom truth. It means we have been placed in a whole different family. This is the family of God, A whole new wonderful life.

What is His inheritance in me?

INHERITANCE:
1. Something legally owned.
2. I am adopted. I am legally His! Rom 8:15. Abba Father.
   Romans 8 tells us nothing can take us out of His hand.
      We are bought with the highest price paid.
         ♥The Precious Blood of Jesus ♥

2 Cor 6:18 *'I will be a Father to you, And you shall be My sons and daughters, Says the Lord Almighty.*

It surely is the application of God's truth in our lives that makes it more than just words. We cannot do it ourselves. It is a super-natural impartation of grace from God that substantiates His Word within and enables us to walk in it.

As we submit to God He pours out His grace. Now grace is the ability to do what God is calling us to do. Is He calling you to forgive? Well, when you submit your anger and unforgiveness to God, He gives grace in abundance. Is He calling you to trust Him? ....→

| Grace to do it is available |

As we renew our mind with the Word of God, He brings His healing power. I don't understand how it happens, I just know it does. He will bring correction, restoration, give us a right spirit, and bestow His Light and Life into our darkness.

We must agree with the Word of God and yield to what His Spirit wants to accomplish. I am convinced there is nothing automatic concerning the workings of the Spirit in our lives. We must choose daily that we want to say, Yes Lord, and remember that faith comes through the Word and by continuing to listen and receive that Word of truth.

JOURNAL ENTRY 10 MARCH.
So what is the hope of His calling?
HOPE: A steady, serene, confident expectation of good. The foundation of hope is faith. Faith is the substance of things hoped for, the basis; the underlying reality on which hopes are built. Even our faith is a gift of God, as He has given each of us a measure.[12]

In order to keep ourselves from discouragement and depression we must choose and determine to protect our minds with the helmet, the hope of salvation.[13] We are saved by hope. Saved from each trial by a steady, confident expectation of good. Not that we already see it. Sometimes it is not forthcoming immediately. We must continue in hope.

Now the God of hope fill you with all joy and peace in believing, that ye may abound in hope, through the power of the Holy Ghost.[14]

It takes the power of the Holy Spirit to enable me to abound in hope, but it is already His will. I don't have to struggle to attain it. Praise God! Here in this truth we can have our minds renewed. We can ask right now. God will do it.

Christ in you, the hope of glory.[15]

Christ in us produces hope. When we are burdened by discouragement, depression, and hopelessness, we can release them to the Lord and receive His Spirit of Hope.

Wherein God, willing more abundantly to show unto the heirs of promise [that's us] the immutability of his counsel, confirmed it by an oath: That by two immutable things, in which it was impossible for God to lie, we might have strong consolation, who have fled for refuge to lay hold upon the hope set before us:
Which hope we have as an anchor of the soul, both sure and steadfast, and which enters into that within the veil.[16]

We can lay hold of the hope that is set before us. The anchor gives stability. The anchor is hope. My foundation is stable because my anchor is hooked into the Eternal One behind the veil, firmly attached to my heart by His love that will never fail. Not only is hope alive [1Peter 1:3] but also:
1. Psalm 16:9 Hope is a hideout and a resting place.
2. Lam 3:26 Hope and quietly
wait for the salvation of the Lord.
3. Zec 9:12 Hope, literally a cord,
tied into God by our hope in final victory.

[The Concordance definition gives the sense of an umbilical cord as tied between mother and fetus, receiving life and provision, growing to maturity]. HOPE IS:
1. a refuge from the storm.
2. a chance for new life to be born out of pain.
3. the cord that binds us to the One
Who holds our future in His hands.

Father, let this truth become established in me.
Thank you Lord. I receive it.

As time passed by, God was indeed implanting these wonderful truths with His supernatural process of reconstruction, regeneration, renewal and establishment. We are in constant growth and change and it comes little by little, every day.

If we relinquish our will for the will of God, things will be more at peace and the struggles will not be so crazy.

JOURNAL ENTRY 21 MARCH.

The Lord is showing me in His Word who I am and where I belong. I claim it as my inheritance, my right in Him; to be where I am in Christ. I am no longer a stranger and wanderer..➔

> I belong to the household of God

Jesus is my foundation, my main stay, my home base. When I cling to my Father, He fixes it. He has made a place especially for me where I fit into His plans. I don't have to defend my right to be there. I am growing right along with everyone else. I don't have to safeguard my position by acting spiritual, that's pious phoniness. God wants us to be real. [People raised in healthy homes may also have this problem]. Only God can reveal it to you.

JOURNAL ENTRY 24 MARCH

So far the Doctrine of Christ has been: according to Ephesians:

2:1 He gave me life when I was dead.
1:8 I am His inheritance - legally His.
2:18 He paid the price, the Blood of Jesus.

More proof: 1 Cor 6:20; 7:23; Hebrews 9:14; 10:1-22; 1 Peter 1:18,19; 1John 1:1-7; Rom 6:5-11;8:14,15, and so much more.

1. I am alive to God! He is legally my Father.
2. I have received the Spirit of Adoption [Gal 4.4-7].
3. The Spirit tells me I am a child of God.

God has now for all time settled it. Galatians 4 tells me the Spirit of Jesus in my heart says He is my Father, and if a son then also an heir of God through Christ. I am to inherit all that Christ has inherited. Romans 8 tells me I'm a joint heir equal with everyone else, and Galatians 3 declares If I belong to Christ then I am of Abraham's seed and heir of the promises and covenants God made with Abraham.

But Father I want to feel it. The lie that I did not belong was instilled as a small child, rejected and unloved. God is healing and restoring. No more in just my imagination, now to become a reality. I've never sat on a Daddy's lap, nor put my head on his shoulder. I've never hugged a daddy and told him I loved him.

But God has told me,

> I've always been your Father, Dory,
> but now you know it. Praise God!

As ye have therefore received Christ Jesus the Lord,
so walk ye in him: Rooted and built up in him,
and stablished in the faith, as ye have been taught.... [17]

We are warned in Colossians chapter two, not to let anyone cheat us out of our inheritance by vain traditions that make God's Word of no effect.

Right here each of us can ask God to show us where man's traditions have blocked His truth from becoming established in us. We can cast those things far from us and fill the empty places with

The entrance of thy words giveth light;
It giveth understanding to the simple. [18]

It's okay to let go of standards that are no longer of benefit. How about, Stay out of the street, you'll get hit by a car. It was valid at three years old, but not now. Let's make room for growth and expansion by eliminating the rubble as God reveals it. God accomplished all in Christ and then

HE PUT US IN CHRIST †
Read the letter to the Ephesians.
Drink into your spirit what God has done for you.

JOURNAL ENTRY 30 MARCH.

Yesterday the Lord told me it is the Father's good pleasure to give me the Kingdom and I'm asking Him to show me what that means. We can't dig around in our own wild imagination and vanity and expect to realize Kingdom truths. Only God can reveal the things of God.[19]

This is why You gave me the Spirit, so I can understand. Please go on and teach me the next principle of the Doctrine of Christ that needs to become part of my foundation. Keep me going in the right direction. So now look at what becomes a reality. In Christ my Lord I have boldness and access - with confidence - by my faith, which He gave me to begin with.

Boldness to enter into the Holiest by the Blood of Jesus. He dedicated for me a new and living way through His flesh so that I may draw near with a true heart,]no fear] with full assurance;[20] made holy and acceptable by Him.[21] I have been made holy and acceptable by His sacrifice on the cross. It is His good pleasure to reveal the mysteries of His will to me,

*And that he will fulfill
all the good pleasures of His goodness.*[22]

JOURNAL ENTRY 11 APRIL.

The foundational principles of the Doctrine of Christ is built on the Father's love. It's explained in Ephesians 3:14-21. God has also been speaking to me about understanding that I am included with all the saints, and He wants me to know of and receive, and be established in the

*depths of his love and be filled
with all the fullness of God.*[24]

I guess I should be able to understand somewhat of God's love - after all these years of walking with Him. The Scriptures say that I might understand along with everyone else just what God's love is all about. But I can only say at this point I know with my mind that He cares about me because of all the things He's done in my life.

So I'm asking You Lord, am I never to feel Your love in my heart, in my innermost being, in my emotions. I feel like my emotions are dead. I need to comprehend why things are this way. Is this what it's all about. Just receive Your love by faith, as fact and believe it; never to feel or experience it? Please tell me, Lord.

Sometime after this entry I was at a meeting of the saints of God and we were singing choruses. They began to sing,

♪ Jesus loves me, this I know,
for the Bible tells me so ♪ ..

This is a little kid's song and it brought me back to my loveless childhood. I couldn't even mouth the words for there was rising up in me that old fear of being left out and never good enough. I was sitting on the edge of a very plush couch with some others and even as resentment was filling my heart I began to weep in frustration of not ever being able to grab hold of the truth which always alluded me.

God used those tears to wash away the pain and then poured His warm oil over me. I sank into the back of that couch and it was as the Spirit of His love engulfing me and drawing me into His heart.

I've never been the same.

Oh how I love the Lord; He knows me inside out
and is so concerned as to spend all the resources
of heaven to heal me.

He has awakened my desire to live life to the fullest of His plan for my life. And my desire is to walk and live in His grace. Thank You Jesus.

JOURNAL ENTRY 2 JUNE

Fear had been the enemy of my faith for so long that my foundation of hope towards God had been shaky and unreal. I've been running on my own determination, a work of the flesh. Lord, I lay it on the altar, tie it to the horns and offer it as a burnt sacrifice.[24] In its place I ask You Lord to cause and establish in me, a faith in God that will move mountains. The Spirit of God replied,

And in His Name, through faith in His Name

> yea, the faith which is by Him will there be
> perfect soundness to your walk with the Lord.

Praise Your Holy Name. I receive this from Your loving hand, Lord. Teach me. [Some time after that I found this word from the Lord confirmed by Scripture in Acts 3:16. Here's more encouragement;

> Be not slothful but followers
> of them who through faith
> and patience inherit the promise.[25]
> Don't give up hope. It is
> Tribulation that works patience.[26]

For some of us there can be plenty of tribulation in waiting, but remember, God is working patience in us while we wait! Romans 15:5 declares that we have a God of Patience. So keep actively believing even when you have to wait for a time to see the answer to your prayers. God already knows our needs, He's saying Trust Me and,

> Show diligence unto the full assurance
> of hope to the end.

1. Faith is a substance, something tangible I can act on.
2. Because of my faith I can know I please God.[A more excellent sacrifice] and I know I stand before Him, righteous [Heb 11:6].
3. Abraham's faith was counted to him as righteousness. God's proof of the pudding is, I am standing before Him knowing I belong. I don't have to defend my right to be here.

UNDATED - BECAUSE OF ETERNITY.
         My New Foundation: Only because
      I have made Jesus my Lord.

Therefore whosoever hears these sayings of mine, and does them, I will liken him unto a wise man which built his house upon a rock. And the rain descended, and the floods came, and the winds blew and beat upon that house; and it fell not: for ....➜

| This house was founded upon a rock.[27] |

I am no longer a stranger and a wanderer. I do belong; a partaker of the household of God. Growing together with the rest of God's family ❤

END OF JOURNAL ENTRIES.

Thus reads one chapter of my life. Because I allowed God to establish me in these things, and not just learn the words as I had been doing, much of the fears, confusion and instability were left behind as I grew stronger in my faith toward God.

In 1987 my husband of almost 20 years decided he wanted his life to go in another direction; [actually it had been for some time]. And that our relationship was irreconcilable and irretrievable, and so he divorced me.

It was the worst experience of my life. Had it not been for God's massive strategy against the stronghold of rejection - I would have lost it. But God wrapped me in His cocoon and separated me unto Himself. In the 3 months it took for the divorce to become final, God gave me the words to write this book; 19 chapters. The first chapter was,

Hope, Expectations and disappointments.
Now it's here.

Sad to say I had built too much hope in my husband and my marriage instead of knowing Psalm 62:5. *My soul, wait thou only upon God; for my expectation is from him. He only is my rock and my salvation; he is my defense; I shall not be moved.*

I loved Mike and prayed he would change, but he didn't.

The verses that helped me the most was Heb 9.14; 10.21,22; 1John 3.19-22; These must be read in the context of the Scriptures. We all have an evil conscience from before Christ, that must be cleansed along with guilt and condemnation

Four years later God showed me I had only written an outline, and over the next 10 years He showed me how to expand all the chapters to tell my story more elaborately. The original name was <u>Handbook on Victory</u>. I'm here to declare God gave me the victory over the flood that came to destroy me. The spirit of divorce says, 'You're not good enough', and tries to render the other party valueless. Ah, but God! - God knew differently. Less than a week after my husband left our home, God confronted this force of evil with His love and

Baptized me in His Spirit of Joy!

The teaching and dealing in my life continues as I walk out each new truth. [New for me, that is]. I would like to encourage you to get out your Bible and turn to Hebrews six. Ask God to lead and guide you into knowing which building stones if any, may be missing or only partially established in your foundation.

The Holy Spirit is your teacher. He will guide you into all truth. What I shared here is only a small portion.

For we are laborers together with God; ye are God's husbandry. Ye are God's building. According to the grace of God which is given unto me, as a wise master builder, I have laid the foundation and another builds thereon. But Let Every Man Take Heed How He Builds Thereupon. For Other Foundation Can No Man Lay Than That Is Laid, Which Is Jesus Christ.[28]

Ever since I found the reality of relationship and fellowship with the Lord back in 1972, I've had a fervor for the things of God that has consumed my life. Surely no one can let such a good thing pass by the wayside, and so I kept pursuing God.

In those past years, there were many times I felt as though a bottomless hole within me, consumed everything God was doing in my life. I just could not seem to find any satisfaction. This is why I felt like I was on a treadmill; never gaining any ground, never getting anywhere. No matter how much time I spent in the Word or seeking God I still felt like I was on half empty.

It was because I had not yet learned how to come into His rest. I strove to please God with a fury within my emotions. I didn't know what it meant to, *Be still and know that I am God.*[29]

But if I will quiet my mind and rest in Him I will know God is trustworthy and with Him all things are possible.[30]

I am also seeing a pattern in what God periodically does in our lives. He uses normal life time experiences to teach us principles of His Kingdom. This pattern I see can readily be compared to the tactics of our Army or Marines, etc. Men who are in training for battle soon find themselves on the firing line. But there also comes a time of what we call R.& R. It is a time of rest and relaxation; a time of gathering personal resources, to be strengthened and encouraged. We may receive new uniforms and weaponry. When we find ourselves once more before the enemy...

We are Stronger - More Efficient,
But more Dependent on God.

Now how does this compare with what God does? Too often when God wants us to rest, we fight to maintain the work we know He has given us. Even though He has lifted the anointing, we may still strive to function in that capacity. Surely we can give up an Ishmael as Abraham did.

Holding on to what God is finished with, will give place to the devil to bring guilt and condemnation because when the anointing has lifted, the work will fade away and we think it's our fault. When we don't learn to be sensitive to the Holy Spirit, satan has opportunity to deceive, to make us feel we have failed and disappointed God; that God is mad at us.

Again in comparison, a Secretary may have many jobs to do, but she or he is still a Secretary. No, God does not take from us the gifts He has given [Rom 11:29]. But if He wants to bring us down another path, then He may be finished with what we were doing,

Most often it is to bring us to a place of rest and restoration of our soul, strengthening our armor, building our faith, healing our wounds; to bring us into a higher place in the Spirit.

Too often we see our self-worth only in the work we can accomplish. God wants us to know we are loved by Him even if we never accomplish anything, because His love is unconditional.

We cannot earn it no matter what we do. He loved us in the womb of our mother when we could do nothing but eat and sleep, stretch out our limbs, and grow and mature. Now translate that into the Spirit realm, and let God grow you up. So, now I can,

Cast my cares on Him because He cares for me.[31]
This is His Sabbath rest. ♪

I'm doing it better every day. Looking back on those days, I stand in awe of God's wondrous patience and love that brought me through those hectic years. Malachi 3:10 says it's okey to prove or test God, so at this writing, I'm proving His hammock and learning how good it is to trust in Him more and more every day, because He is trustworthy.

Thank You God, You know exactly where I am.
You know exactly what I need. I am growing up in You and becoming that tree planted by Your River of Life.
I can spread out my roots
and rest here in Your presence.
♥

The foundation of God stands sure, having this seal. The Lord knows them that are his.[32] *And they that shall be of thee shall*

build the old waste places; thou shalt raise up the foundations of many generations, and thou shalt be called the repairer of the breach, the restorer of paths to dwell in.[33]

STUDY GUIDE

1. What are the foundations stones of the Kingdom according to Heb chapter 6?
2. If our Doctrines of Christ are muddied up how can we possibly stand on a sure foundation? 1Co 3: no condemnation. Let God's fire burn the tares now so we can receive the reward later. Let's do it His way. Tares can be false wheat, false doctrine. Not knowing the truth of Who God really is.
3. Where can we begin to grasp these fundamental truths?
4. If we don't know who we are in Christ how can we function in the Kingdom? Are we still a stranger? What does God say about this? Isa 26:3-4.
5. We all have a very active imagination. Is it a good idea to think about what God might be like - and go from there? Isa 56:8-9, Judges 21:25.
6. How can we find out the real truth about Who God is? Mt 1:21; Jer 29.
7. What happened to Abraham because he dared to hope in God? Rom 4.
8. What is the hope of His calling? How can we know about it?
9. What is the link between hope and faith? Heb 11.
10 . What produces hope in us? Col 1.
11. Why has hope been compared with an anchor? Heb 6.
12. Why is it important to be rooted in Christ? Col 2.
13. The Father has birthed in us a living hope. Why? 1Pet 3.
14. Is it really possible to know God? 1Jn 2; 1Pet 1
15. Can hope cause us to know God? Heb 7.
16. How do we be still, and patient before God?
    1. Right focus. 2. Surrender. 3.Trust.
    4. Patience. 5. Time apart with God.

PRAYER: Thank you Lord that I can know the hope of Your calling for my life and that the eyes of my understanding are being enlightened.

To know You Lord
Is the hunger of my heart
To worship You in all I do
To feel Your love flowing through me
Like a river of the water of life
Coming from the throne of God
And from the Lamb
To be that tree of righteousness
Planted by Your river
To drink of Your living stream
To be all that You made me to be
Is the hunger of my heart.

Come into My throne room, child
Sit with me and drink of My love
Let My hand of grace overcome
The troubles and trials of life.
In your weakness I shall strengthen you
In your failures, come to Me
And in time you will surrender
All of life that you could be.

♥♥

SCRIPTURES

1. Ps 127:1
2. Ep 2:10
3. He 4:10
4. 1Pe 5:1
5. 1Th 3:13
6. Ps 89:21
7. 2Ch 20:20
8. Ps 115:3
9. 2Co 11:4
10. Je 29:13
11. Ep 1:18
12. Ro 12:3
and Mt 11:27
24 Ps 118:27
25. He 6:11-12
26. Ro 5:3
27. Mt 7:24-25
28. 1Co 3:9-11
29. Ps 46:10
30. Is 32:17-18
31. 1Pe 5:7
32. 2Ti 2:19
33. Is 58:12

THE GIFT OF LIFE

> *But unto you that fear my name shall*
> *the Sun of righteousness arise*
> *with healing in his wings;*
> *and ye shall go forth, and grow up*
> *as calves of the stall.*[1]

Calves of the stall are grain fed - well taken care of. They are protected from harsh weather and attacks from wild animals. While living on a ranch some years ago I saw some range calves that were minus their tails. I was told the coyotes run them down at night and sometimes they escape but they pay a price. Calves of the stall are kept safe from weather and predators; and watched over by their owner-master.

CHRISTIANITY IS NOT A RELIGION
IT IS RELATIONSHIP.

Webster's Dictionary defines

#1. Religion as the service and worship of God or the supernatural [itdoesn't matter which]; commitment or devotion to, or observance to a religious faith; institutionalized religious attitudes, beliefs and practices. The implication here given is something you do, or something you get.

#2. Relationship on the other hand is defined as - The state or character of being. We have a difference here between knowing about Jesus; and knowing Him personally. It can be defined this way:
A. Religion: knowing about Jesus or merely acknowledging his existence.[2]
B. Relationship: having kindred fellowship on the foundation of personal intimate knowledge.

For the Kingdom of God is not meat or drink,
but righteousness, peace and joy
In the Holy Ghost.

The Kingdom of God is not a ritual of taking in and putting out; a ceremony of works guaranteed to make heads turn, or the performance of the expected standard for pleasing men. The Pharisees did that and Jesus called them whitewashed graves, looking great on the outside; hypocrites. Sometimes this is caused by fear. We're afraid if we don't look right, that others will judge us. If we can just be honest with ourselves and with God, He will stand with us. We don't have to set any performance records.

Rom 14:17-18 *for the kingdom of God is not eating and drinking, but righteousness and peace and joy in the Holy Spirit.*

The Kingdom of God is not what you say or do or think. The Kingdom of God is the eternal union of God and man that brings forth the fullness of the New Creation; the new man walking in resurrection life with King Jesus sitting on the throne, His laws inscribed in our heart [Heb 8:10].

Many people think of religion in the context of what we do when we get to church. We may be indoctrinated into thinking that God stuff is what automatically happens on Sunday if we are not too tired from the night before; a duty to be carried out because we were raised in church. It may become a spectator sport that includes wearing our finest to go hear an excellent orator speak on the issues of the day.

God's purposes for His people are established on the foundation of relationship and fellowship.[5] He desires that we enter into - participate - partake of the very life of God in our innermost being. A new-born infant is brought into our families and tenderly cared for, nurtured and is a member of - experiencing the vital every day life and resources of the family. A new person, born of its seed, inheriting its traits; a partaker, part and parcel of all this family unit contains.

This natural experience is the analogy, type and shadow of the spiritual experience of a born from above [of incorruptible seed][6] believer in Christ, a family member of the Kingdom of God; the offspring of the eternal Father.[7]

The natural will pass away. Only that which belongs to the Kingdom of God will go on through eternity.

We can live a life of praise and worship as we come into a true knowledge of our God and King - our Lord and Master. Jesus said *God is Spirit and they that worship Him must worship in spirit and truth*.[8] The true knowledge of God is what Jesus came to reveal. *And this is eternal life, that they may know you the only true God.*[9]

In the temple there were prayers and worship, sacrifice and praise, constantly being offered up to God.

My house shall be called a house of prayer.

Now we are His house, His temple.
[Isaiah 56:7]. Worship and praise brings us into His presence and in this place, we get to know Him. We hear and experience many things that settle down in our heart because we are sometimes ignorant of spiritual truths. Paul tells us God does not want us to be ignorant. This means a lack of information. So, know this ....→

> The born-again believer IS the temple of the living God

My people perish because of a lack of knowledge,

because we don't read the Word enough, and sometimes we only half believe it. We must develop confidence in His Word. It is Truth. Matthew 13 tells us the parable of the farmer planting the seed. The Word is the seed.

If God's Word Is the Seed of Life -
Are the Words of Our Mouth,
The Seed of Our Life?
What Is Coming out of Our Mouth?

As we desire to be established in truth - the deceiver comes along with his lies and deception. He points his arrows at our fears and doubts, and repeats what he said to Eve,

Yea, hath God said....

He tries to make us believe that God is a hard task master; that we have to strive to please Him. Paul tells us satan tries to corrupt our minds: to pine or waste, to shrivel or wither, spoil, ruin, defile. The glorious truth of the gospel in all its simplicity [for even a three year old can be led to salvation] will renew our minds and train us to reject satan's lies. The seed is waiting to take root in our hearts. God is now ready to bring His truth to bear, that we may,

Receive with meekness the engrafted word which is able to save our souls.[10]

As He begets in us His Word of truth[11] we must relinquish to God even those religious ideas and ideals that we cherish in our heart. In laying our beliefs on the altar,[12] God will help us sort them out. We can even here, right now, have a spiritual yard sale. Up on the table we can place:

- Religious tradition-
- Commandments of men-
- False expectations-
- Our brand of theology-
- Ritual, religiosity-
- Facades, hypocrisy-

- Opinions, attitudes- • Vain imaginations-
- Churchianity [that's going to church to be seen of men]
- All our Ishmaels [that's religious stuff we do without God].
- Other things God is showing us hidden in our attic.

Now Father has seen your AD - and He's come to purchase,
>for a higher price than you bargained;
>The Precious Blood of His Only Begotten Son.

As we put these things into His hand we can approach Him with purity and sincerity; the innocence of a child, and allow His restoration. God knows we are unable to receive all He has for us at one time. He desires His fullness for us. He doesn't want us shortchanged. And so here we come again. He'll lift us up to reach the fruit on the higher branches this time, and the tender shoots that come forth because of the Son shine [Jer 17:7-8].

We cannot know God in an unredeemed, unrenewed mind. Romans 8:6-7 [Amp] tells us,
Now the mind of the flesh [which is sense and reason without the Holy Spirit] is death [death that comprises
 all the miseries arising from sin both here and hereafter].
But the mind of the [Holy] Spirit is life and [soul] peace [both now and forever]. [That is] because the mind of the flesh
 [with its carnal thoughts and purposes] is hostile to God, for it does not submit itself to God's law; indeed it cannot.

If you are a child of God the Holy Spirit dwells in you and directs you. You have access to His wisdom; access to the mind of Christ [1Co 2:16]. When we are born-again into His Kingdom we have much to learn - and unlearn.
David recognized this in Psalm 119:7.
>*I shall praise thee with uprightness of heart,*
>*when I shall have learned thy righteous judgments.*

Our awesome Jehovah-Jireh, the God Who sees our need;[13] our Provider can supply the true bread and wine to minister to our hungry and thirsty hearts. The overcomer of Revelation 2 will eat of the hidden manna.
>*These things saith he who has the sharp sword with two edges, hold fast my name and don't deny my faith.*[14]

Hebrews 4 tells us the double edged sword is the Word. It divides soul works and spirit faith. As the overcomer lays down the works of his soul,[15] and comes into His rest, he may dine on the hidden manna of deeper fellowship with Jesus; the written, and living Word.

2Peter 1 tells us we become partakers of the Divine Nature through knowing God and Jesus our Lord. This happens through fellowship [partner, companion, associate, sharer, having things in common].

Saints of God it is harvest time. The Holy Spirit is ready for His truth to bear witness to your spirit.[16] Ask Him to separate the wheat from the tares as you seek Him with all your heart.[17].....➔ The Word says to:

> God's Word brings true life, true nourishment; from the Living Bread.

Resist the devil and he will flee from you, draw near to God and He will draw near to you.[18]

This is a promise of which I have experienced immediate results. There are also times when I've prayed for a need that was not answered so spontaneously. The Word tells us we can be confident that if we pray in His will,

We know he hears us and we will have what we ask because we believe that we receive them.[19]

His phone number is Jeremiah 33:3. He doesn't have a party line, nor an answering machine. He will though, sometimes put us on hold so He can work patience in us. This causes endurance and faith.[20] We also must be aware that when we pray for our mountain to be removed, God has to get out the mountain moving equipment to bring it to pass. In other words, certain things have to line up for His power to be released.

First of all, our unrelinquishing faith and trust in God and His Word. Yes, God has made all provision for us before the world was; but remember *it is only faith that pleases Him* and brings the reward. God loves us and wants us to know where we stand in Him. Fear, doubt and unbelief has its own reward. But remember this also,

If we confess our sins... [1Jn 1:9].

It is so wonderful to come into His rest, and develop the ability to wait for His perfect solution. In Isaiah 40:31 the word wait means: 'bind together by twisting'. Meditate on this and let God teach you. The Kingdom of God is the government of God being borne out in His people; holiness, obedience, righteousness - His sovereign rule - and - His government to be established in His people, each individual of us.[21]

Mankind has always naturally been in rebellion toward God and separated from Him. Only obedience to the known will of God will allow us to partake of His,
Holiness without which no man shall see God.[22]
Search me oh God and know my heart,
try me and know my thoughts.[23]
Even as we release ourselves to God, He is investing His Divine Nature within us.[24] He takes our unbalanced personality into His heart and heals.
Of his own will begot he us with the word of truth, that we should be a kind of first fruit of his creatures.[25] *According to his abundant mercy, he has begotten us again unto a living hope by the resurrection of Jesus Christ to an inheritance incorruptible, undefiled, reserved in heaven for you who are kept by the power of God through faith unto salvation.*[26]
We are born again of incorruptible seed,
Which liveth and abideth forever............................→ **THE WORD OF GOD.**
The life of God that flows from the Holy Spirit within us, continues to cleanse and set us free as we choose to obey and walk in His will.[27] In order to make room for Him we must get rid of what stands in His way - as John the Baptist said -
He must increase - I must decrease.[28]

Jesus said there was not a greater prophet than John the Baptist. John's father was Zacharias the priest. The name Zacharias means: Yah has remembered, to mark so as to remember. What did God have to remember; His covenant promises.

Isaiah 40:3 *The voice of one crying in the wilderness: Prepare the way of the Lord;*
Luke 7:27 *This is he of whom it is written:'Behold, I send My messenger before Your face, Who will prepare Your way before You.'*
And so... *In the fullness of time God sent forth His Son.*[29]

Zacharias was chosen to birth the son who would prepare the way of the Lord. He was a priest of the tribe of Levi. The Levites were the tribe anointed of God to serve Him in the Temple. The Old Testament priest ministered the type and shadow, the unblemished lamb sacrificed for the sins of Israel on the altar in the Temple.

John knew what were the duties of the priest. He learned them as a boy growing up, living in the house of a priest, as a descendent of Levi. This heritage is found in Numbers 18 and was the best of the Temple offerings; wine, wheat and meat. John ate locusts and wild honey. He renounced the prestige and influence - the holy garments of the priest - to live in the desert wilderness, to wear camel's hair.

John gave up his priestly inheritance
handed down by his father.

It is quite likely Moses understood exactly what the blood sacrifice was all about; how God would use it as a type and shadow of the Savior that would shed His Blood for the sins of the world.

He probably taught these truths to Aaron and his sons as they were anointed for the duties of the priesthood. But through many generations of disobedience, rebellion and corruption; the love, honor and respect for the holiness of God was set aside for more worldly ambitions.

Malachi brings an indictment of curses from God for the pollution the priests had brought into the temple. Their gross idolatry and profiteering from the anointing brought God's wrath and finally His silence. Four hundred years passed in which the truths of the Kingdom became buried under ritual and law. Any lover of God would have their heart broken to read Ezekiel 8-10.

But God had a people! Zacharias was one of them; chosen by God to birth and raise up His first prophet in 400 years. John must have heard hundreds of times, about the sacrificial lamb. John also saw the ritual when he went to the temple with his family. Imagine the enormity of the revelation of John 1:29,

Behold the lamb of God
who taketh away the sin of the world.

Because he did not hold his worldly inheritance as a thing to be grasped, John touched not the type and shadow, but the reality.

He touched the Precious Lamb, the Unique Holiest of All.

A close encounter of the highest kind.

We can lay our self-will on the altar for God's will. The Kingdom of God is the forming of Christ in the born-again believer.[30] The Holy Spirit will change our heart and mind in every place that we are corrupted by our sinful Adam nature and from glory to glory - one experience of His presence to another - remake us into the image of Jesus [31].

I have been crucified with Christ, it is no longer I who live, but Christ lives in me; and the life which I now live in the flesh I live by faith in the Son of God.[32]

Are you willing to die to the lusts of your flesh so that the fruit of the Spirit may take seed and flourish - that you might take on the very nature of your Lord Jesus Christ.

In Matthew chapters 5-7 Jesus explains clearly how to live and function as a mature son of the Most High God. Are these keys to the Kingdom? We can take each portion and compare it with our life. As we see the inconsistencies remember the Holy Spirit Himself makes intercession for us.[33] And our Great High Priest Jesus also stands before the throne of God in our behalf.[34]

Wherefore also we pray always for you, that our God would count you worthy of this calling, and fulfill all the good pleasure of his goodness, and the work of faith with power, that the name of our Lord Jesus Christ may be glorified in you, and ye in Him according to the grace of our God and the Lord Jesus Christ.[35]

Psalm24 reveals who it is that may inherit the Kingdom of God, who it is that may stand before Jesus in His Holy Place. It is that one who opens the door of their heart and allows the King of Glory to enter in, to rule and reign - to sit upon the throne of their life. So, who is your king?........................→

Christ in us, the hope of glory.[36]

He Is the King of kings, the Lord of lords
I am the resurrection and the life. Our King is Jesus. If He is living within us to rule and reign then His Kingdom will be expressed through us. Jesus said the Kingdom does not

> A Kingdom must have a King.

come with observation; the Kingdom is within us. We sing a lot about Jesus being our King - but is the government of God being wrought out within us?

*Thy Kingdom come, thy will be done,
in earth as it is in heaven.*

This verse clearly explains what the Kingdom is all about: God's will being performed! It is God's intention to have His will performed in us.[37] His will is His determination, His choice, decree, volition, desire, pleasure, delight. His delight is in His people. The Kingdom of Heaven is the residence of God. Again, The Kingdom of God is, *righteousness and peace and joy in the Holy Spirit.* We live in this Kingdom right now, to experience His peace, to know His presence. This is the Gift of Life!

So as His rule and reign and sovereign will is expressed through us and in us, there we enthrone the King of Glory. We are not God, we are His dwelling place. Where God is concerned we have been given a choice as to what we are and what we may become. The word choose and its variations are in the Bible almost 100 times. Joshua 24:15 brings us to -

Choose you this day whom ye will serve.

The Kingdom of God is a way of life,

The only way TO life!

God has given each of us a very important and valuable gift. It is called our free will. He has made this gift inviolate, and He will not touch it without our permission. In each and every attitude of the heart can we ask God to perform His will and die to our own intentions.

Probably the greatest struggle of our lives

is the one we battle to maintain control.

Philippians 2:13 says He works in us to cause us to choose His way. The word work comes from: energy - positive, effectual power to move in our behalf the moment we yield to Him,

Not my will but Thine be done.

Even Jesus had the opportunity to express His own will.[38] We retain the power of choice each time; so to which one will we give rein. God will allow rebels to spend eternity in the lake of fire if it is their will to not accept His free gift of Eternal Life.[39] I heard an interesting quote:

A man convinced against his will

is of the same opinion - still.

Religion is: Man seeking his own god because we are religious creatures and we must have something to worship and we are sometimes not too particular of what that might wind up being, but it will be a god created in our image so we can understand him without too much effort. Relationship deals with the heart through choices we consciously make, that influence our attitudes. The revelation of Who God is comes to us through our developing relationship.

Of course that is how we build any relationship. We have to spend time with Him as with others whom we desire to know better. *I will give them a heart to know me that I am the Lord; and they shall be my people and I will be their God.*[40]

ALWAYS AND EVER
THE GOOD PLEASURE OF HIS WILL. ♥

Our loving Creator God is totally capable of bringing each of His creation into a significant bond of union with Him. The purpose of which is to know Him as we are known, and of becoming all we were meant to be in Christ.

This involves being re-created into His image[41] so we can fellowship with Him on His level. He became like us so that we could become like Him.[42] For He said,
You be holy, for I am holy.[43]
But God does not give commands that are impossible for us to fulfill. God's Holy Spirit dwells in us. The more we give place to His Holy Spirit the more we be holy as He is holy. [1Cor 2.12] *Now we have received the Spirit who is from God that we might know the things that have been freely given to us by God.*

Overcomers - that's what we are. We are now partakers of His Kingdom. His gifts are freely given to us that we might be overcomers in this world. He delights to show us how His will can be accomplished. In doing a word study of the original Greek we find the word image as used in two Scriptures.

Romans 8:29 tells us we are being conformed to the image of the Son. 2Cor 4:4 proclaims Christ as the image of God. The word image is the same and means the same in both instances. Glory to God! The fruits of the character and likeness of God are being developed in us.

God created each of us as unique individuals. When we are given our heavenly bodies - we will still retain our individuality. We will not be melded into the cosmos and lose that identity. Remember after the resurrection, the disciples recognized Jesus for Who He was. We were created in the image and likeness of God. When the Bible speaks of us bearing the likeness of the heavenly it means that our personality/character will become as the fruit of the Spirit. This is a part of God's character credentials. We will be like

Him. We will have to let go of all that defiles [1Co 15:49]. Read 1Co 2:9-10 Let the mercy and grace and loving kindness of our eternal Father wash over us as this truth becomes the ground we stand on. We have neither seen nor heard, nor even thought about the things God has already prepared for those who love Him...................➡

> But He reveals them to us by His Spirit Who knows the things of God.

2Peter 1:4-8 is a further character reference of the image God is developing in us. We begin with faith in God. Let your Wonderful Counselor cause you to develop these traits. None of us have arrived; God is accompanying us on this awesome journey. As we realize Kingdom truth and our inheritance in Christ through His precious Blood, our boldness and authority in Christ over the enemy will have him on the run. Satan's access to us is totally through deception, because we are sometimes ignorant. He's been around 6,000 years and is a master of deception. Only in Christ, through His name and the power of the Blood do we have God's wisdom and authority, and always keep in mind Philippians 2: 5-8. For,

> We wrestle not against flesh and blood,
> but principalities and powers in high places.[44]

All of us grew up with some sort of system of standards; and I'm not saying this is all wrong. I'm sure we would have anarchy in the world without some rules and regulations. Some of us though, were so stamped with the seal of compliance that we have a hard time realizing the freedom of grace and mercy in our spirit. If the line we had to walk was critical and narrow with no leeway for the mistakes of growing up, then we become critical and give no room for the faults of the human predicament, in ourselves or others. We may become cold, rigid and impersonal and transfer this formalism, ritual, into the gospel as our god.

Then all we read in the Word becomes an extension of those rules and regulations. Too much of what we hear in Church, in seminars, at retreats, from other Christians and from the Bible stops between our ears and becomes more knowledge. We are safe in thinking if we comply, we're doing it right. It all becomes ritual on the outside, when the real God wants to touch your inside; all those places that wounded you.

CHRISTIANITY IS NOT RELIGIOSITY OR CHURCHIANITY.
IT IS RELATIONSHIP. ♡
THIS IS THE FATHER'S GOOD PLEASURE. ❤

From all these negative attitudes we may become walking libraries with a ready answer for all problems. We may even have a standard cliche' for the wounded spirit of our brethren. But behind our mask there is a real longing for reality. We begin to see that head knowledge is of little value when we ourselves are hurting, and have no substantial answers.

As in all transactions with God there comes a choice. There is always a choice - and the choice is always with us. You see God has already chosen,

For we are his workmanship, created in Christ Jesus
for good works, which God prepared beforehand
that we should walk in them.[45]

He has made the provision to come forth at the appointed time. God has already provided. The appointed time is when we choose to say, Yes Lord, I want all you have for me. He settled it once for all time before the foundation of the world that we,

Should be holy and without blame
before Him in love, having predestined us
unto the adoption of sons by Jesus Christ to himself,
according to the good pleasure of His will to the praise of
the glory of his grace through which he hath
made us accepted in the Beloved.[46]

Then we may read in John 17 as Jesus is speaking to the Father. He says that He [Christ] gives eternal life to all that He [the Father] has given Him [Christ]. Dear ones, this means that we are a gift from our Father God to our Lord and Savior Jesus; the only true Master of the universe.[47]

God deposited our inheritance in escrow through the Holy Spirit before the foundation of the world.[48] [Escrow: the state of a deed put in care of a another, until certain conditions are fulfilled.] The first party, the Father; the second party, the Lamb slain from the foundation of the world.[49] The third party, God's Holy Spirit, all loving us so much that we will bow before Him;

Acknowledging His Majesty,
making Jesus the Lord of your life.

It May Be a Long Road
But We Are Transitioned
At The Foot of The Cross.

The word 'from' specifies completion. One of the comforting principles of the Word is that God called forth all the provision we would ever need, before He created the universe [Rev 13.8].

On the cross Jesus declared, It is finished!!
and now His purposes would be brought to completion. All the conditions were fulfilled.

His divine power has given [bestow gratuitously, an offering, a gift, a present!] to us all things that pertain to life and godliness...given us exceedingly great and precious promises, that by these ye might be partakers of the divine nature.[50]

This is an awesome statement. These provisions are already in effect to accomplish His will in our life; that is to say we might be brought back into the Father's presence and re-created into the image of His Son. The third party stamps His seal on us. The Holy Spirit sees to it that we may partake of our wonderful heritage.

It is God who confirms and makes us steadfast and establishes us [in joint fellowship] with you in Christ, and has consecrated and anointed us [enduing us with the gifts of the Holy Spirit]; [He has also appropriated and acknowledged us as His by] putting His seal upon us and

> *giving us His [Holy] Spirit in our hearts as the security deposit and guarantee [of the fulfillment of His promise].*[51]

It is of unique importance to recognize that being conformed to the image of the Son comes to us by and through the presence of the Lord. How many can tell of their salvation experience, of His presence and the sweet assurance of His love; of His healing, how the warmth of His touch banished the pain and fear; and times of repentance that His peace washed away guilt and shame. The natural conclusion is the more we seek His face the more we experience His presence. It is His presence[55] that brings transition. In Winds of Change, by Donald Rumble, Destiny Image; he says,

> God is the only One I know of
> Who builds in an earthquake.

God receives us as we are. He loves us as we are. He uses us in His service as we are. In sharing the wonders of Christ with our fellow traveler, we can sense His peace and encouragement. Yet He cares too much to leave us as we are. If all our answers are in Christ, where would be the best place to abide except in His presence.

> *He who dwells in the secret place of the most high shall abide under the shadow of the Almighty.*

[And check out Ps 16:11!]

> *Oh Taste And See That The Lord Is Good*[56]

And this in John 6   *I am the bread of life. He who comes to me shall never hunger, and he who believes in me shall never thirst. He who believes in me has everlasting life. I am the bread of life. One may eat of it and not die. I am the living bread which came down from heaven. If anyone eats this bread, he will live forever; and the bread that I shall give is my flesh, which I shall give for the life of the world. Unless you eat the flesh of the Son of Man and drink his Blood you have no life in you.*

> *Whoever eats my flesh and drinks my Blood has eternal life and I will raise him up at the last day. My flesh is food indeed and my Blood is drink indeed. He who eats my flesh and drinks my Blood abides in me and I in him. He who feeds on me will live because of me. Does this offend you?*

> *It Is the Spirit who gives life; The flesh profits nothing.*

Those people who heard Him were horrified. Many walked away.

The admonition to eat His flesh and drink His Blood is an invitation to total commitment, to profound communion; a depth of intimacy never before known of, or even heard. *The words that I speak to you are spirit and they are life.*

We are being re-created into His image.

This awesome, magnificent passage in John Chapter six, is telling us of the only way to receive the life of God. We are made partakers of Christ, partakers of His very nature; and this is eternal life and resurrection [Heb 3:14].

When we eat and drink of Him, we receive His life, His character, His ways, His virtue, His wisdom. These words are Spirit and they are life. We can't make this happen; the flesh profits nothing. But we can yield our flesh to the workings of the Spirit. He will bring it to pass. God is saying this: He wants to become a part of - no, not a part of - He wants to 'become' our experience. He wants to be the very basis of life within us; [Gal 2:20] our entire motivation for living; the Source and the Resource. Through obedience to His commandments and yielding to His will, we become the dwelling place of God.[57]

Christ in us is our hope of glory.

See what John 14:21-23 has to say.

He who has My commandments and keeps them, it is he who loves Me. And he who loves Me will be loved by My Father, and I will love him and manifest Myself to him.
Judas [not Iscariot] said to Him, Lord, how is it that You will manifest Yourself to us, and not to the world?
Jesus answered and said to him,
If anyone loves Me, he will keep My word;
and My Father will love him, and We will come to him and make our home with him.

At the point of salvation, the Holy Spirit comes to dwell in our spirit. We receive His eternal life at that moment. From there we grow into mature sons and daughters of God. This is our inheritance and Father's good pleasure. There was a specific purpose for Jesus to expound on being the Bread of Life. We all know bread feeds and nurtures. He could have left it there, but didn't. Verse 57 is astounding! *As I live by the Father, so he that eats me even he shall live by me.* We've all read,

If you see me you see the Father.

Verse 57 tells us as Jesus is one with the Father, so we may become one with Jesus. As Jesus manifested the Father, so

may we manifest the Son in our life, as we take into account v. 63. And Peter answers,
> Where else is there to go?
> You have the words of eternal life. ❤

This is our rightful inheritance of which we may partake. The very life of God permeating our entire being. No wonder we will rise from the dead at His glorious appearing!

God will set you free to receive His grace and mercy; His Gift of Life. Now a person can be offered a gift for a hundred years and never take advantage of the giving.

We receive a gift because we choose to receive it.

The flow of life is like the flow of a river. If it comes to a standstill it is no longer capable of sustaining and growing and expanding the living force within. That's why Jesus said we would need,
> A well of water springing up,[59]

so we would not stagnate.

The Gift of Life is yours now. Receive it, and say thank you. Don't listen to the devil saying it's too late for you cause you didn't get it the first time around. He's a liar. He used to say that to me all the time, and because B.C., I was always a day late and a dollar short, I always missed it; until I renewed my mind with the Word! Psalm 119:89 declares;
> Forever oh God, thy word is settled in heaven.
> Thy faithfulness is unto all generations.
> Thou hast established the earth, and it abideth. They continue this day according to thine ordinances, for all are thy servants. And this I recall, therefore I have hope and expectation.
> Great is Thy Faithfulness.

No left - overs, and plenty to spare .... ➜

> His mercies and compassions fail not, they are new every morning.

Jeremiah is in the middle of a nation being chastened by God, and yet he declares the faithfulness of God [Lamentations 3].

Isaiah 55:11 tells us His Word will not return to Him empty of the promises He sent forth to accomplish; but it will prosper and grow in whatsoever He purposed. No matter what is happening in your life right now, God is faithful and will bring you through. Jesus has come to say unto you,
> *The Spirit of the Lord is upon me, because he hath anointed me to preach the gospel to the poor; he hath sent me to*

heal the brokenhearted; to preach deliverance to the captives, and recovering of sight to the blind, to set at liberty them that are bruised.[60]

Isaiah reveals the compassion of God.

Neither let the eunuch say I am dry tree. For thus saith the Lord unto the eunuchs that keep my Sabbaths, and choose the things that please me, and take hold of my covenant: Even to them will I give in mine house and within my walls a place and a name better than of sons and of daughters; I will give them an everlasting name, that shall not be cut off.[61]

    A eunuch is a person who has not produced or reproduced. Many of us have been eunuchs in our spirit. Until this day we may be dammed up with stagnant water, perhaps by fears or unforgiveness.

    Let the Spirit of God reveal this. If you will let go and forgive and surrender striving to keep the law or someone else's standards; release it all to your Lord, He will pour through you His Living Water that will produce His Life in you; and in its turn will reproduce that Life in others. Speak to your Lord. Tell Him what you want. He longs to hear your voice. Lift your hands and praise your God for His marvelous Gift of Life.

How excellent is thy lovingkindness, oh God! Therefore the children of men put their trust under the shadow of thy wings. They shall be abundantly satisfied with the fatness of thy house and thou shalt make them drink of the river of thy pleasures, for with thee is the fountain of life.[62]

    Remember Barabbas? He was the first person to actually be given life in exchange for Jesus' life. Sentenced to death for insurrection [rebellion] and murder, Jesus traded places with him.

    Barabbas wanted to run far from that crowd lest he be returned to his hapless fate. Yet his attention must have been drawn to this One Who opened not His mouth to His own defense; *Who went as a sheep to the slaughter.*

    Barabbas heard with his ears the forgiveness sent forth to those of whom would commit such a despicable act, the murder of an innocent man. Yet Barabbas was just as glad as I am that Jesus died in his place; died for his offenses and mine. Jesus literally died in the place of Barabbas..➜

| The beginning of the Great Exchange. |

Barabbas walked away a free man. He did not have to pay the death penalty for his crimes. This fact was an historical reality for Barabbas. It is just as much a reality for you and me. Jesus went to the cross instead of Barabbas; instead of you and me! He was the first of many -
Bar - son of; Abba - Father.

BAR-ABBA'S - SONS OF THE FATHER.
It is His good pleasure. ♥

I go to prepare a place for you,

A deeper, higher walk in the realm of the Spirit of which we know nothing. But please read 1Cor 2:9-16 for yourself.

There are many concepts in the Word that are basic principles of the Kingdom of God. He longs to reveal Himself to us. We cannot truly understand the fullness of why the mighty Creator desires to dwell in His puny creatures. The more we search the Word, the hidden manna will be revealed to us. Such is the word of John 14:23; abode means staying place and it comes from the same Greek word as mansions in John 14:2.

Are we His many mansions? That place where God has chosen as His resting place, His abode?

We can read the last chapter of the Book. We can know the end results. We can come to realize the fullness of our inheritance. Do you just want it or do you intend to have it!

Our adoption into God's family is a legal transaction. Read Ephesians Chapter one. Here is the voucher that we've been sealed by the Holy Spirit. He is the,

Earnest of our inheritance until the redemption of the purchased possession, unto the praise of His glory .[63]

This is Father's Good Pleasure

As we wait on God we become absolutely dependent on what He's going to do, and saints that's exactly what He wants. Jehovah Jireh, truly our Provider. Pr 30:8 asks,

Feed me with food convenient for me.

This is not physical food, but it means to feed our spirit with what we need to receive His life. The word convenient is from Strong's Concordance #2706 and means - enactment, to apportion, hack, inscribe as to cut in stone [Jer 31.31].

Our covenant with the Creator of the universe gives Him permission to inscribe - engrave His laws in our heart. Then because of His great love, we automatically want to please Him. Christianity is not what God is doing to us or for us. It is what God is doing 'in' us. It is what we are becoming. Remember -

2 Cor 6:16-18 *For you are the temple of the living God. As God has said: I will dwell in them And walk among them. I will be their God, and they shall be My people. Therefore Come out from among them And be separate, says the Lord . Do not touch what is unclean, And I will receive you. 'I will be a Father to you, And you shall be My sons and daughters, Says the Lord Almighty.*

Recently I was reading the comic strip Ziggy. [Christians are allowed to read the funnies] He said, 'With so much to do, sometimes it's nice just to be!! That must be why we're called human beings - and not human doings'! This was just a side note, but the reality is true.

Again we look at Romans 8 and Ephesians 1 for some clues. Here the Word tells us we are adopted [meaning, the placing of a son] into the family of God and sealed by His Holy Spirit. Saints of God, this means we are a stamped and sealed legal document. We are a purchased possession.

God's file cabinet is the Holy Spirit Who always keeps His records straight. The Holy Spirit is the earnest of our inheritance. So - on our spirit in large letters is engraved;

REDEEMED BY THE BLOOD OF THE LAMB.

Our adversary the devil can read this, because he is a spirit. But he will always make us question who we are; and especially, Did God really say that? The reason he can harass us is that we don't always acknowledge who we are in Christ. We allow our emotions to go haywire because of fear, doubt and unbelief.

Nevertheless God has declared your plundered soul to be unshackled. Your Emancipation Proclamation is a legal document. It has been signed in Blood, sealed and delivered to the highest court - the Eternal Judge. Praise Him forever more!

Your Divine Intercessor is there to plead your case. The litigation is in your favor. The thief has been stripped of his cloak of secrecy and his dominion and rulership over you is forever smashed, broken and cast under the feet of your mighty Redeemer.

Heb 7:25-26 *Therefore He is also able to save to the uttermost those who come to God through Him, since He always lives to make intercession for them.*

At this point we may want to examine our hearts to be sure we have legal access to the Life of God by being born again into His Kingdom. Have we told God, Thank you for Jesus. Paul asked,

Who shall deliver me from the body of this death?
Then he said, *I thank God through Jesus Christ.*[64]
As we speak with our mouth and receive Jesus as our Savior and Lord,[65] we are accepted into the Kingdom of God. Now we can legitimately partake of the Bread of Life.

When Peter recognized Jesus as the Son of the living God, this truth was revealed to him by the Father. Jesus declared......,,,,,,,,,,,,,,,,,,,,,,,,,,,,,....→

> On this Rock of truth, I will build my church! [Matt 16]

Not the truth of who Peter was; His name was changed and he denied Jesus three times! But more profoundly, the truth of Who Jesus IS!

Col 1:15-19 *He is the image of the invisible God, the firstborn over all creation. For by Him all things were created that are in heaven and that are on earth, visible and invisible, whether thrones or dominions or principalities or powers. All things were created through Him and for Him. And He is before all things, and in Him all things consist. And He is the head of the body, the church, who is the beginning, the firstborn from the dead, that in all things He may have the preeminence.*

The true Church of Christ can not be built on flesh and blood. It takes the mighty supernatural power of the Living God to re-create us into the holiness of our Creator. Only the precious Blood of Jesus can save us and make us His own; complete in Christ.

When this arrow of truth pierces our heart, we are born again and enter the Kingdom of God. He is the Corner Stone of the building; the foundation on which His lively stones,[66] [that's us] *are fitly built together for a habitation of God.*[67]

A building is raised one brick or stone at a time. Jesus is building His Church out of individuals as each comes to the same truth as revealed to them by the Father [1Co 3:9-11].

In crusades there may be hundreds that come to the Lord at the same time. But each had to come to terms with what the Spirit was speaking to their heart. Each individual had to decide for him/her self. No one else can make this decision for us [Acts 2:37-38]. God doesn't have any grandkids.

No matter what another has done in your name, the only way we can enter the Kingdom of God is by being born from above ourselves, because we have chosen to invite the Lord Jesus into our life; to be our Savior and Lord. No one else can do this for us. This happens when we recognize Jesus as The Only Begotten Son of God, that He died for us, that He rose again from the dead.
[Rom 10:9]. We speak with our mouth and receive Jesus as our Savior and Lord - [John 1.12].

John the Apostle of love, writes about Life 43 times in his gospel. In his first Epistle he tells us of the Word of Life,
That which we have heard and seen with our eyes, looked upon and handled, that which is called Eternal Life;
is the same Gift of Life that you and I may also have fellowship with, that our joy may be full. Oh God, how I thank you that your gift of Life did not depend on any works I've been able to do, but rather on what I could not.

The Holy Spirit validates us with His stamp and seal of approval and we have [Romans 8.15].
Received the Spirit of adoption [sonship] whereby we cry Abba Father, and the Spirit bears witness with our spirit that we are the children of God.

♪ I'm Not My Own, I Belong to Jesus -
I'm Not My Own, I'm His
Bought With a Price - The Blood of Jesus,
I'm Not My Own - I'm His. ♫
[Author unknown]

You gave me Your Life, Your Love
And called me to be Your own
Blood bought
Family brought,
I am Kingdom saved
No longer a slave
I will worship You, that You may know
My gratitude is buried in
My soul, my heart, my mind
Forever You will be
The love of my life ❤

THE GIFT OF LIFE FROM GOD OUR FATHER

Our Name Has Been Written in the Book of Life and We Inherit Many Gifts from Being a Child of the Most High God. Paul begins his letters with
*Grace be to you and peace from God our Father
and the Lord Jesus Christ.*

Here's the Story.

These Gifts are From the Prince of Life (Acts 3)
To Receive the Promise of Life (2 Timothy 1)
That We Might Have Abundant Life (John 10)
With Christ Who is Our Way of Life. (Col 3; Acts 2)
    In Him was Life (John 1)
He is the Light of Life (John 1)
Who Gave us the Breath of Life (Acts 7)
To Receive Newness of Life (Romans 6)
And all That Pertains to Life (1 Corinthians 6)
So We Could Change Our Manner of Life. (Acts 26)
    Jesus Has Given Us the Bread of Life (John 6)
That We Might Walk in the Grace of Life (1 Peter 3)
Through the Word of Life. (Philippians 2)
And with the Promise of Life (2 Timothy 1)
That is an Endless Life (Hebrews 7)
The Hope of Everlasting Life (John 6; Titus 3)
    We Receive the Crown of Life. (James 1; Revelation 2)
And the Spirit of Life (Romans 8)
He Pours Out on Us the Water of Life (Revelation 21.22)
That We May Drink from the River of Life (Rev 22:1)
And The Gift of Resurrection Life (John 11)
That We May Eat of the Tree of Life (Revelation 2.22)

*And he showed me a pure river of water of life,
clear as crystal, proceeding from the throne of God
and of the Lamb.*

And the Spirit and the bride say, "Come!" And let him who hears say, "Come!" And let him who thirsts come. Whoever desires, let him take the water of life freely. (Rev 22:17)

❤

STUDY GUIDE

1. What is the real meaning of Christianity? Eph 3.
2. What is the Kingdom of God? Rom 14.
3. What happens when we choose to walk in the Kingdom? 2Pet 1.
4. Why does God want us to partake of His inheritance? 2Th
5. How is our being born into the world, a type of the reality of being born into God's Kingdom? 1Pet 1,2.
6. Who is it that God will allow to stand in His holy place? Ps 24.
7. What is the hardest human attribute to overcome? 1Jn 2:15-16 Amplified.
8. Just as Adam was searching for a comparable mate, so is God looking for a people with whom He might relate. Since He is so far above all that we are, what does God have to do in us? Rom 8.
9. If we are to receive His life [increase],
      what must we do? [decrease] Jn 3.30
10. His provision is already in place. 2Pet 1.
11. We're sealed by the Holy Spirit.   Eph 1.13-14. God's First Security Heavenly Bank Treasurer.
12. Can we trust God? Is He faithful? Ps 36.
13. No other creature has the privilege of praying,

Once I was dead - now I'm alive.
I'm so grateful to You Lord
for giving me Your Life and Your love.

♫ **HALLELUJAH** ♫

Your revelation so sweet to my ears
Will speak of Your love
down through the years
Growing and knowing this life in You
Such a joy to my heart
Is knowing the truth
You really are the only way
And I want to walk in Your path
So show me each step that I must take
To know You is all that I ask ❤

SCRIPTURES

1. Mal 4:2
2. James 2:19
3. Rom 14:17
4. Jn 14:23
5. 2Co 6:16-18
6. 1Pe 1:23
7. Acts 17:28-29
8. Jn 4:23
9. Jn 17:3
10. Js 1:21
11. Js 1:18
12. Ps 118:27
13. Ge 22:14
14. Re 2:12,13
15. Heb 4:12-5
16. Rom 8:14-16
17. Ps 27:8
18. Js 5:6-8
19. 1Jn 5:13-15
20. Js 1:1-2
21. 2Pe 1:3-11
22. Heb 12:14
23. Ps 139:23
24. 2Pe 1:4
25. Js 1:18
26. 1Pe 1:3-4
27. 1Jn 1:7-9
28. Jn 3:30
29. Ga 4:4
30. Ga 4:19
31. Rom 8:28-29
32. Ga 2:20
33. Rom 8:26-27
34. Heb 4:14
35. 2Th 1:11-12
36. Co 1:27
37. Ph 2:13
38. Lk 22:42
39. Jn 3:16-20
40. Je 24:7
41. Rom 8:29
42. Heb 2:14
43. 1Pe 1:15-16
44. Ep 6:2
45. Ep 2:10
46. Ep 1:4-6
47. 1Ti 6:15
48. Ep 1:9-14
49. Re 13:8
50. 2Pe 1:3-4
51. 2Co 1:21-22 Amp
53. Co 3:16
54. Ps 107:43
55. Ps 91:14-1
56. Ps 34:8
57. Jn 14:17,23
59. Jn 4:14
60. Lk 4:18
61. Is 56:4-5
62. Ps 36:7-9
63. Ep 1:13-14
64. Rom 7:24-25
65. Rom 10:10-13
66. 1Pe 2:5
67. Ep 2:20-22
68. Rom 8:15-16 and 1Co 3:11

*But whoever listens to me will dwell safely,
And will be secure, without fear of evil."*
Prov 1:33

♥

THE FEAR OF MAN

He gives you beauty for ashes, the oil of joy for mourning,
the garment of praise for the spirit of heaviness,
that you might be called a tree of righteousness,
the planting of the Lord,
that He might be glorified.[28]

Oh Lord, the Reality of Your Kingdom
Has Totally Overwhelmed Me.
I Am Your Bride. You Have Chosen Me -
An 'Are-Not' of the World To Manifest Your Glory,
To Be a Witness of Your Love To Other 'Are-Nots'.
Thank You God   [1 Cor 1.27-28].

Who are you that shall be afraid of a man that shall die,
and of the son of man who shall be made like grass, and
forget [Who I am] the Lord your maker.[1] *Sanctify the Lord*
of hosts himself, and let him be your fear, and let him be
your dread, and he shall be for a sanctuary.[2]

Another of our greatest enemies is The Fear of Man.

Fear and anxiety is one of man's greatest enemy for it can and will hinder the Lord's work in His people. The fear of evil was at the top of my list and God was gracious and merciful, because It hides and we're not even aware it is there to torment. Too many people are hindered by this enemy and it goes back to the beginning of time. As early as Genesis it is recorded that Cain feared what man would do to him when his sin of murder was found out.

Some Bible Commentaries state there were probably 30 to 50 thousand people on the earth by this time, and certainly many cities and villages. Cain and Abel were probably 100 years old and more when Abel was murdered. In the genealogy of our beginnings, men are recorded to have been over a hundred years old when they had certain named sons. Adam and Eve lived over 900 years. It is recorded they had many more children. One Jewish tradition states Adam had 300 sons and daughters and they had children, etc.

It is natural to suppose there were many other children, [male and female] for people lived many hundreds of years. The Bible's genealogical records however, are interested in only one factor; to trace the lineage of the sons of God as opposed to the sons of men.

We must realize that time and years did not exist in the garden. Adam was ageless in the garden. When he was cast out
 into the world he began to age in years and had children. Seth was given to Adam when he was 130 years old, after Abel was murdered.

Abel and Seth were sons of the Kingdom. Seth means, appointed or substituted. He was chosen to inaugurate the godly line which would eventually birth the Savior of the world. Noah was a progeny of Seth. [Noah died 50 years before Abram was born].

When Seth had the first male child of this line, Enosh, *Then began men to call on the name of the Lord.*

Chapter 4 gives the lineage of Cain, so-called the sons of men, in the Scripture. By the time we get to verse 24 it is obvious this family inherited the sins of their father.

Then chapter 5 records only the lineage from Seth to Noah, because we need to understand our Godly heritage. God is making it clear just where His nation came from, and who are the people that He used to bring about His plan of redemption. Our natural genealogy comes from many nations; but we are joined with God's people as we are born again into His family and -

> We didn't come out of nowhere. We have roots and foundation because of Abraham [Romans 4].

Then the Bible tells us men multiplied on the earth and had sons and daughters. Satan only reproduces by inhabiting men's souls or bodies. Also know that when one plays with fire they will get burned. When one fellowships with depravity, it will corrupt even the most moral aptitude. Satan had been well aware of One to come that would crush his head. He tried every trick to make sure He would never be born, or that He would be trapped by sin; totally polluted by the world and flesh before He could carry out His plan.

> Satan never knew the Son of God Himself would come, and certainly never knew what He would do to set us free from his lies and deception.

God set a mark on Cain, lest anyone finding him should kill him.[2] Why would arrogant Cain fear what man would do? Because sin makes us afraid of exposure and judgment.

> That's why these deeds are done in darkness.

Some proclaim this mark made him black and that's where the black race came from. I personally do not believe this. [Perhaps at the tower of Babel, God did more than change their language]. We can read for ourselves that Noah descended from Seth, not Cain. All of Cain's descendants died in the flood. Only Noah, his sons and their wives survived the flood and we are all descended from these. God destroyed all but Noah and his family in the flood because...

The wickedness of man was very great, and every imagination of the thoughts of his heart was only evil continually.

Men had become so perverted that it grieved God. The nature of man has not improved in 6,000 years. Matter of fact, man's nature has been more vilified down through the centuries.

After the flood, it didn't take long for one of Noah's sons to manifest who his friends had been. In three generations Ham produced Nimrod, the builder of Babylon, citadel of the occult.

Nimrod's name means rebellion.

In these early chapters, God carefully draws a line between the holy and the profane. Chapter 11 gives the generations of Shem, again picking up on God's people, from whom came Abraham. Bible historians claim that Shem killed his nephew Nimrod, because he was so evil. He was the 'creator' of Babylon.

Getting back to Noah, It is realistic to see that God had to cleanse the earth of animal life too, except for what was brought into the ark. Their perverted life style probably matched Romans 1:21-27. God had to have hand picked every animal for the ark and brought them to Noah. Otherwise how could Noah have even found a pair of each animal on the earth.

I just wish he had swatted those mosquitoes and bugs.

In that state of depravity we must conclude the population did not ignore this preacher of righteousness and let him get on with his building program. That a boat that size would be built on dry land?- we can be sure there was criticism, taunting, ridicule and jeering from the crowd, that would have to be confronted within Noah's heart; but He'd heard from God! And Noah made God's grace sufficient. For 120 years he tried to warn them - they would not listen. How many of us would have prevailed for that long, trusting God to protect us.

Gen 7.9-10 says God sent all His choice of animals in to the ark and then it says in verse 10, the door stayed open for 7more days... time for anyone else to get in there; but alas - no one did.

Remember Ham the rebel, was the father of Canaan. Ham's descendants were cursed because of his disrespect for Noah. Perhaps Ham did more than just look at his father. It is clear that Ham was mocking his father as he reported to his brothers. Was Ham infected with the seed of Cain by association, as was Lot's family?

Obviously this son rebelled against authority and did his own thing, as did Cain. Just five generations from Cain, Lamech murdered a man for offending him, and believed he was justified. The heart was hardened to the fear of God. The spirit of Cain spread rapidly to infect God's creation.

That spirit produced massive carnality and rebellion. Archaeologists have found remnants of Canaanite perversion that would defy the imagination; An Insult To Our Humanity. On the other hand, Shem and Japheth were blessed. Canaan would be their servants.

In Genesis 12 God told Abram to journey to the land of Canaan. Abram and his caravan moved south into the arms of his enemies. Genesis 9&10 gives us the background for the Canaanite's hatred and jealousy of any descendant of Shem.

Perhaps this explains some of the hostility the Israelites encountered on their way to their promised land; and why God wanted them destroyed off the face of the earth. If other nations intermarried with the Canaanites, [and that is very likely], they would have been polluted also. This is why Israel was forbidden to do the same. Is it possible? God told Abram, [Gen 15].

Know of a surety, [it will happen]! *Your seed will be in bondage, Until the iniquity of the Amorites is full.*

Amorites - the name used to personify the inhabitants of Canaan, became more wicked as the generations passed.

Now think about this. If the sons of Israel had been left in the land they would also have been polluted. This is proven by their rebellion in later generations after Joshua died. They intermarried with the nations. Even king Solomon had hundreds of heathen wives which by the way, caused his downfall.

But here God has kept His inheritance pure. They were kept in a bubble in Goshen. It occurs to me that God was using this time [400 years] to build a nation out of 70 people, to be used by God as a witness of His righteousness. Some believe there were at least a million Israelites that came out of Egypt. [See Gen 15.12-16]. I'm not implying God made slaves of His people in Egypt - I'm saying He knew it would happen.

His nation was not able to give their sons and daughters to the Egyptians or any other. God was keeping them safe. Now I know they were treated without mercy, but it was the reason God would destroy Egypt. This is why God wants us to love our neighbors. God's people are of great value. And...

This is why God could fulfill His covenant with them as Abraham's seed, because they were still his pure seed!

We can see how Abram's fear of man had just cause in these warring tribes that constantly attacked travelers through the land. Two of the fears that torment us is the fear of man and the fear of death.[4] May I insert here that the fear of death could be responsible for the tremendous pressure we come under when we try to die to self; self-preservation kicks in. When the fear of death is dealt with, we are more readily able to pursue our decision to take up our cross and follow Jesus.

Abram was motivated by each of these fears as he continued on south into Egypt because of famine, and exposed his wife Sarai to the harem of pharaoh. The promised seed was to come through Sarai. She also had to choose to trust in God. Her fears certainly could have caused much anxiety. In Genesis 12 and 20, Sarai again finds herself a pawn in the hands of Egypt's king.

Perhaps her deliverance from pharaoh's court was the turning point in her life. Perhaps her trust in the God of her husband was reinforced also. She walked in awesome trust, even as she submitted and called Abraham, 'lord', and God nailed Abimelech to the floor as the fear of God came on him.

Sarah's womb was being prepared to bear God's promise. Perhaps she had already conceived. God would not allow her to be defiled. I wonder that she was again made to be a virgin and her womb revitalized to be able to carry a child. Sarai yielded to God and her faith grew to the proportion that would enable her to conceive. We can be sure God's blessing on her was magnificent as she held forth her first and only child, at the age of ninety years.

No wonder they called him laughter.[5]

Genesis chapter 15 blood covenant was for the land of promise, and the tribes that would occupy this land, the nation of Israel. God made this covenant with Abram before he sired Ishmael - his carnal solution to God's promise. Because of the blood covenant and God's immutability, He was not free to seek another progenitor of His holy nation.

Genesis 16 infers Sarai and Abram were perhaps feeling pressured to accomplish what God obviously had forgotten. After several years of waiting they were intimidated and provoked to make it happen, and so they had Ishmael to contend with.

God would not allow flesh to touch His covenant promise so he waited 13 more years. Abram had much time to think about what he had done. God had to bring him to a place of,

fully persuaded [Rom 4.21]
and obedience. Scripture reveals God made blood covenant with Abram twice, twenty years apart. The Holy Spirit did not dwell in him as He does us.
He calls Abram His friend because...... ➜

> There came face to face trust that could not be dissuaded.

The blood covenant for circumcision revealed in chapter 17, was for the promised child. Here at the age of 99 Abram is renamed Abraham. It was through this blood covenant of circumcision that he became the father of many nations. Sarai was renamed Sarah, mother of nations.

The covenant blood of circumcision pierced through the veil of Sarah's barrenness and produced many nations. When the Blood of Jesus pierces through the barrenness of our heart, it is circumcised into covenant,[6] to produce a people of one nation, a holy nation unto our God.[7]

Abram and Sarai were brought out of Ur of the Chaldees, an idolatrous nation. As far as God is concerned there are only two nations. One of darkness and one of light![8]

God birthed His holy nation through Abraham and Sarah. And so we all must be transferred into His holy nation by birth into His Kingdom of light. [See Eph 2 and Col 1:12-13]. Only our trust in God enables us to overcome our fear of man.

The Lord is on my side; I will not fear.

What can man do to me?[9]

Abram went to Egypt to escape the famine. How ironic that centuries later God would bring more than a million of Abraham's descendants into this same desert and sustain them there for 40 years. Abram also journeyed full circle back to his place of beginnings and sacrificed to God, perhaps in repentance.[10] Hai means ruin, iniquity, perverse. I believe Abram learned how to trust in God day by day, just as we must.

God revealed Himself as Abram's shield and exceeding great reward, and there was covenant made between God and man. Abram acknowledged the Lord God as El Shaddai - Master - Owner. Psalm 62:8 tells us to,

Trust in Him at all times...pour out your heart before Him.

Abram grieved to have a son, an heir of his own seed. God wanted to give him so much more. In Gen 15:6,

He believed God and it was counted to him for righteousness.

Because one man so long ago chose to trust God, he received the seal of the righteousness of faith, that he might,

Be the father of all them that believe that righteousness might be imputed unto them also, who walk in the steps of the faith of our father Abraham.[11]

Only in eternity will we see the full impact of what our faith has really accomplished in the Kingdom of God. In Gen 15:9-18 Abram comes into covenant with God through blood sacrifice - just as we do through the Blood of Jesus. Now Abraham and...

Because of this covenant Abraham continued to receive deeper revelation of Who God is and God continued to carry out His plan. The All sufficient One, Strengthener, Nourisher, Almighty God had spoken. He shared His heart and revealed how He would separate and draw to Himself a people; a holy nation by the power of His will and His good pleasure. It was the power of this revelation in covenant with a faithful God that enabled Abraham to depend on God as he walked up the mountain with his beloved son, his promised son, Isaac.

Here now comes the ultimate test; turning Isaac over to God completely. I've wondered if perhaps due to the circumstances, Abraham and Sarah had made Isaac a idol. We sometimes tend to do that with our Isaacs. Put your idol on the altar... Burn it up!

Perhaps his mind was bombarded by thoughts of the heathen gods and their child sacrifices as the devil would try to bring fear on him. Did God really say that? His credibility was at stake here; against all the idolatry of the surrounding nations that were sure to hear of what Abraham had done. Yet he was called,

A friend of God.

His reputation and credibility were tied into God. Abraham already knew what he would do before he started up that hill. The Scripture is silent as to how Isaac responded. Isaac was not really Abraham's only son.[12] Because he was the child of promise, Isaac was the type and shadow of another Child of Promise;[13] *the Lamb brought in silence to the slaughter* - in total submission to His Father. Mt. Moriah is near Jerusalem; Calvary is a part of this range of mountains. Jesus said,

*Abraham rejoiced to see my day
and he saw it and was glad.*[14]

The implication is that Abraham had a vision of the Son of God sacrificed on these mountains [Jn 8:6]. Our obedience and trust in the same Lord God of Abraham, Isaac and Jacob, despite the circumstance, can bring awesome rewards.

Eye hath not seen nor ear heard, neither hath entered into the heart of man the things which God hath prepared for them that love Him. But God hath revealed them to us by His Spirit.[15] *The eyes of the Lord are upon the righteous, and his ears are open to their cry.*[16]

In Exodus 2:14-15 Moses responds to the fear of death and fear of man by fleeing from Egypt. In Exodus 4:1&10 he tries to manipulate God and argue out of what God wants him to do. When we run from our fears we can't deal with them.

After 40 years in the desert Moses was still not willing to go back and face the people he ran from. Sort of, 'Here I am Lord, send Aaron'. Verse 14 says God got angry.

God has made provision for us, yet we still squirm when obedience is required. Even after seeing God's power [Ex 4:3,6,7], Moses still backed off. But as he went on with God, He continued to reveal His true nature to Moses and his boldness increased. His faith and trust in God strengthened him to lead a nation out of bondage in Egypt and through the desert for forty years.

When his brother and sister rebelled against His leadership, he humbled himself before the Lord. It must have broken his heart to see God's judgment fall on her. Miriam, who was faithful to watch over her tiny brother in a river full of crocodiles. And Aaron with whom he faced an outraged pharaoh.

Aaron was struck with astonishment and humility as the cloud lifted and left him staring at the filthiness of his self-righteousness; leprosy rotting his sister's flesh off her body.

Because Aaron was anointed high priest, sanctified and set apart for God, to minister in the place of the Shekinah Glory, God did not allow the leprosy to touch him. But Aaron was just as much admonished by God's anger. We can be sure the fear of the Lord fell on him. He knew immediately the profound depth of his own sin. Moses' trust in God also enabled him to face Korah and 250 men that rebelled against his authority. Instead of defending his position he again fell on his face before God.

In researching genealogies, we find that Korah was actually a first cousin of Moses. Some of us face more intimidation from our own families than from anyone else. John 7:5 and Mark 3:21 tells us even Jesus' family came against Him at one point. They thought He'd lost His mind.

In Joshua Chapter one, God speaks to Joshua's fears four times. His courage helped him to stand against the other ten men, many years before, when they returned from spying out the land.

Be strong and of good courage. Be not afraid neither be thou dismayed. [Don't faint, be discouraged or terrified]..................➡

> As I was with Moses so I will be with you.

Joshua would take Moses' place as leader when the children of Israel went into the land of promise. Here is an awesome duplication of their deliverance at the Red Sea. Though there was no enemy chasing them, the people had no reasonable way to cross over Jordan at this time. The spring rains had rendered the river impassable.

When Israel came out of Egypt, those of a slave mentality, those that feared man; He would not allow into His land of promise, though they were still His people. But now this new generation born in the desert - this new man; circumcised in Gilgal and into covenant, baptized in the

Jordan, kept the Passover and came under the blood covenant of Moses.

This new generation is now ready to come into their inheritance; to conquer the enemy and receive their covenant blessings. The reproach of Egypt, the stigma of slavery, had been rolled away and the manna from heaven was no more. No more maintenance in the desert, now provision in the promised land.

As they breathed in the fresh air of their inheritance, Joshua is confronted with the Captain of the Lord's hosts.

Are you for us, or our adversaries?
This man standing with sword drawn says,
No! I'm not for you or for them. I'm not here to take sides, I'm here to take over!

Now comes the time of judgment. Will the fear of man cause them to compromise? Will they follow in their parent's footsteps? The sword is the Word, the law; the dividing asunder of all that is not holy unto God.

Righteousness exalts a nation.

I am for the one who will come before Me in righteousness and justice; respect and fear of Who I Am!

Joshua fell on his face and worshiped. Remember Joshua spent long hours in the Holy Place communing with God. He knew His voice. Joshua knew he could trust his God. [Ex 33:11-17].

This visit from the Lord Jehovah assured Joshua of God's presence... Moses dared not go without Him; neither would Joshua. Nor should we! God is no respecter of persons. He is here showing Joshua exactly how Israel can defeat the enemy. He obeyed the Lord's every command no matter how preposterous it sounded.

Because Joshua obeyed, Jericho was destroyed.

The coveting of the spoil from Jericho the accursed city, was an accursed thing before a holy God.[17] One of the meanings of the word Jericho is fragrant. Verse 17 says the city is accursed and devoted. The Hebrew word used, means dedicated to be destroyed, and devoted. This is saying the treasures of Jericho were cursed to them and devoted to God.

That is what the tithe is. The 10% tithe of our income is dedicated to God, but if we keep it, it will be a curse to us. it will fall through the holes in our pockets [Hag 1:6 and read what Malachi 3 has to say]. Have you felt that no matter what you do there is never enough money? Haggai says,

Consider your ways.
Considering all this, why would God want an accursed city named Fragrance.

Well - Jericho was the tithe of the promised land!
The first fruits of their conquest.

It must be offered to God as a sacrifice, taking nothing for themselves. The first fruits of our land offered to God, is a sweet fragrance of our obedience and our submission to our Lord. Read Malachi 3:11.

The fear of the Lord is the beginning of Wisdom.
And I will rebuke the devourer for your sakes..

But Achan polluted the camp with his sin. He made Israel a curse. The Lord of Armies now stood with Israel's enemy at Ai.

Because Achan disobeyed, HE was destroyed.

Joshua immediately fell on his face before God. Joshua constantly watched Moses to see how it was done. Joshua did not fear the men of Ai, he feared God, and sought His God on how to deal with it.

How interesting in the light of how king Saul dealt with the issue of totally destroying the Amelekites. Here is revealed Saul's independent spirit that responds to the fear of man and not the fear of the Lord, which would have been the beginning of his wisdom [1Sam 13].

Because of the activities of the people, Saul is goaded by his own insecurities to do something, even if it's wrong. Then in Chapter 15 his heart of rebellion is really exposed. King Saul was told to utterly destroy the Amelekites and spare them not, But see our whining king who does stupid things.

The people also rebelled.

They probably took note of all the cattle and wanted to keep some of it. And Saul, being the coward he was - allowed them. So we must also be careful of whose leadership we submit ourselves. Whatever our covering is, that is to what we will begin to respond. Verse 9 tells us Saul and the people spared what their eyes told them was good, [Remember Eve!] Verse 15, Saul releases himself of responsibility and says, *They the people did it.*

The fear of man teaches us to manipulate other people or allows them to manipulate us. The greatest victory satan has over this whole issue is that we're afraid to tell anyone we're afraid, and are concerned with what they may think of us.

Saul was replete with self-deception. If we look at the name of the king he spared, we get insight into reality. Agag: means 'flame' [ie. passion] He was a descendent of Esau, a man of the earth, flesh; in contrast to his twin brother Jacob, a man after God, renamed Israel. Saul still insists he has,

Obeyed the voice of the Lord and gone the way which the Lord hath sent me.

Saul relied on his own ingenuity, constantly running around in circles, making foolish decisions, causing confusion among his men.

Saul spared the flesh, the King of Self!

Self-will brought deception; rebellion and stubbornness moved in right behind it bringing witchcraft and idolatry. All because he gave in to the fear of what others might think of him. He was a king filled with pride and feared the people would reject him as their king. He was a man pleaser.

1Samuel 18 demonstrates how far Saul's flesh was dragging him to jealousy and rage. He saw the favor of God and man with David, and being withdrawn from himself. He would stop at nothing to save face. We can see Saul does not accept the Lord as his God, He is Samuel's God. We can readily see how Saul is swayed by the people's opinion. Saul declares,

Because I feared the people, I obeyed their voice.

And because of all this, God rejected him as king and tore the throne from him. Remember what Adam lost because he would not take responsibility. If you know Jesus as your personal Savior then the Kingdom of God dwells within you. The Spirit of Truth dwells within you, and John 17...

If any man love me, he will keep my words and my Father will love him, and we will come unto him and make our abode with him.

Jesus promises to be with us until the end of the age.

Fear not, for I am with you.
For it is the Father's good pleasure
to give you the Kingdom. ❤

As Joshua told his people to do, so must we -

Choose ye this day whom you will serve.[18]

Judges six tells of Gideon - in the lineup of men of faith in the eleventh chapter of Hebrews. Yet his fear of man drove him to tear down his father's altars at night because,

He feared his father's household.
His obedience to God strengthened and encouraged him also, that he was able to carry out God's marching orders.

King David was one who shared with us, the tremendous personal battles he fought. He was not ashamed before His God, and wanted so much to have clean hands and a pure heart that he openly confessed his sins and shortcomings. It is to our blessing that he was willing to do this as revealed in his Psalms.

Many of us have grown mightily in the Lord because of his beautiful Psalms. Not only does He share his revelations of Who God is, but also how God delivered Him from his fears.

David had much opportunity to fear man or to give in to the fear of evil. But with each juncture He turned to God and began to praise and worship. He could have killed king Saul on several occasions and put an end to his running from this lunatic, but he chose to do it God's way.

Ps 105:15 *Saying, "Do not touch My anointed ones, And do My prophets no harm."*

> *But thou O Lord, are a shield for me;*
> *my glory, and the lifter of mine head.*

I'm reminded also of Job's quandary -
> *The thing I greatly feared has come upon me*
> *and what I dreaded has happened to me.*

Some believe that Job's problem was pride. I think maybe it was the sin of presumption for all of them. [Ps 19.13, see Job 38]. As God begins to reveal Himself to Job, he finally answers [42.3]
Therefore have I uttered that which I understood not; things too wonderful for me, which I knew not.

Here in 1Kings 17 we have Elijah the Tishbite [meaning recourse]. God's recourse to His holy nation gone mad with an idolatrous king and his blasphemous heathen wife; was a man that would bring God's fiery judgment.

Suddenly - Elijah pops into view. When he opens his mouth, he closes the heavens for three years. God does not give this kind of power to just anybody. But know this; Elijah was a man with a hidden history in God.

The other men in the Bible have recorded how God raised them up, and often gives their genealogy. This is not to say they did not have a history with God. But with Elijah it was so graphic that he seemed to come out of nowhere. God has birthed him for a time such as this, as He did Esther.

The forming of a man of God transpires in the secret place of the Most High; and a history with God is produced in the crucible of obedience. When and where God told him to go - he went. First the brook Cherith, then Zarephath. This city was the center of Sidonian idolatry. Ashtoreth was worshiped by Jezebel because she was Sidonian. Here we have her worst enemy, hidden in God right under her nose. Ahab and Jezebel sent forth armies for three years, to search for Elijah.

Until God brought him out, they could not find him!!
Elijah challenged 450 prophets of Baal, on a mountain top filled with 400 more of Jezebel's priests, and how many Israelite worshipers of Baal. When they were proven to be false prophets, Elijah slew all of them. He stood against 1000 idolatrous priests and many of his own people who had broken covenant with God, in the courage of the Lord. But when Jezebel threatened to kill him, he ran. Beersheba is 90 miles from that mountain.

Situations in our lives can be overwhelming and just one more straw can break us. Elijah asks the Lord to take him home. Total discouragement came over him. He gave up even to the point that he thought he was the only one left in all of Israel that still loved God.

Elijah allowed self pity and fear to rule over the situation. But God drew Elijah out of his pit and sent him about his prophet' business.[19] For some years he trained the one who would wear his mantle.[20] And finally God takes Elijah as he would enter the heavenlies in a whirlwind. Now Elisha asks,

Where is the Lord God of Elijah?
Where was He for Peter and Paul; for young Timothy
and Barnabas, especially for Stephen!
Where is He for you? He's in that still
small voice of peace and rest;
in the secret place of trusting God.
Jeremiah had the fear of man.
*Be not afraid of their faces, gird up thy loins and arise and
speak unto them all that I command thee; be not
dismayed at their faces, lest I confound thee before them.*
There are many places in the Word that people feared the Lord; but God doesn't want us to be afraid of Him. The Fear

of the Lord means to approach Him with respect and honor to His glory and majesty. We are approaching a Holy God, the Creator of the universe and all that is in it; His Majesty our King.

Sometimes we look at faces to see if we're acceptable. If God tells us to do something, many times we judge what are the circumstances before we be obedient. We allow the fear of rejection, the fear of judgment and criticism, to come be our master. Many prophecies in the Church are withheld because of the fear of man.

The book of Hebrews tells us the Word of God is like a two-edged sword, dividing the soul and spirit. When the fear in our soul overpowers our capability to walk in the spirit, we need to turn to the power of the Word for what is needed to conquer the enemy.

Psalm 29 is a prolific allegory on how we may gain the victory. In the opening verses, realize that only as we praise and worship the Lord, can we recognize Who He is and that He is Sovereign over all the earth. At whatever depth the flood of waters takes you, the Lord is there. What is the voice of the Lord saying in your flood of circumstances? Praise and worship magnifies the Lord in our sight. How big is your God! David cried,

Bless the Lord, oh my soul, and all that is within me, bless His Holy Name.[21]

As the Lord inhabits the praises of His people, He becomes enthroned at the flood. Then when we look, all we see is the Lord.

He is high and lifted up, and his train fills the temple.[22]
If I be lifted up, I will draw all men unto me.[23]

That does not always mean unbelievers. Jesus will draw His people closer to Himself as we lift Him up. The fear of man may cause us to avoid people and places to which the Lord could be leading. It can bring us into restlessness, depression, and even lies, to escape the real problem.

Other great men of God could have been crippled by their fears. The Word shows us they were no different than we are today. But God is still faithful. God tells His prophet Ezekiel, [2.6]

And thou, son of man,...be not afraid of their words, nor be dismayed at their looks.

God says you speak my words whether they want to hear it or not! Fear brings compromise. 2Cor 4:1-6 speaks of our ministry in the Lord to the Body of Christ. Unless we've allowed God to deal with our fear of man, there can be an underhanded way in which we sometimes share the gospel.

We have an enthusiasm to bring forth the Good News, but fear creeps in and causes us to withhold the things that we think will offend people. I don't believe we should go around offending others, but the gospel itself is an offense to those who do not receive the love of the truth. God wants us to be bold in Him, [not in our flesh]. If the fear is there, we make adjustments, according to their reaction.

Sometimes we're guilty of hypocrisy as was Peter. His fear of death caused him to deny Jesus three times. His fear of man caused him to compromise and his duplicity caused others to stumble.[24] But in Acts 5:29 Peter defies the Pharisees and obeys God. He must have been delivered from the fear of man.

The calling of God on our lives does not immediately produce a perfect image of the Son. The calling of God is in the Spirit realm. We have a soul desperately in need of restoration. God will do it from glory to glory, day at a time, walking and trusting as our soul and spirit come into one accord.

Paul speaks of being troubled on every side; *conflicts without, fears within*.[25] This can only be referring to what man was doing to him and his ministry. He would preach the Word and when he had to leave, the wolves would come in, attempting to devour the flock.[26] And the Jews were always trying to kill him. They almost succeeded. God gave him back his life.[27] He had to trust God. The next verse says,

Nevertheless God is faithful.

Paul boldly proclaims he has been approved by God and entrusted with the gospel to speak, whether it pleases men or not. It is God that tests the heart. The fear of man will cause one to falter in their commitment to God. Pretty soon they are playing head games. 'Did God really say that to me, I wonder if I'm really supposed to be here'?

Double-mindedness and confusion sets in, just as the Lord told Jeremiah it would [1:17]. And then we walk in fear - afraid to even want to hear the voice of the Lord - so we shut Him out, cut Him off; afraid He's gonna tell us to do something of which we are not capable.................➜

> Put on the whole armor of God - and stand.

But read Jer 1:18-19; did God send Jeremiah to carry out His orders in his own flesh, in his own strength? Or did God make of Jeremiah - a warring machine, and a man to stand with him. Did He not make of His people [51:20] a weapon of war - a battle ax to destroy the works of the enemy?

The fear of man is nothing more than lies poking into our insecurities. Those of whom God appoints, He also anoints. This is grace-ability; grace [strength manifested in our weakness] to obey - and ability to carry it out.

Deuteronomy chapter one is very interesting to apply here in this place. Because the people were so many, Moses was told to appoint leaders, captains and judges. They were charged to not fear the face of man. What would it cause? Respect of persons; the favor of one against the other. Unrighteous judgment, perhaps to cause hardship or even death to an innocent man.

Israel's fear of man kept them in the desert forty years [Num 13:33]. They could not enter His rest. The fear of man caused unbelief, deception, sin against the Lord, rebellion, unrest, defeat, presumption, and grieving of spirit.

This fear of man is nothing to wink at. It can be deadly to our walk in the Spirit and can keep us out of the will of God. The truth is - even if we are trying to impress someone - it is because we have the fear of man; and we're making them like a god, giving them charge over our behavior and emotions.

Sometimes we do it for attention; to make other's aware that we are alive. Child of God, you are precious in your Father's sight. If you will turn to your Savior and Redeemer, He will give you the assurance of His love and care. The Holy Spirit will show you your place in the body of Christ where you belong, and bring you into His perfect plan for your life.

In a previous chapter I've shared some scripture on fear such as 2Tim 1:7 and 1John 4:18. Fear becomes our enemy through the negative workings of our thought life. When our mind becomes tormented by fear we fail to walk in the power and authority God has made available. It is then exceedingly hard to trust God and receive the love that casts out fear. When we know that we know Him,[28] because we keep His commandments, then His love is brought to its fullness in us. In the security that comes from this relationship there is no place for fear to stand.

Most if not all the people used so powerfully by God as recorded in the Bible, had to overcome as do we, the same obstacles to their faith. Men and women though used of God in supernatural ways still must overcome their flesh and learn to trust in God. It is not for nothing that we find in 1Cor 10:13 these words from an understanding Creator;

> *There hath no temptation taken you but such as is common to man, but God is faithful, who will not suffer you to be tempted above that you are able; but will with the temptation also make a way to escape, that ye may be able to bear it.* The Amplified Bible says.............➔

Escape to a [safe] landing place.

God is faithful. Do we have this truth established deep in our heart? Have we examined our concept of God? Oftentimes it is based on what other people have told us, our vain imaginations or our past experiences and disappointments with others.

Some of our theology is based on what movies or television programs we've seen. It should be based on the truth of the Word of God, the Bible; the unfolding of the identity of the Creator of the universe. God tells us in Ephesians 1:17,18 that His desire for us is that we may receive the knowledge and revelation of Who He is. All through Scripture God tells us it is His will for us to know Him.

I have asked God to take all my notions, ideas and imaginations of a religious God and replace them with His Spirit of Truth. Too often we have our god in our little religious box and declare that He can or can't do this or that. Will the real God please stand up! *Fear God and let Him be for a sanctuary*.

He will give us favor with man. Then the manipulation and control and fear of man stops. We are warned not to trust in man and make flesh our arm, or strength.[29] We may not look for the approval of man that we might be strengthened by that approval, or put off by their dissension.

How often as a child did we cringe at this look of disapproval from a parent. On the other hand, if your parents deem you a good girl, you kill yourself trying to live up to that image. Because we are imperfect and fail many things, condemnation comes heavy trying to please when your heart knows the truth.

Their expectations are set at a level you cannot reach. So every time someone overloads you and you can't perform - the anger and guilt rises. The resentment comes, for they have discovered your weaknesses. You cannot please them. The fear of man comes in many different forms. Nor can we allow people's reaction to be our barometer for God's work in us. At one time I allowed that, but - no more!

The fear of man brings a snare.[30]
The fear of the Lord is the beginning of wisdom.[31]

God has a place of maturity and leadership, in Him, for all His people. He does not want us continually on milk. There comes a time for us to eat the meat and draw from the Well because of what Jesus has accomplished IN US. This has nothing to do with sitting in the pew on Sunday. The Word commands us to not forsake the assembling of ourselves together.

Maturity does not negate the need to listen to an anointed Bible teacher, nor does it bring us to a place where we no longer need to be teachable. It has to do with growing up in the Word so that it becomes the Living Water flowing out of our belly, or inner heart, from which others may drink.

There can be a place of embarrassment within us from the many times we failed to perform rightly and people either laughed or ridiculed us. I remember when I was in the fifth grade I transferred to a new school. There were already feelings that I was not acceptable but I thought - new school, new start.   My first week in class I mispronounced a girl's name out loud so the whole class heard me. I was so wounded by their laughter that, until recently, I would automatically reject listening to a person's name as I was being introduced.....➜

It was my excuse that I did not remember it, thereby eliminating any chance of ever being embarrassed like that again. God has shown me down through the years how good it feels when people remember my name. Lately He's been helping me be more

| Praise God, He knows us by our name. |

sensitive and listen; and if I goof, so what. People are gracious and glad to tell me again what their name is. The Word speaks of our name being written in the Book of Life.

Just as Jesus suffered outside the gate, we are enjoined to go forth unto Him bearing His reproach. If any one had the right to the Fear of Man syndrome, it was Jesus. It is constantly recorded in Scripture how they were plotting to kill Him! But He had been so dependent on the Father, *Not My will but Thine*, was His life's theme. On the cross in total submission to the Father's will, the fear of man died with Him, totally overcome. This enemy of ours, the Fear of Man, was nailed to the cross of Jesus!

And death, where is your sting!
O grave where is your victory!
Death is swallowed up in victory.[32]

Jesus knew the Father. The people of the Bible trusted in God because they knew Him. We too can know God. Have you got His phone number? He has a 24 hour a day hot line. Jeremiah 33:3 *Call unto me, and I will answer thee, and show thee great and mighty things, of which you know not.*

Fear is a spirit. It is not from God. It only comes from the enemy. *I sought the Lord and he heard me and delivered me out of all my fears.*[33]
And again there shall be heard in this place which ye say shall be desolate,...The voice of joy, and the voice of gladness; the voice of the bridegroom, and the voice of the bride, the voice of them who shall say, praise the Lord of hosts, for the Lord is good; for his mercy endures forever; and of those who shall bring the sacrifice of praise unto the house of the Lord.[34]

You see, God has not given us a spirit of fear, but of love, power and a sound mind.
Ye have not received the spirit of bondage again to fear; but ye have received the Spirit of adoption whereby we cry, Abba, Father.[35] *For in Him dwells all the fullness of the Godhead bodily and we are complete in Him.*

This is God's purpose.

We are buried and risen with Him, dead to sin, alive in Him. He blotted out the handwriting of ordinances [the law] took it out of the way - nailed it to His cross. Spoiled principalities and powers, shamed them, triumphed over them and gave us the victory. [36] The example of these men's lives have been given to us because fear makes us believe that we are the only one trapped in this corner. But Jehovah

Jireh - the God who sees, is ever ready to supply our need, as He did theirs.

There is another twist to this fear of man syndrome. Too often we look at someone who seems to be so much closer to God than we are - so much more mature than we are. We believe they really have it all together, and we place them on a pedestal. Nothing ever seems to go wrong in their life. They immediately know what to do in every trial; they never have any problems. Or so we think!

What happens here is, we begin to imagine that they judge everyone else's life. They are perfect and will criticize me if I expose my faults to them. This could keep you from coming into God's will.

A respecter of persons [Lev 19:15] will always have the fear of man and be afraid of judgment and criticism. There can never be real relationship with them, only cordiality. It's a pity because that other person most likely does not want to be set apart on a pedestal. That's what it does. It sets apart and isolates them. Maybe they would rather be liked for themselves and drawn into your circle.

They do not have it all together. They are growing in the Lord just like every one else - and believe it or not, they hurt sometimes too. But in your respecting - you have isolated them from your friendship. Rejection hurts them just as much as it hurts everyone else..➜

> Even God is not a respecter of persons!

There may be some readers to whom God has spoken, told some things of Kingdom matters. The fear of man has caused you to re-evaluate the Word of God according to opinions and decisions; according to the climate and consensus of those with whom you have to do. Your joy has been gone, your peace has been gone, and you may only be experiencing the outer court thanksgiving in your heart. Romans 14:17 tells us,

> *The Kingdom of God is righteousness,*
> *peace and joy in the Holy Ghost.*

God knows where you are. Turn your heart back to Him. His Spirit will not let you go. Even as fellowship with the Lord and Bible reading time has been dry and barren, you keep insisting all is well with your soul. My friend, if you will go back and do the last thing God asked you to do - you will again experience what the devil ripped off from you through fear. If you don't remember, ask; God will tell you.

> Lord, I praise You and thank You that
> I don't have to be intimidated or controlled
> by what other people think of me.
> You are my Rock, my fortress, my deliverer, my God,
> my defense, my high tower. I hide myself in You.

Bible heroes were just people used of God. In spite of their shortcomings [which by the way the Bible does not try to hide], God used them for awesome tasks to bring about the restoration of His Kingdom on the earth. Hey, it's His Kingdom and His work. If it's not done His way, It will not get done.

All God is asking is for us to trust Him and obey. That's what they did! And God helped them overcome all that stood in their way of victory. So wonderfully set free can God's people be, from the fear of man and the fear of death. The burning stake, the lions or the sword had no power over the Christians of centuries past who were martyred for the cause of the Kingdom. If God is for us what does it matter what others do?

In many countries there is still deadly persecution for those who would defy the world's religious system. Remember, we are not of this world   [Jn 17].

Daniel's three friends would not bow down and so must we never. Our God is able to deliver us safely into eternity with His love, grace, and mercy. Those young men came out of the furnace with not one singed hair. And if they hadn't, just read and remember Mt 10:28,

Fear not them who kill the body, but are not able to kill the soul; but rather fear him who is able to destroy both soul and body in hell.   And always remember -

> *Ye shall not need to fight in this battle; set yourselves, stand ye still, [in His peace and rest], and see the salvation of the Lord with you.*[37] *Cast your cares on the Lord for he cares for you.*[38]
> We can - with myriads of God's people before us,
> SHOUT!
> *Let the Redeemed of the Lord Say So -
> Who Has Been Redeemed
> Out of The Hands of The Enemy.* [39]

The enemy builds a counterfeit city; God is rebuilding the original. His city, the legitimate - and we know what the finishing touches will be, so let's focus now on the journey.

Have you ever thought about why Jesus loves Jerusalem so much? Have you ever thought that maybe this was the exact site of the Garden of Eden where God walked and talked with Adam? The Word tells us that He will rule and reign from Jerusalem.

So why is Jerusalem so important to God?

Matt 23:37   *O Jerusalem, Jerusalem, the one who kills the prophets and stones those who are sent to her! How often I wanted to gather your children together, as a hen gathers her chicks under her wings, but you were not willing!* [Why not any other city?]

Mark 11 - On the way to Jerusalem He saw a fig tree; the place where the first man, Adam, turned from Him; covered with fig leaves, hiding in his sin as if his Creator, the lover of his soul, wouldn't see him. Like a little girl with a lollipop in her mouth, denies she got into the candy.

Now comes Jesus to curse the fig tree because it had no fruit; no real life in it. [Mk 11.13&21]. We know Jesus came to set us free from bondage to darkness, so He began at the beginning where the root of 'our sin nature was birthed'.

God always begins at the beginning with anything He wants us to understand. So Jesus curses the fig tree down to the root; thus beginning His journey to the cross - His goal, the end of - *He shall bruise thy head* [Gen 3.15]. This means the authority the enemy had over us would be done with, at the cross; total, finished. Remember - *'It Is Finished'*.
And now Lk 10.19 *I give you the authority over all the power of the enemy,*

Jesus went to the place where man first rejected Him and cursed it at its root. *Let no one eat fruit from you ever again.* Here is the beginning of the demise of the sin nature that plagues all of mankind. It began right here at the fig tree. Adam was given authority over the earth - and he gave it to satan
Lk 4.5-6 *and I [satan] give it to whoever I please.*

The garden - the place where man first rejected Him; He bound Himself there in prayer to His Father's purpose. Remember the garden - to pay the price for Adam's betrayal. And at the cross *Jesus said - It Is Finished! So Jesus was* Buried and resurrected here in Jerusalem.

This is how Jesus feels about Jerusalem - and more.
Matt 5:34-35 *But I say to you, do not swear at all: neither by heaven, for it is God's throne; nor by the earth, for it is His footstool; nor by Jerusalem, for it is the city of the great King.*

Zech 3:2 *The Lord who has chosen Jerusalem rebuke you! Is this not a brand plucked from the fire?*
2 Chron 11:16-17 *Those from all the tribes of Israel, such as set their heart to seek the Lord God of Israel, came to Jerusalem to sacrifice to the Lord God of their fathers.*

Matt 5:35-36 *nor by Jerusalem, for it is the city of the great King.* Luke 2:39 *she gave thanks to the Lord, and spoke of Him to all those who looked for redemption in Jerusalem.*
Acts 1:8 *and you shall be witnesses to Me in Jerusalem,*
Heb 12:22 *The city of the living God, the heavenly Jerusalem,*

Rev 21:10-11 *and showed me the great city, the holy Jerusalem, descending out of heaven from God,*
See Rev 21. Especially v.22. And in the end God will rule there. Jerusalem - the City of Peace.

There are hundreds of Scripture pertaining to Jerusalem. And we know the Temple of God has always been in Jerusalem.

So - Is Jerusalem the site of the Garden of Eden ?

STUDY GUIDE

1. Who was the first person in the Bible, recorded to have the fear of man?
2. If we're going to live for God, it's going to cost us. Do you suppose Noah had lots of help from the public to build the ark?
3. What did Abram's fear of man cause him to do with Sarai?.
4. What is one other fear that usually accompanies the fear of man?

5. What does God say about this subject? Mt 10.
6. Our powerful leader Moses - how did he respond?
7. How about Joshua. Can God help us the way He helped Joshua?
8. Gideon, our mighty man of valor had to face the wrath of his own father. Should you obey man or fear God?
9. Ah! King David - he told it all on himself. He's helped me a lot, how about you?
10. Jeremiah the prophet of doom. Every time he opened his mouth he made somebody mad.
11. Ezekiel also had a message for a rebellious people. God's strong hand and grace on this son of man brought him through.
12. According to 2Cor 4 what can happen in ministry if we have the fear of man?
13. Elijah - mighty slayer of Baal, ran from a woman's threats. We can move mightily in the anointing and then afterwards tend to forget Who is our Source. He wanted to die but God had more for him to do.
14. Peter learned the hard way.
15. Paul found God's grace through his trials [2Cor 12.9].
16. Are you intimidated by other people's frowns? Do you back off? What if God sent you? Will you seek God for deliverance from this enemy of your soul?

PRAYER: Father I ask You to show me the instances that I am responding to the fear of man that I may overcome this enemy of my soul. There are many reasons why I have walked in this fear. I ask you to reveal the roots of my fears that I may be set free to serve You completely. I turn my eyes away from man and onto You, the Lord of my life.

*Cursed are those who put their trust in mere humans
and turn their heart away from the Lord.
They are like stunted shrubs in the desert,
with no hope for the future.
They will live in the barren wilderness,
on the salty flats where no one lives.
But blessed are those who trust in the Lord
and have made the Lord their hope and confidence.
They are like trees along the riverbank
with roots that reach deep into the water.
Such trees are not bothered by the heat or worried*

by long months of drought. Their leaves stay green, and they go right on producing delicious fruit.
[Jer 17:5-8 NLT].

The will of God is all I need
And to His call I will ever heed
His glory is what He shares with me
My faith is that He cares for me
His love sets me heart on fire
He will always be my one desire
God wrapped me in His love and grace
One day I'll see Him face to face
I've been stamped and sealed,
I belong to Him
Cause He has set me free from sin
With Glory He has covered me
In Christ I will always be
I am His true inheritance ❤

SCRIPTURES

1. Is 51: 12-13
2. Is 8:13-14
3. Mt 22:30
4. He 2:11
5. He 11:11
6. Ro 2:29
7. 1Co 15:46
8. 1Pe 2:9-10
9. Ps 118:6
10. Ge 13:3-4
11. Ro 4:1-13
12. Ge 22:2
13. Is 9:6
14. Jn 8:56
15. 1Co 2:9-10
16. Ps 34:15
17. Jo 6:18
18. Jo 24:15
19. 1Ki 19:9
20. 1K 19:16
21. Ps 103:1
22. Is 6:1
23. Jn 12:32
24. Ga 2:11-14
25. 2Co 7:5
26. Ac 20:29
27. Ac 14:19-20
28. 1Jn 2:3
29. Je 17:5
30. Pr 29:25
31. Pr 9:10
32. 1Co 15:54-55
33. Ps 34:4
34. Je 33:11
35. Ro 8:15
36. Co 2:9,15
37. 2Ch 20:17
38. 1Pe 5:7
39. Ps 107:2

THE FEAR OF MEN

The Lord hath been witness between thee and the wife of thy youth, against whom thou hast dealt treacherously; yet she is your companion, and the wife of thy covenant. And did not he make one? Yet had he the residue of the spirit. And why one? That he might seek a godly seed.[1]

The father figure that was established as the foundation of the family unit, was designed to stabilize and foster a nurturing atmosphere to rear the children God has loaned to us. Yet this designated leader has in too many homes, become a drunk, a womanizer, a child abuser, a wife beater, and in some instances a murderer. What a tragedy it is that we have lost sight of the blessings our God purposed for the family. [Pr 17:6].

*Children's children are the crown of old men,
and the glory of children is their father*

Glory means to gleam, embellish, boast, to beautify. God had some definite reasons for structuring the family unit as He did. Malachi 2:11-17 tells us a great deal of how God feels about what happens in some homes.

Mostly He hates what it does to people.....→

> God hates divorce.

The aftermath of divorce leaves children in no-man's land. Their heart is full of fear and insecurity, and they are torn between loyalty to both parents. Too often they believe it is all their fault.

He calls it treachery when a man breaks covenant with his wife; a covenant reminiscent of His covenant with mankind. That they would be one, inseparable. He deposits a residue [a remnant, a portion] of His Spirit to bind them together. And why;

That God might seek after a godly seed.

A little girl learns at her Father's knee if she can trust men, and she will look for the same character and integrity in her choice of mate. A little boy who watches his Dad treat his Mother with respect and love will respect himself, and choose for a mate a young lady that will nurture his children with care and patience, to become the godly seed for whom our Creator seeks.

In these past some generations the family unit has been eroding and disintegrating to the point that untold numbers of American children don't even know who their father is, and do not have a sense of identity. Too many of today's children are being raised by women of whom were never meant to bear the stress of being head of the home, nor meant to take the place of father to their children. These women are frustrated and angry and don't really know why. Too often the next man in the house abuses them and the children, physically or sexually.

The violence in homes across the nation leaves wounds and scars that bury themselves deep and cause more anger and rage down through the generations. The children grow up never sure from one day to the next if they will even have their basic needs met. Many never do. Many go to bed hungry, battered or both. This scenario is not reserved only for the under-privileged.

Drunkenness, drugs, violence and especially incest are running rampant in every layer of our society, as is attested by our daily papers and T.V. A broken heart and wounded spirit gives birth to its kind wherever it is found. Those people whose lives have been devastated by one of these reason or another, deal with much emotional pain and fear - of men, authority, and ultimately - Father God. And know that these men also most likely come from an abusive home. It is learned behavior - to love or not!

And women do not escape this behavior. They have a hard time raising children with the love they never got.

One of the most important family factors is the covering of the father; the spiritual protection that his headship provides for his children. And this also applies to unbelievers. God's family laws never change and are applicable to all. Unprotected, uncovered kids are prey for pedophiles and homosexuals. These men [and in many cases, women] are sensitive to children who are not receiving the covering love and attention they warrant. Spirits of lust and perversion may be transferred to the child in the midst of this traumatic terror and anxiety; at the moment of the encounter.

These children [most often we're currently dealing with the adult child] also may need deliverance from the spirit of child molestation. Taken by surprise and anxiety, these children are also open to the transference of spirits of lust and perversion. Their feet may now be set on the road to promiscuity. There is much pain and heartache in their future.

I am not implying this scenario for all, but for the ones who suffer from these things; please know that your merciful compassionate Lord sees you where you are and will deliver you as you turn to Him. Begin with forgiveness for all your abusers. This does not have to be passed down to your generations.

I was approached twice by pedophiles in my childhood. The anxiety and terror of being victimized, lived with me for many years even though I was able to run from them. In later years God brought me to much needed deliverance.

Some of us are able to push things into a dark closet and go about the business of every day. But God sees our tears at night when all alone with the pounding of our broken heart in our ears; the tossing and turning, the nightmares, the strain of relationships - the headaches - the bitterness and rage that consumes us every time we contrive to get even, or be justified.

Too often the offended is drawn into the same lifestyle. And so family relationships are destroyed and homes disintegrated, because the future homes of many little girls and boys are totally wrecked before they reach adolescence; all as a result of the non-restraint of self serving attitudes. Very often, abused children become bullies in the playground and grow up to be abusers.

It's evident that verbal abuse can be just as harmful as any other. A sense of worthlessness can bring disaster to a family. Emotional neglect is another kind of severe abuse. Most times the anger or rage that rises up, is totally unexplainable. Emotions turn on a dime and once again we have war. We must be aware these things did not all of a sudden spring up out of nowhere. They were happening years ago, just no one ever heard much about it. Girls who were raped or abused in their home were threatened with more abuse, or made to feel that what happened, was their fault, so they kept quiet. Most times they are warned to keep quiet.

Many of these women are still suffering the results of the social climate of their day, afraid to tell anyone what their father or uncle or brother did to them; perhaps over a long period of time. These days families are more aware of the help that is available. They are freer to turn towards that help; although we know the only true resolution of this problem, or any other for that matter, is in Jesus.

In the world system there is at least

some understanding, now.

In previous generations there was none. The adults that are in their late 40's and upward did not have that help readily available. Now I know even today there may be many younger people that for some reason were never helped either. I do not want to diminish from any one's desperate need.

It is almost [if not entirely] impossible for other people to relate to or understand the consequences of this tragedy in one's life. The husband of a woman who has this sexual violation in her little girl emotions is puzzled, angry, hurt; and many times in total frustration, sues for divorce because his wife fights him in bed. He can not understand that, though she may desperately love him and need him; she is in reality experiencing in her subconscious again and again, that frightening account of being raped by an uncle, a brother, a stranger, and yes, even her own father.

A little boy may be used by his frustrated mother to fill the emotional needs left empty by her husband. He is forced into a role his immaturity can never bear, especially if he is allowed entrance to her bedroom or bath anytime he chooses, at an age much beyond the reasonable innocence barrier. This is a form of emotional incest, which produces inordinate soul-ties. Perhaps he also has this access to His older sister.

Though he may at the time, enjoy the attention and the central position in his mother's life, there are forces at work that neither of them are aware. He has lost his innocence and his sense of identity of who he really is................➔

> He strives to relate to adults as an equal.

The emotional pattern of being a little boy growing up secure in his father's house has been traumatically altered. He is responsible to take care of mom when he is only capable of giving hugs. Too often this house also has an abusive father and husband, and the boy will try to protect his mother from these things. His lack of power here, only fuels the fire for future emotional outbursts and the fear of impotency.

Sometimes the father is aware that his wife has turned to his son for comfort, and makes matters worse by jealous outbursts. None of them know how to stop this recurring nightmare. Satan has a stronghold in this family and will use every opportunity to bring about discord and strife.

This child is developing a disrespect for his parents, and probably all other authority figures. He has fits of explosive anger and rage that seem to have no reason. His mind and his body seem disconnected and his spirit becomes buried under pain and confusion. He will be desperately hungry for a father figure to nurture him and so may be prey for a pedophile or compelled by a homosexual. One of the deepest roots of homosexuality is incest and a father that doesn't care. There are others. The bottom line here is the desperate need for love and acceptance. Emotional or real, the payment may be the same.

He may live out his anxieties in his marriage bed and never nail down his own masculine identity; or perhaps be driven to the perverted use of women. Sexual perversions represent extreme attempts to overcome rejection and anger. He may develop a hatred and disdain for women, and must control them sometimes to the point of slavery. If he's in charge of all her activities, then he has a handle on his own emotions; or so he thinks.

His relationship with his future wife may never reach a balance point, because every time she has a legitimate need and pulls on him, he gets inordinately angry. Frustration rises and the old pressures cause him to lash out at her. This can also be true for inordinate girl/father relationships.

If a little girl is being molested, she must learn to control her environment. The imagination is very inventive and creates all kinds of options; one being, to separate from the abuse and create another personality. That one is being abused, not me. This is called Multiple Personalities. If you think these ideas are preposterous, talk to one of those who have already reached adulthood. They will recognize themselves. Fear and anger are ruling factors in her life.

If you keep reading you will find there is healing for these things that torment you.

These childhood wounds may be deeply buried in our inner most being, and we are not aware of them in our every day memories. The pain can be too great to bear and so our merciful Creator has built within us the capacity to forget. Our subconscious can get mighty full of debris in some cases. Most often there is a dread and shame within our soul, but to put a finger on the exact cause many times escapes us.

The effects on our personality and our emotions can be diverse, so that totally opposite results are produced. In any given group of people there can range different levels of promiscuity to emotional coldness and withdrawal. These elements will be modified by other factors present in the person's life.

Through the anger of their telling and perhaps not believed, mixed with the rejection, violence and fear that may already be a part of every day, the little girl grows up with getting even, in her heart. Too often a young lady becomes promiscuous to fill that hunger for nurturing left unfulfilled by her father, but also believes she is punishing men at the same time. If she has been abandoned, abused or molested by her father, there comes a belief that she is punishing men by being promiscuous even though the hatred of men may be a ruling factor in her behavioral patterns.

But they always looking for a father.
Please try to understand the gross perversion of truth that satan propagates. Both ends war against the middle. Confusion of soul reigns, and satan loves it. As she goes from one lover to the next, the wounds of rejection cut deeper. After all, she is looking for the daddy that never loved her. But all she is left with is frustration, emptiness and guilt.

The hatred of men becomes more firmly imbedded, because none can fill that absented role. No other man can fill that need, but she keeps searching. It may become established that, should she marry, this woman may not be capable of true intimacy with her husband. Her soul is fragmented by many soul ties produced by fornication. This happens to both parties [1Co 6:16]. The foundational blessing of this home has been ripped off, before it began.

Now match her up with the young man whose life we just studied, and we have an interesting scenario. Two people will live a life of frustration never having that God-given need satisfied, and...their children will suffer the consequences.

On the other hand, one may wall her [or him] self into a private world and to a greater or lesser degree; become centered there. If I let myself go, to trust anyone and lose control, it may happen again. This can also torment a teenager, or a women that was raped as an adult with no childhood molestation. Coming from within and without, there is much guilt, shame and condemnation.

Thank God there is not one condition of our humanity that is left out of the Word of God. This wonderful Book tells it like it is. God has exposed all because He understands that we need to know where we can find the answers to our predicaments.

Even His much loved David, whose life story is covered in seven books of the Bible and more, is not hidden. His sin with Bathsheba and the murder of her husband; resulting in family nightmare, is shown for what it was. 2Samuel 13 reveals how the iniquity of the father effects the children. Some have thought David got away with what he did. Perhaps this idea occurred to his son Amnon. So Amnon decided he would give in to his lust also. After all there is no terrible price to pay.

The pain he caused his sister Tamar was the least on his mind. Yet this one act cost him his life, and there was also propagated again, a murderer in the family. But that was only the beginning of the king's sorrows. And Tamar; she believed her life was over. Her shame was more than she could bear. She was deemed of no value. I doubt that she was placated by Amnon's death, even though her own brother took vengeance.

When these things happen, we feel alone and abandoned. We are unable sometimes to get a handle on life. We long to partake of the social activities in our community but we are always lonely in a crowd, unable to cope with the reality of relationships. We have been violated, used, deemed unworthy to take our rightful place in the human race. Too often it is an uncle, a father or even a stranger. It is devastating to our soul.

We relegate ourselves to stay on the outside, looking in. Always a spectator - never a participator of the festivities. And still we ask,

> Is there no one that understands? Is there no one that can rescue me? I'm drowning in my own self pity! I'm angry at the world that allowed this when I was helpless to defend myself. Where is justice? Who will make them pay for destroying my life?

Yes, there is Someone that understands. There is Someone Who will rescue you from the pain. There is healing for every person that has this horrific experience in your life. First please forgive the ones that harmed you. Unforgiveness will keep you trapped in the maze of pain. It has brought a bitterness deep in your soul. You may not feel like you can do this, but forgiving the rapist is a decision. If you choose to do this, God will help you. Set your heart on releasing all this to the Lord, and know He has forgiven you for your anger, resentment and wanting to get even. God understands. So now after forgiveness, you can expect God to fill your heart with His love and mercy, compassion and understanding, and most of all, His peace.

I pray Lord God, with Your mighty healing hand, touch this person and bring restoration and healing to their emotions. Heal this broken heart and wounded spirit. Lord God, by the power of the Blood of Jesus, please drive out the enemy's stronghold. It is the anointing the breaks the yoke. The anointing for deliverance and healing is possible every time we go to the Lord for help.

So right now in the Name of Jesus, I break the power of this yoke of bondage and burden off you. In the name of Jesus I sever every soul tie to those people. Let them go, give them to the Lord. Rom 12.19 tells us...*Beloved, don't be obsessed with taking revenge, but leave that to God's righteous justice. For the Scriptures say: Vengeance is mine, I will repay, says the Lord.*
[From the Passion Translation by Brian Simmons].

This torment and nightmares must leave. You were not to blame. Lift up your heart to the Lord. He loves you and wants to make you free of all this. Lord Jesus, please bring peace here in this place. Now Lord I ask that Your Life and Your Love flow through this child of Yours that is so dear to You. Let them know they belong to You and You will never leave them. Strengthen and encourage them to let go of the pain and shame. Help them to walk in the newness of Your life.

Right now you can speak to your Lord and thank Him for what He has done for you and in you.

These emotions can also be evident in the life of a person that was rejected by their parents. Unwanted, they may have been terribly abused. A physically battered child lives a life of desperation. All behavior is learned. A new born infant has no experiences to draw from. There can be however, stamped on the emotions even before birth -

REJECTED!

If a woman is battered during pregnancy by her husband or live-in, then violence and fear can be transmitted to her baby. These little ones are totally dependent on their environment for survival. Some don't make it! For the ones that do, there can be many dark days of depression and unexplained fears that are hard to overcome, or even understand.

If a woman tries to abort her baby and is unsuccessful, a spirit of the fear of death and fear to live may torment these people. All our emotions, positive and negative, are a product of our life experiences. Actually, our emotions were given to us by our Creator to enable us to do just that... to live, experience life.

We can use our emotions as a barometer to help us know what's going on inside our heart in order to bring these things to God for healing. We also must understand that our own perception of life is what's stamped there. We do not always perceive reality the way others do. That's why siblings can recollect a family situation from different viewpoints. Some of us can react to our past with violent emotions; others with no emotions; totally turned off, closed shop, shut down, and could not care less. Now I understand many of us have had a very healthy and fulfilling childhood. For these I praise God.

It is for the others I write.

God has given me much understanding of circumstances that some people have been raised with; and from my own background, I am very sensitive to the pain some others have experienced.

Being aware of the Scripture that says the iniquity of the fathers will be handed down to the fourth generation; Scripture also tells us we are accountable for our own sins. There is no doubt that it is the consequences of iniquity that is being referred to here.

If a man is bound up in pornography and adultery, his children may be given over to the forces of sexual sins. We may need deliverance from the sins of the fathers, and the curses that are handed down through the generations. And remember we are accountable for our own sin before God. How are we responding to all this?

*All have sinned and come short
of the Glory of God.*[2]

Perhaps that is the focus of the whole issue. We are constantly missing the mark; the high calling of God. The fact is we are responsible for how we react or respond to what happens to us. If we can say about ourselves, I never received love how can I be expected to give it? We also must validate that for others. If our parents grew up rejected, with no outward show of love, and indeed abused, neglected, or trashed in their growing up, how could they in turn have shown us love?

All behavior is learned. This is not given as an excuse, but rather for understanding. Jesus' final words on the cross were,
> Forgive them Father, they know not what they do.

> We cannot continue to blame others,
> we can only do what the Word commands.
> That is forgive them - Seventy times seven.

It matters not if your parents worked their fingers to the bone for you, so that you would have a better life. If you never understood in your heart and felt in your emotions that they loved you, then you may very well have perceived yourself as rejected by your parents. Perhaps you were set aside as they pursued their career. The emptiness of heart can be unbearable.

There is sin in the world and humanity comes severely short of the glory of God. We must remember that satan is the god of the world. He rules and reigns over all that is of the world. But saints, we are not of this world.[3] The devil hates God's creation, that's us, and has our destruction as his goal; however, *Jesus came to destroy the works of the devil*![4]

The world cannot forgive for they know not the Father's mercy and grace. Forgiveness is a powerful piece of machinery in the Kingdom of God; used to plow through the works of the devil in our lives. That is why the death of Jesus has such significance. He FORGAVE His murderers! And beloved of God we are all responsible, because we all needed a Savior. His death was used by God to break the power of sin over mankind. Yes! All this was planned and determined by God before the foundation of the world [Rev 13.8]. The very nature of God in the capacity of forgiveness dwells in the Savior of the World. See 2Cor 5:21.

> He died that we might have Life.
> WHAT A MASSIVE EXCHANGE!

Yet we must remember no one took His life. He gave it up willingly because He knew we didn't have a chance otherwise![5] Now He offers us the Ministry of Reconciliation. 2 Cor 5:17-19 *Therefore, if anyone is in Christ, he is a new creation; old things have passed away; behold, all things have become new. Now all things are of God, who has reconciled us to Himself through Jesus Christ, and has given us the ministry of reconciliation, that is, that God was in Christ reconciling the world to Himself, not imputing their trespasses to them, and has committed to us the word of reconciliation.*

This means reconciliation with Father God. It also means reconciling with our world, the things and people with which we have to do. It will be glorious in eternity. But what about the gory here and now. God wants to flow through you, His healing waters. Are you experiencing the Life of God within you right now? ....→

> It Is a decision! God has given us a free will and so, we must choose.

Ask for it - and receive it!

There may be other messages in this passage in John; where the Pharisees threw a prostitute before Jesus and demanded to know if He was going to keep the law of mandatory stoning. Jesus totally ignored their accusations [she was caught in the act] and proceeded to write something in the dirt.

Do you suppose He could have written. Where's the man? The law demanded both parties be stoned, but they did not bring the man with whom she was caught. When He stooped the second time was He writing the imaginations of their heart [Mt 5:28]. Were they being reminded of their own sexual sins? They scrambled outta there! But Jesus knew where she was coming from and He told her,

Neither do I condemn thee, go and sin no more.

The power of forgiveness can wash away a lifetime of pain. It can bring wholeness and healing and restoration to a broken heart. When Jesus died on the cross an explosion of God's forgiveness was loosed into the universe along with the grace and love we need for the ability to forgive those who have so terribly offended us. As we forgive, God's forgiveness sets us free [Mt 6:14].

If we are being re-created into the image of Jesus then we must have available to us all that was available to Him. If forgiveness is a part of His very nature, then we have ready access to it. The pain of these issues in our lives can be so great that try as we may, we can't hardly speak the words of forgiveness. At this time I would ask your gracious Heavenly

Father to do for you what you can't do for yourself; that is, give you a heart of forgiveness.
But, If you say you can't forgive it's the same as, I won't.
It involves the will. Forgiveness is not,
I repeat is not, a sentimental feeling.
And I am asking God to help you make that decision with your will no matter how angry you are. Decide to do it and God will pour out His grace. Even as you are turning to God for the grace you need at this time, He is there with you to answer your need. *And it shall come to pass that before they call I will answer;*
and while they are yet speaking, I will hear.[6]

God's grace may be unmerited favor but I believe it is so much more than that. It is God's grace that enables us to do the will of the Father. The Lord coined a word for me awhile back. Graceability; the grace that gives us the ability.

I had a vision recently of a little child sitting in a wading pool, laughing with joy, playfully splashing water all over itself. God told me that's how He wants us to receive His grace.
Isn't God funny?
I pray right now for an abundance of God's
graceability to be present here and now as you read these words, so you can and will forgive.
- It Is Not Sufficient For You to Say,
Yes, I Can Forgive.
- That Sounds Good, But You Are Not Doing It.
- You Are Only Saying You Can.

Let go of all your hatred, resentment, bitterness, anger, rebellion, self pity, self- rightousness and anger toward God for letting it happen; and unforgiveness. If it was the only attention you got, and you liked it cause it felt good, it is still satan's perversion of God's best. Ask for forgiveness and restoration.

As you release these things to God He will loose His healing power through you to restore all that was stolen from you. God is in the business of restoration. He's in the business of healing. Forgiveness releases His tender mercies into your heart, that you can receive His wondrous love. You need no longer be a victim.
If we confess our sins,

God is faithful and just to forgive us our sins and to cleanse us from all unrighteousness.

It's not that we are guilty of the offense.

Our sin comes from our response.

Unforgiveness has little effect on the person we won't forgive. It is the effect on us, that has such devastating power. It's the bitterness in our gut that causes the spastic colon, ulcers, depression, yes and even arthritis may be caused by our sin; it is *rottenness and drying of the bones.*[7]

I had unforgiveness for many things, down in the marrow of my bones and yes, true bitterness. It was only the mercy of God that He held me in His arms as I forgave all that almost destroyed my life [on top of three abusive marriages that left me knowing I was still unlovable and rejected]. Jesus comes to us one day at a time to deal with those things that are destroying us.

Read Romans 8 and then chapter 12. It shows us how to walk in His grace and blessing. But we have to follow all of His directions if we are to receive all He has for us. Some parts are easy; but know our flesh must die. God has so much more for us.

He doesn't give us more than we can bear. This is when His Mt 11:22 yoke comes in handy. He bears the burden with us, and then removes it by His mighty love. What it takes to receive this is a decision to let go. [Heb 13:5 Ampl].

He [God] Himself has said, I will not in any way fail you or give you up nor leave you without support. I will not, I will not, I will not in any degree leave you helpless nor forsake nor let you down, relax my hold on you! Assuredly not!

So here in Romans is His direction for you.

Repay no one evil for evil. Never avenge yourself, but leave the way open for God to take care of it: for it is written, vengeance is Mine, I will repay, says the Lord.

Do not let yourself be overcome by evil, but overcome [master] evil with good.

Please read the whole chapter for context. And while you're at it also read Psalm 18, and remember we are dealing with spiritual warfare. This is the important part; He cleanses us from ALL unrighteousness. That is - the effect of the sin. Right now God wants to heal and cleanse the destruction that resides in your emotions, memories, your soul, your body. He sets your spirit free to be who He intended you to be.

Many times we experience physical illness and psychological infractions because of what is transpiring in our souls; and our mind runs rampant through memories to keep them current. The fear of men can be joined with a hatred of men which can also bring a hatred and demeaning of self.

To blame and shame one's self for what happened can be used by our subconsciousness to batter and bruise, until we say, 'What's the use, no one can understand what I have been through'. Well,

- There Is One Who Understands.
- There Is One to Whom You Can Turn.
- There Is One Who Can And Wills to Heal You.
- He Came to Make You Whole.

His Name Is Jesus.

So if you want healing from the Lord hold still for the operation and yield to His intensive care. Let God do it His way.

He healed many different ways in the Bible. Let Him be God. Oftentimes we do not receive from God because even though we have faith to believe and want to receive; we are hindered because we want what we want, when we want it.

Give the Lord the opportunity to restore. This may be over a period of time. It took time for you to get where you are. It takes time to untangle messes.

God would say unto you .... ➜

> Receive the blessing I want to give you.

Another tragic result of fractured family relationships is the ongoing occurrence of illegitimate children; born or even conceived out of wedlock.

No matter how our society has condoned it or even fostered this behavior and demoralization of our value system - it is still sin in the eyes of God. When we read about Lot and his daughters after the angels took them out of Sodom, we see that his daughters committed incest with their father and produced two sons, Ammon and Moab.

Growing up in Sodom and Gomorrah, Lot's children learned the severe consequences of living in the midst of perversion. I've wondered what Lot did when he found out what had happened. The curse on illegitimate progeny is to be an outcast. There are several ways that we can be deemed an outcast, but this one carries a curse. Please keep reading. *Those of illegitimate birth, an Ammonite and a Moabite shall not enter into the congregation of the Lord unto the 10th generation.*

Now watch for God's provision!
And please don't stop reading!

The Ammonites and the Moabites were constantly at war with the children of Israel. They came from the same ancestors. Lot was Abram's nephew. But one [Isaac], was legitimate and blessed of God. Ammon and Moab were not; but if you read about when Joshua entered the land, these two were also given a place.

In many ways the Old Testament is a physical example of the spiritual war we fight now [Eph 6:12-18]. So the battle with Ammon and Moab has impact in the spirit realm today. We know the devil wants to keep us all out of the Kingdom by blinding us to God's truth. As the Holy Spirit draws us, we can indeed be born again and become a child of God.

Herein lies the problem. Just as Ammon and Moab fought with Israel constantly, so the spirit of this curse will battle with the Christian who has this curse on them. Our salvation is not at stake here, it is our victory to overcome and walk in holiness, and know that we know we do belong in the family of God; that is constantly under attack. This is why deliverance has been made available.

No! These things that happened were not your fault. See why it is so important to read and study the Word. Now we can understand the goodness of God. Now, we know we can be delivered and set free from this curse.

Until we are, there will always be a problem trying to relate to the body of Christ as a member, and a striving to enter into praise and worship and yet be frustrated beyond understanding. We can praise God for His awesome grace. He has made provision.

Gal 3:13 tells us, *Christ hath redeemed us from the curse of the law, being made a curse for us; for it is written, cursed is everyone that hangs on a tree.*

Jesus was also called illegitimate [Jn 8:41]. His ignominious sacrifice came from an incomprehensible compassion dwelling in the very heart of God. He took every curse on Himself so His people could be free. It's your inheritance. Take it and stand against the devil in the power of the Blood and in the Name of Jesus. The curse is broken and you are free.

That the blessing of Abraham might come on [you] through Jesus Christ, that [you] might receive the promise of the Spirit through faith.[9]

At this time I want to be sure that first, you have forgiven all who hurt you, then it is just as important to confess your own sin of anger, bitterness, hatred etc.; that God will forgive you. Next it is important for you to forgive yourself. We can carry around a lot of the blame/shame for a lifetime; but we don't have to.

I shared the Scriptures Hebrews 9.11-15; 10.19-23; 1Jn 3.19-22 Read and study these until they become part of who you are in Christ.

At this time you may want to re-evaluate your thoughts and pictures of Jesus and God. In our system of things we have a habit of lumping similar items together. We sort ideas into categories to keep our thoughts somewhat in order..........................➜

> It is the nature of humans to do this.

So as the Bible speaks of God - HE, we somehow in our mind lump God into our category of male. Perhaps we have evaluated God the Father in the same way as the other males in our life that have hurt us, rejected and abandoned us.

#1. Perhaps you had a father who left you, or you could never please, no matter what you did. So it is natural to believe that no matter how you strive to please God you never will, but you keep trying anyhow.

#2. No matter how obedient you try to be, you fail miserably [because you are trying to keep the law]. You become rebellious.

#3. You cannot get close to God because all males have a disdain for women.

#4. Jesus is OK because my brother was my friend, but I'll stay away from God the Father; I'll stay out of His way.

#5. God the Father is O.K. but my brother is the one that hurt me. I'll just bypass Jesus and get right to the Source.

#6. I'll never be good enough.

No you won't my friend, because it's not your goodness that saves you, it's the goodness of God.[10]

If our heart condemns us God is greater than our heart and knows all things, Beloved if our heart condemns us not then we have confidence toward God.[11] By this perceive we the love of God, because he laid down his life for us.[12]

God made provision even for single Moms. Read Ps 68:5 and Isaiah 54, and trust Him. Now pray and speak these Scriptures right from your heart.

How much more shall the Blood of Christ, who through the eternal Spirit offered himself without spot to God, purge [my] conscience from dead works to serve the living God? [Hebrews 9:14 and this one, 10:22]

[I will now] draw near with a true heart in full assurance of faith; [my] heart is sprinkled from an evil conscience, and [my] body is washed with pure water. [I will] hold fast the confession of [my] faith without wavering, for He is faithful that promised.

God already had this planned just for you to partake of it now, because Jesus fulfilled all this 2000 years ago, before you were born - so what could you have done to earn this blessing. What conditions could you have met? None were possible.

Right here you can take that pain of being a victim and an outcast that has kept you in fear and bondage and give it to your Savior, Deliverer, and Healer. You can receive the gift of unconditional love right now. The truth will set you free. Just say,

Jesus, I receive it now.

Perhaps these concerns have been your burden. Perhaps you can come up with a few more of your own. Release them to God Who loves you so much He was willing to leave His rightful Throne of Glory to enable you to live life to the fullest.

You CAN experience freedom in Christ.

There are many men also, who have never known the love of a father; never been encouraged with a kind word or shown respect by a real Dad. Many boys are the victims of brutal child abuse, if not the harshness of a man who was afraid to show his children tenderness. Many boys live with constant criticism and nagging because of childlike behavior and immaturity.

Too often this little boy grows up not knowing who he is; sometimes not knowing what he is! He comes into manhood and is still bound by the anger and rage of betrayal in his heart. Insecurity and confusion prevent him from standing in his rightful place as the head of his own house. He is continuously trying to prove his manhood, sometimes even to a father, long deceased. But this proving ground has many paths of destruction.

Proverbs 6 and 7 reveals what can transpire in a man's soul when he walks on this path. All this, because there is a little boy inside trying to get his dad's approval; or trying to be a man through macho behavior.

Whoever said, boys don't cry. Who laid down that rule! I'll tell you who. It was the author of pain and disintegration. The one who only has destruction in mind for us. The one who wants to destroy our emotions and rob us of the full capacity for love and intimacy.

The foregoing scenarios can be applied to both male and female. Please know this; the same ministry of healing and wholeness is available for women and for men, for boys and for girls. Jesus came to heal the broken hearted 'Whosoevers'. We are all precious in God's sight.

We are a hurting people. That's why we all need Jesus. We have all been ripped off in one way or another. Jesus came to repair the breach. He came to restore us that we might come into our rightful inheritance in the Kingdom of God. But we have to receive from Him. Jesus makes it available to all who will come to Him. And Jesus brings us to the Father.

We Must Always Remember God's Love is Unconditional.

Nothing you do or don't do can change this fact -

that He loves you- Unconditionally.

Don't allow your past to keep you in a grave.

The thief comes not but to steal, and to kill and to destroy; I am come that they might have LIFE, and that they might have it MORE ABUNDANTLY.[13] *Stand fast, therefore, in the liberty with which Christ has made you free, and be not entangled again with the yoke of bondage.*[14]

In John chapters 15-17 Jesus reveals the Father and declares the reason why He came to earth. I pray that you will read these verses until you have a deep understanding and a new revelation of Who He is.

Jesus came to show us the Father. He came to reveal that His Father is *our* Father. He came to reveal that God is a loving Father, not anything like our earthly fathers. Even the most loving earthly father is no match for God the Father. His love and mercy are unparalleled. He led me to write a book called 'Abba Father' and showed me how I can love and trust Him as my Father.

Now this Father God has been waiting for a long time to show you how much He loves you. He will cover you over with His banner of love and hold you securely in His arms. Don't be afraid. Don't let the devil rip you off any longer. If you have asked Jesus to come into your life and be your Savior and Lord then you are a child of God and this is your inheritance. Reach out to Him and He will come running towards you, just as the father of the prodigal son. SO -

Lift your hands and praise Him. Lift your cup and He will fill it to overflowing. Won't you say,

THANK YOU FATHER, FOR YOUR LOVE.
I RECEIVE IT NOW.

My father abandoned us, left my Mother with 5 children under the age of 8. I was 3 years old. He was very abusive to all of us. It took God many years of Him healing my emotions to allow me to see that Father God loves me. Jesus came to reveal His Father. If you will ask Him to show you Who He is - He will.

Now you are in position to receive the ministry of His Fatherhood. His Word tells us that when our mother and father put us down that He will pick us up. In every letter that Paul wrote, he exposes the heart of the Father right there in the beginning.

Grace be unto you, and peace, from God our Father.
Receive His grace and peace as He covers you with His unconditional love from His Father's heart. He's always had His eye on you, waiting for the day you would turn to Him. Your turn to receive is now.

For this cause I bow my knees unto the Father of our Lord Jesus Christ, of whom the whole family in heaven and earth is named, that he would grant you, according to his riches in glory, to be strengthened with might by his Spirit in the inner man; that Christ may dwell in your hearts by faith; that ye, being rooted and grounded in love, May be able to comprehend with all saints, what is the breadth, and length, and depth, and height, and to know the love of Christ, which passes knowledge, that ye may be filled with all the fullness of God. Now to him who is able to do exceedingly abundantly above all that we ask or think, according to the power that works in us..[14]

> Praise and Honor
> and Glory
> to Him Forever.

Abundant mercy, grace to the fore
Came with the Christ, that much and more
He brought His Kingdom, He brought the Gift of Life
And through His death came the end of strife
The law was dead, It is finished came the declaration
For in the beginning came the preparation
He knew all along what was destiny
Yet He came to propose
To bring a war, to bring an end
The enemy at last was revealed and disposed.

Thank You my ABBA - FATHER.

♥

STUDY GUIDE

1. One of the signs of severe anger caused by child abuse of any kind, can be the condition of our teeth and gums. A dentist can spot teeth grinders though the person may be unaware. Very often it causes a lose of our teeth, because clenching loosens the roots and can cause gum disease. If you have this problem know that God can help you. Through the healing of my emotions, God helped me to deal with my angers and fears. Talk to Him about it. He loves you.

2. God is prepared to release you from these burdens of pain and stress. All the anxiety and fears, the anger, resentment, bitterness, and everything else you are carrying; can be thrown into the sea of forgetfulness. How you do that is go to the Lord, humble yourself before Him, and He will draw you

near to Him. Even as His love is flowing through you, you can give all this into His hands.

He will give you grace to go day by day through this valley. You need no longer be a victim to the past. As He shows you each negative emotion, such as hatred for those people, you forgive them, you ask forgiveness for yourself from God for your sin of unforgiveness and hatred; and you forgive yourself. This is the circle of forgiveness that slams the door in satan's face. Then ask God to cleanse you [1Jn 1:9]. Then you tell hatred to go from your life. You will no longer give it place [Eph 4:27].

Be clothed with humility; for God resists the proud, and gives grace to the humble. Humble yourself therefore, under the mighty hand of God, that he may exalt you in due time, casting all your cares upon him; for he cares for you. Be sober, be vigilant, because your adversary the devil, like a roaring lion walks about, seeking whom he may devour. Whom resist steadfast in the faith, knowing that the same afflictions are accomplished in your brethren that are in the world. But the God of all grace, who has called us unto eternal glory by Christ Jesus, after you have suffered [died to self] make you perfect, establish, strengthen and settle you. To him be all glory and dominion forever and ever. Amen [1Peter 5:5-11].

3. Can you look in a mirror and say, I love you and I accept you just the way you are. And thank You God, that You love me just the way I am. You're changing me back to the way you designed in the beginning; in Your image and likeness to reflect Your glory, and to walk in the fruit of the Spirit; and You are helping me grow in my faith and trust in You, day by day.

SCRIPTURES

1. Mal 2:14-15
2. Rom 3:23
3. Jn 17:14
4. 1Jn 3:8
5. Jn 10:17-18
6. Isaiah 65:24
7. Pr 14:30&17:22
8. Dt 23:9
9. Gal 3:14
10. Rom 2:4
11. 1Jn 3:20
12. 1Jn 3:16
13. Jn 10:10
14. Gal 5:1
15. Ep 3:14-21

The longing to love and be loved
Only God can fulfill that need
For one of whom has never loved
The magic - the illusion is constant in the heart
But soul knows truth
And right from wrong is 'herant from youth.
To grow to be masterful Of love's life dream
Can never be as one would seem
The hunger to be loved A desperate need indeed
Can only be fulfilled By one who shares the dream
The Lord of mercy, grace and love
Foresaw the wretched heart reject
To never know the love We have the right to expect
But God is no illusion He created us as such
Because of His great love He died for us to touch.

One day God said to me -
*'Has any one ever told you - You are beautiful.
You should have seen Me smile the day you were born'.*
The Bride of Christ,
Each One So Beautiful
And Loved by the
LORD of LIFE.

Only You can satisfy the hunger of my soul
Only You can reach the depths of my being
Its only You that has loved me
Its only You to Whom I can turn
You've put a longing in my heart
To answer the call,
to surrender all
So let Your love burn -
let my heart burn
Until I am one with You.

❤

FEAR OF LOSING CONTROL

Why do the peoples imagine a vain thing. They take counsel together against the Lord and his anointed saying, Let us break their bands asunder and cast away their cord from us. He that sits in the heavens shall laugh; the Lord shall have them in derision.[1]

Not long after man took his first step into life - he determined to decide for himself what was good for him. Not understanding there would be consequences, he snapped closed the umbrella of God's protection. He ventured out to conquer the world on his own terms.

Even after thousands of years of historical [and hysterical] failure, mankind still pursues independence. Yet that very independence may cause instability, insecurity, and fear; mostly fear that we have made the wrong decision about the issues of our life. Of course we do make some right choices to achieve some goals but anxiety rules over situations more often than not. So we must manipulate people and conditions to maintain the control so we'll always come out on top. For a Christian this can still be a disastrous way of life..................................➔

> Because of fear we become double-minded James 1.8.

Maintaining control can bind us from achieving the one goal most of us want to reach. It could hinder our growth in the Kingdom of God; perhaps prevent us from completely surrendering to God. If we've made Him Savior.

As we mature in walking in the Spirit, we do give different issues over to God, but the fear of giving up all control interferes with the overall Lordship of Jesus Christ. We fear what will happen if we do let go. We maintain faith in the fear, instead of faith and trust in God.

We cannot make our own plans - ask God to bless them - and expect His anointing to cover us. That would signify our will being done, not His. If we will flow with the Spirit,

He will direct our path,[4]

because He works with us, *To will and do of His good pleasure,*[5] Only God can see and know what will happen down the road of our decision. When Jesus taught us to pray, He said exactly what He meant, *Thy will be done on earth as it is in heaven.*[6] The next step is to acknowledge Him as Lord. We do that as we trust in Him to take care of each situation.

God's sovereignty must be recognized. It must be His plan. He must carry it out; notwithstanding many times through His people, His body on the earth. But it's His choice. If we can't or won't yield a situation to God, He can accomplish little in that arena. But of what enormous Kingdom value if our plans were birthed in the heart of God.

What awesome possibilities shall come forth for His glory and exaltation; His majesty enthroned in the very center of our lives.

In trying to control situations we can and do become frustrated with God because perhaps things are not happening fast enough, nor going the way we want. The desire to read His Word, pray and praise Him sort of drifts in and out of our daily experience, little by little. We easily become discouraged.

As we live out our lives, circumstances occur that we automatically deal with. We do this either with anxiety and frustration or in peace and trusting God. The concern is not, will events take place; the concern is who is in charge of the issues, and the outcome.

Fear is often expressed in anger. The purpose of this composition is an attempt to reveal some fears that hinder our receiving all God has for us. Everything that is established in our life has a root somewhere. Sometimes we have to take an axe to the root[7] of old issues, so we can get on with God.

Many times in our growing up we experience a helplessness; an inability to control what's happening to us. Those people that rightly had, or illegally took control of our lives, may not have always managed it wisely. If situations got out of hand, the results could have been devastating to our emotional well being. Our angry reaction to that frustrated impotence [our temper tantrums if you please], only served to establish patterns of blowing our cool when we do not get our own way.

As adults we invent many sophisticated methods to hide our anger, and still maintain control. What can we though, hide from the Lord. When God called to Adam in the garden and said,

Where are you?

It was not because Adam had succeeded in hiding in the bushes. It was a loving Father asking His son if he understood how wanting control over his own life, had separated him from God. We might say to ourselves, Where am I? Anger can also be a satisfying emotion. We're getting even. BUT............→

> Anger is a very negative and seductive emotion.

> Be angry and sin not. Let not the sun go down on your wrath.[8]

What do you do with your anger? Have you nursed it? Kept it close to your heart, as you choose the time and place to explode! Do you manipulate people with it? A father with a short fuse keeps his family thermostat set on anxiety.

> If you live according to the flesh you will die, but if by the Spirit you put to death the deeds of the body, you will live. For as many as are led by the Spirit of God, these are the sons of God.[9]

Only what's done through the Spirit of God has eternal value and brings Life. What is done through the self-centered desires of what is our thing can only bring death to that situation. No flesh will glory in God's presence. There are also times when we deceive ourselves by convincing us and others that we are, a responsible person. [This has nothing to do with raising our children].

We take responsibility for this or that issue to deal with, or we feel responsible to do this or that for a certain person; etc. Sometimes this is a cloak for controlling a circumstance or the people involved. It boils down to motive. Only God can search our heart and reveal the truth. We must be sure to understand that,

> To whom ye yield yourselves servants [bond-slaves] to obey, his servants, [bond-slaves] ye are whom ye obey whether of sin to death or of obedience unto righteousness because of the infirmity [weakness] of your flesh.[10]

Controlling and manipulating people and situations has its roots in witchcraft. Gal 5:20 tells us this is a work of the flesh but we can be sure satan is somewhere in there helping to raise King Self to a place of prominence. In our rebellion toward God we may easily give place to the devil.

> God resists the proud and gives grace to the humble.[11]

Giving up our right to anything constitutes a change of motives and attitudes, and finding His grace and peace.

Demanding our rights translates into being in control of that issue. The drive to meet our need may result in frustration, anxiety and anger, even sometimes rage.

We don't have the resources to meet all our needs and no other person was created to do so. Only God is able - Who is ever ready to bless us with His peace and rest [Heb 4:9] as He works out the details in the fulfillment of His will in our lives; to bring us to wholeness in spirit, soul and body [1Th 5:23].

Manipulation and control also comes in another form, that of judgment and criticism of others. Buried in the midst of this gross abomination to God [1Co 4], is hidden our own agenda to change people into our own image. If they are not behaving according to our criteria, we take on the responsibility to change them; but we do it behind their back, and share all their discrepancies with the world; as if our emotional outburst will have this kind of effect.

Our need to control is usually rooted in our fear of losing control. We manipulate people, situations, and solutions. In our ignorance God may become a name on our list. God has committed Himself to bringing our lives into the fullness of His inheritance.[12]

He is also committed to leading us into a life totally dependent on Him.[13] An independent spirit is a spirit in rebellion to God. The bottom line to being a son of God is total dependence on the Father. If you want to see how to do that, look unto Jesus.

The Son can do nothing of himself, but what he sees the Father do, for whatever things he does, these also does the Son likewise.[14] *He was equal with God, yet he made himself of no reputation and took upon himself the form of a servant.*[15]

So we come to a place of realizing that other people controlling our lives can bring destruction. We ourselves when controlling our lives, can bring frustration and disaster. The ultimate lie of the world system: take control of your life! The real truth is there are too many hidden variables that we cannot take into consideration. Look at Luke Chapter twelve. This rich man thought he was in total control of his life and goods - for many years to come - But -

This night your soul is required of you.

I'm not declaring that if one does not yield to God that they die. It is clear that no matter what comes into your life or how long a life you live, when God is in control then,
All things work together for good to them that love God and are called according to his purpose.[16]
Matt 18:3-5 *Assuredly, I say to you, unless you are converted and become as little children, you will by no means enter the kingdom of heaven. Therefore whoever humbles himself as this little child is the greatest in the kingdom of heaven.*

In our knot hole view of life's parade, our evaluation of circumstances is many times stretched into our unrenewed imagination and fantasy sets in. Many of our decisions are based on these two elements. This is why our mind must be continually renewed by the washing of the *Water of the Word* [Eph 5:26].

But our gracious and merciful loving Father, Who can search the hidden motives of our heart, and spans from eternity to everlasting, can see our problems from every angle, start to finish.

He already has the solution worked out to bring our lives into divine order. Oftentimes we take control because our emotions are going haywire. There can be that spirit of fear pushing us into not waiting on God. Don't you understand? You will always have tribulation in your life. The issue is, how will you handle it?

We must learn to wait on God. Patience is something that comes over time, of not demanding our thing, now! The Word says patience is worked in us through tribulation. We all fight that word, so we make the foolish statement that we will not pray for patience because it will bring tribulation into our lives.

We would do well to read this verse in context. I pray you will stop and study this in Romans 5:1-5. It is an awesome passage revealing the maturing of the saints of God. It begins with being justified by faith and goes on to His grace that we may rejoice in hope of the glory of God, and to glory in tribulation.

These are times of testing our integrity, giving us the opportunity to resist the enemy and turn to God; realizing how He strengthens us to go through the rough times if we depend on Him and not on our own resources. This not only works in us patience to wait on Him and come into His rest;

but brings us to experience the presence of God, to deliver us from shame and release into our heart the magnificent love of God.

It is a ploy of the devil to get us to fight this whole idea by taking it out of context. Jesus tells us in John 16:33 that in the world we will have tribulation. It will come whether we want it or not. But God assures us and tells us that in 1Jn 5:4-5

Jesus has overcome the world.

Remember Abraham and Sarah. Taking control of God's promise produced Ishmael - the bane of Israel's existence for all these centuries. Rebekah and her son Jacob also took matters into their own hands. God had promised the older would serve the younger - so Jacob stole the birthright and the blessing from his older twin brother. He would fulfill his destiny his own way; never mind what was God's plan.

The life of Jacob is recorded from Genesis 25-50. Jacob - the supplanter, [i.e., to take the place of - by treachery]. Always in control of his life by hidden agendas and fraud. Even though he had an awesome encounter with the God of his fathers at Bethel, and chapter 28 tells us of God's covenant promises to him; Jacob continued to live out deceiving ways.

How interesting that the man to whom God sent Jacob was also a deceiver! He duped Jacob into marrying Rachael's sister first; cheated Jacob out of some wages and would have sent him away empty-handed except for God's hand in controlling the genetics and breeding process.

After seeing his best of flocks stolen out from under his nose, Laban was furious when he discovered the theft of his household idols. Perhaps Rachel took her father's icons as they were leaving Haran in case her husband's god didn't come through and wanted that protection to fall back on.

Jacob did not know she had stolen them, just as he had stolen from others. Jacob believed he was so in control of things that he unknowingly cursed his beloved Rachel with death before he even thought about it. [Gen 31& 35.18].

Jacob paid back with the substance of his house; his beloved wife Rachel, the one for whom he had worked 14 years. She died in childbirth. She never lived to see her babies grow up. In the end, both Jacob and Laban reaped what they sowed.

Now here in Genesis 32:22-32, Jacob must come to terms with God and with his heart. We must all come to the place called Jabbok; the place of pouring out, of emptying, to utterly make void; and have our nature changed. We can have an astounding born-again experience and yet still continue in our old ways. The contenders: soul verses spirit! Which will rule and reign?

We rule over our soul through our spirit in which we have given Holy Spirit permission to lead and guide us.
And God said unto Jacob, what is thy name? This is like God asking Adam, *Where are you?* Did God not remember Jacob's name? He wanted Jacob [and Adam] to realize and understand what and where he was; bring him to his senses.

The fear of man can and will control us.
Jacob was terrified that Esau would kill him and his family. Isn't that what happens when the bottom falls out of our plans. A great terror and fear of evil comes on us as we think of what people will do to us when they realize we have been conniving and manipulating them. Now confronted with the harvest of what he has sowed, Jacob prays, and God delivers him.

Isn't it interesting that his sons also learned to be deceivers, [Gen 37]. They found an easy solution for their hatred and jealousy of their brother, Joseph. They also paid a high price [Gen 43-50].

How it must have tortured Jacob to have his beloved son Joseph taken from him; a situation he could not control. And the despair when he was forced to let go of Benjamin [Gen 45]. Both of these boys were the only sons of Rachel, his most beloved wife. And think of how it soaked down into the depths of Jacob's being - as Joseph unfolded the story of his life in Egypt...

God was in charge all this time.
Because of submission to letting God be in charge, Joseph was raised second to the throne of pharaoh, and was able to save from the famine, God's inheritance in the earth.

And so, after many years of God dealing with Jacob, we come to the end of his life and we see a humble man blessing his sons and worshiping God [Gen 49]. No longer Jacob: arrogant conniver; now he is Israel: and has favor with God and man.

Many times we don't realize and understand what we're doing but God can open our eyes. He is ever ready to deliver us from our own worst enemy - US! Now we allow Jesus to be Lord of all; to rule and reign with Christ; changed into His image, from glory to glory. There is healing and deliverance as we humbly come before our Lord and Savior.

You can release all your burdens to your Lord.

And therefore will the Lord wait, that he may be gracious unto you, and therefore will he be exalted, that he may have mercy upon you; for the Lord is a God of justice; blessed are all they that wait for him...He will be very gracious unto thee at the voice of thy cry; when he shall hear it, he will answer thee.[17]

Standing in faith, trusting in God, peace in your heart, with full assurance of hope - this is waiting on God.

And having done all, to stand.[18]

Unless we renounce our right to control, He cannot work out His perfect plan for us that stretches down the road on which He has planted our feet. God wants us to freely release ourselves into His capable hands. God's love for us is never-ending and so out of proportion to what we actually deserve; but He loves us anyway.

I will instruct thee and teach thee in the way which thou shalt go. I will guide thee with mine eye.[19]

God doesn't want to control us like puppets. He wants us to let go of the controls so He can lead and guide.

For it is God who works in you to will and to do of his good pleasure. ♡

Can you imagine that you are God's good pleasure? Isn't that a delightful thought? Did you ever realize that it was God's good pleasure to give us the fragrance of a rose - and then to give us the ability to smell it?

God is a lot more concerned with maturing us than we are. Sometimes we are bound by fear of the unknown. Because God's motivation is to bring us into a relationship of trust and rest in Him - He does not always show us the process, although He does tell us about the reward for our faith in His Word.

Too often our fears speak too loud for us to hear His words of peace. We feel safer in our pit rather than be exposed in the open to, Only God knows what! If God has seemed to quit on you and you're not getting answers to your dilemma there is all probability that you are terrified to make yourself vulnerable. Webster's dictionary tells us vulnerable means; capable of receiving injuries. The capability is there and that's what we fear. At some point we've declared, I'll never let them hurt me again.

The reality is you will keep on being hurt until you release it and yourself to God. A wound can only begin to heal when it is cleansed of all the dirt and infection. It has been taught how we can live on the right side of the But - I've been devastated,

BUT - God can deliver me.

If we fear to give up control because all hell will break loose; the reality is this. Between our fears and stubbornness lies the arena that satan is having a field day. The situation keeps getting worse and there's no relief in sight. Well, there is no hope in our own answers, anyway. So there can be no victory. God will renew our mind if we decide to do things His way.

Rom 12:1-2 *I beseech you therefore, brethren, by the mercies of God, that you present your bodies a living sacrifice, holy, acceptable to God, which is your reasonable service. And do not be conformed to this world, but be transformed by the renewing of your mind, that you may prove what is that good and acceptable and perfect will of God.*

God's Word says; He is my defender, my provider, healer, deliverer, my high tower,[20] we can abide under the shadow of His wings, in His secret place, in His pavilion; we can trust in Him,

1 Peter 5:6-7 *Therefore humble yourselves under the mighty hand of God, that He may exalt you in due time, casting all your care upon Him, for He cares for you.*

He is compassionate, merciful, forgiving and gracious.

And, He loves you so much that He died for you.

God is waiting on us to realize we do not have the resources within ourselves to fix it. We cannot change situations and people by our fears, anger, resentment and control. Valuable changes come about only by choosing to yield the situation to God.

If we confess our sins he is faithful and just to forgive us our sins and to cleanse us from all unrighteousness.[21]

The Father is waiting and searching for the heart that would depend on Him, as He waited and longed for the Prodigal Son. I know He is speaking of us, His wandering children.

That boy never stopped being a son, he was an unprofitable one! He wanted control of his own life. As we forgive each and all that shared in our hurtful experiences we must be aware of our responsibility in reacting as we did. Anger, even hatred and bitterness could be harbored in our heart. Give it all to God.

As we forgive, so our Father forgives us, and cleanses us from the results of our sin. He can help us form new habit patterns as we break the power of the old ones through the Blood of Jesus. Resist the devil. Draw near to God and repent of any anger and rebellion toward Him. Full awareness of the truth of Jesus' words in Jn 15, *Without me ye can do nothing*, breaks the power of satan's lies that established the fear of losing control; If I'm in charge, nothing can hurt me. David's trust in God and recognizing His Lordship enabled David to abandon his life into his Lord God Almighty. He could declare in Psalm 4,

I will both lie down in peace, and sleep;
for thou Lord, only makes me to dwell in safety.

Consider this young man a mere shepherd - anointed king over Israel. But he did not march up to the palace and demand his crown and robe. I believe David hid many things in his heart. He'd learned to wait on God. David had already turned the reins of his life over to his Lord, and declared,

Blessed are all they who put their trust in him.[22]

David learned as we must, how to rule over his own heart before he would rule over a city.[23] Young David began to learn the way of submission to authority. I wonder what went through his mind when Saul threw that first spear. He had several options. The Bible tells us,

Offenses will come, but woe to that man
by whom the offense cometh.[24]

What Saul did to David was by our standards, outrageous! God had a definite plan in mind, but He didn't say. Hindsight is a great teacher if it is allowed. David ran, and lived in caves but he would not demand his rights, stand up to the authority God put over him, nor take control of his life by returning the spear.

God is looking for a totally - empty of Self - vessel through which to manifest the Kingdom of God. David's throne - the anointing and authority - will be remembered throughout eternity, because David's anointing and authority was developed in the heart of God; not in the vain imaginations of a power seeker.

When his son Absalom tried to usurp the Kingdom he did not defend himself. David said, *Hey, Who does it belong to, anyway!* [See Ps 27:13-14]. Even the One to whom the worlds belong, gave up His rights and became an empty vessel for the Father to manifest through Him, the Kingdom of God. [Heb 11.6]

He is a rewarder of them that diligently seek him
Now, Who better is there that we can give ourselves to, than a loving Father God, Who holds the worlds in His hands, and created you for His good pleasure.[25] He is faithful. We can trust in Him above all else. Because of our nature, we need God to fence us in. Psalm 32 portrays a horse that must be bridled, *Lest they come near unto thee.*

This is speaking of a wild stallion, one that is used to running free.

No bridle, no restraints. He rears his head on a strong stiff neck and races into the wind, to go where he chooses. He can hardly be caught. When he is cornered he rages at the one who would dare to quell his independent spirit. This passage also speaks of a mule, known for its stubbornness.

If we jump the fence and run when things get hard, we may never know how God wanted to plant us into the very source of Life; to be established in His prosperity and increase and bring forth the life of God into our environment.

In verse 8 God speaks to the submissive spirit that chooses the leadership of the Holy Spirit - our guide - our counselor. He dwells within us and longs to lead us in His path of righteousness.

Paul was like a wild stallion, until Jesus stood in the road of his madness and confronted his own personal ideas of how he should serve his God. He would even control the religious ideals of others.

As he yielded to the Lord's harness, that independent spirit was broken and Paul became the Master's bondslave. In Romans 1 He declares himself to be a servant of Jesus Christ. The same word, which means bondslave, he uses in Romans 6:20.

When ye were [bondslaves] of sin...what fruit had ye then in those things of which ye are now ashamed. For the end of those things is death. But now being made free from sin and became [bondslaves] to God, ye have your fruit unto holiness, and in the end everlasting life. SO -

Choose ye this day who you will serve.[26]
You cannot serve two masters.[27]
Your full inheritance in the Kingdom of God awaits your choice. And,
*I will instruct thee and teach thee
in the way which thou shalt go;
I will guide thee with mine eye.
Be not like the horse or mule,
that have no understanding,
whose mouth must be held in
with bit and bridle,
lest they come near unto you.*

A rebellious horse is controlled by a short bridle, so he can't have his head. He is held in.

And if ye be without chastisement, of which all are partakers, then ye are bastards, and not sons.[28]

If life has been turmoil, with frustration, chaos and confusion; if you lack direction - and it seems you are swimming upstream in mud - ask God if rebellion and an independent spirit is at the root. Then you may quickly choose 1 John 1:9. Then read Exodus 21:1-6, and after that, ask God to pierce your ears so you can hear that still small voice.

Jesus was tempted in all ways,[29] and could have chosen to do his own thing. He didn't. Jesus is our forerunner. Total dependence on the Father. He did it first. There was however, nothing available to Jesus that is not available for us.

#1. Jesus did not have a sin nature.

He took ours to the cross; it died with Him, and went to the place of the dead, sheol. It's still there. That was our Adam nature. The thing that compelled us to sin.

It takes a while for our spirit to realize it doesn't have to fight with the old man, as it did before. In continuing to reckon him dead, our spirit grows in submission to the Holy Spirit Who dwells within.

The object is for our soul [personality, character, intentions of our heart] to come into subjection to our spirit which is in submission to the Holy Spirit. If the Old Man no

longer rules over our soul we will learn to yield more easily. As we appropriate His death on the cross, we can reckon our old man dead and we are,
> *United together in his death,*
> *and in the likeness of his resurrection life.*[30]

Likeness is from a root word meaning, in the same place together. By the Spirit, we were on the cross with Jesus and our old nature paid the penalty for sin - death. We were resurrected with Him, now we can, *Put on the new man.*[31]

Water baptism is for us, the analogy of His death and resurrection. We are raised the New Man in Him [Col 2.12].

#2. Jesus was empowered with the Holy Spirit and declared to be the Son of God when He was baptized by John. So all the resources that were available to Jesus are available to us; to enable us to walk in victory. And if that's not enough

#3. He also gives us His strength and His love to help us will to do His will. And do not forget GRACE [Phil 3.13].

John 14:12-13 *Most assuredly, I say to you, he who believes in Me, the works that I do he will do also; and greater works than these he will do, because I go to My Father.*

Jesus was in constant communication with His Father. We have an open door into the presence of our Father.[32]

1Cor 4:20 tells us, *The Kingdom of God is not in word, but in power.*

It is not just a matter of what we say in our choosing the righteous path. It is the fact that we are choosing to do His will. This attitude of submission gives our loving God the opportunity to meet us where we are. He pours upon us the same grace and peace Jesus had in every trial that came His way; especially peace in Gethsemane when He knew He was to be crucified. [Mt 10:38-39].

This is the place of breaking that soulish man of self-will and self-love; of having an opinion about everything; always knowing what to do in every situation through our own will power; depending on our own strength to carry us through.

And please note that our flesh, our mind and our emotions can be very deceiving. We have learned to protect our inner feelings; so to God is asking us to exchange them for the fruit of the Spirit. Now change does not come all at once nor in our timing. We have to take one day at a time.

We give all we have, all we know about, over to God [Mt 10:26]
> God's purpose is to bring us to the cross.
> To die to our self - determination.
> Nothing is hidden from Him.

But there are aspects to our personality and deep things in our heart that are unknown to us. The Holy Spirit Who dwells in our spirit knows everything about us. He is there to help us make our decisions according to the Word of God.

Very often we believe we have given something over to God, but there seems to be no rest in our heart. As we pray and trust in the promises of God we may ask God to search our hearts, and see if there be any specific place we are maintaining control. Sometimes we have to go deeper.

We can also ask God to show any stronghold of the enemy so we can use our God-given authority to kick it out of our life. Rom 2:4 It is the goodness of God that leads us to repentance. And Psalm 140:7 declares:

O God, the Lord, the strength of my salvation,
thou hast covered my head in the day of battle.

Not only does He give His angels charge over us to keep us in all our ways as we walk with God, and they encamp around us according to Psalm 91; but He also covers us with His presence as we choose to go to battle with the enemy of our soul, to break us free from bondage, as we see the truth of the Word and choose to walk in it.

John 8:31-32 *Then Jesus said to those Jews who believed Him, If you abide in My word, you are My disciples indeed. And you shall know the truth, and the truth shall make you free.*

There may be a lot of changes in our life, but it is more important to remember that we are 'becoming'. The more we give to God, the old self, we are becoming more like Jesus. We were created in His image and He's getting us back there as we are becoming more like Him.

The Israelites were given manna in the desert. The word manna translates into, What is this? We know that God's Word is our manna for today, our Bread of Life. Jesus is the Living Bread; the Bible is the Written Bread. As we read it and desire to feed on it, we can ask questions. What is this? What does it mean? What does it mean to me? How can I

apply it to my life? Remember each gathered according to his need. Pr 30:8 says,
> Feed me with food convenient for me.

As we feed on and apply His Word - His Manna, to our lives, then He will sustain our lives as we increase,

Eph 4.13 *In wisdom and stature and in favor with God and man... Till we all come in the unity of faith, and the knowledge of the Son of God, unto a perfect man, unto the measure of the stature of the fullness of Christ.*

Perhaps the greatest battle for some of us, is to let go of our past. We can be paralyzed by our past. Many cannot move on with God because they will not let go. It rules our emotions and decisions as though it were a tyrant. But if we think it is all we have, we are afraid to let go. We think familiar pain is better than the unknown.

No, we cannot know every detail of that which God has in store, but He gives wonderful revelation and joy as we travel down the road with Him. You can safely place your past into God's loving hand. Let go and let God handle it for you.

And if we will submit and yield to our gracious merciful loving Savior, He will teach us to trust in Him. Then we can deal with the fear to let go. Fear is a spirit [2Tim 1:7]. Determine you will no longer give it place; that you are going to pray and trust in the Name of your Lord Jesus.

You have authority over the devil through the mighty Name of Jesus and the Blood He shed on the cross for you. Satan was defeated by the Blood of Jesus and it is a mighty tool in your hand to dislodge any unwanted visitors. He can no longer stay. He is there by deception, hiding in our ignorance of his presence. Mark 16 tells us Jesus has given us ALL authority over ALL the enemy. Tell him, The Blood of Jesus is against you. You have to leave!

It is the Holy Spirit within, showing you the root of the problem. Pay attention to how He is leading you. You prayed for guidance. You prayed for help. He will even show you how to pray, listen for His voice. Listen for His direction. Right now you can give Him all your stress and anxiety.

We are in a spiritual battle. We have to be trained just like our Army and Marines. We are given equipment just as they are, to help us come out on the winning side. The Holy Spirit will always make us overcomers if we follow His direction. We are given our armor in Ephesians chapter six. Study this passage and pray that God gives you understanding. He will teach you and guide you in learning how to defeat the enemy.

It is mandatory we all learn spiritual warfare, because God wants to fulfill Psalm 149 in His people. The nations, nobles and kings are the principalities and powers mentioned in this chapter, Ephesians six.

God desires to do a quick work but some of us are escape artists. I'm grateful to know the cross does not hold its victim forever. Resurrection life is our inheritance. When we die to controlling our life, resurrection happens!

Don't let the fear of losing control stop you from giving your life to Jesus. Actually you will be more in control as you seek His wisdom in matters of your life. You always have your free will.

I pray it will be for God's life in you.

Only in this breaking of our soulish power, can new life come forth. We are such a proud and self-righteous people. God resists the proud, He is for ones that will obey Him. He knows best. But He is not a hard task-master.

I thank God He comes back time after time, to help us. How wonderful it would be if we had with others, the patience God has with us. His loving-kindness and mercy are new every morning.[33]

He chose us in him before the foundation of the world, that we should be holy and without blame before him in love, having predestined us unto the adoption of sons by Jesus Christ to himself, according to the good pleasure of his will.

♥♥♥

If we seek Him daily and delight to know His ways, Then shall your light break forth like the morning, and your health shall spring forth speedily, and your righteousness shall go before you, and the glory of the Lord shall be your rear guard. Then shall you call and the Lord shall answer; you shall cry and He shall say, Here I Am. [34]

He has made everything beautiful in it's time. Also He has put eternity in their hearts, except that no one can find out the work that God does from the beginning to end. I know that there is nothing better for them than to rejoice.[35] *I know that whatever God does, it shall be forever. Nothing can be added to it and nothing taken from it. God does it, that men should fear before Him.* [Eccl 3.11]

STUDY GUIDE

1. Why is it so important to trust in God?
2. The world teaches us to take control of our life. When we come into the Kingdom, we operate from the same manual. What must we do?
3. Would you say that some of the anger you display now, is a response to not being able to control situations in your past.
4. Is it true or false that we can really be in control, or are we being manipulated by the enemy of our soul, Paul the Apostle of grace - so arrogant and presumptuous as to assume he knew Who God was and what He wanted; that he demanded people worship God as he said - not allowing God to be God - Paul wanted to be in control. But God also saw in Paul a heart for truth, and so He pierced his heart with Truth - and out poured grace; enough for Paul and running over to bless those he once persecuted to death. It is God's mercy that allows us to be who we are and make our own decisions. Paul saw God's mercy as he came face to face with himself - there on the road to Damascus.
5. Is God really able to help us? 2Tim 1:12; Rom 8:28; 2Cor 9:8
6. What is it that pushes us into controlling our life? What does the Word say about it?
7. Doing our own thing is another name for rebellion and independence. What does God say about this?
8. Did Jesus do His own thing or the Father's will?
Heb 10:9 *then He said, "Behold, I have come to do Your will, O God."*
9. How did Jesus make it possible for us to follow in His footsteps?
10. At this time you may want to ask the Holy Spirit to search your heart and evaluate your motives.
11. What can be some of the first steps of walking in newness of life?
   Eph 4:22-24; Rom 12:1-2; Pr 3:5-8; Ps 62:5-8

PRAYER: So many 'what ifs' flood my mind, it's hard to sort them out. I look to You Lord, to help me let go and I trust in You to take me step by step. I choose now to let You be in charge of my life.

Ps 5:11 But let all those rejoice who put their trust in You; Let them ever shout for joy,

It's freedom that You've given me
To seek a place called home
Freedom from my
slave sick soul
To be Your very own
To walk in grace and mercy
To know You as my Lord
And walk in heavenly places
According to Your Word
To know who I am in You
So at last I would belong
That in Your grace and mercy
I would be strong
Not led by all the darkness
That snares in unbelief
But to walk by Your Spirit
For my soul in sweet release ❤

SCRIPTURE

1. Ps 2:1-4
2. 1Ti 6:15
3. Ph 2:12
4. Pr 3:5-8
5. Ph 2:13
6. Mt 6:10
7. Lk 3:9
8. Eph 4:26
9. Rom 8:13-14
10. Rom 6:16-19
11. James 5:6
12. Eph 1:13-14
13. Jn 1:12-13
14. Jn 5:19
15. Ph 2:7
16. Rom 8:28-30
17. Isa 30:18-19
18. Eph 6:13
19. Ps 32:8
20. Ps 144,2
21. 1Jn 1:9
22. Ps 2:12
23. Pr 25-28; and 16:32
24. Lk 17:1
25. Lk 12:32
26. Josh 24:15
27. Mt 6:24
28. Heb 12:8
29. Heb 4:15
30. Rom 6
31. Eph 4:24
32. He 10:19-22
33. Lam 3
34. Isa 58:8-9
35. Ec 3:11-14

VICTORY OVER FEAR.

> *And this is the victory that overcame the world,
> even our faith.*[1]

When God created man in His own image He proclaimed that creation to be very good. Psalm 119:1 tells us,
> *The heavens declare the glory of God,
> and the firmament shows his handiwork.*

Of all God's creation, man is the most precious to Him, made in His own image. He has chosen man as His inheritance:[2]
Isaiah 43:7 *Even every one who is called by my name; for I have created him for my glory; I have formed him; yea, I have made him*

To share with us all He is and all He has.[3]

God is Spirit and He communicates with us through His Spirit, so He had to make us spirit also. We are a soul [our identity, personality, character], with a spirit, walking around in a body. Among other attributes, God has identity, character, and personality, and so we are. His unlimited imagination has made each person unique. We are created in the image of God.

We were given a physical body that we might relate to the physical world in which we live. We communicate with God through our spirit which has been awakened by His indwelling Spirit. We communicate with our society through our soul. Within our soul dwells our emotions, our will and attitudes that motivate our life - our self-awareness.

When Adam sinned his spirit died. His spiritual perception
was gone. He could no longer communicate with God as he had before. Adam's spirit had been bonded to God in relationship, but God cannot fellowship with sin and rebellion, and so the bond was broken. And of course, their body began to decay as also did the rest of creation. Adam had been created so perfectly that it took 930 years for him to die.

The wages of sin is death. As the centuries passed by so did the process of sin and decay increase and cause man to perish within a few short years. All Adam's progeny have been born with a dead spirit and a sin-nature, incapable of relationship with their Creator. When we are born again the Holy Spirit comes to dwell within our spirit and imparts eternal life. We are again brought into union with our Creator, of one accord with our Father.

To be renewed in the spirit of our mind is vital for our Kingdom survival.[4] We are transformed by the process of this renewing.[5] The Holy Spirit gives us the power of choice to use our will to rule over our soul. Attitudes and physical habit patterns can be changed to line up with His Word. As our mind is renewed we become more and more capable of making choices according to the will of God. *It is God Who works in us to will and to do of his good pleasure.*[6] So God makes the changes corresponding to our cooperation.

Romans 6.19 *Even so now, yield your members servants to righteousness unto holiness.*

Before we learn to walk in the Spirit of God - before our spirit man rises up and we begin to understand the spirit realm of God's creation, we live in our soul, our emotions and feelings. We see, hear and experience many things that disturb us because we can't understand with our flesh what is happening. Before we are born again we can't communicate with God through our spirit. We are well aware of a spirit world or dimension but most often it produces anxiety, confusion and deception. It can also make us curious and apprehensive. Some of our fears had their beginnings in our dark bedroom so many years ago with imaginary noises in the closet or under the bed.

When I was very young my older sister played hooky and hid in my bedroom closet. No one knew where she was. When she heard Mother's plans to call the police she decided she had better come out. She was sitting on a storage box and had to get off - my room was dark - the door was closed. What do you think was going on in my head and my emotions as she groped around to find the closet door. I tried to cry out but my throat was paralyzed with fear. She heard my whimpering and said to me, Shut up stupid, it's only me. This added offense to the fear I bore for years.

Our fantasies may give way to the fear of evil which comes from not understanding the unknown. The forces of darkness take advantage of our ignorance and helplessness. Even as adults this fear of evil can be tormenting. God in His great mercy delivered me from the fear of evil, fear of the dark and many others.

There are some who may falter in their Christian walk because of the fear of evil. Somehow our minds connect the fear of the supernatural with anything we don't understand in the Kingdom of God. Satan will continue to keep us in bondage for as long as he can. Remember every area of our life that is not established on trust in God, the enemy has a place of fear or uncertainty on which to stand - giving an opportunity for his lies to speak. He also takes advantage of our curiosity to lead us in the path of witchcraft and divination through astrology, ouija boards and the like. In these last years we can turn on the TV and always find a program or movie exhibiting the black arts.

These days we are flooded with demonic activity. An unbeliever would probably zone it out, or it would sear their mind. This is exactly the plan of the destroyer. I'm always amazed as people share with me some of the spooky games they played as children and reveal the many times they experimented with seances and table lifting; with ghost stories and games such as bloody Mary. As they remember the power they felt and other manifestations from the Kingdom of darkness they begin to realize how they opened doors for the enemy to gain ground for destruction as he leads them further into deception. Hidden within all this activity is the spirit of the fear of evil that may never manifest itself as such, until that person decides to live for God in spirit and in truth.

The devil entices young ones into the world of fantasy by many avenues. We must understand that when we give him an inch he will never stop until he has our whole life in his control. He works under cover and makes evil seem good or at least of no harm until he has his victim bound. There was no TV in my childhood. Programs dealing with the occult came much later. I dream of Jeannie and Samantha were programs used mightily by satan to entice people to seek and discover psychic abilities; used to pull them deeper into occult experiences.

Now-a-days TV and movies are much more blatant. TM and the martial arts are other avenues of mind control the enemy uses to bind us. There are many doors into the supernatural realm that will entrap. These things seem innocent of themselves - but it behooves us to investigate the foundations of such activities.

Anything that makes us self sufficient, has a root of evil and is sure to branch out into satan's domain. Some things seem harmless because we don't understand the roots. What happens because of a lack of knowledge? If we will give God permission to search our heart and try us, and see if there be any wicked way in us; not defend any activity we took part in, He will answer!

His purging and refining fire will torch the ground the enemy stands on. Anything of Kingdom value will remain. Yes Lord, I surrender. I ask You to begin to cleanse me of all that does not please You. He will take you step by step into His secret place of rest and cover you with His arms of love as the Blood of Jesus puts the enemy to flight. *When we confess our sin he is faithful and just to forgive us and cleanse us of all unrighteousness* ....➔

> He will teach us spiritual warfare.
> [Eph 6:12-18]

Please remember the things of God *are* supernatural. Certainly they are not of this world.[7] Now God has set natural laws of the universe in motion and that is what continues to operate such as gravity, etc. For one who has not yet matured in the Lord, the mysterious ways of the spirit realm, good or evil, may bring apprehension. Often a person needs deliverance from the spirit of the fear of evil before they can receive the baptism in the Holy Spirit [that was me]. Many of God's wonders - we have no understanding. God has given us supernatural gifts through the Holy Spirit, over the enemy. There are strongholds of resistance we must learn to break through, by the power of the name of Jesus, and His Blood.

I continue to marvel at our merciful and gracious God that moves in our lives in spite of our immaturity or unbelief. But we must be sure to understand that His highest purpose is to bring us into a foundational faith and trust. We can see that it is only faith that pleases God; and there is the other half of the Scripture many people overlook;

We must believe that he is and that he is a rewarder of them that diligently seek him.[8]

Some of us are afraid to look for the reward because we fear God in an unhealthy way. We only see Him as condemning or unreachable because of the qualities of other relationships. Some of us don't even know what a reward is.

The Holy Spirit begins a work in us that we might expand our borders of trust, and the fear of evil rises up. If we give up control of our situation we will be vulnerable to all kinds of disasters. Everything will fall apart. The roots of negative experiences give place to the growth and strength of fear. Strongholds of self-protection and walls of resistance are surrounded by the fear to let go. It takes longer to write about this and read it, than it does for the spirit of fear to grip our heart and tell us, NO! An apprehensive fear may rule in situations that will bring distrust or dread concerning the future, a foreboding; anticipation of disappointment, anxiety [for instance in the arena of believing for healing]. But, this does not have the authority to continue in your life. [2Tim 1].

*God has not given [you] a spirit of fear,
but of love, power and a sound mind*

Allow the peace from God your Father, and the Lord Jesus Christ to rule, [umpire, to arbitrate, govern, prevail] in your heart and mind [Cor 3:15]. ....→

| Jehovah Jireh, The God Who sees our need. |

Deliverance is yours now! Resist the devil, draw near to God. Ask Him to show you how to pray as you ought. Yes, I was set free from the spirit of the fear of evil.

As we grow in Him we can come to trust that He will act in our behalf. But more than that - God desires to bless and fulfill our lives so that we can receive from Him and become a channel of blessing for others. Perhaps there are prayer needs that have taken especially long for God to answer. Being on my emergency priority list I thought surely God would take care of it soon. As the months and years went by without response I began to despair and became bitter. [it was a part of my anger at God] The longer I waited the more I feared that God had forgotten me and left me behind. I became angry with people who would tell me I didn't have enough faith. Fear then would take over to prove to me that God would never provide for me because of my own inadequacy. Oftentimes it can be our own family that seems to knock the pins out from under. I didn't realize any faith I had was overshadowed by bitterness and fear; coupled with rejection ...

Fear can be a mighty stronghold.

One day I was graphically delivered from all that, and rose to a new understanding of the God who rescued me.

Hebrews 12:15 shows us that bitterness can spring up from not walking in the grace of God as we wait for Him to respond to our walking in faith. The enemy binds our heart with fear that God has left us, or that we deserve punishment not love.

What happens here is this. Jesus is the Alpha and Omega, the beginning and the end of our faith. Alpha [start]--- Omega [end]. In between [---] is our resting place as He brings about the answer. This is the place to know - This is the place to walk in His grace. Ask and receive it.

Our prayers can be defiled by bitterness if we haven't learned to wait on God - our faith goes out the window. God wants to deliver us from fear and give us a sound mind; the mind of Christ.[9] Then we can understand God is building our house to withstand the assaults of the enemy [Mt 7:25], to walk through this life strong and mature. This is a timely process not one night stands. Construction and establishment takes place through our fiery trials - each brick taken from the oven in its turn, to produce our heavenly mansion, the image of the Son.

The Sermon on the Mount in Matthew 5-7 is the way of a born again believer, walking in the Spirit, living for God, obedient to His Word and receiving a daily supply of grace. The Our Father in the middle of the Sermon declares God's purposes for us; to recognize Who He is, that we can know the will of God and affirms His intention to set us free from the fear of Evil. He has seated us in heavenly places with Christ Jesus [Eph 2.6]. The enemy is under our feet. We have the authority. We can possess our land, fly a new flag, declare new ownership.

Some of us are so overcome by fear because of childhood insecurities and rejection that we lack self esteem and oftentimes suffer an identity crisis on a daily basis. Before any of us launch out to find ourselves, remember that being changed into His image means we carry His I.D. papers in our heart. We no longer need be vulnerable to the lies we once believed. We no longer need to withdraw or panic because of stressful situations.

Use the Scriptures to defeat him, as did Jesus; and He is making me strong in Him. I'm learning to trust Him more.

We are all given a measure of faith. We can aim our faith in the right direction and forgive those people of whom have seemingly failed to give support. The fear of betrayal can hinder one from fulfilling commitments. Ask God to deal with your fear, doubt and unbelief. Deliverance is ours! If one is hesitant in making any firm decisions to the point of anxiety or frustration, perhaps double-mindedness is the culprit. At the bottom of all this can be a fear of failure; or the fear of criticism. Were you put down or embarrassed by wrong judgments in the past?

Did you decide it would be better if you never made another decision? It's easy to manipulate situations so that one is never truly responsible for the outcome. Did others ever say 'You never do anything right'! There can be an agony of soul as we identify ourselves with always being wrong. We can look back in our lives and see that no matter what we tried to do, it always seemed to backfire. It causes a defeatist attitude. God is right here now to deliver from the anguish and condemnation of defeat. Is there a fear of judgment? Lift up this burden to the Lord and He will give you rest. [Rom 8:1]. 1John 4:18 proclaims,

> There is no fear in love; but perfect love casts out fear, because fear hath torment. [how well we know that]
> But he who fears has not been made perfect in love.

That last part seems to condemn us for we are helpless to perfect our love. Let's look at verse 19.

> We love him because he first loved us.

So it is God who initiates the love and since we know He's the perfect One, not us, it must be His perfect love' that is operating. See v. 17 Amplified,

> Love has been perfected [done, complete, accomplished] among us.

That means the love is growing - maturing in us as we yield day by day to the working of God in us. Revelation 2.4-5 says *You have left your first love, remember therefore from where you have fallen*. But what is your first love? *Remember we love Him because He first loved us*. Well, our first love is His love towards us. We don't get born-again until we can see that He loves us. His love penetrates our heart. But in the passing of time we tend to forget how incredible is His love for us.

Things don't always happen the way we think it should, and we may get angry at God and turn away from Him. We forget about how much He loves us unconditionally, He'll always be there for us, He does not leave us, but sometimes we turn our back on Him.

Rom 5.5 *Now hope does not disappoint, because the love of God has been poured out in our hearts by the Holy Spirit who was given to us. For when we were still without strength, in due time Christ died for the ungodly. For scarcely for a righteous man will one die; yet perhaps for a good man someone would even dare to die. But God demonstrates His own love toward us, in that while we were still sinners, Christ died for us. Much more then, having now been justified by His Blood, we shall be saved from wrath through Him. For if when we were enemies we were reconciled to God through the death of His Son, much more, having been reconciled, we shall be saved by His life. And not only that, but we also rejoice in God through our Lord Jesus Christ, through whom we have now received the reconciliation.* BECAUSE...

Gal 4:4-5 *When the fullness of the time had come, God sent forth His Son, born of a woman, born under the law, to redeem those who were under the law, that we might receive the adoption as sons.* Rom 5:5-11 CHRIST TOOK OUR PLACE...

Remember the cross? It was the line of division. Jesus took our sin... 2 Cor 5:21 *For He made Him who knew no sin to be sin for us, that we might become the righteousness of God in Him.* Can we understand that He actually became our sin, died in it and took it all into the depths of hell. When He arose from the dead - He left it there. It's still there - writhing in confusion - wha - wha hoppin'!

When we decide to die to our sin nature; choose to walk in the light of the Kingdom of God; Jahvahshua - *Jesus is salvation*, becomes our new lifestyle. This satan no longer has authority over us to keep us in sin. This power was broken at he cross.

Ps 27:14 *Wait on the Lord; Be of good courage, And He shall strengthen your heart; Wait, I say, on the Lord!*
Isa 40:31 *But those who wait on the Lord Shall renew their strength; They shall mount up with wings like eagles, They shall run and not be weary, They shall walk and not faint.*

He does everything in His time. We think we know how to work out our lives, but we don't. We've made a big mess. Only with God's love can we wait on Him to have, *All things working together for good....* We need to learn to wait upon the Lord, He will renew us. Trust Him, He loves you. [Isaiah 40.31] He sent His Holy Spirit

I wish I had known all this at a young age; my life would not have been such a mess. There was a time that I believed it was all not worth it and one afternoon I lay on my bed and believed I'd be better off dead. I did not have the nerve to kill myself but in my heart I believed my life was useless. I had no idea what was the consequences of such an attitude; but many years later, God delivered me from a spirit of suicide. He knows all about us. Thank You Jesus.

Heb 4:12-13 *For the word of God is living and powerful, and sharper than any two-edged sword, piercing even to the division of soul and spirit, and of joints and marrow, and is a discerner of the thoughts and intents of the heart. And there is no creature hidden from His sight, but all things are naked and open to the eyes of Him to whom we must give account.*

I am grateful God knows all about me. He knows what I need and what to correct. My life in God has brought me peace.

John 14:26-27 *But the Helper, the Holy Spirit, whom the Father will send in My name, He will teach you all things, and bring to your remembrance all things that I said to you. Peace I leave with you, My peace I give to you; not as the world gives do I give to you. Let not your heart be troubled, neither let it be afraid.*

Many of us have been intimidated by the word `perfect' but Strong's Concordance lists its meaning as; complete, full age, to adjust, restore. The implication here; a fully mature piece of fruit. Yet the fruit had to pass through stages of development and growth to reach the fully mature or perfect stage of its existence.

We are in process to be perfect as He is perfect.

We don't expect our babies and children to be perfect, neither does our Father in heaven expect us to be there without a period of growth. They must grow to maturity and so must we. The love is perfected by God, not us. We just yield. [Eph 4:24; Col 3:10].

For we are His workmanship, created in Christ Jesus unto good works, which God hath before ordained that we should walk in them[10]

This word workmanship is referring to that new man, *Created in righteousness and true holiness and renewed in knowledge after the image of him who created him.*

Here is what it means to put on the new man.

Strong's Concordance #4746: sinking into
[be enclosed in]; invest, or equip as a soldier.
ie.,#1722: instrumentality, position, relationship of rest.
#1416: to sink, to go down into, set.

When there is little emotional warmth in one's life it many times translates into the physical realm. I was always cold. I found myself of necessity arriving in Alaska at one time of my life, and decided that I would spend much time indoors wrapped in a blanket. I was very apprehensive and the more I prayed the more God comforted me. Prices are very high in Alaska and a warm goose down parka can cost 200 to 300 dollars.

The first week we were there my eye caught a sign - Parka for Sale. This was in July! I got an almost brand new goose-down parka for $40.00. As the temperature dropped lower and lower I was able to venture out into impossible to fathom [unless you've been there] 40-50 degrees below zero. I thanked God for providing for me so graciously. Snuggling into that coat of the warmest kind and pulling the hood over my head, I knew in my heart I could rest easy. My anxiety over being cold had physical as well as emotional ground.

The memories of that small child in me, always being cold in those New York blizzards, and having to walk uphill, [yes, I really did, but not both ways!] a long way to school; were left in the past. And by analogy, we can sink down into that new man created specifically so that we can function in an alien atmosphere.

We can learn how to respond in God's righteousness to the scenarios in which we find ourselves. The world, the flesh and the devil pulls on us to entrap. But we have been equipped - enclosed in a new mentality; a position of resting in God and being assured we have victory in Him. This New Man - His workmanship created specifically for good works; put it on! Walk around in it! Realize it comes in your size and the enormous price has already been paid. It's yours as you partake of God's provision.

As we submit ourselves in obedience to the will of God, He draws us into deeper relationship with Him.
Eph 4:22-24 *that you put off, concerning your former conduct, the old man which grows corrupt according to the deceitful lusts, and be renewed in the spirit of your mind, and that you put on the new man which was created according to God, in true righteousness and holiness.*

But whosoever hearkens unto me will dwell safely and shall be secure without fear of evil.[11]

The closer we allow God to draw us, the more He reveals Himself to us. He enables us to expand our capacity to trust in Him. Psalm 29 first brings us to praise and magnify the Lord and lift Him up in our sight. When the enemy comes in like a flood, and we are overtaken by circumstances... we put our eyes on Jesus. This is His purpose. Then we can see that the Lord sits as King, the Lord sits enthroned high above the flood. As King He blesses us with His peace because He has control over the wind and the waves.

There are many storms in our life that threaten to overwhelm us. These fears are real to us and we can never learn to handle them. We must be totally delivered from them. *For this purpose was the Son of God manifested, that he might destroy the works of the devil.*[12] Then we experience His peace. And *If the Son therefore shall make you free ye shall be free indeed.* Why? *Because you shall know the truth!*[13] The devil's power over you is broken, destroyed. Only lies, deception and fear keep us in his darkness. Find Truth! Come out into the light [1Jn 1:7]. Also look at Psalms 119:130 and 18:28.

My God will lighten my darkness.

When Peter walked on the water, he only began to sink when he took his eyes off Jesus and looked at the wind and waves coming at him [Mt 14:30]. When we look at the storms of life around us we can't be looking at Jesus. With compassion and love Jesus reached down and took hold of Peter's hand and walked him back to the boat. But remember, Peter walked on water! In reading the account of Abraham in Romans four we find that he kept his eyes on the Lord and the promises, no matter what he perceived was happening. Abraham was just as human as we are and remember this also; he had to learn how to trust and obey, just as we do.

He would have to overcome his fears and trust completely in El Shaddai, the All Sufficient One. He continued to believe and the Word declares in verse 21, *He was fully persuaded.*

Fear is the sin of disbelief in God. But the Lord declares, *I did not come to condemn but to save.*[14]

God's view of sin is 'missing the mark'; missing out on the good things He wants us to have and experience. I read in a magazine some years ago........➜

Fear blocks logical thinking and makes creative solutions to problems impossible. Remember we have access to the mind of Christ, and He gives wisdom without reproach. So don't lose hope. As

> Sin is not harmful because it's wrong,
> sin is wrong because it's harmful.

we feed on the Word, study and meditate on it, let it become established within us; then hope is revived and faith produces its resurrection power and life within.

Fear not...Have no fear, I am with thee.[16]
For the Kingdom of God is not food and drink,
but righteousness, peace and joy in the Holy Ghost.[15]

We can claim God's sure promise of forgiveness, cleansing and renewal. Arise from your bed of ambiguity and get on with life. We need constant reassurance as little children and the Father gives it. Dependence on God is not the opposite of strength or maturity. Look at Jesus. He was afraid of nothing, yet totally dependent on His Father. He was not afraid of truth, nor of man's opinion nor unpopularity.

He walked away from mobs and stood calmly before Annas, Caiaphas and Pilate. Jesus is forever calling us to a simple sturdy faith. Remember He was a man totally dependent on Father God. Let's not be consumed by the fears of our imaginations.

Preoccupation with self can be a breeding ground for fear. Facing up to what we fear, whether real or in our mind, [and to us that is real] we can trust God to take us through. This is a great step of growth in our character and spiritual maturity. We can rid ourselves of all our fears. *We wrestle not against flesh and blood.* Are men our antagonists or the evil rulers of the unseen world using them against us.

Put on the whole armor of God - [Eph 6]
- Integrity is our coat of mail
- Truth is our belt.
- Salvation is our helmet.
- Faith is our shield.
- The Word is our fortress.
- Prayer is our strength.
- Feet shod with the stability of the gospel of peace.

We can learn Kingdom strategy for we are in the middle of a war. Even as preparations for a battle are made in the General's tent - so Daniel's three friends had already decided in their heart how they would handle the king's mandate .
See Daniel 3.6-23 for the whole story. Here is their answer.

Dan 3:16 *Shadrach, Meshach, and Abed-Nego answered and said to the king, O Nebuchadnezzar, we have no need to answer you in this matter. If that is the case, our God whom we serve is able to deliver us from the burning* fiery furnace, and He will deliver us from your hand, O king. But if not, let it be known to you, O king, that we do not serve your gods, nor will we worship the gold image which you have set up.

We can allow God to have dealings with us so that when trials come, we've already settled it in our heart. We've already confronted the real enemy, which is often rooted in our own flesh. When we die to our flesh, then the Spirit rules peace in our heart and mind. Our spirit man gets stronger and stronger as we trust and depend on God. Then in a time of trouble that spirit man rises up to take authority over the enemy and,

Having done all to stand.
Paul shares what God told him as he was going through a tremendous storm; *My grace is sufficient for thee.* [17]

His strength is brought to it's fullness in us through our weakness. Walking in His grace by faith, enables us to overcome our enemies. Their power is short-circuited by our faith in the Name of Jesus, and His Blood shed on the cross that defeated the devil.

We are love children born-again of a loving Father God.
But as many as received him, to them gave he the power to become the sons of God, even to them that believe on his name; which were born not of blood, nor of the will of the flesh, nor of the will of man, but of God. [18]
If we are born-again of incorruptible seed through the Word of God.[19] then we may,
Behold what manner of love the Father hath bestowed upon us, that we should be called the children of God. [20]

We love Him because He first loved us. There is so much more evidence of His love recorded in the Word of God. I would exhort you to do more research. There is more grace and peace from God recorded in His Word than we can imagine and -

We are rooted and grounded in His love.
Yet in all these things we are more than conquerors through him that loved us. For I am persuaded that neither death nor life, nor angels nor principalities nor powers, nor things present nor things to come, nor height nor depth, nor any other created thing, shall be able to separate us from the love of God which is in Christ Jesus our Lord. [21]

This passage reminds me of Ephesians 3:18. We live in a three dimensional world. Here in the Word we are seeing a fourth. *May we be able to comprehend, with all the saints, what is the breadth, and length, and depth and height...* [of His love].

The word breadth is from a root word meaning to shape, fabricate, mold, to form. Is this fourth dimension of His love; the forming, molding, shaping and fabricating, [in other words construct, manufacture, create], of us, the object of His love?

Is God recreating us INTO His perfect love?

There is a song the Body of Christ sings, Lord make me an instrument of love. God's love is a covering - and so much more. *Romans 6:13 declares, Yield yourselves unto God as those that are alive from the dead, and your members as instruments of righteousness unto God.*

Just as we become the righteousness of God in Christ, so we become an instrument of love. It is no longer what we do - it is what we are becoming. Just as the Kingdom of God is not what we do or say or think. We are becoming the channel of God's love to the world. He said greater works would we do. We are His body; His hands, His feet, His heart. We are becoming, from glory to glory - becoming, as the government and rulership of God is developed in us.

All things were done in Christ and then we were put in Christ, established in the Kingdom through what He did for us, and what He is doing *in* us.

And the word 'depth' means 'profound, as going down'. I can tell you this; that the love of God is still reaching down into the depths of my soul to heal and restore.

I don't ever want Him to ever stop.

God draws us ever closer to His heart day by day because we are precious to Him. He sees the pain of insecurity and fear that torments us. His love is powerful enough to overcome all our fears and bring us into safety. He is our Hiding Place, our Pavilion, [means to entwine, fence, hedge in for protection]. *If a man love me, he will keep my words; and my Father will love him, and we will come unto him, and make our abode with him.*[22]

[abode: a staying, residence, mansion]. In that fourth dimension of God's love, we become that love...

Just as God is Love! [2Cor 13.11].

We may take on His personality as we humble ourselves and allow Him to change us. Jesus can manifest what He is to a lost and dying world as He uses us as His instrument. No wonder Paul declares that nothing can separate us from the love of God. What one is, cannot be detached from itself.

But now says the Lord who created you, and he who formed you, Fear not, for I have redeemed you; I have called you by YOUR name; YOU ARE MINE. When you pass through the waters, I will be with you; and through the rivers, they shall not overflow you. When you walk through the fire, you shall not be burned, nor shall the flame scorch you, for I am the Lord your God, the Holy One of Israel, your Savior.[23]

Please note this is WHEN - not IF... And Praise the Lord Your God, Your Savior, the Holy One of Israel.

Many of us go through life never sure of who we are. Because of hard things that come our way we no sooner [sort of] recover from one painful experience when here comes another. Pretty soon we withdraw from life and become very passive. We walk on egg shells, afraid to really live. Since we have developed no resources to change things, we flow with the current and become non-important to the world around us. We lose any sense of identity we may have had, and become a non-person. Now most other people do not have the slightest idea that this has happened and we do not know how to tell them. Besides, we become very defensive and yes, even prideful; as though to say, 'You have stolen everything else from me, leave me to my non-person status. At least that Is mine'.

The result of this emotional surrender is that we take unto ourselves the identity of our environment, ie., people and circumstances. It will usually be all negative because we have no inherent positive resources to draw from. We are definitely not creative and don't know how to be............................➔

| These become the resources to which we relate. |

There is tremendous fear in not knowing who we really are. I remember many years ago I asked myself that question. I did not then have an answer.

When we live with tormenting fears we do tend to store up many unidentifiable dead negatives. More isolation.

Though things are the way they are, if we are a child of God, The Spirit of God is moving to awaken us to the Life He has deposited therein. No matter what has occurred in our past when we didn't know Jesus, His mighty creative power is able to change whatever it is that keeps us from experiencing His Life and Joy.

Eph 3.20 *Now unto him who is able to do exceedingly abundantly above all that we ask or think, according to the power that works in us.* Yes, He is able to give us an identity, in Him. For some of us this new creation is a doubly powerful miracle of restoration. It happened to me! It can be yours. This chapter tells much of how the Lord delivered me from fear. The fact is, I did not have some fears. My life was tormented by anxieties and fears that had their roots buried deep into my identity as a castaway - not ever sure of who I was or where I belonged.

Condemnation, guilt and shame tortured my mind as I re-hashed at night the mistakes of the day; always being in the wrong place at the wrong time. How glad I am that,

The Lord doth build up Jerusalem; He gathers together the outcasts of Israel. He heals the broken in heart and binds up their wounds.[24] *For I will restore health unto thee, and I will heal thee of thy wounds, saith the Lord, because they called thee an outcast.*[25]

Because of the precious Blood of Jesus our conscience can be purged from dead works - so that,

If our hearts condemn us; God is greater than our hearts and knows all things.[26]

Fear leaves us powerless, we cannot receive love from anyone, and our mind makes us think we will never belong. Well now, our fears, anxieties and apprehensions can be left in the past as we reach out for new life in Christ. As our trust in God pervades each attitude and emotion we can be free from the fear of evil. In turn, we can walk in, *power, love and a sound mind* [2Tim 1.7].

For this we can give praises to the
most High God, our heavenly Father.

Dear Reader, if some of these things are troubling you and have held you back in your commitment to live for God, know that Jesus can and will bring victory. We can look to Him and pray,

Lord Jesus, please do for me what I can't do for myself. I give You all the grieving and dead works that are in me. Give me Your Life, and establish my identity in You.

As I gave up my right to be angry and bitter, God brought to my heart,

Where sin abounded, grace abounded much more.[27]
And I praised God for filling that now emptied place with His grace and His love. Now you can get ready for God to move in His awesome resurrection power. He brought us out, so He could bring us in! Remember the Old Testament is given us for an example. God shows us all through His wonderful Word how much He loves us and wants to take care of us. He's our Father!

He will show you how to walk in authority over your enemies, [Eph 6.10-18; And 2 Cor10.3-5]. He will teach you spiritual warfare. Pay attention to His Word, learn to run to Him for instructions. In everything you do - ask His wisdom, depend on Him, He will always be there for you.

Deut 6:23 tells us how He brought Israel out of bondage to Egypt, and into His glorious inheritance. He brings us out of bondage to the world and the devil and into His glorious inheritance. Let Him lead you and guide you. His love for us is so great that He will never give up on us. He never gives us more than we can handle. A friend said the Lord told her, *The part you can't handle is what I carry for you.* [Remember footprints in the sand].
Give to Him that part you can't handle. He is ever ready to begin to deliver us and heal us, the instant we turn to Him. Thank you Father, for bringing me out of fear and into You - [Mt 11.28-30].

Fear Not Little Flock For it Is Your Father's Good Pleasure To Give You the Kingdom. [Lk 12:32 & Ps 35:27]
It is imperative that we learn to trust God to the utmost. He alone can keep us safe in Him, no matter what is happening. Get it clear in your heart - 'I will never deny His name'. Heb 13:5 *For He Himself has said, "I will never leave you nor forsake you.*

John 8:31-32 *If you abide in My word, you are My disciples indeed. And you shall know the truth, and the truth shall make you free.*
John 8:36 *Therefore if the Son makes you free, you shall be free indeed.*

We are the Master's masterpiece
Formed by His own right hand
His image down to the last concern
To have at His command
He only wants to love us
And bring us freely alive
But in our rebellion, pride of life,
We've turned to our own archive
We were created to be His own
To live in His tender care
So He did what was of the gravest sort -
To die - shed His Blood lay bare -
On the cross of indignity
He hung before His nation
He carried out His Father's will
To reconcile creation
So now we are His masterpiece
Reborn for Him alone
To walk the path He plied for us
Until we get back home.

♥

STUDY GUIDE

1. We were created in God's image, to fellowship with Him. We relate to the world through our physical senses. We relate to God through what?
2. Not understanding the supernatural world can cause what?
3. What does God respond to?
4. Much confusion in our lives comes from what?
5. God wants to help us walk in 2Tim 1:7.
6. What are some of your fears? God wants to set you free?
7. What do you have to do to be set free? Heb 11:6, Pr 3:5, 1Pet 5:7, Ph 4:6. Being set free from any fear is not an isolated incident in our life. It is a part of the Master's plan to bring us to 2Co 1:10 and Eph 3:19.
8. There's almost 2 pages in Strong's Concordance of Scripture verses on fear. Do you suppose God has the answers?

9. God is looking for a heart that will trust Him. See what He told Joshua. We all need that assurance, and God gives it. See Ps 91.
10. God's love for us is greater than anything in the universe. When we draw near to Him, He responds with peace and love.
11. Will you forgive those who didn't protect you from these things? Talk to God about it. He'll show you what to do.

PRAYER: I realize fear prevents me from trusting in You. Your Word tells me I can walk in the Spirit of liberty. If You'll show me the door, I'll walk through it. I'll trust You to guide me and teach me - and enable me. I ask You to bring me day by day, out into freedom in Christ. I put my life into your capable hands.

> Oh How Jesus Loves Us,
> He Died to Make Us Free
> To Love Him and to Worship Him -
> And to know Our Father God

SCRIPTURES

1. 1Jn 5:4
2. Ep 1:18
3. 2Pe 1:3-4
4. Ep 4:22-24
5. Ro 12:2
6. Ph 2:13
7. Jn 18:36
8. He 11:6
9. 1Co 2:16
10. Ep 2:10
11. Pr 1:33
12. 1Jn 3:8
13. Jn 8:32,36
14. Jn 3:17
15. Ro 14:1
16. Dt 31:6
17. 2Co 12:9
18. Jn 1:12-13
19. 1Pe 1:23
20. 1Jn 3:1
21. Ro 8:3739
22. Jn 14:23
23. Is 43:13
24. Ps 147:23

WHO AND WHAT IS THIS MAN OF SIN - THE BEAST; AND WHAT IS HIS MARK?

We must be careful to understand the consequences of 'who do we follow';

Luke 6:46-49 *"But why do you call Me 'Lord, Lord,' and not do the things which I say? Whoever comes to Me, and hears My sayings and does them, I will show you whom he is like: He is like a man building a house, who dug deep and laid the foundation on the rock. And when the flood arose, the stream beat vehemently against that house, and could not shake it, for it was founded on the rock. But he who heard and did nothing is like a man who built a house on the earth without a foundation, against which the stream beat vehemently; and immediately it fell. And the ruin of that house was great."*

This Scripture really tells it like it is. What foundation do you want under you, that will keep you for eternity. Is it God - or not! This text tells what happens to the one with no foundation in Christ. SO... If we do not invite Jesus to be the Lord in our temple, then it is an open doorway for...

2 Thess 2:3-4 *The man of sin is revealed, the son of perdition, who opposes and exalts himself above all that is called God or that is worshiped, so that he sits as God in the temple of God, showing himself that he is God.*

So which God will you worship? To whom do you belong?

And - where/what is the temple of God???

The Word says...

1 Cor 3:16-17 *Do you not know that you are the temple of God and that the Spirit of God dwells in you? If anyone defiles the temple of God, God will destroy him. For the temple of God is holy, which temple you are.* AND...

2 Cor 6:16 *And what agreement has the temple of God with idols? For you are the temple of the living God.*

Man was created to be the temple of God; but satan wants us to be *his* temple; to worship him. From the garden until now, that has always been his goal. But we must...

Col 3:2-4 *Set your mind on things above, not on things on the earth. For you died, and your life is hidden with Christ in God.*

But what if your life is not hidden in God - you are stuck with the sin-nature that was passed down from Adam.

We are all born with a 'sin-nature'. The only thing that changes our nature - is to be born again into the Kingdom of God. Unless you are 'born again', you will live for your own pleasure.

Now, this man of sin has the same sin nature as the unbeliever, so that [2Thes 2.4] *he sits as god in this temple* [of unbelief], *showing himself that he is god,* and he rules there.

Actually, he is always there in our life until we make Jesus the Lord of our life, because until then, we are in control of our life, or at least we think we are. This satan will speak to our mind 'in the first person' so we think the thought is ours and we will most often act on it. These thoughts are to make sure that we are in control of it all - what is in our best self interest.

The unbeliever and the man of sin both have the same nature and want to be their own god. Remember the garden episode - *'you will be as gods'?* And who else wanted to be God? *Lucifer, son of the morning...*

Isa 14:13-14   *'I will ascend into heaven, I will exalt my throne above the stars of God; I will also sit on the mount of the congregation On the farthest sides of the north; I will ascend above the heights of the clouds, I will be like the Most High.'*

Actually, anyone who is not born-again into the Kingdom of God, has the sin-nature and is already the temple of the man of sin. Understand that this is why we are trapped in sin until we turn to Jesus. We dwell in darkness and are controlled by our sin-nature. Our sin nature can never be any different, until we...

Col 1:12-14   *Give thanks to the Father who has qualified us to be partakers of the inheritance of the saints in the light. He* [wants to]... *has delivered us from the power of darkness and conveyed us into the kingdom of the Son of His love, in whom we have redemption through His Blood, the forgiveness of sins.*

An unbeliever is already deceived by the master of deception. Just recognize what a life without God is all about; did we live there for a long time? And just as the believer is the temple of God; the unbeliever is ruled by the enemy of their soul, to do his works. He lives in their temple; has always lived in the temple of the unbeliever. So Who Lives in Your Temple?

Ephesians 2.2-3 *according to the prince of the power of the air, the spirit who now works in the sons of disobedience...*

The unbeliever is already - because we are born with a sin nature, we are naturally -

The temple of the antichrist spirit.

We are all born to be 'born-again' into the Kingdom of God, but it is our choice. We have a free will. Do we want to be our own god or will we choose the God Who created us to be a part of His family. But understand this... Our soul is lost unless we ask Jesus to be our Savior; invite Him to live in us. *He stands at your door* and knocks. Will you open your heart to Him [Rev 3.20]

John 1:12 *But as many as received Him, [Jesus], to them He gave the right to become children of God, to those who believe in His name: who were born, not of blood, nor of the will of the flesh, nor of the will of man, but of God.*

John 14.15-19 *If you love Me, keep My commandments. And I will pray the Father, and He will give you another Helper, that He may abide with you forever — the Spirit of truth, whom the world cannot receive, because it neither sees Him nor knows Him; but you know Him, for He dwells with you and will be in you. I will not leave you orphans; I will come to you.*

The only way to be saved from cunning lies is to give your heart and soul to Jesus Who died for your salvation. Remember Jesus, *in whom we have redemption through His Blood, the forgiveness of sins.*

If we walk in the image of God we are holy as He is holy, having the mind of Christ, only wanting God's will. God does this in us as we turn to Him.

If we worship the image of the beast, it's because we are like him - his temple; self-serving, satisfying only our flesh, our mind captivated by the world and what it can give us. The terrible truth of the matter is, we don't know an evil spirit has control of our life.
BUT...

Colossians 2.6-11 *As you have received Christ Jesus the Lord, so walk in Him, rooted and built up in Him and established in the faith, as you have been taught, abounding in it with thanksgiving. Beware lest anyone cheat you through philosophy and empty deceit, according to the tradition of men, according to the basic principles of the world, and not according to Christ.*

I'm writing all these verses because many Christians, young ones and older Christians who don't really read the Bible or may not understand what I'm trying to say; that God will keep you safe if you have done John 1.12, *received Him into your life.* No matter what happens, please trust Jesus - no matter what,

And please don't ever deny His Name.

Heb 13:5-6 *For He Himself has said, I will never leave you nor forsake you. So we may boldly say: The Lord is my helper; I will not fear. What can man do to me?* Read Mark 8.34-38;

Luke 12.29-32 If we will not deny Him, *It is Father's good pleasure to give us the Kingdom. Remember, Greater is He that is in us than he that is in the world.* We must know that God has a hard grip on the believer, that He will never let us go [Romans 8].

1 Corinthians 6.17 *But he who is joined to the Lord is one spirit with Him.* What more can He do for us? Be Amazed! We are saved by faith because of God's grace. Divine redemption is actually the living experience with One Who has been raised from the dead, Jesus Himself, by the power of the Holy Spirit, is alive in each lover of God.

♬ *I'm not my own, I belong to Jesus, I'm His.*
Bought with a price, the Blood of Jesus, I'm His ♬

Not Religion - It is Relationship!

If we acknowledge that Jesus died - shed His blood on the cross for our sin - and ask forgiveness for our sins; then our sin-nature died with Him and we now take on the nature of God. The Holy Spirit now lives in us and He will send ...

John 14:26 *The Helper, the Holy Spirit, whom the Father will send in My name, He will teach you all things.*

1 John 2.20-27 *But you have an anointing from the Holy One, and you know all things. I have not written to you because you do not know the truth, but because you know it, and that no lie is of the truth.*

John 14:23 *Jesus answered and said unto him, If a man love me, he will keep my words: and my Father will love him, and we will come unto him, and make our abode with him.*

Let Truth Abide in You.

Even if we are confronted with some 'authority' who will demand we worship this image, this beast; Rev 13 talks about who is worshiped - or not. Remember the three boys who were thrown into the oven because they would not worship the king's image [read Daniel 3]. Who showed up in the flames with them? If we have a fear of death, then we must turn to Jesus to resolve this. It will cause us to compromise; very dangerous to our life in Christ.

Just know that even if we die we must not deny the precious name of Jesus Who died on the cross for our salvation and eternal life; and we will immediately be in the presence of our Father. And please don't fear for your children; God has His angels around them. God can snatch them out at any time. They will with you, be immediately in the presence of God. Rev 21.22; - 23.5. Read it.

So, do you want to know what the mark of the beast is? **Worship is The key! Who do you worship?**
Ephesians 1.13-14   Every believer is already sealed by the Holy Spirit. All this has to do with Who it is that we worship. Oh yes, and Revelation 2.29   *And of those who keep the words of this book, Worship God.*

Rev 13 reveals what is the mark of the beast - Verse 8. *All who dwell on the earth will worship him, whose names have not been written in the Book of Life of the Lamb slain from the foundation of the world.* Read Revelation the whole 13th chapter. It talks about those who will worship the beast - or not.

Rev 13:8 *All who dwell on the earth will worship him, whose names have not been written in the Book of Life of the Lamb slain from the foundation of the world.*

SO - DO YOU GET IT!

The mark on our forehead and hand is
Who do you believe in -'who do you worship
and who do you serve?'

I did a research on where the mark originally came from...
We are sealed by the Holy Spirit, marked by Him...Eph 1.11-14. This next Scripture is from Ezekiel, when God destroyed the temple because the priests had become corrupt. Please read it Ch 8-9.

Ezek 9:3-7   *Now the glory of the God of Israel had gone up from the cherub, where it had been, to the threshold of the temple. And He called to the man clothed with linen,* who had the writer's inkhorn at his side; and the Lord said to him, "Go through the midst of the city, through the midst of Jerusalem, and put a mark on the foreheads of the men who sigh and cry over all the abominations that are done within it. To the others He said in my hearing, "Go after him through the city and kill; do not let your eye spare, nor have any pity. Utterly slay old and young men, maidens and little children and women; but do not come near anyone on whom is the mark; and begin at My sanctuary." So they began with the elders who were before the temple. Then He said to them, "Defile the temple, and fill the courts with the slain. Go out!" And they went out and killed in the city.

[Remember children are taught by their parents. That's why the nations were wiped out by Joshua, all of them. But innocent children will live for eternity with God]. So, He began with the priests who used the law against His people.

This is how God feels about those who are marked by Him.

Those who loved Him. And where did all this begin.

It began when Moses delivered Israel out of Egypt.

Exodus 12. 21-28 has Israel marking their house with the blood against the death angel. This was the Lord's Passover. Verse *51 And the Lord brought the children of Israel out of the land of Egypt by their armies.*

Gen 46.3 & 27. Imagine that...from 70 people God has made them 'armies' Some say more than a million people came out.

Ex 13 Now, before they get to the Red Sea, Moses is teaching them about the God Who delivered them from slavery. After 400 years they lost track of the God of Abraham. They did not know him. God revealed Himself to Moses; 'I AM THAT I AM'.

This chapter also reveals [verse 9] that God will 'mark', His people above all that live on the earth. There is none like us, those who love the LORD GOD.

Ex 13:8-10 *This is done because of what the Lord did for me when I came up from Egypt. It shall be as a sign to you on your hand and as a memorial between your eyes, that the Lord's law may be in your mouth; for with a strong hand the Lord has brought you out of Egypt.* These Words Pertain to Us Also.

Deut 6:6-10 *And these words which I command you today shall be in your heart. You shall teach them diligently* to your children, and shall talk of them when you sit in your house, when you walk by the way, when you lie down, and when you rise up. You shall bind them as a sign on your hand, and they shall be as frontlets between your eyes. You shall write them on the doorposts of your house and on your gates.

Deut 11:18-20   Therefore you shall lay up these words of mine in your heart and in your soul, and bind them as a sign on your hand, and they shall be as frontlets between your eyes. You shall teach them to your children, speaking of them when you sit in your house, when you walk by the way, when you lie down, and when you rise up. [please do more research, there is more].

Between your eyes is your mind - who is your mind stayed on? Who do you worship? The sign on your hand is who do you obey? This is all about what you think and what you do pertaining to your spiritual life. Your mind and your hand. Do you love God and do you obey Him. What you think about is where your heart is. And the works of your hand...

John 14:15   "If you love Me, keep My commandments".

Here is the revelation on what the mark means and where it started.

THE MARK, the SEAL, the TOKEN, the SIGN - what they mean.
MARK Rev 13 to stamp as a badge of servitude
TOKEN Ex 13 evidence, monument, memorial
SIGN Ex 13 same thing
SEAL Eph 1 to stamp, to fence in, to protect, imprint.

With God, this is a spiritual sign, not a physical mark on our forehead; Faith in Christ, and Jn 14. *Do my commandments*.
For Rev 13. 17 There may occur a physical mark, who knows. But it is faith in self and 'Do as I please'. Not really knowing who you are serving will cause you to bow to the beast.

I hope this gives a good understanding.

God always begins at the beginning. It is crucial to your understanding that we begin at the beginning. Moses is teaching His people - commands them to remember this day - the beginning of their deliverance out of the darkness of slavery even before they have left Goshen because of the blood of the lamb on their doorpost, and as they are crossing the desert.

[Please forgive repetition and please understand]

It Always Begins with the Blood.

First it must be understood that ....

2 Tim 3:16   *All Scripture is given by inspiration of God, and is profitable for doctrine, for reproof, for correction, for instruction in righteousness, that the man of God may be complete, thoroughly equipped for every good work.*

2 Peter 1:20-21   *knowing this first, that no prophecy of Scripture is of any private interpretation, for prophecy never came by the will of man, but holy men of God spoke as they were moved by the Holy Spirit.*

The witness of Scripture is woven through out the Word so that we can be sure it is not just an arbitrary word of man. So let's see how far this research will take us as we journey through the Word to establish what God wants us to understand.

It begins as far back as the

Exodus of Israel from Egypt.

Ex 12:21-27   *Then Moses called for all the elders of Israel and said to them, Pick out and take lambs for yourselves according to your families, and kill the Passover lamb. And you shall take a bunch of hyssop, dip it in the blood that is in the basin, and strike the lintel and the two doorposts with the blood that is in the basin. And none of you shall go out of the door of his house until morning. For the Lord will pass through to strike the Egyptians; and when He sees the blood on the lintel and on the two doorposts, the Lord will pass over the door and not allow the destroyer to come into your houses to strike you.*

It is the Passover sacrifice of the Lord, who passed over the houses of the children of Israel in Egypt when He struck the Egyptians and delivered Israel. It's like all the junk that happened to them from when Jacob first entered Goshen - He brought them in, now He's bringing them out.

After 400 years - God is taking them out.

So lets be clear about what God wants His people to remember. It was the blood of the lamb that set them apart; and because they covered their threshold with blood, they would be released from bondage. The destroyer would not harm them. And so, six hundred thousand men plus women and children set out into the desert for where, they knew not.

And we must remember that it was and is the Blood of the Lamb - Jesus - that brings us out of our darkness.

Col 1:12-14   *giving thanks to the Father who has qualified us to be partakers of the inheritance of the saints in the light. He has delivered us from the power of darkness and conveyed us into the kingdom of the Son of His love, in whom we have redemption through His blood, the forgiveness of sins.*

Now, even as Israel was crossing this great expanse of wilderness, and before they came to the Red Sea, Moses was instructing them further on what they were to remember. It was crucial to their relationship with the God Who had just devastated a once powerful nation and its many gods; and now here He is...

A God they did not know.

Ex 13:3   *And Moses said to the people: Remember this day in which you went out of Egypt, out of the house of bondage; for by strength of hand the Lord brought you out of this place.*

REMEMBER THIS DAY.

This was a commandment to be physically observed just as the law was to be observed; that this people would remember always the Passover; that it was the mighty hand of God Who brought them safely out of bondage to Egypt.

Ex 13:8-10   *And you shall tell your son in that day, saying, 'This is done because of what the Lord did for me when I came up from Egypt.' It shall be as a sign to you on your hand and as a memorial between your eyes, that the Lord's law may be in your mouth; for with a strong hand the Lord has brought you out of Egypt. You shall therefore keep this ordinance in its season from year to year.*

What does this mean for application sake? *A memorial between your eyes* - it's your mind. What and who is your mind stayed on?

Isa 26:3   *You will keep him in perfect peace, Whose mind is stayed on You, Because he trusts in You.*

Yes, God wants Himself to be the One we focus on for our life's standard. And the *sign upon your hand* - who do we obey, whose works do we do?

WoW - it all started here when God first began to deliver His people out of bondage to the evil of man and devil. Ths marking of God's people is repeated several times throughout the Word of God.

But now God is about to show Himself to Israel in a way they should not ever forget. This God they just now found is about to show them exactly Who He is! Ex 14.13-31.

The sea parted for them and drowned their enemy.

How could they ever forget?

Well, I know the 'sea parted' for me in a big way when Mike left. I know I could have wound up a 'bag lady' but for His loving kindness for me. And I'll not forget His mercy.

But getting back to the issue at hand...

Now we know copycat devil uses the same context in Rev 13.17. *And, here is wisdom*. 666 is the number of the natural man; body, soul and man's spirit, the unredeemed, unbeliever. BUT

Rev 15:2 *those who have the victory over the beast, over his image and over his mark and over the number of his name* - Is the born again believer - lover of God and His Word

If we don't want to give up our sin-nature for the nature and image of God then we maintain the soul-nature, body, soul and spirit. Remember man was created in the sixth day. [666] still the number of unredeemed man.

The image of the Beast and the unbeliever

have the same sin-nature.

The born-again in Christ is the image of God,

recreated as we were meant to be from the beginning.

So to continue with the covenant that was passed down to us through Jesus, repeated several times in His Word...

Deut 11 *Therefore you shall love the Lord your God, and keep His charge, His statutes, His judgments, and His commandments always. Therefore you shall lay up these words of mine in your heart and in your soul, and bind them as a sign on your hand, and they shall be as frontlets between your eyes. You shall teach them to your children, speaking of them when you sit in your house, when you walk by the way, when you lie down, and when you rise up. For if you carefully keep all these commandments which I command you to do — to love the Lord your God, to walk in all His ways, and to hold fast to Him...*They were marked by God as to belong to Him.

See also these verses, Exodus 13.8-16; Deuteronomy 6.6-9, 11.18; Rev 14.1 in context as two and more witnesses of the 'mark'. Do more Research.

Four times from Exodus to Deuteronomy the instructions are given to remember what God has done for His people; to get their mind wrapped around the fact that now the God they will serve has made them free; and the works of their hand shall be to love the *Lord thy God* and obey His Word. So has this witness been given as truth? This nation was raised up to walk in the ways of God.

They Have Been Sealed, Marked by God To Be His Own People; And They Are to Pass it down to All Generations.

Deut 11:18-19 *Therefore you shall lay up these words of mine in your heart and in your soul, and bind them as a sign on your hand, and they shall be as frontlets between your eyes.*

We must bind God's truth to our heart and soul, so it will be a part of our identity; who we are in Christ.

As we can see, there is the witness of this commandment given several times to affirm what God has said. Israel has been marked and sealed by God to remember their deliverance from bondage to Egypt and slavery.

AND WHAT DID GOD DO FOR US?

We Are Always to Remember What God Did for Us!

Eph 1:13-15 *In Him you also trusted, after you heard the word of truth, the gospel of your salvation; in whom also, having believed, you were sealed with the Holy Spirit of promise, who is the guarantee of our inheritance until the redemption of the purchased possession, to the praise of His glory.*

2 Cor 1:21-22 *God, who also has sealed us and given us the Spirit in our hearts as a guarantee..*

1 Cor 11:24-26 *And when He had given thanks, He broke it and said, "Take, eat; this is My body which is broken for you; do this in remembrance of Me." In the same manner He also took the cup after supper, saying, "This cup is the new covenant in My blood. This do, as often as you drink it, in remembrance of Me." For as often as you eat this bread and drink this cup, you proclaim the Lord's death till He comes.*

This is to always remember - not to make an idol out of it.

Rev 12.11 And we overcome satan by the Blood of the Lamb and the word of our testimony. We will not deny Jesus and the Blood He shed for our redemption.
1 Peter 5:6-7 Therefore humble yourselves under the mighty hand of God, that He may exalt you in due time, casting all your care upon Him, for He cares for you.
The seal and mark of God that the Christian bears, is that we remember Jesus brought us out of darkness into His glorious light.
Col 1:12-14 Giving thanks to the Father who has qualified us to be partakers of the inheritance of the saints in the light. He has delivered us from the power of darkness and conveyed us into the kingdom of the Son of His love, in whom we have redemption through His blood, the forgiveness of sins.
[Col 1] It is the mind that remembers Who it is that we worship, and our hand that is always ready to do God's bidding. The works of our hand -
John 14.15 If you love Me, keep my commandments.
Eph 1:13 In Him you also trusted, after you heard the word of truth, the gospel of your salvation; in whom also, having believed, you were sealed with the Holy Spirit of promise,
Eph 4:30-31 and do not grieve the Holy Spirit of God, by whom you were sealed for the day of redemption.
2 Cor 1:21-22 God, who also has sealed us and given us the Spirit in our hearts as a guarantee...   And then there is...
This mark of God follows us now into Revelation.
Rev 7:3-4 Do not harm the earth, the sea, or the trees till we have sealed the servants of our God on their foreheads.
Rev 9:4-5 They were commanded not to harm the grass of the earth, or any green thing, or any tree, but only those men who do not *have the seal of God on their foreheads*; it only means our mind, who do we think about and who do we worship.
The true Christian has already been marked and sealed by the Blood of the Lamb. Please research these Scriptures for proof witness. Eph 4.30; Rev 9.4; 14.1; 2.13; 12.17; 15.2-3; 2C 1.22; John 3.33; 6.27; 2Tim2.19; 1 John 1.3; 2.22-24; 4.13-19; 5.4-5; 2 John 1.9; Rev 15.2-3; 7.3.

The mark and the seal basically mean the same thing.
Ephesians 1:7-14 *In Him we have redemption through His blood, the forgiveness of sins, according to the riches of His grace which He made to abound toward us in all wisdom and prudence, having made known to us the mystery of His will,*

according to His good pleasure which He purposed in Himself, that in the dispensation of the fullness of the times He might gather together in one, all things in Christ, both which are in heaven and which are on earth — in Him. In Him you also trusted, after you heard the word of truth, the gospel of your salvation; in whom also, having believed, you were sealed with the Holy Spirit of promise, who is the guarantee of our inheritance until the redemption of the purchased possession, to the praise of His glory.

So do you understand what the seal or mark of God is for the true Christian? It is the knowledge that Jesus shed His Blood for our redemption. We know the lamb's blood for Israel was the shadow of the Blood Jesus shed for us. So He did the same for us. We are marked and sealed by our God, as long as we confess Jesus is our Lord.

Col 1:9-14 *That you may be filled with the knowledge of His will in all wisdom and spiritual understanding; that you may walk worthy of the Lord, fully pleasing Him, being fruitful in every good work and increasing in the knowledge of God; strengthened with all might, according to His glorious power, for all patience and longsuffering with joy;*

Just know in the bottom of your soul and spirit that... *He brought us out of the power of darkness and has translated us into the kingdom of His dear Son, Jesus ...*

Into our promised land.

1 John 2:20-29 *But you have an anointing from the Holy One, and you know all things. I have not written to you because you do not know the truth, but because you know it, and that no lie is of the truth. Who is a liar but he who denies that Jesus is the Christ? He is antichrist who denies the Father and the Son. Whoever denies the Son does not have the Father either; he who acknowledges the Son has the Father also.*

Therefore let that abide in you which you heard from the beginning. If what you heard from the beginning abides in you, you also will abide in the Son and in the Father. And this is the promise that He has promised us — eternal life.

These things I have written to you concerning those who try to deceive you. But the anointing which you have received from Him abides in you, and is true, and is not a lie, and just as it has taught you, you will abide in Him.

Yes, We Are The Children of God
marked and sealed for Him only.

28 *And now, little children, abide in Him, that when He appears, we may have confidence and not be ashamed before Him at His coming. If you know that He is righteous, you know that everyone who practices righteousness is born of Him.*

So we born-again children of the Most High God are marked and sealed to Him, never to be abandoned or forsaken. *If you love me, keep my commandments* [John 14]. Rev 13 Marks off Who Will Be Worshiped and Who Will Not. Verses 16-18 *the mark of the beast, the imitator.* BUT...

What happens to those who will not - read Matt 13.29-51. Read all about the wheat and the tares. Who goes and who stays.

NOW DO YOU KNOW THE SECRET TO THE MARK OF THE BEAST? IT IS - WHO DO YOU WORSHIP!!!.

What you worship changes you into that image.

The image of God or the image of the beast.

Sorry to keep repeating. I just want you to understand what we are up against and what are the real issues.

THE IMAGE - THE MARK. What do you think the Mark is? See Rev 13:4; 8; 12; 15; 14:11; 16:2. And 1Thess 4.13-18.

Always Read Scripture in Context.

It is all about - who do you worship and who do you serve.
The question is - Who do you worship, God or the beast? To worship God is all through the Bible. And the sin-nature is also described in finality.

Rev 21.8 *But the cowardly, unbelieving, abominable, murderers, sexually immoral, sorcerers, idolaters, and all liars shall have their part in the lake which burns with fire and brimstone, which is the second death.*

So what-who will we choose?

Rev 13:15-17 *He causes as many as would not worship the image of the beast to be killed. He causes all, both small and great, rich and poor, free and slave, to receive a mark on their right hand or on their foreheads.*

To Cause...'his determination, his intention', his threats of death - says you can't buy food unless you worship him.

LOL, God fed Israel in the desert for 40 years.

He will try to frighten many to turn and worship him; but child of God - you must determine now! Who you belong to and Who you will worship. This decision must be foremost in your heart. Filled with the Spirit of God, there is only one decision to make -

'I Will Not Deny the Name of Jesus'!

Most of us are aware of the many martyrs who gave their life to stand for Jesus. This satan will try to make us afraid, but 'We are more than a conqueror in Christ Jesus.

Isa 54:15-17 *Whoever assembles against you shall fall for your sake. Behold, I have created the blacksmith Who blows the coals in the fire, Who brings forth an instrument for his work; And I have created the spoiler to destroy. No weapon formed against you shall prosper, And every tongue which rises against you in judgment You shall condemn. This is the heritage of the servants of the Lord, And their righteousness is from Me, Says the Lord.*

So - do you know who is the spoiler?
That's right - US!

Isa 54:15-17 *Whoever assembles against you shall fall for your sake.*

Rev 21:6-9 *And He said to me, "It is done! I am the Alpha and the Omega, the Beginning and the End. I will give of the fountain of the water of life freely to him who thirsts. He who overcomes shall inherit all things, and I will be his God and he shall be My son.*

Rev 13.16 *To receive a mark in their right hand or in their foreheads?* Well now, where did this come from? We heard it before in Exodus 13. We have a copycat loose on the earth. The carnal unredeemed man is marked; he has the same nature [image] as the beast, [read Romans 1.18-2.16, and Rev 21.8].

And what is an image? Man was created in the image and likeness of God. So the believer in Christ looks like God and acts like Him. It is your character, personality, your nature; it is how other people see you, how they know you, how you act. The Christian is known for Godlike qualities; how we act toward others with God's love. We are re-created into the image and likeness of God. Because we have received Jesus as our Savior and Lord, our sin nature has been taken to the cross and Jesus brought it down to Hell. He Left it there when He rose from the dead. It's still there.

The unbeliever acts out in their carnal nature doing what they please no matter what. Read Romans to see what the nature is, of the unbeliever. Jesus brought us out of this and marked us as belonging to Him. Thank You Jesus.

The unbelievers' image is the same as the beast.

To worship something is to adhere to what is just like you. The unbeliever still has the sin-nature and this is the nature of the beast and the man of sin.

Rev 13:15,17 To worship his image is that you are just like him, have the same nature. 666 is the # of a man; body, soul, spirit. **It is the number of the natural man.**

But the Christian has been born again – we have the image and nature of God. Our sin nature has been brought to the cross and to hell, its still there.

Exodus 13 tells us when the 'mark' was initiated. By God. Satan is a copycat. We are marked and sealed by God Eph 1:13.

The mark of God is to worship Him. The mark of the beast is to worship him. To worship is to give your heart in agreement. God has been marking His people for a long time. God's Word is the place to find Truth. If we pay attention, there is no place in our life for fear.

Moses was teaching them about the God Who had just delivered them out of slavery. 'You will know Him and obey Him'. The God they should know and worship was about to make a path through the Red Sea and drown their enemies. And... He was about to give them the criteria of how they should live and treat others.

It was the 10 commandments engraved in stone.

If you are sealed by the Holy Spirit, you cannot take the mark. Actually it is not something you 'take', it's something you already are; which is only the decision to not identify with Jesus, to deny Him and to identify with the sin nature of the beast - that is, we are our own god. And ...   [I cannot say this enough times]-

It is to worship him because the unbeliever has the sin-nature, not redeemed by the sacrifice of Jesus, Who died to save you from the lake of fire. The beast and the sin-nature are synonymous. To 'take the mark' means that you worship the beast [satan]; it means you deny knowing Jesus.

The unbeliever is just like the beast. Of course he will give his allegiance to him. They want the same things.

Colossians 3.1-4 *If then you were raised with Christ, seek those things which are above, where Christ is, sitting at the right hand of God. Set your mind on things above, not on things on the earth. For you died, and your life is hidden with Christ in God. When Christ who is our life appears, then you also will appear with Him in glory.* John 14.16-18,21,23, 27;16.33;17.26.

Remember. Atheism believes there is no God. An Agnostic - is there really a God? *A double minded man is unstable in all his ways* [James 1], and easily deceived.

Revelation 13.18 Understand '666', It tells us, it is the number of a man. Six is the number of a carnal man, so - body, soul, and [man's] spirit is of a carnal nature to begin with; [thank you Adam]. and we were created on the sixth day...Another But... read 1 John 5.11-13 - He gives life to our spirit, soul and body [in the resurrection] as we accept Him. And understand what is the mark ... IT IS WORSHIP.

We need to stand on The Word because God does not lie. He gives us assurance. It All Boils down to One Thing. Do You Believe the Word of God - or Not? Adam Did Not! *He decided that he would do his own thing - and be in charge of his life.*

> Not enough said Adam, I want to explore
> Not what I have with You Lord, I want much more,
> There's other ways and things to do
> On the other side of the gate
> To taste and see the wrong and right
> And where should I put my faith
> I'll try this, and I'll try that, And then I will decide
> But OH! If I could just turn back
> I know now, I gave up my life. ☹

As Adam betrayed his position in the Spirit realm, they were no longer covered by the glory and they were naked. Now they would hide in fear of the presence of the Lord. Adam had face to face with his Creator; he was covered with the glory of God. He met with God face to face. He was shown the mysteries of the universe; and was given dominion over all the earth. But Adam made a decision that would rob them of all this. He decided that his Creator-God, was not enough. He wanted to be in charge. So unbeknownst to Adam who didn't think it through - He handed over to satan the authority over the earth.

Matt 4:8-9   *Again, the devil took Him up on an exceedingly high mountain, and showed Him all the kingdoms of the world and their glory. And he said to Him, "All these things I will give You if You will fall down and worship me."*

That's a brazen statement unless it belonged to him. And Jesus knew it did. That's why He came; to take it back for us.

You have the power to decide for yourself. What will it be? Make your own decisions - to ask Jesus into your life? He will restore all things Whatever it was that Adam gave up.

If Adam only would have repented instead of putting the blame on someone else. So now, he becomes worldly, carnal, to do as he pleases, to live by his self-will. After he disobeyed God, it was too late to turn back, and so, they lost their identity in God. But God must have forgiven them, for He covered them with the blood and skins of a lamb. And for us....again -

Ephesians 1.7-14   *In Him we have redemption through His Blood, the forgiveness of sins, according to the riches of His grace which He made to abound toward us in all wisdom and prudence...in Him you also trusted, after you heard the word of truth, the Gospel of your salvation; in whom also, having believed, you were sealed with the Holy Spirit of promise, who is the guarantee of our inheritance until the redemption of the purchased possession, to the praise of His glory.*

This all sounds like such a complete salvation; saved into the arms of One who is madly in love with each of us.. So What Is Our Inheritance, Who Are We - And to Whom Do We Belong? We Are Bought with a Price -

The Greatest Price of All in the Universe -

The Precious Blood of our Creator God.

John 17.9-20   *I do not pray that You should take them out of the world, but that You should keep them from the evil one.*

This happens when we run to Him. To want to live for

Jesus Is the Greatest Life Style Possible.

John 17:20-23   *I do not pray for these alone, but also for those who will believe in Me through their word; that they all may be one, as You, Father, are in Me, and I in You;*

John 14.23   Jesus answered and said to him, If anyone loves Me, he will keep My word; and My Father will love him, and We will come to him and make Our home with him.
   Yes, *it is Christ in you, the hope of glory.*
So we should know how Jesus looks after us in the worst of times.
Rev 9:4-5 Read it, *The angels were commanded not to harm the grass of the earth, or any green thing, or any tree, but only those men <u>who do not have the seal of God on their foreheads.</u>*

He knows who we all are and where we are. And we are sealed to Him, no one can take us away from Him.

John 17:15   *I do not pray that You should take them out of the world, but that You should keep them from the evil one.*
   It is obvious that we must learn to trust in God - to put all our life into His hands. It is the only thing we can do. And after all is said and done - the words of Jesus spell true -
John 14.15   *If you love me, keep my commandments.*
It's not good enough to say 'I love Jesus', then go about your own business. God will help us every time if we turn to Him..
   Philippians 2.12-16. Working out your own salvation means to cooperate with God for the changes He arranges. These next verses here are from The Passion Translation by Brian Simmons.
Eph 2.10   *We have become His poetry.*
Heb 10.36   *Revealing the poetry of God's will.*
James 1.22   *Always let His Word become like poetry written and fulfilled by your life.*
Ps 42.8   *Through the night I sing His songs.*
You see... *The joy of the Lord really is our strength.*
   Jesus is so in love with His creation. He died an agonizing death to set us free from the enemy of our soul who had us so deceived and enslaved by his lies.
2Pet 3.19 *People are slaves to whatever overcomes them*
   Rom 6.20 Paul declares he is a bondslave of Jesus.

Be sure to know Who it is that has your attention.

And remember, we have resurrection power working in us.
Col 2:12-13   *buried with Him in baptism, in which you also were raised with Him through faith in the working of God, who raised Him from the dead.*

So, baptism is a symbol of death, burial and resurrection.
I've given you all the Scripture - look them up, believe and be safe.

> Our life in the present world
> is almost exclusively a time of preparation
> If we make our pilgrimage upon the earth
> the focus of our ambitions and joys
> we shall have made the greatest mistake
> which it is possible for a human being to make
> We are being prepared to live with God
> and serve Him forever and ever
> and what will we be like after
> a billion years have rolled by?
> Robert B. Thompson, Trumpet Ministries

Yes, we will be like God -

recreated in His image and Likeness ❤

SO NOW - WHO OR WHAT ARE THE TWO WITNESSES?

The Bible reveals all we ever need to know about life, the Kingdom of God and the world we live in.

Deut 19:15-16 by the mouth of two or three <u>witnesses</u> the matter shall be established.

Matt 18:16 that by the mouth of two or three <u>witnesses</u> every word may be established.

Luke 24:44-45 Then He said to them, These are the words which I spoke to you while I was still with you,.. <u>And He opened their understanding, that they might comprehend the Scriptures</u>.

See Deut 31.26; 4.26; 31.21; Jos 22.34; 1Sam 12.5...

The Word Is a Witness to Itself. The Word of God is a witness. Remember He sent them out two by Two.

Luke 9:1-6 Then He called His twelve disciples together and gave them power and authority over all demons, and to cure diseases. He sent them to preach the kingdom of God and to heal the sick. And He said to them, "Take nothing for the journey, neither staffs nor bag nor bread nor money; and do not have two tunics apiece. So they departed and went through the towns, preaching the gospel and healing everywhere.

What did they have - only the Word they had been taught.

Acts 1.8, Rev 11. Jesus taught them for 3½ years all about the Kingdom of God; now they would receive on the day of Pentecost - Acts 1:8 *But you shall receive power when the Holy Spirit has come upon you; and you shall be witnesses to Me in Jerusalem, and in all Judea and Samaria, and to the end of the earth."*

They had the Word in their heart, so what did they do? They taught the Word that had been exploded by the anointing; tongues of fire, each one a witness to His love.

The fire of His Word sets a fire in the heart of the believer.

That's how Jesus sent them out; nothing but the men and the Word they were taught. And this is the evangelist that stands on a street corner or in a church giving his testimony - or to a neighbor, the witness of his faith, or going around the world [Acts 1.8].

This Is the Two Witnesses - the Believer and the Word of God. There will be more than two witnesses in Jerusalem, Now all over the world. The Believer And The Word, God's People Sharing God's Love all over the earth.

It's not a mystery, It's a revelation
The Kingdom of God Has come in its power
Alive and well in this very hour
By the Sword and His Spirit We live by the Word
Because, sons of God We have made Jesus Lord
And now we will conquer The enemy of our land.

God's presence destroys despair when we cultivate a thankful heart and live immersed in gratefulness. God's presence surrounds our lives with a ring of fire that is His glory, and that fire will set off the land mines of hell hidden in the weeds of our lives. Instead of stepping on death, we begin walking in freedom. The distant explosions will remind us that -

God has gone before us and the way is now clear.
Anonymous

WHO IS THE 144,000 ?

Rev 14:1-5   *Then I looked, and behold, a Lamb standing on Mount Zion, and with Him one hundred and forty-four thousand, having His Father's name written on their foreheads. And I heard a voice from heaven, like the voice of many waters, and like the voice of loud thunder. And I heard the sound of harpists playing their harps. They sang as it were a new song before the throne, before the four living creatures, and the elders; and no one could learn that song except the hundred and forty-four thousand who were redeemed from the earth. These are the ones who were not defiled with women, for they are virgins. These are the ones who follow the Lamb wherever He goes. These were redeemed from among men, being firstfruits to God and to the Lamb. And in their mouth was found no deceit, for they are without fault before the throne of God.*

Surely we know that God is not saving only 144,000 of the people He loves. This is the number of the government of God. There are billions of us lovers of God. We can look at another 144.000 in Rev 7. All representing the body of Christ.

Rev 7:1-10   *After these things I saw four angels standing at the four corners of the earth, holding the four winds of the earth, that the wind should not blow on the earth, on the sea, or on any tree. Then I saw another angel ascending from the east, having the seal of the living God. And he cried with a loud voice to the four angels to whom it was granted to harm the earth and the sea, saying, Do not harm the earth, the sea, or the trees till we have sealed the servants of our God on their foreheads. And I heard the number of those who were sealed. One hundred and forty-four thousand of all the tribes of the children of Israel were sealed:*

of the tribe of Judah twelve thousand were sealed;
of the tribe of Reuben twelve thousand were sealed;
of the tribe of Gad twelve thousand were sealed;
of the tribe of Asher twelve thousand were sealed;
of the tribe of Naphtali twelve thousand were sealed;
of the tribe of Manasseh twelve thousand were sealed;
of the tribe of Simeon twelve thousand were sealed;
of the tribe of Levi twelve thousand were sealed;
of the tribe of Issachar twelve thousand were sealed;

of the tribe of Zebulun twelve thousand were sealed;
of the tribe of Joseph twelve thousand were sealed;
of the tribe of Benjamin twelve thousand were sealed.
A Multitude from the Great Tribulation

Please look at Rev 1:3 *Blessed is he who reads and those who hear the words of this prophecy, and keep those things which are written in it; for the time is near.*

Did you get that? Revelation is a book of prophecy. We have to seek the wisdom and knowledge of the Lord to understand it.

Prov 2:6 *For the Lord gives wisdom; From His mouth come knowledge and understanding;*

Prov 4:*7 Wisdom is the principal thing; Therefore get wisdom. And in all your getting, get understanding.*

So I decided to research what that list of the sons of Israel mean. First I realized that these names were not listed in the order of their birth and Manasseh was not a son of Jacob, he was the first born son of Joseph; and the tribe of Dan was missing because they went into idolatry.

Rev 7:9 *After these things I looked, and behold, a great multitude which no one could number, of all nations, tribes, peoples, and tongues, standing before the throne and before the Lamb.* So this is a representative of a great multitude; and as I researched, I found the meaning of each name in Genesis.

THESE ARE THE SONS OF GOD

A graphic example of our life in the Kingdom is shown as we examine Jacob's sons, the twelve tribes of Israel. The servants of God are depicted in these twelve tribes...See Genesis 30 and 35.23, for the correct order of their birth. Reuben, Simeon, Levi, Judah, Dan, Naphtali, Gad, Asher, Issachar, Zebulun, Joseph, Benjamin.

Hebrew genealogy always counts sons on the order of their birth. Reuben was the first born and Manasseh was not one of the 12 tribes of Israel. Judah was the fourth born son, but here in Revelation he is listed first; [Rev 7.4-8]. and Dan is left out. Judges 18.30-31 This tribe became idol worshipers; and Jeroboam, king of the northern kingdom set up idols in their territory [1 Kings 12].

So, is this listing in Revelation 7 really the order of the tribes of Israel, the sons of Jacob, in the order they were born? No.

Perhaps I am wrong in this, but it sure sounds like this listing in Revelation refers to the born again sons and daughters of our Most High God, which is the Bride of Christ; not the ancient tribes of Israel; although they were the pattern which were themselves as chosen by God, a shadow of the reality of the whole Body of Christ, born-again and redeemed from the slave master.

So here is the body of Christ, the bride, marked, sealed and protected from the evil one. Here is the identity of the sons of God, Jew and Gentile, the body of Christ.

You will find the meaning of their names in Genesis as they were born to the wives of Jacob - Israel, but now attributed to the whole body of Christ, because of what the names mean and the order in which they are now listed. These sons of Israel have become a picture of our spiritual life and shows the progression of the believer in Christ. And these were the stones on the ephod which the priest wore into the presence of God - the Holy of Holies. Exodus 35-39 will explain what was the ephod.

1. Judah - Praise
2. Reuben - Behold a Son
3. Gad - a Great Company
4. Asher - Joy or Fulfillment of Joy
5. Naphtali - to Overcome
6. Manasseh - to Forget the Past
    [born to Joseph in Egypt]
7. Simeon - the Lord Hears
   [My Sheep Will Hear My Voice]
8. Levi - to Be Joined
9. Issachar - the Price Is Paid
10. Zebulun - Dwelling Place   ]
11. Joseph - Added to or Fruitful, He Will Increase
12. Benjamin - Son of My Right Hand

Does this Describe the Inheritance
Of the Body of Christ?

Here's what it all means...
1. to praise God for our salvation,
2. adopted as His child,
3. Into His family,
4. filled with His joy,

5. faith and grace to overcome the enemy,
6. to forget our past,
7. to listen for His voice,
8. be joined to Christ,
9. because the price has been paid,
10. we are His dwelling place - He lives in us,
11. we develop the fruit of the Spirit living for God,
12. and we are the son of His right hand [Gen 35.18].

God Has Taken Away Our Reproach
And Gentiles are Grafted in.
[Romans 11.11-25].

♥

Oh Hallelujah
Our God reigns
And He shall come
with the armies of heaven
to draw His people unto
Himself. That we may live
in His presence for eternity.

♥

TRUSTING IN GOD

*Trust in the Lord with all thine heart
and lean not unto thine own understanding.
In all thy ways acknowledge him
and he shall direct thy paths.
Be not wise in thine own eyes,
fear the Lord and depart from evil.
It will be health to thy flesh
and strength to thy bones.*[1]

I came into the Kingdom of God with a racquetball heart that learned never to trust anyone. In all the years before I was born again, my life had no meaning nor goals. Relationships were a facade; a game played out by people just trying to get through the day. There was no reality - no stability.

The yawning chasm between me and another was stocked with illusions and niceties until an offense built an impossible wall. Then came rejection and loneliness. No place was found for a U-turn and so another friend would be gone from the scene.

I suppose my general anger and negative attitudes offended and turned people off. But I thank God He is changing my attitudes and motives. I've come to realize I can't please everybody and everyone is not going to like me. I have also found that to have friends, one must show themselves friendly. *And there is a friend who sticks closer than a brother.*[2]

I thank God He has enabled me to deal with my hostilities,[3] and has given me a love for people.

Our dealings with people, either in friendship or business, is mostly based on past experience and expectations. If God heals past wounds and our expectations are from Him,[4] then the offenses that come our way can easily be forgiven............................➜

> Relationships can then carry on and grow into something wonderful.

Unable to trust that the next person is not going to betray, makes one feel isolated from society. Though people may try to be a friend; if there is a history of fear to trust anyone then it's difficult to receive any friendship offered. There's always the thought, This is too good to last, and we wait for the axe to fall.

In the foundation of every person's life there is built a measure of trust. This is a powerful force of either positive or negative influence of which will commandeer that one's motivation for their entire life - unless a greater force dislodges it.

The basic foundation of trust that enables a little one to run with safety and surety into the arms of their caretaker, will carry them onward in confidence and assurance, in self worth and a positive value system; meeting life head-on, no matter what.

But in total contrast, if there was established a fear to trust and no assurance of safety; there will develop confusion, anxiety, fear, a question of identity and an attitude of rejection - of self and others.

Withdrawal, anger, resentment and no sense of purpose are attitudes that prevail in one who has no ground of basic trust that the community in which they live is a secure place to be. Most often this one will seek and find a back door of escape from offenses; but once again will there be loneliness and fear.

The Lord knew exactly what it would take to bind up my wounded heart, and so He sent me compassionate ones with His love and tenderness that would help me overcome the harshness and isolation I had so often encountered, B.C.

I remember in the early 60's I had a job working nights in a book factory. Our department sewed or stapled the pages together at the binding, after they were printed.

Even after being several weeks in the shop - I still found myself eating supper alone. I worked nights.

I tried to please my coworkers by learning quickly what was expected of me.   [I had not yet met the Lord].

One night a thousand books came to my machine for sewing on an industrial sewing machine. They get run through onerightafteranother and are cut apart at the other end of the table. They must be kept straight as they come off the machine or the next one sews crooked or breaks the needle.

The needles were supplied by the foreman, and after three were broken he was getting upset with me. I tried to understand and explain why the cutting girl was pulling the books and causing the needle breakage.

When I asked her to please do it different, she exploded violently and threatened to put those scissors through me. Ten other people were in the shop and not one tried to explain what this madness was all about!

The girls' friend joined her in threatening and cursing me. I was totally astounded and had no desire to wear a pair of scissors, for I'm certain she was capable of carrying our her threats. Please know that I did not have a relationship with Jesus at this time. I was terrified of her.

Without answering I picked up my purse, said goodnight to the foreman and went home. Later on I found out their anger came from the fact that my production quota was much more than theirs and they had the boss snowed that they were doing their best and more was impossible.

Perhaps they felt their job was on the line. Even the foreman stayed clear of these women who had turned so violent. They had been employed there for several years - so it was me that had to go. So sad because I really liked that job.

Please understand I had all my life been running on nervous energy. I did everything in a hurry. I guess I thought if I got this task done - then I would find the meaning of life and begin to see some purpose for my existence.

I was like a bee going from one place to another, never knowing what it meant to come to a place of rest. Sometimes I felt that life was a demolition derby and one could not leave the arena.

> I'm so glad Jesus reached into my pit
> and pulled me out.

After being saved I realized there were some things in the Word about trusting in God. I got out my Concordance and began looking at this. Since I had nothing to compare with my experiences in the realm of trusting anyone, this was a new concept. I had over the years developed a trust that everything I did would end up in defeat. [I know God was behind my research to find the answer].

There are precious promises given to the one who will put their trust in God. The opening verse of this chapter promises health and prosperity for trusting in Him. I learned to love His Word and to pray the Scriptures as He further established me in His Kingdom. Ps 62:5-8,

> How I thank you Lord, that you are my
> foundation rock. I can depend on you,
> for you have saved me and want to
> protect me in the face of my enemy.

I don't have to panic when
the unexpected happens.
You are my strength. I can hide in you
and not be afraid. Oh God, teach me
to trust in you at all times, for Lord -
I have no where else to go;
there is no other.

As I learned to wait on Him and let my expectations be of God, my life began to take on significant changes as I share in other chapters more fully. I looked up all the verses on trusting God and chose to make it the desire of my heart to do it; to let it become a way of life for me, not just words.

I made those verses a personal matter and thanked God for every one. I wrote them down and let them feed my hungry spirit. I identified with Job at one time of deep trouble; but I cried out...............➜

> *Though he slay me, yet will I trust him.*[5]

I was an immature Christian at the time and did not realize how the enemy of my soul was trying to destroy what little faith I had in God.

It was a season of great difficulty. My emotions were boomeranging off the walls so to speak. I felt like I was on fire I hurt so bad. That lying devil told me to curse God and die.[6] I was living in Montana at the time and there were many winding dirt roads to travel. One morning I had to go to town and in trying to navigate first this way, then that - the sun continued to almost blind me. It seemed no matter which direction I was headed I couldn't get the sun out of my face. I was beginning to get annoyed, but God spoke to me very clearly. He said...

You see Honey, no matter where you go
or which way you turn you'll always be in my sight.

Such a peace came over me. Everything was going to be O.K. God was asking me to be patient, hope and wait. He was still there in the middle of this crisis that was trying to drown me.

Because we are alive, events will happen, merely because we are alive! We respond to life out of what is already in our heart attitudes. As we grow up in the Lord, He corrects our course that we may respond according to His principles;

Peace, Love, and Joy in the Holy Ghost.

In that time of teaching me what it meant to trust and rely on Him, He also gave me a scripture,
> These things I have spoken unto you
> that in me ye might have peace.
> In the world ye shall have tribulation
> [because you are alive]
> but be of good cheer, I have overcome the world.[7]

I have since realized that Jesus is sharing with us the same peace He had, even in facing His crucifixion.

And think about this; Jesus so trusted His Father for provision that He appointed as one of the twelve, a thief - and put him in charge of the money bag! [Jn 12:6]

We can give up control of our time and accept God's control. Instead of looking at the succession of events in our daily lives as part of the pressure of the flow of time, we can accept the condition that He is in charge and will guide us in making the most of the opportunities He sends us. We are free from worry about the past or the future and are able to live in the now moment.

We can look at circumstances as a challenge to choose to adjust our natural tendencies away from anxiety or anger, and take on the character of Jesus; love, forgiveness, long-suffering, etc.

As I came to trust more in God I began to see that people are vulnerable, their flesh is weak and they will fail me continuously. They can't meet the needs of my heart and can't understand me anyway. Only God has the resources to fulfill my life. If my expectations are of God and my trust is in Him, I am no longer easily offended, I am quick to forgive and I have decided to turn off my defense mechanisms. So, when offenses come, I try to give others much leeway to be themselves. We are all in process, eh? I love the peace God gave me one day as He lead me to read,

> Blessed is the man that trusts in the Lord and whose hope the Lord is, for he shall be like a tree planted by the waters and spreads out her roots by the river, and shall not see
> when heat cometh, but her leaf shall be green
> and shall not be anxious in the year of drought,
> neither shall cease from yielding fruit.[8]

Anxiety shows up at our door when we think God is not moving fast enough, but this tree planted by the River of Life has come into the Hebrews four Sabbath rest of God.

I want to be that tree.

One does not reconstruct the many years of devastation with one book or a word from the Lord, or someone telling us to hang in there. It takes a daily walking with the Spirit of God and learning to trust in Jesus as He unlocks each dark closet memory and experience, to heal and restore.

It is these impressed on our heart from which we draw our decisions concerning the issues of our life.[9] Not everyone has been effected in negative ways, in their childhood; but to those who were,   Your Only Hope is in Jesus!

It is His desire for His precious children to put their trust in Him. Trusting in God cannot prevail until faith comes to rest in God. But our faith should not be supported by circumstances, positive or negative. We can all have faith in fear. Job 3:25 declares,

The thing I greatly feared has come upon me,
and what I dreaded has happened to me.

God showed me that I had placed my faith in my ability to believe. This of course, fluctuated according to my senses. We need to, *Have faith in God*.[10] For this verse of Scripture, the word '*in*' has been inserted by the publishers. The original Greek says...

'Have God's faith'. That's why,
All things are possible to them that believe.

We can depend on the integrity of God's Word.

The reason God wants us to set our mind on things above,[11] and not on circumstances, is that only one of these factors never changes.[12] We are so indoctrinated into making things happen to satisfy or justify any given situation as we see it.

We may even want to conform our faith according to what we hear or see in another's life. We consistently adjust the evidence until it suits our perceived need. Because of fear we imagine what would be a good solution to our problem and then try to carry it out, trusting in ourselves.

Since we are hardly ever able to evaluate the true consequences of our judgments and decisions, we are constantly tracing rabbit trails. Hence anxiety and frustration settle down in our bones ever ready to tantalize our flesh.

If our faith in God rests in and grows only because of the blessings we receive from God, then our faith in God will rest on and decrease when we don't get our prayers answered according to expectations.

If God answers one prayer in a certain way, we may look for the same results the next time. When it doesn't happen, disappointment settles in, then comes what? You name it. What happens to you?

Do you lose your faith?

We may compare this situation with a small child being put in his crib to go to sleep. Mom leaves the room and what happens. Fear comes on him. The child goes into a crying fit because Mom has left him. Well, has she abandoned him? Of course not. He has to learn to trust that she will be there when he wakes up.

If we're having a hard time going through a trial perhaps it's because we are trying to get it together, and anxiously, fearfully, watching over all the pieces of this puzzle. Very often there is fear mixed in with our faith and we have a hard time finding the line of division.

Often we confess trust in God but still are trying to figure things out. Sometimes our efforts boil down to the redundant. Jesus constantly focused on faith in God and not in the circumstances. Look up these Scriptures and you'll see how this happened.

Mt 8:26   Faith in the face of the storm.
Mt 15:28 She would not be deterred.
Mk 5:34   She overcame all the circumstances.
Mk 5:36   Jairus almost detoured.
          Jesus kept him focused.
Lk 7:9   Here is a man with true vision.
Lk 18:8   Will there be anyone totally centered in on God, and not on what they see.

According to Strong's Concordance the word faith is found just once in the gospel of John. *Be not faithless, but believing.*[13] Is this because the entire gospel of John focuses on Jesus and the trust walk of a true son of God?

As the living Father sent me, and I live because of the Father, so he who feeds on me will live because of me.[14] ....→ | Believer's intimacy! ♥

Colossians three gives us behavioral criteria the Lord is looking for. Verse 8 tells us we must also put away filthy language out of our mouth. Corrupt communication can be any negative confession first of all because it defiles us. [You can have what you say. Mark 11:23 works both ways.]

And secondly - it is disparaging to the Redeemer Who died to raise you up and to set you in heavenly places [Eph 2:6]. He died that we might live yet we speak death over circumstances,

What the use, what good is it to try.

It will never happen for me.

No one cares about me anyway.

And we have perfect faith that our negative confession will come to pass. And it will! We must renew our minds. Psalm 62 says;

> *Trust in him at all times, Oh people, pour out your heart to him, for God is our refuge.*

And this Scripture begins with
Let all your expectations be of God.

When we trust in God and have really decided to relinquish our life to Him, the covenant promises God has made with His people comes to pass in our life. We can't make it happen. God has already made the provision.

He does it so He will receive the glory. [15]

Submitting to Him, yielding control, and resting in His love will allow God to bring us step by step into His wholeness.

There are many things in our past that are hidden in our sub-conscience that deeply effect our present life of which we have little or no awareness or understanding. For instance, I have met others besides myself that were tormented by fear, yet had no conscious connecting line to the past, from which these fears certainly were rudimentary.

And so we must trust God to do that of which we are incapable; to change us into a trusting son of God. This miracle of healing that I'm about to share is true and actually happened the way I describe it.

Somewhere in my younger years of growing up I had a recurring dream that made no sense to me at the time. I only thought of it as one of many nightmares that tormented my efforts to sleep.

The years of walking with the Lord however, has brought healings into the very depth of my soul, reaching into the darkness where a dreadfully wounded little girl was hiding; afraid she would be found and required to face the charge of worthlessness - and cast aside once more.

A child, growing securely under the loving hand of parents that nurture and especially a father who takes his responsibility to heart in the care of his offspring, will be

founded on the rock of trust,
the basis on which a healthy stable life is built.

On the other hand, rejection or the fear of abandonment that is a significant part of a child's life, is probably one of the most destructive forces ever devised by the enemy of our souls.

As I have shared in other chapters of this book, my father was gone long periods of time in earlier years and finally abandoned our family when I was three years old. At this same time I suffered rejection from my mother and siblings, and this continues. If I want to contact them, I must initiate the phone call. And It' OK.

[This was happening way in the past years.
Now In these years I have good relationships with them].
If it hadn't been for God I would still be in much pain from this, but forgiveness and love has so filled my heart for them that I am glad to keep in touch with them no matter what the cost. Actually, as they went about their own life, there was little time for me.

[At this time of writing 2023, I am really the only one left of my family; and here I am soon to be 91 years old. But I know where they all are and I will see them soon. Praise God].

Satan works diligently to disengage the family unit so that the children and the offended spouse are opened to rejection and fear. He especially focuses in on the father, to force him to leave; or at least to not function in the role for which he was created.

Whether the father is in the home or gone - if he does not nurture his children, protect them, give them their identity, affirm their personhood, take his place as head of his home, and actively participate in their growing process; then a child may perceive him/herself as rejected by their father.

Many fathers work 12 hours a day to give their family things - or use work [or hobbies] to escape family responsibilities. The most important thing we can give our family - our kids, is our time.

The wounds and brokenness of rejection can go so deep as to the marrow of the bones,[16] and may be passed down through the generations to the children and the children's children. In this way satan tries to disintegrate families before any true relationships can be formed.

A person can be so hungry for love and acceptance that they mistake lust for love and marry without the judgment of a sound heart. They settle for the counterfeit. Shortly into the marriage, the honeymoon is over and the demands begin to surface that manipulate and control the other.

Often both partners are love hungry and do not know the true source of Life. The roots of instability reach out branches of fear and rejection and yet another generation is caught in the web of deception............................→

> Family dynamics define our Identity.

If it's negative, we can become so identified with rejection that we may see ourselves an outcast in the very center of our family or any other given group in which we find ourselves; even after we've been born again. The inability to trust our caretakers as a child, lies at the root of the rejection syndrome. The Bible tells us we can take an axe to that root, and destroy the lies it is feeding on. The Bible tells us when our father and mother forsake us, the Lord will take us up [Ps 27:10].

Old Testament law [Dt 25:5-10] provided for a man's name to be perpetuated if he died before siring children. The man's kin would marry his widow and raise up children in his name. That way his inheritance would not be lost. In Genesis 38 we discover how man's disdain can pervert God's intentions.

It is not so capricious that wife and children take on the father's name. A family name is to be respected and honored. The family name tells us who we are. It marks out our identity.

Rejection by our mother can cause deep wounds, bitterness, rage, hatred, self pity, insecurity, etc. But rejection by the father is all that plus, a greater perversion and misinterpretation of what God instituted in the family structure, and of His purposes;

That we would receive God our Creator

As our real Father.

The identification process of our mind becomes firmly embedded in the subconscious. Everything heard about God the Father is siphoned through the pain and agony of our childhood. He is cruel and unjust, and does not care about me.

We do need to understand that a person cannot give what they don't have. So we must acknowledge that our parents probably inherited these traits from their parents. Hence the generational sins are passed down to continue until someone forgives and breaks the curses from their blood line.

It's amazing how many females I have prayed with, in the arena of their father's rejection; God heals their pain - and for the first time they recognize their femininity and start wearing make-up and dresses.

I ministered to a young girl bent on homosexuality - raped and used by her father, and preacher grandfather; that one day came to show me the new pair of nylons she'd bought and was wearing, even under her new dress pants and pretty blouse.

I'd never seen her in anything but jeans and mannish attire. She was well on her way to being completely healed in Christ. As she forgave them, she released judgment of them into God's hand, and He ministered healing and deliverance into her broken life. Now she is free from the fear of God, and may receive all God has for her. I haven't seen her for years but I know God is continuing the process.

The family unit was created by God to represent the Kingdom of God, the Fatherhood of God; the analogy of sons and daughters born-again[17] into His family, accepted with unconditional love.................→

> Accepted in the Beloved. ♥

When the position of earthly fatherhood is warped and distorted, the child may grow up to compare these negative attributes with the character of God.

Until the Spirit of God heals these things it is impossible to relate to God the Father and have relationship based on this ideal. There is only bitter experiences to draw from, overshadowed by the fear and terror of rejection and abandonment by God.

It has been studied over the years and reaffirmed that what a person thinks of their earthly father, is usually what they believe about God. I can confirm this from my own life without reading the reports. My father abandoned me - so would God.

After I was born again, I had to deal with the assumed possibility of this scenario, because then I probably would have carried out my thoughts of suicide.

But for me, God had other plans.

God is faithful. His Spirit works diligently all through our lives to capture and enrapture us within His magnificent, loving arms. He will never let us go. And He will deliver us from the lies and deceptions of satan.

> Our Father God has created within Himself
> A place called home
> It is an ever expanding place
> Of acceptance, warmth and love.
> It was deliberately
> Formed in the center of His Being,
> Surrounded by His arms of love,
> So that all His children would fit,
> And be forever safe.

In praying with a certain lady, God revealed that because of massive childhood rejection [that was still recurring through her family] was so fearful as to allow a deceiving reprobate spirit to cause her to believe she was unapproved of and rejected by God, when in fact she loved Jesus and determined to discover the root of her fears. We quickly got rid of that fellow and she commenced to see the truth of God's Word, that she also is loved and accepted by her Father in heaven.

Even as we begin to overcome these lies of the enemy and God brings healing to our soul and mind we must remember that not every one will like us and want to spend 12 hours a day in our company. And we must stop looking for man's approval. There are offenses that will come.[18]

Sometimes we are reproached for the name of Christ - often we are repudiated because - believe it or not we can be obnoxious and give others an occasion.

It is important to realize that we will be rejected somewhere, sometime, by somebody. We need to work on our hostile attitudes and downright anger at life, because we feel cheated, duped, taken advantage of.

Beloved of God, brothers and sisters, we must come to a place where we can lay down our right to be justified. Lay all this dross down and ask the Spirit of God to bring us out of our cocoon and be released into the flight stage; become a part of the solution instead of always the center of the problem. Some of us don't have anger, we are an angry people, but we must not....

Sin, and let the sun go down on our anger.[19]

*God is our refuge and strength,
a very present help in trouble.*
He is ever present, even within you.
The battle is not yours, but the Lord's.
2Chronicles 20 is a chapter in the Bible everyone should be familiar with. It is an awesome declaration of God's deliverance in the face of tremendous odds. God's solution will astound you and help you realize the power of trusting in God. Read it all.

King Jehoshaphat is warned that a great multitude was coming against Jerusalem. Three nations joined forces against Jehoshophat. These enemies came together to assault and conquer the tribes of Judea.
*A great multitude is coming against you
and behold they are in Hazazon-tamar
[which is Engedi].*
This word Engedi means an eye, Jehovah sees!
This passage is so exciting.
Jehoshaphat declared a fast throughout all Judah! All the cities of Judah came together and sought the Lord, *to ask help of the Lord*; and he prayed. First, Jehoshaphat declared Who his God is; and Who was his God, no one but Jehovah; and
*Are you not our God, and in your hand
is there not power and might,
so that none is able to withstand you?*
Now he stands in the covenant God made with Solomon. *When evil comes, if we stand in this house and cry to you, that you will hear and help us.* So they came into the presence of their God. This is where the grace, the favor, the blessings of the Lord are bestowed upon us. The presence of God will go with us as we trust Him to be our covering and protection; and He will be the judge of our enemies!

And now Jehoshaphat lays out his problem before the Lord. God knows all about our problem, He knew before the beginning of time all the troubles that would come our way. He wants us to realize how helpless we are. Remember,
Without me, you can do nothing, declares the Lord.
O our God, will you not judge them? For we have no might against this great company that comes against us, neither do we know what to do, but our eyes are on you.

Now, can you easily pray what Jehoshaphat prayed? Can you put all your trust in a God you can't see, or perhaps you haven't had prayers answered for a while, or has your prayer time been kinda at loose ends.

Would now be a good time to ask forgiveness, to forgive yourself, to humble yourself before the God that loves you so much He died for you so that He could be the Lord of your life and be your provider? Right at this time the word says ,

All Judah stood before the Lord, with their little ones, their wives and their children.

They put all their lives in the hands of the Lord. The burden of all this belonged to their God. It was not for them to try to solve this problem. Why don't you speak to Him about it right now. Whatever burden you are carrying, the shoulders of our mighty Redeemer are strong enough to carry it all.

Then upon Jahaziel...,came the Spirit of the Lord in the midst of the congregation.

He was a son of Asaph, a most beloved of God's anointed priesthood, and had a rich inheritance in God. God is right in the middle of our dilemmas also, to choose the right person at the right time to come along side us; to encourage, to remind us of Who is charge.

Verse 14 tells us, *Then upon Jahaziel...* , his name means 'beheld of God', *came the Spirit of the Lord in the midst of the congregation.* Son of Zechariah [God remembers]; son of Benaiah [Yah has built]; son of Jeiel [carried away of God]; son of Mattaniah [gift of Yah] these were the sons of Asaph, [a singer, a worshiper, a musical composer, and wrote more than 10 psalms], a most beloved of God's anointed priesthood, and had a rich inheritance in God.

Does God not remember us? Has He not built us into His temple? Are we not carried away of God? And according to John 17.2,6,9,11,12,24, We are a gift from the Father - to His Son. Jesus Christ is God's love gift to the world, and believers are the Father's love gift to Jesus Christ. God beholds us as His precious jewels; He has made us worthy to be called the temple of God; His desire is to fill us with all the fulness of God and to know His unsearchable, uncompromising, unconditional love for us.

But now, just remember how rich is

your inheritance because of Jesus. ❤
God was already with them. He declared that the battle was not theirs but the Lord's. When we trust God, He takes care of our business. He is watching! In verse 16 of this passage, the word Ziz means to twinkle, shine, to show forth. The Lord shows us the enemy clearly, Because The battle is not yours, it is God's!

God's light exposes the works of darkness.
Jeruel means founded of God. He chooses the time and place. How much more clear can it be that God knows all our problems and will show us how to deal with them.
> You shall not need to fight in this battle;
> set yourselves, stand still and see
> the salvation of the Lord with you...
> fear not nor be dismayed.

Three nations came against the tribes of Judah. Researching the root meaning of the names of these nations, you will find they relate to the lust of the flesh, the lust of the eye and the pride of life. These things can run rampant in someone who always feels victimized; and they will feel justified in it.

But we can learn to walk in the peace of God.

This is the place of power! The place of trusting God!
The first thing Jehoshaphat did was fall on his face with all the people and worshiped the Lord.
> Then all the priesthood stood up to praise the
> Lord God of Israel with a loud voice on high.

Searching 1Peter will find that we are -
> A royal priesthood, a holy nation unto our God.

We have the same power and authority to come before the Lord to petition, to receive an answer and then to trust Him to help us. In the middle of all this we have praise and thanksgiving going on in our heart. This is the place of power.

Then they went to battle - Judah [praise] went first. They rose early in the morning and went forth into the wilderness of Tekoa. This word means a 'trumpet. [They were already declaring their victory]. As they went forth, Jehoshaphat warned them,
> Believe in the Lord your God, so shall you be established;
> Believe His prophet, so shall you prosper.

How does this fit into our lives today - We must trust our God because He is trustworthy. And it is the Word that speaks to us today. We must believe and trust the Word of God. The Word that comes forth from God will not return to Him void of His promise [Isaiah 55.11].

They were sounding the voice of victory even as they were marching into battle. Jehoshaphat encouraged them to only believe, as he appointed the singers to praise the beauty of holiness, and say,

Praise the Lord for his mercy endures forever.
When they began to sing, the Lord turned the enemy on each other, and when Judah came to the watchtower in the wilderness,

They looked unto the multitudes and behold they were dead bodies fallen to the earth, and none escaped.
These three tribes actually killed each other. There was no battle to be fought, all because His people chose to trust in God and praise Him in their circumstances. The Scripture tells us they were three days gathering the spoil. It reminds me of the three days Jesus was in the grave to ransom us from the enemy and give us back the riches of His glorious inheritance.

The secret of overcoming and getting on with Kingdom business is to invite the Spirit of God to have dealings with you on a daily basis. God has a portion to give us every day, of His life and His love. We have so many walls of defense around us that even as God is trying to pour His life into us, we may hinder the process by our fears and apprehension. Each time God has ministered to me, He has wrapped me in His arms of love and protection as He declares,

Fear not for I have redeemed thee,
I have called thee by name, thou art mine.
He has become
my Defense, my High Tower.
He is also yours!
Praise His Holy Name.

God had the following words forever recorded in His Word because He knew we would take on loads of burdens and responsibilities that our shoulders were never meant to carry. They can cause a grieving spirit, a heavy heart, anxieties, fears, many things; BUT - we seem to forget - He took them all to the cross.

Some burdens come out of our human compassion for those who are hurting, but God showed me that He hung on a cross of wood, symbolic of our humanity. He took on the burden of our humanity. So Father, in Jesus name, let us know the depth of Your love that wants to carry all our burdens, and in realizing this, cause us to give them to You, and to understand that You are most willing to take them from us.

Matt 11:28-30 *Come to Me, all you who labor and are heavy-laden and overburdened, and I will cause you to rest. [I will ease and relieve and refresh your souls]. Take My yoke upon you and learn of Me, for I am gentle [meek] and humble [lowly] in heart, and you will find rest [relief and ease and refreshment and recreation and blessed quiet] for your souls. For My yoke is wholesome [useful, good — not harsh, sharp, or pressing, but comfortable, gracious, and pleasant], and My burden is light and easy to be borne.* [and Jer 6:16].

We don't really know or understand the fulness of what God wants to do for us. We can do nothing of value without Him, as pertains to relationships. We must acknowledge that we can do little - but that He does it for us and in us. He only wants our cooperation. Will you choose to let Him?

Phil 2:12-13 *work out your own salvation with fear and trembling; for it is God who works in you both to will and to do for His good pleasure.*

This means cooperate with Him and ...

Everything from God must be received, so we can ask God to knock down our walls of defense as He did Jericho, and through the healing process have our lives changed one day at a time. We can be made whole. I challenge you to step out and speak to your Lord and Savior. Ask Him to do this work in you. The way has already been provided, it's your inheritance. He wants your cooperation, to yield to His will.

*Be followers of them who through faith
and patience inherit the promises.*[23]

And give all the glory to God. He is worthy.

God wants to extend our goals and cast off our limits that we may receive the reward of our faith. God has so much more for us than we can possibly imagine.

Since the Lord is eternally present in the past, the future, the here and now; He is able to transcend all obstacles to walk with us in the spirit of our memories and deep within our subconscious, unearth all long forgotten pain..➜

Some refer to this work of God as inner healing.

As Pastor James Robison describes it, 'If inner healing is the ongoing, sanctifying work of the Holy Spirit within us to conform us to the image of Jesus, then we need it'.

Whatever the reader would like to call it - it is real, it is a miracle of healing the past. It is happening to me - and continues. The enemy is an opportunist and begins to oppress and trouble our life at the most vulnerable times - as children and when we experience stress and pain; and as most already know, because of sin.

John and Paula Sanford [Healing the Wounded Spirit, Victory House Inc, Tulsa, OK] says it like this. Picture an old dry well with sticks and leaves, spiders and insect litter at the bottom. As a great rain would fill up the well so all the litter would rise to the surface; in the same way the water of the Holy Spirit forces to the surface whatever rotten old things have been lying dormant in our natures. The first function of the Holy Spirit Who is called Holy is to convict us of sin. He Himself dislodges and causes these old things to rise up within us. He is neither surprised nor offended. He knew all along. We are the only ones astonished at what is revealed. Now one minute at a time - one hour, one day - here a little there a little - the Holy Spirit is wise and does not drive us into mental breakdown.

Ex 23:30-31 *Little by little I will drive them out from before you, until you have increased, and you inherit the land.*

Yes, now Holy Spirit gives us control; we no longer have to fight with this enemy of our soul. There is 'Freedom in Christ'.

Now we can begin to pray, and if needed - He'll send along a prayer partner. Isaiah 53 which speaks of the crucifixion of Jesus tells us *He bore our griefs and carried our sorrows - He was wounded for our transgression - by His stripes we are healed.* When Jesus went to the cross He accomplished three things:
1. the forgiveness of our sin -
2. the healing of our body -
3. the healing and restoration of our soul [see Ps 23:3]

Trusting in God to do this work does not include purposefully visualizing Jesus to do certain things. We cannot determine in our mind before hand, to manipulate or control the outcome of God's work in us. We cannot manipulate and control the Spirit of God. This device may draw the attention of another spirit that will be glad to accommodate patterns of self will.

I've prayed with people for the healing of their wounded past and have seen Jesus touch them or hug them in my mind's eye. I neither expect it nor plan for it.

But this is a part of the ministry of the Spirit as explained in Eph 1:17-18

And the gifts of the Spirit [1Co 12].

It was a blessing and confirmation to my heart that Jesus was accomplishing what we were praying for and at the same time, the person experienced the presence of God.

In every instance if God is not glorified, if people are not led to give pre-eminence to Jesus, if He is not lifted up - then we must assume the signs and wonders are not from God. We can submit ourselves to the searching of the Spirit of God,[26] that He might wash us clean from the pollution of the world, the flesh and the devil. Remember Simon in Acts 8.

God is looking for clean vessels through whom to pour out His Kingdom resources upon a hungry hurting world. Jesus told Peter,

Satan hath desired to have you, that he may sift you as wheat; but I have prayed for thee, that thy faith fail not.
And when thou art converted strengthen thy brethren.[27]

We are more able to understand the pain of others because of our own, and there must be the capacity to love without judgement.[28] He is the Great Shepherd, and He is the Door. He guards the way to His sheepfold.

Jesus will give us His unconditional love to rule in our hearts that it may pour out to others. True ministry comes forth from His love. We are His hands, His feet, His heart.

When we are led by the Holy Spirit to minister to someone in this capacity, each situation and encounter brings such a flow of God's mercy and deep love to set the captive free. I stand in awe of His personal attendance to healing His people in their minds and their brokenness.

Secular ways only serve to keep the pain current. Sometimes the scheme is to brainwash by hypnosis; the counterfeit of the renewing of the mind, and it has no fruitful benefits. There will be no real healing; only greater bondage.

If any have already experienced this, confess it to God, ask for and receive Healing, Deliverance, and Restoration.

Using secular methods is like putting a band-aid on a broken arm. Guided imagery is not ministering through the gifts of the Holy Spirit. We all have an imagination and it can be activated by just a word or thought, not led by the Holy Spirit. We must pray and invite God's Spirit to control these sessions. In the renewing of our mind we can begin to walk out that good and acceptable and perfect will of God. We can have a sanctified imagination that is not given over to worldly causes and always in submission to God.

We must walk in the Spirit, be led by the Spirit, know the Father's heart for the given circumstance, be able to discern the Holy Spirit - an evil spirit or man's spirit. This is by the gift of the discerning of spirits.[29]

A person cannot strive to operate in these gifts or any others because they belong to the Holy Spirit - it's His ministry, His presence. He uses yielded vessel to operate through, because we are the physical body of Christ on the earth.

Getting back to the recurring dream of my childhood, it had been many years since I'd even thought of it. So God began to filter bits and pieces day by day, back into my conscience mind. It occurred to me that these ideas were familiar but to remember why, I couldn't. It was buried very deeply. I asked the Lord what was He trying to show me, and what did these things mean.

In my dream I was a little girl rising from my bed of sleep and going over to the bedroom closet. My concern was with the upper shelves which had their own doors high up by the ceiling. This kind of closet really was in my childhood bedroom.

Behind those doors I knew someone was hiding in the dark. I was the only one who knew she was there and it was up to me to bring her food. I constantly had to apologize to her for forgetting. She constantly reminded me to not tell anyone she was there.

She frightened me, because she was dressed in rags, unkempt and forlorn and always pulled back into the shadows. There was so much of her familiar to me though I couldn't then say what it was. I only know I continued to go to her in my dreams. She existed in darkness, terrified, alone and never grew any older.

When we commit our lives to God He is totally in commitment and covenant to bring to wholeness that which has been broken and devastated in our former life B.C. - or before Christ. Redemption is not only for eternity - God wants to redeem each and every area of our life; changing us [our personality, motives, attitudes, emotions, our ways of thinking and doing, etc. into the image of Christ.[30]

Transformed - Metamorphosis
like a caterpillar into a gorgeous butterfly.

When I was born again through His incorruptible seed,[31] I began to read the Word and saw how ludicrous was my life in comparison with what God was saying. That's why even my Christian walk was a facade. I had to hurry up and be all the Word said I was - so that I could belong.

God helped me to see He wanted to make me real, but I had no idea what that meant. Oh God, my whole life has been lived on the edge of inconsistency, how can it possibly be any different? But with God all things are possible, and He continued to bring me one day at a time into wholeness and reality.

As Jesus went with me back into my bedroom of the past I was confronted with that closet and the mysterious figure hiding in the dark. The Lord asked me to help her get down but I was overcome by a paralyzing fear. Greatly terrified, I began to realize I was that little girl. It was then that I saw and experienced the full meaning of this dream and the impact it had on me.

I saw how the seed of rejection had grown into the fears and anxieties that dominated my life. Stunted in growth - frozen in time - afraid for life to find me out. How could I present this nightmare to a pure and holy Jesus. I was so ashamed that He would know my secret..➔

> I was a phony, a counterfeit; and I did not belong.

Even though I was starved to receive His life I was incapable of bringing this truth about myself out into the light. I was a throwaway, of no real value to anyone. No one was really interested in what I had to say or what was happening to me. The best I could invent for myself was wishing I was someone else. No matter how this sounds - it was real for me.

These things haunted me even in my adult life.

The forces of death and darkness, fear and loneliness had such a grip on me they dared to try to hold me in their power, even in the presence of Jesus. But you know what; you can throw all kinds of trash into the River of Life and this River will continue to flow pure and clean. Nothing you can come up with can ever pollute the holiness of our Eternal Lord of Glory.

He took it all unto Himself on the cross of Calvary. He brought it all with Him into the realms of death. He left it all there, when He arose, victorious over the works of the devil.

The Lord Jesus simply asked me if it was okey with me if He helped her come down. I could only look at Him and hope He knew what my heart was crying out for; to be set free. As He reached up, that dying little girl grasped His hands and climbed down into the Lord of Life.

He took into Himself all the pain, the shame, the death and fear, the darkness - most of all, the rejection and loneliness, and gave me

Acceptance in the Beloved according to the good pleasure of His will. [32] ♡

And the question is this; can we trust God in His mercy, to tear through the very fabric of our being. Can we trust

Jehovah Jireh, The God That Sees!

Psalm 139 reveals the intimate relationship and fellowship we were created for. He would search the inner depths of our soul. With the same compassion and love that drove Him to the cross to reconcile us to Himself, He would lift out from our broken heart, the pain - the anguish - the agony. He would dispel our fear. He would quiet our mind. He is looking for responding trust to a passionate love poured out from the Father's heart. And please know it is never too late. He healed that wounded child in a 50 year old adult!

As God has chosen to forgive us so we must choose to forgive. We have long carried the burden of demand for justice and vindication. Now is the time; now is the hour; release all to

THE ONE WHO CREATED YOU FOR HIS PLEASURE.

And I will cause him to draw near, and he shall approach unto me; for who is this that engaged his heart to approach unto me? saith the Lord, and ye shall be my people and I will be your God.[33]

At one time I was under severe attack by satan through some people who were yielded to his ways. I became

very defensive and came against them vocally and in prayer. Because I knew I was covered by the Blood, I continued to seek God to discover why they had this access to me. First God gave me Romans 12.
Recompense to no man evil for evil, avenge not yourself, vengeance is mine, I will repay saith the Lord, overcome evil with good.
Then He reminded me of Paul's thorn.
My grace is sufficient.
It will fix your thorn and anything else that troubles you.
There are Scriptures to confirm again and again what God says about this subject. 1Peter 3:9-17 - *Not rendering evil for evil...*
1Thes 5:15 - *See that none render evil for evil unto any man...*
2Samuel 16:5-13 - Even if others say you are justified..
Proverbs 20:22 - *Do not say I will repay evil, wait expectantly for the Lord and He will rescue you...*

Then He lowered the boom! After writing a whole book about dying to self and being totally yielded to God, I was still manifesting self-righteousness. I was reminded of when Achan sinned at Jericho. He thought that since God gave them the victory over the city and they could slay them all; 'Well, we must be the greatest to have God's favor, so we must be deserving of a reward'.

His self-righteousness proved to be a snare. Suddenly the enemy had favor against God's people. That's why 5:13-14 is so powerful. 'I Am for the pure in heart'. Self-righteousness will cause Proverbs 24:17-18 to manifest.
Rejoice not when thine enemy falls, and let not thine heart be glad when he stumbles, lest the Lord see it, and it shall displease Him, and He turn away His wrath from him... [and expend it on you, a worse offender]
[Ampl]
Who among us shall dwell with the devouring fire?
Who among us shall dwell with everlasting burnings?
He that walks righteously!
When something is burned up, those strings can no longer be pulled, and Jesus can bring resurrection life into that arena. Trusting in God, letting our expectations be only of Him, allowing the good pleasure of His will to work in us day by day,[34] we can be sure,
He is able to keep that which we have

committed unto him against that day.[35]
*Lean on, trust in and be confident in the Lord
with all your heart and mind and do not rely on your own
insight or understanding. In all your ways know, recognize,
and acknowledge Him, and He shall direct and make
straight and plain your paths. Be not wise in your own
eyes; reverently fear and worship the Lord
and turn [entirely] away from evil.
It shall be health to your nerves and sinews,
and marrow and moistening to your bones.*[36]

There are many issues of life that need drastic correction. The issue of top priority is, are you ready to throw yourself on the mercy of the highest court in the universe.

Remember Romans 12,
*By the mercies of God - through, in, and because of!
The mercy - in His mercy present your body.*
Mercy: compassion, pity, merciful,
of tender mercy -

And remember the word in this verse

is plural - many mercies,

An abundance for everyone.

Because I forgave and let God handle the consequences - I was found innocent and redeemed.

We are surrounded by His mercies. His everlasting love is upon us and in us and through us to bring us into His peace. When we choose God's ways, we can walk on His path. Are you ready to put your foot into His footprint?
[I did one time and He healed my fractured talus bone.

Lord, I thank You that I can safely place my life in Your hands and that You are faithful and worthy of my confidence. If I have Jesus, I have everything. In all my ways, I can ask You; and You will lead and guide me.

Our Father God is so totally aware of everything in our life. He knows exactly what it will take to bring us step by step - to grow in grace and virtue in His Kingdom. We are all in the pruning and growing stage. When we trust our lives into His hands and allow Him to choose   [Psalm 47]
*The food convenient for us,
then we can be sure He will bring us into safety.
For the Lord Most High
Is Awe Inspiring, He Is a Great King
Over All the Earth. He Will Choose*

Our Inheritance for Us ❤
Here in Your presence I rest in Your love
Here in Your presence In Spirit I move
Only what You ask of me
Will I choose to do Your will
But for this very moment
I will be still.

Oh Give Thanks to the Lord
For He Is Good.
He Is Absolutely So Good.

❤

STUDY GUIDE

1. Are you able to freely trust God in the issues of your life?
2. Do you hesitate - wondering if this time you ought to handle it yourself?
3. Do you panic easily, not remembering there is Someone to Whom   you can turn?
4. Have you found the Rock of Hope; and faith to feel safe when you do turn to God?
5. Have you forgiven any and all who may have contributed to your anxiety or fear to trust?
6. Have you begun your study on the word trust? [God's trustworthiness?]
7. Have you made some new decisions; to renew your mind and draw closer to God.
8. Are you releasing your life into His hands and trusting Him to bring restoration and wholeness?
9. Sometimes our emotional pain makes us think we're going crazy. The devil wants you to maintain the status quo. If you are a child of the Most High God, you have the resources to evict him. Find out the truth, for it will make you free. He's already been defeated by the cross. Victory is yours. The Holy Spirit will lead and guide you into all truth.

PRAYER: Lord Jesus, You know exactly what I need and exactly the right time I need it. I humble myself and draw close to You. Thank you for the grace to trust you with my life.

Some things were never meant to be
We make mistakes in the course of our life
We sometimes pursue a forbidden path
Not knowing the trouble out-of-sight
We try and try to make it work
Blinded by self-satisfaction
We ride along on stress and fear
And never take any action
We live a life of loneliness
As though it will be alright
But in the final course of life
It dissolves into the night.
So Lord Jesus, I give to You
The life You have given me
For the plans and purpose
You already have
Cause that's what was meant to be.

♥

SCRIPTURES

1. Pr 3:5,6
2. Pr 18:24
3. 1Jn 1:9
4. Ps 62:5-8
5. Jn 13:15
6. Job 2:9
7. Jn 16:33
8. Je 17:7-8
9. Pr 4:23.10.
   Mk 11:22
11. Co 3:2
12. Ma 3:6
13. Jo 20:27
14. Jo 6:57
15. Ep 2:10
16. Pr 17:22
17. 2Co 6:16-18
18. Mt 18. 6-7
19. Ep 4:26
20. Ps 46:1
21. Ep 1:18
22. 2Pe 1:3-11
23. He 6:12
24. Is 54:2
25. He 11:6
26. Ps 139:23
27. Lk 22:31-32
28. 1Co 4:5-7
29. 1Jn 4:1
30. 2Co 3:8
31. 1Pe 1:23
32. Ep 1:5
33. Je 30: 21-22
34. Ph 2:13
35. 2Ti 1:12
36. Pr 3:5-7
37. Ps 47:2,4

TRUST SCRIPTURES

I became an adult and still did not know what it meant to trust anyone. But it is imperative that we learn to trust God, for that is what our relationship with Him is built on. One day God spoke to me about this issue and wanted to teach me; so I learned it all from His Word. ?where else? I wrote them down and took His Word into my heart.

You can also pray these into your life. Of course it is a journey, this life in Christ. Things don't change over night. But God wants us to learn how to trust in Him. This may be a further growing in the Lord, or it can be a new beginning. Remember It is a process. One day at a time.

I have heard that the very center of all Scripture verses in the Bible is Psalm 118. 8. Could there be any words more appropriate than this one, in a book of instructions by our God.

> *It is better to trust in the Lord*
> *than to put confidence in man.*

It would be a blessing to all who would meditate on the following verses and pray them into your life. Here is an example.

Psalm 2:12: Blessed are all those who put their trust in Him.
PRAYER: Lord, cause me to trust in You more every day, that I may receive Your blessings. Forgive me for not trusting. Thank You for Your gift of salvation.

> [If you don't understand the meaning of any verse then do James 1.5, and may God pour out His grace on you, as you search for a deeper relationship with your Lord].

This next verse is one of the greatest promises in His Word.
John 14:15-18 *If you love Me, keep My commandments. And I will pray the Father, and He will give you another Helper, that He may abide with you forever — the Spirit of truth, whom the world cannot receive, because it neither sees Him nor knows Him; but you know Him, for He dwells with you and will be in you. I will not leave you orphans; I will come to you.*

Every day we go deeper into God as we learn to walk
and live in His ways so that the blessings and treasures
of God are ours. It is a day by day learning
to trust Him more and more ♥

Psalms 4:5: I Offer the sacrifices of righteousness, And I put my trust in the LORD. [For example, what are the sacrifices of righteousness? Here are some]
Ps 118:19-21 Open to me the gates of righteousness; I will go through them, And I will praise the Lord. This is the gate of the Lord, Through which the righteous shall enter. I will praise You,
For You have answered me, And have become my salvation.
Deut 33:19 They shall call the peoples to the mountain; There they shall offer sacrifices of righteousness; For they shall partake of the abundance of the seas And of treasures hidden in the sand.
Psalms 11:1 Faith in the LORD's Righteousness. In the LORD I put my trust.

Psalms 5:11: But let all those rejoice who put their trust in You; Let them ever shout for joy, because You defend them; Let those also who love My name Be joyful in Me.
Psalms 7:1: O LORD my God, in You I put my trust; Save me And deliver me, [God will save us every day from the things that try to come against us because we belong to Him and we trust Him].
Psalms 9:10: And those who know My name will put their trust in Me; For You, LORD, will never forsake me as I seek to know You more.

Psalms 13:1: I Trust in the Salvation of the LORD.
Psalms 16:1: Preserve me, O God, for in You I put my trust.
Psalms 17:7: I will Show My marvelous lovingkindness by My right hand, I will save those who trust in Me.
Psalms 18:2: The LORD is my rock and my fortress and my deliverer; My God, my strength, in whom I will trust; My shield and the horn of my salvation, my stronghold.
Psalms 18:30: As for God, His way is perfect; The word of the LORD is proven; He is a shield to all who trust in Him.

Psalms 25:2, 20: O God, I trust in You; Let me not be ashamed; Let not my enemies triumph over me, for I put my trust in you.
Psalms 31:1: In You, O LORD, I put my trust; Let me never be ashamed; Deliver me in My righteousness.
Psalms 31:14:, I will trust in You, O LORD; I say, 'You are my God'.

Psalms 31:19: Oh, how great is Your goodness, Which You have laid up for those who fear You, Which You have prepared for those who trust in You, In the presence of the sons of men! Psalms 34:1: [The Happiness of Those Who Trust in God]
I will bless the LORD at all times; His praise shall continually be in my mouth
Psalms 34:22: The LORD redeems the soul of His servants, And none of those who trust in Him shall be condemned.
Psalms 36:7: How precious is Thy lovingkindness, O God! Therefore the children of men put their trust under the shadow of Your wings.
Psalms 37:3: Trust in the LORD, and do good; Dwell in the land, and feed on His faithfulness.

Psalms 40:3: He has put a new song in my mouth Praise to our God; Many will see it and fear, And will trust in the LORD.
Psalms 40:4: Blessed is that man who makes the LORD his trust, Psalms 56:3: Whenever I am afraid, I will trust in You.
Psalms 56:11: In God I have put my trust; I will not be afraid. What can man do to me?
Psalms 62:8: Trust in Him at all times, you people; Pour out Your heart before Him; God is a refuge for us.
Psalms 64:10: The righteous shall be glad in the LORD, and trust in Him. And all the upright in heart shall glory.
Psalms 71:1: God the Rock of my Salvation In You, O LORD, I put my trust; Let me never be put to shame.

Matt 6:32-33 For your heavenly Father knows that you need all these things. But seek first the kingdom of God and His righteousness, and all these things shall be added to you.
Phil 3:8-10 That I may gain Christ and be found in Him, not having my own righteousness, which is from the law, but that which is through faith in Christ, the righteousness which is from God by faith.

Remember at Jesus baptism:
Matt 3:15 But Jesus answered and said to him, "Permit it to be so now, for thus it is fitting for us to fulfill all righteousness." Then he allowed Him.
    He was fulfilling our journey into His righteousness.
        And He began at the beginning.

2 Cor 5:21   *For He made Him [Jesus] who knew no sin, to be sin for us, that we might become the righteousness of God in Him.*

[Jesus traded our sin for His righteousness].

Eph 6:14-15   [The armor of God] *Stand therefore, having girded your waist with truth, having put on the breast plate of righteousness...*
Prov 3:5-6   [WHEN WE] *Trust in the Lord with all your heart, And lean not on your own understanding; In all your ways acknowledge Him, And He shall direct your path.*
[Then we will experience ...
John 14:26   *Peace I leave with you, My peace I give to you; not as the world gives do I give to you. Let not your heart be troubled, neither let it be afraid*   [because God says]

Jer 33:3   *Call to Me, and I will answer you,*
           and show you great and mighty things,
                which you do not know.' ❤

THIS IS YOUR DESTINY.
    DO YOU BELIEVE IT!!   DO YOU RECEIVE IT???

To enlighten all men and make plain to them what is the plan of the mystery kept hidden through the ages and concealed until now in the mind of God Who created all things... [Col 1.26]

Eph 3 *The purpose is that through the church the complicated, many sided wisdom of God in all its infinite variety and innumerable aspects might now be made known, His eternal and timeless purpose, carried into effect in the person of Christ Jesus our Lord.*

[That] He grant you out of the rich treasury of His glory to be strengthened and reinforced with mighty power in the inner man by the Holy Spirit, Himself indwelling your innermost being and personality. May Christ through your faith actually dwell, settle down, abide, make His home in your hearts!

May you be rooted deep in love and founded securely on love. That you may have the power and be strong to apprehend and grasp with all the saints, God's devoted people, the experience of that love, what is the breadth and length and height and depth of it.

That you may really come to know practically, through experience for yourself, the love of Christ which far surpasses mere knowledge, without experience; that you may be filled through all your being unto all the fullness of God; and may have the richest measure of the divine Presence, and become a body wholly filled and flooded with God Himself. Amplified Bible]

<pre>
       I would seek Your face Lord,
          Not Your hand to give
         I would seek communion,
            For in this do I live
         I've had many an answer
           For special needs of mine
        But they compare as nothing,
             If I can't be Thine
        The closeness of Your Spirit,
          Your touch upon my heart
      The knowledge You have given me
            That we will never part
     Oh Lord my God, my Precious One,
          Your love has lifted me
       Because You've given all of You,
             I give my all to Thee

       I have a Father, He knows my name
      He calls me to His side, again and again
            He sees me where I am,
              And where I will go
         His plans for me too wonderful,
            He reveals so I will know
           Eternity - for at His side,
            I'll rule and reign with Him
           Because by His precious Blood,
            He redeemed me from my sin
              So I'm free to worship
             With all my heart and soul
           And live with Him forever,
             In the Kingdom of His love ❤
</pre>

HOPE, EXPECTATIONS, DISAPPOINTMENTS.

This chapter was written; actually the very first of all the chapters and books I have ever written. It was given to me while my husband of 20 years, was divorcing me. One night God began to download the story of all the fears of my hope, expectations and disappointment coming to fruition. All these words were filling my mind till I was begging God to please let me sleep. But no, *He said, Get up and write these things down. It is the first chapter of your book.* God told me years before that I would write a book so ... Here it is. He called it 'Handbook on Victory'. It had 19 chapters. Now changed to 'Our Inheritance'.

God had given me His unconditional love for Mike no matter what he did or didn't do. It was the only way I could survive this lifeless marriage. I was a runner all my life from hard things; but God told me if I didn't run He would help me; so I stayed. God wanted to do some things in me that ... well; He gave me Deuteronomy 8.2-3. That will explain. And I should say that 3 years before this, God told me He was taking me into a desert place and to keep my eyes on Him.

It took me a long time of realizing Mike would not change his life. I lived with so many years of his adultery; finally God took him out of my life, and not too many years later, he had a heart attack I had prayed so long for him to come back to God - that was my hope. My expectation was in the Word and trusting in God to change him. So many friends said trust Him.

But my disappointment; well in the end, God told me -
'I cannot come against his free will.'
For too long I believed God would change him, but now...
I had to get back to focusing more on God.

We all at some time have to deal with our prospective of life and eternity. Those things which are worked and established from the moment of re-birth are fixed in us forever. We are actually step by step walking deeper and further into the Kingdom. We will never stop growing; maturing in the knowledge of God, if we have made Him Lord.

The most valued thing we must appreciate
is learning to trust God; to put our life in His hands,
and to know how much He loves us.

Remember the many dimensional qualities of His love. This is not a vacation; something extraordinary we do to get away from it all - a fantasy that relieves the stress of life. All the struggles of today are working toward the victories of tomorrow. Every triumph is not likened to a trophy which may or may not fall off the mantle - break - and be forgotten. What we have gained in Christ will go with us, on and on and on throughout eternity. This Kingdom of God thing, is reality! Buried in our heart of hearts.

So I was learning at the deepest point of my fears, anxieties, faith and hope dashed; depression, shame and guilt, that God is still on His throne and His love for me is still overwhelming. With so much going around in my head, I had to listen carefully to what God was saying.

My soul, wait thou only upon God; for my expectation is from him. In God is my salvation and glory, my refuge is in God. Pour out your heart before him.[1]

It was in 1980 when I first heard the concept of letting my expectations be of God and not of myself, other people, or circumstances. A big part of my world was crashing down around my head. The events were totally opposite of what I thought would happen and I was not handling it very well.

Oftentimes we want something so much that we convince ourselves it is God's will and that He's behind us all the way. People tell us how God came through for them or we read into the Word, an answer that was never meant to be applied to our situation.

I've come to realize that God doesn't always change the world for us, but He will certainly change us in the world, if we allow Him to. God's purpose is to bring each of His kids into an intimate union with Him that will enable us to trust Him implicitly in every facet of our life.............................➜

When we commit ourselves to Him, He is totally committed to bringing us into wholeness. Often times we don't like the way God works in our lives but then most of us didn't want to brush our teeth or eat veggies when we were young, either.

> We are invited into His presence where there is fulness of joy.

We don't always know what's best for us, though we think we do. Our society today is all for a quick fix, but our God has eternity in mind.

The day we each took that step into the Kingdom of God through the door of salvation, eternity was birthed in our heart. God's gift of everlasting life is not only something of quantity, but mostly quality.

It is the place of future habitation with which we must be concerned. The Bible teaches that times and seasons will cease. Years as we know them will no longer exist, and there will be no night.[2] It would be a good thing to be done with some things - now.

Allow God to 'take out the trash' now.

Eternal life abides in the believer now.[3] Those changes of which God is accomplishing in our personality and character are to prepare us to live in the presence of a magnificent, holy God. He is interested in relationship. It is evident from Scripture that the God of Whom the heaven of heavens cannot contain, desires the fellowship of His creation.

Man is the crescendo; the clashing of the cymbals; The finality of God's creation. His masterpiece. Oh but listen to this;

Jer 24:7 *And I will give them an heart to know me, that I am the Lord: and they shall be my people, and I will be their God: for they shall return unto me with their whole heart.*

John 17:3 And this is life eternal, that they might know thee the only true God, and Jesus Christ, whom thou hast sent.

John 14:21,23 He that hath my commandments, and keeps them, he it is that loves me: and he that loves me shall be loved of my Father, and I will love him, and will manifest myself to him. Jesus answered and said unto him, If a man love me, he will keep my words: and my Father will love him, and we will come unto him, and make our abode with him.

John 17:26 And I have declared unto them thy name, and will declare it: that the love wherewith thou hast loved me may be in them, and I in them.

Ex 34:14 [But] *for you shall worship no other god, for the Lord, whose name is Jealous, is a jealous God,*

Isa 60:1-2 *Arise, shine; for thy light is come, and the glory of the Lord is risen upon thee. For, behold, the darkness shall cover the earth, and gross darkness the people: but the Lord shall arise upon thee, and his glory shall be seen upon thee.*

Every blessing counted for Israel flows down to us, His born again lovers, because of Jesus.

Eph 2:14-22 *For He Himself is our peace, who has made both one, and has broken down the middle wall of separation, having abolished in His flesh the enmity, that is, the law of command- ments contained in ordinances, so as to create in Himself one new man from the two, thus making peace, and that He might reconcile them both to God in one body through the cross, thereby putting to death the enmity. And He came and preached peace to you who were afar off and to those who were near. For through Him we both have access by one Spirit to the Father.*

Christ Our Cornerstone

Now, therefore, you are no longer strangers and foreigners, but fellow citizens with the saints and members of the household of God, having been built on the foundation of the apostles and prophets, Jesus Christ Himself being the chief cornerstone, in whom the whole building, being fitted together, grows into a holy temple in the Lord, in whom you also are being built together for a dwelling place of God in the Spirit.

His glory will be seen upon us. Do you know what that means?

Understanding just this small portion, can we conceive that the whole Bible is the story of love; the intimate relationship between the Creator and His creation. The whole reason Jesus came was to reveal this to us and then make it possible for us to receive it.

1 John 3:1 *Behold what manner of love the Father has bestowed on us, that we should be called children of God!*
1 John 4:19 *We love him, because he first loved us.*

All through John's New Testament writings [the Gospel, I, II, III John] there reveals a Father Who yearns for His children to know Him; to bring to bear an intimacy afore unknown. As He becomes our focal point of hope and expectations, we will never be disappointed.

We become partaker of His glorious life source from that moment of being born into His Kingdom; born on the earth then *Born from above, of incorruptible seed; by the Word of God, the Word of truth; not by the will of man but of God's own will.*[6]

The purpose of the Spirit of God coming to dwell within is to impart His divine nature;[7] grow us up in Him and conform us to the image of His Son, Jesus. Our work here on the earth is to pay attention to our schoolmaster, the Holy Spirit.

We are endowed with a free will that permits us to make our own plans and goals and God will not overrule. Remember God allowed even Adam the freedom of choice, and man lost his dominion over the earth. But if we do pay attention;

John 14:26 *But the Helper, the Holy Spirit, whom the Father will send in My name, He will teach you all things,*

I will instruct thee and teach thee in the way which thou shalt go; I will guide thee with mine eye.[8]

We may take into account that God has a specific path for each of us. We may also rejoice in how His Spirit gives us compassion for another going through a similar trial and can readily see variations, because we are so different. God does not lump us all together and hope the right one gets the right thing. We are so precious to Him that He knew us in the womb, and called us by name.

Abraham's mighty trust in God did not lead him to part the Red Sea. David was not responsible to hold rain in the heavenlies for 3 years, and Paul did not call down fire to consume a sacrifice.

We are not all called to be missionaries in Africa, or even to pastor a church in our own city. We are unique and special and God has a cleft in His heart that waits to be filled with the one specified for that place; anointed to carry out His will for our life.

The will of God for our life is not bound up in our Isaacs, but with God Himself. We sometimes get so carried away with ministries, that we have more regard for the works, and there we place all our hopes and expectations. He created us for relationship; not for our doing, but for our being.

It would be a tragic mistake to focus on producing satisfaction or gain, even for His glory. He is more than capable of glorifying Himself. Ministry belongs to the Holy Spirit. We are never given charge of the gifts of the Spirit. When we have the relationship with our Father that brings us into His presence; He pours out His anointing through us to accomplish His will.

We are invited to walk the path He has predestined but He will not force us. God desires to have a people for Himself, to share in His glory, His joy, His life. If we choose to be partaker, we shall have to do it His way. Anything else does lead to frustration. As the writer of Hebrews declares,

Follow peace with all men and holiness, without which no man shall see the Lord; looking diligently lest any man fail of the grace of God, lest any root of bitterness springing up trouble you and by it many be defiled.

This scripture comes in the context of our Father chastening and correcting His kids. We are exhorted to praise Him in the midst, receive His correction and continue on the path He has chosen for us. But especially to lean on God's grace; look for it - covet it. If we don't, a root of bitterness may spring up.................➜

> We can become a stubborn rebellious brat.

If we hold onto grudges and try to justify ourselves, we cannot receive His correction and rebellion will have its way. In the end, it can possibly cause us to turn from God. Read about Esau in the same chapter. God will allow us to go our own way, as also did the prodigal son because of free will.

Yet the father still yearned and waited for that heart to again long for home. God implants the seeds of hope and faith in our hearts as we turn to Him in repentance and though this candle may flicker [because of our lapses in faith], God will not allow it to die for He knows those who belong to Him.

The Lord will not cast off his people,
neither will he forsake his inheritance.[10]

Abraham is an example purposely given us in the Word to encourage us to continue in hope, trusting in God. He was given the promise that,

He would be the heir of the world,[11]
and he dared to believe !

Because he believed, God was able to carry out His massive strategy that brought us to the place we are. Imagine that your salvation began to take effect on the earth [God's part/man's part] 4,000 years ago because one man dared to believe and put his hope and expectation in God. And it was counted unto him for righteousness.

It is very clear in God's Word, that He accomplishes His will on the earth through man. He looked for a man. He found one in Abram of the Chaldees, a descendent of Shem, son of Noah. Through blood covenant with Abraham, God ushered into the world the promised child that birthed the Promised Child.

Because it was earthborn man who caused the breach between man and God, Jesus the Son of God took on humanity, became earthborn to destroy the breach. But there had to be a genealogy to prove his right of passage into our world. And so God began at the beginning............................➔

> God had to do all this through earthborn man.

Abraham answered the call of God. What marvelous works God can accomplish through one man or woman who answers the call of God. Abraham was made the father of many nations so that, through his natural Seed - Jesus, God could become the Father of one nation. The God Who looked for a man is the God of hope [Rom 15:13].

He took one man out of a city. He took one nation out from the midst of another nation [Deut 4:32-34]. Verse 32 asks,

*Since the day God created the earth
has there been such a thing as this?*

But now, He is removing one holy people from the entire world to bring them unto Himself;

*...a holy nation, a royal priesthood, a people of his own,
that we may show forth the praises of him who hath called
you out of darkness into his marvelous light.*[12]

He called Abram out of darkness; out of idolatry, out of the world. And so He calls us. But always remember,

Abraham was called...A friend of God -

and that means they had a relationship.

Through that relationship, Abraham was able to accomplish exactly that for which he was created. God brought correction to his course whenever he veered; and then the decisions Abraham made flowed from that point of contact.

Abraham's expectations and hopes were in God's hand as he walked up the mountain with his beloved son. *Didn't God say...?* was foremost on his mind, and he reckoned that Isaac would have to be brought back from the dead.

He would obey no matter what the cost! Wasn't Sarah's womb dead and he was one hundred years old when God gave resurrection life? Romans 4:18 declares,

*Who against hope believed in hope,
that he might become the father of many nations.*

Contrary to all he could see with his eyes, Abraham staggered not at the promise, he was fully persuaded. What does it mean to be fully persuaded? We all know that sometimes we pray trying to trust in God and in His Word, though it doesn't always seem to be real. We may go back and forth in fear, doubt and unbelief. If we're honest with ourselves we know James 1:6-8 double mindedness may hold true for us at any given moment. The passage is not there to condemn. It was put there because it is real in many people's lives at one time or another.

But we never have to stay where we are - because of Jesus. We are all in different stages of growth in the Kingdom. For the Christian what God is saying is, If you're doing this, come to Me. I'll show you a better way.

His condemnation and wrath are for those of whom will never turn their face toward Jesus, the One Who died for them. Thank You Jesus, that you died for me.

God told Abram about his promised son when he was 75 years old. Twenty five years later it came to pass.

Faith is not some magic formula. Faith is a gift from God. ...that must be exercised through a trusting relationship in order to evolve fully persuaded [Heb 5:14]; to believe for the impossible. Not blind faith, but that which stands consistently on the faithfulness of God,[13] and knowing what is God's will for the situation.

All things are possible to them that believe and join their will in cooperation with God's perfect will. Because Abraham was fully persuaded, God was able to bring forth those things that were not - bring forth the capacity to procreate life from a source long since dried up and dead.

- Are you praying for what looks impossible
   to the natural eye?
- Are you fully persuaded that you want it?
- Are you fully persuaded it is God's will?
- Are you fully persuaded He is able?
- Are you fully persuaded He'll to do it for you?

If you are, then do what Abraham did, as recorded in Romans 4; *call those things which are not as though they were.* Fully persuaded is the Omega of trust.

Please may I add from my own heart; let's not with prayer and supplication, tell God how to do His job. It's a waste of time. I know, I've tried it. 1 Cor 14:15 *I will pray with the spirit, and I will also pray with the understanding.*

Sometimes our long prayers are only a list of details for God to fill. We can't manipulate God to do things our way. We must be sure also, that we are not deceived by our own persuasion. That means, if we refuse to give up what God has removed from our life, then our own emotions may dupe us into hanging onto false hope.

The enemy can then lead us deeper into deception and even anger at God for not answering our prayer according to our false expectations. Allowing God to search out the depths of our heart, will set us free to receive from Him.

Stand in faith that He's doing it, no matter how long it takes. Remember Ishmael? Halfway through the 25 years Abraham wavered. God got him back on track. When you trust in God your faith binds itself to expectation and hope in the God of hope, and you become fully persuaded.

Oftentimes we fear that God truly does not want to do some of the really important things for us. At one time I was delivered from the fear of the sin of presumption. How dare I presume God wanted to do for me?

Well the Word tells me I've been adopted into His family and He is my Father. This was a new concept for me because I grew up without a father. I'm learning that a loving father will take care of his kids.

Mk 1:40-41 tell us about a leper. There is more here than meets casual reading. Could we possibly imagine the excruciating pain of rejection and fear this man bore day and night; the disgust and loathing he saw in his former friend's eyes, and perhaps even from his family.

Being a cast-a-way, deemed of no value to society, I see him crouching behind a tree watching from afar in astonishment, scarcely breathing, as he saw Jesus healing all who came to Him. Lepers were forbidden by law to come near people. He would have been stoned. Not until the crowd thinned out did he dare venture out into the open. By then he could hardly contain himself.

He ran and fell at the feet of Jesus.

I have seen your marvelous works. I know what you can do - but will you do this for me? Jesus was moved with compassion for this precious man who had become the off-scouring of the earth and the word translated touched really means to attach oneself. **Jesus hugged him!**

I think this man was fully persuaded that God cared about him and for him. I have to believe he went running and screaming and laughing hysterically as he, *began to publish it much and to spread abroad the matter....➜* Let's take a look at another man. There were not many in this day of whom hadn't heard of Jesus, and more than that, listened and witnessed His marvelous works among men.

> It was more than his body that was healed that day!

But still came mockers, still unbelievers. The thieves on the cross with Jesus, until now, were one or the other. Mt 27:44 and Mk 15:32 tell us they reviled Him even as they hung at His side. Yet seeing this man in the middle still pouring out His love, still living what He preached - there came the moment of truth to one tortured soul.

This nameless thief was confronted with Truth.
Suddenly life and death became reality, and another man became fully persuaded.

In John 18.38 Pilate asks Jesus What is truth? Jesus has just told him that truth only comes from God. But Pilate didn't wait for an explanation. He'd already made up his mind because the pharisees were intimidating him.

Where are you in this? Are you or are you not, persuaded that truth resides only in Jesus. We are believing so many lies. When we believe a lie, it becomes truth to us. If we want reality, look to the written Word and the Living Word, Jesus.

Truth comes to the mind - head knowledge -

Reality lives in the heart - deep n our soul.
So if you find yourself wondering whether God will do for you, know that Jesus has the answer. He always has the answer because He IS the answer. Our confession is agreeing with God that there is something needing correction.

Looking at the first chapter of James we can see that God is totally willing to give us the wisdom to know how to deal with our dilemmas. He can show us the specific trouble spot.

We may be going through a time of anxiety and frustration and not even know why. A fearful man is double-minded and unstable, pushed one way then the other. Doubt and unbelief will drive us up and down the ladder of faith.

Because of discouragement and the over burdens of stress, failures in the past, we become passive and depression sets in.

*Let not that man suppose he will receive
anything from the Lord.*

But don't stop there, keep reading.

It would certainly be advantageous to examine and reconsider our hopes and expectations. Perhaps we would not have so many disappointments. Get out your Bible and see for yourself.

The Word says He is a God of order and this chapter of James can be seen as progressive. Going through the fiery trials that lead to fully persuaded, God has provided all we need. The trials we encounter may be used of God to mature and change us into His image - trial by trial - glory to glory.

James 1:7 is not shaking the finger at us for our failures. God is telling us He can help us get it right so that there comes a free flow of His provision into our lives. Verse 9, well we can recognize we have no resources of our own. Our lifeline comes from heavenly places.

Abraham was not perfect any more than we are. He learned to trust. He staggered not at the promises of God through unbelief. Some of us need deliverance from the spirit of unbelief. Abraham was strong in faith. Through the years of walking with God he learned that God is indeed faithful to His promises. And he learned as we must, God will do it His way!

The Bible doesn't hide the humanness of God's people. I'm grateful for that. I can see by reading the history of ol' Abe, that he made a lot of mistakes. But he was in covenant with God. Since I am in covenant with God I can walk in hope...

That God will bring correction to my course.

Abraham is given as an example - the father of all in Christ because he dared to believe. But we can readily see he also learned obedience through suffering. He also had to die to all his agendas. He also had to give up his will for God's will. He also had to choose.

Now we all have been given a measure of faith.[14] Take that measure of faith and apply it to the circumstance you're going through right now. You needed a measure of faith to believe for salvation. You no longer need it for salvation. Put it somewhere else. Put it in the place you are believing God to move super naturally - the if He doesn't, *it's just not gonna to happen* place. We have access to His grace, and can rejoice in hope.

Anything that is not of faith is sin.[15] But praise God - sin can be dealt with because of the Blood of Jesus. Back in Romans 5, we have been justified by faith, we have peace with God,

In 1John 5:16 he tells us there is a sin unto death that we are not to pray for. He reveals what it is in the first chapter, verse 8,10, *If we say we have no sin we deceive ourselves, the truth is not in us and we make him a liar.* And this is it...

We don't need the Blood of the cross. Our hope is in ourselves. No need to be justified. No need for grace. This is the sin unto death. Spiritual death that cannot enter the Kingdom of God. No need for God. But the love of God reaches out to all who will recognize that we have sinned and desperately need a Savior. Then we may appropriate 1Jn 2:1-

We have an advocate with the Father, Jesus Christ the righteous and he is our propitiation. Now hope makes not ashamed because the love of God is shed abroad in our hearts by the Holy Spirit who is given unto us.

❤❤❤

The Word emphatically declares we were predestined, [marked out, determined before hand] and sealed with the Holy Spirit of promise.[16] But then there are others....

Luke 16*:15   And He said to them, You are those who justify yourselves before men, but God knows your hearts. For what is highly esteemed among men is an abomination in the sight of God.*

The events of Abraham's life show us what God will do for a person standing in hope and expectations. Receiving the promises of God may be fortified in our heart by knowing and experiencing the true meaning of these words. All this comes through believing that -

God is trustworthy and worthy of our trust.

2Peter 1:4 tells us about God's exceeding great and precious promises that enable us to partake of His divine nature. Webster's Dictionary says promise means this: An assurance given by one person to another - AND - reasonable ground for hope and expectation. To partake: all the words boil down to, joint heirs.....➜

> He is our hope.
> He is our expectation.
> [Ps 62]
> And He will never disappoint us.

Do we believe that God is faithful and worthy of our trust? Do we stand on this ground of trust? Only by faith do we have access to the promises of God.

Without faith it is impossible to please God; but we also must put our faith in the hope of the reward for that faith.[17] And...*This is the victory that overcomes the world, even our faith.*[18] Now the *God of hope fill you with all joy and peace in believing, that you may abound in hope through the power of the Holy Spirit.*[19]

Hope is defined as a steady serene confident expectation of good. For those of us who learned we could not place our hope in anything or anybody - for those of us who have never had any hope...

Hallelujah! - Grab hold of this truth.

First God gives us joy and peace [a place of safety to stand] in believing, so we may see that it's okey to begin to hope; and to receive the gift of hope from the God of hope. As we place our expectations in Him, we may anticipate with pleasure what God has planned for us.

In drawing near to God our hearts may begin to condemn us that, 'You are not good enough'. But knowing that God's love is *greater than our condemning heart,*[20] can wipe out these lies from satan with His Word of Truth. God knows where we are and wants to bring us into confidence and full assurance of faith.[21] For the Word says,

> *He predestinated us unto the adoption of sons by Jesus Christ himself, according to the good pleasure of his will, to the praise of the glory of his grace through whom he hath made us acceptable in the Beloved.*[22]

So we can come against satan's lies with 2Corinthians 10:4-5 and replace our thoughts with Phil 4:8. It is imperative we study the Word. *Think on these things*, and renew your mind. We can pull down every imagination of fear and mistrust and bring it into captivity in the name of Jesus. Every knee must bow!

We must remove our faith in the devil's lies and deposit that faith into the Word of God's truth. We don't need any more faith. Just aim it in the right direction. If you had the faith of a mustard seed, you could move mountains.[23] And be sure the faith you are standing on is not faith in your own ability to believe. Many have fallen into that trap! Jesus, in Mark 11:22 says, *Have faith in God*, but the literal translation is.............→

> Have The Faith Of God!

That is, have the same kind of faith God has that spoke to creation and expected a response. The same kind of faith Jesus had when He spoke to the fig tree and expected it to die at His command. His faith is a gift to us. We need only walk in it.

Then the hope that God gave us hooks into the faith that God gave us to believe for the promises that God covenanted with us. The boldness that rises up in our heart allows us to enter into the presence of God knowing we have a right to be there because God said so.[24] [see Eph 2.8] Turn On Your Receiver!!!

I had expectations, but they were halfway in other people, and not completely in God. Because of the stronghold of the fear of rejection and to be abandoned one more time; I allowed this to overshadow my faith in God to do the impossible for me.

I was continually disappointed. Still living in the old ways, I yet hadn't heard there was a reward. That's why it's so important to read the Word and think on these things. We must also realize that we cannot make these things happen. Oftentimes we fear that what we believe, is all in our head and it seems impossible that it can ever be reality. We strive to make it real and such frustration overtakes our life, we become more pulled into ourselves.

The whole truth of the matter is that we cannot make it real, because then it would be that we earned this faith, therefore God has to reward it. Faith is a gift from God, and He gives each a measure; the measure of which will enable us to be that for which we were created. Our fears and frustrations make it difficult for God to get through to us. The answer to our dilemma is in 1Peter 5:6-7 *Therefore humble yourselves under the mighty hand of God, that He may exalt you in due time, casting all your care upon the Lord, for He cares for you,*

At this point please meditate on Phil 2:13.

This is how we work out our own salvation with fear and trembling. Trusting in the only trustworthy God.

It is important to cooperate with Him.

Now we can grow in the Spirit to a point of letting the Spirit of Hope overcome the spirit of fear and disappointment. Such hope in God will never delude or shame, because His love is shed abroad in our hearts.[25] Remembering past disappointments brings the fear that God might not stand on His Word - this time.

Isaiah 43:18-19 tells us to *Remember not the former things*.

The power of the tongue to recite the past builds a wall around the disasters and destruction and holds them fast to our future. Isaiah continues to tell us,

Behold, I will do a new thing...rivers in the desert...This people have I formed for myself; they shall show forth my praise.

Stop reciting the past - awake to a new day. Expect the Lord to come into your world. Our hearts need to be sprinkled from this evil conscience; that is, the dread of disappointments. Remember the end of our faith is being fully persuaded.

Let us hold fast the confession of our faith [hope] without wavering for he who has promised is faithful.[26]

Abram had expectations. His human reasoning of hope gave way to faith in the God of hope. He believed and abounded in hope.

What will you do for me, seeing as I have no child.[27]

-Abraham- Who against hope believed in hope.[28]

Everything would appear to Abram's senses as unreasonable. Sarai was past the age of child bearing, and getting older every year. But with each passing year he grew in faith as he saw God keep His covenant promises.

He didn't have the Spirit of God living in him and didn't have the Law to go by. Abram just had to choose to believe. We have the indwelling Spirit to help us make this choice - to believe God. If you are in covenant relationship with the living God then He is,

The author and finisher of your faith.[29]

But what if someone comes to you with unbelief to discourage? The Word says,

Will their unbelief make the faithfulness of God without effect. Certainly not! Indeed let God be true and every man a liar.[30]

After Ishmael was born, 13 years passed in which it seems, God was silent. I imagine it gave Abram a long time to contemplate the error he made. He tried to bring about God's promise through human effort. He did not understand the far reaching implications of this Promised Son.

No flesh will glory as God moves to sovereignly carry out His will. In those 13 years God could have looked for some one else with whom to carry out His plan of redemption. Ah, but God is a covenant God - a faithful God of integrity.

Since he already knew Abram and Sarai would try to fulfill His will in their flesh - He made a blood covenant with Abram that could not be broken; because God swore by His own Self,[31] because God cannot lie. Here is the foundation that God's promises stand on - Covenant faithfulness contracted through Blood sacrifice binding then; and now,

How much more shall the Blood of Christ...the mediator of the New Covenant, [that] they who are called might receive the promise of eternal inheritance. [32]

He knows exactly what we will do with His promises. He waits until we are fully persuaded, because it is only faith that moves the hand of God![33] This kind of faith ceases from its own works and rests in God [Heb 4] His covenant is based on His faithfulness, not ours..➔

It is true that when we yield to His will He can then carry out His plan for our life - sometimes in immediate response and sometimes there's a waiting on God.

> When we stand on the Word, other things begin to happen.

Because it is impossible for God to ever prove false or deceive us, we who have fled to Him for refuge shall have mighty indwelling strength and strong encouragement to grasp and hold fast the hope appointed for us and set before us. Now we hook up to this hope as a sure and steadfast anchor attached to our soul. It cannot slip and it cannot break down under whoever steps out upon it. A hope that reaches further and enters into the very certainty of the presence within the veil.[34]

If we look at circumstances and the people involved with our situation, with the eye of criticism and judgment, murmuring and complaining; then where is there any room for, *Singing and making melody in our hearts to the Lord,*[35] and letting, *The word of Christ dwell in us richly.*[36]

It is Jesus our Great High Priest Who is within the veil. Hope is our anchor in Jesus. Take your anchor of hope and throw it into the Holy Presence behind the veil, rooted in Jesus. We can receive the truth and acknowledge that this is our inheritance. God purposes to finish what He started. Paul was fully persuaded as he shared with Timothy the covenant assurance that,

He is able to keep that which we commit to him against that day.[37]

He will do whatever is necessary to hold on to us. He will never let go. He is faithful. It's my job to want to be in God's will. It's His job to keep me in His will.
Look at Isaiah 26:3-4 and 12.

Thou wilt keep him in perfect peace, whose mind is stayed on thee, because he trusts in thee. Lord, thou wilt ordain peace for us; for thou also hast wrought [or done] in us and for us all our works [Ampl].

If we are to let God be God, we must not be offended if He does not fit into our little mold we've labeled - GOD AND JESUS. Allow the Spirit of God to reveal and teach. We must not imagine up our own god by declaring what He will or will not do, according to our own fears and disappointments.

Because of our constant drive to get our needs met we learn to manipulate and control circumstances and people. If we're in charge we won't get hurt. But our own list of expectations hinders the flow of what God wants to do for us.

Here again we can have a yard sale. Your Heavenly Father is ready to carry away:
1. All your disappointments, hopes, dreams and failures that were based on false expectations.
2. All unforgiveness of ourselves for failing; and to others for not meeting our needs. If we never failed, we would not need God, but in our humanity we don't always do things right.

To hold on to these things can lead to idolatry and employ devious measures, demanding from others, things for which they were never created. In the midst of our despair and distress, we can give our God the opportunity to show His love and grace.

You can do it - now is the time to forgive.

God wants to pour out the riches of His Kingdom on His people [Phil 4:19]. Most of us need the riches of His restoration & healing in our emotions, mind and broken heart.

We carry around too much pain. Our world becomes so small we have a hard time extending our horizon. BUT...

It Is Father's Good Pleasure
To Give You the Kingdom.

Isa 54:1-6 *Sing, O barren, You who have not borne! Break forth into singing, and cry aloud, Enlarge the place of your tent, And let them stretch out the curtains of your dwellings; Do not spare; Lengthen your cords, And strengthen your stakes. For you shall expand to the right and to the left, And your descendants will inherit the nations, And make the desolate cities inhabited. "Do not fear, for you will not be ashamed; Neither be disgraced, for you will not be put to shame; For you will forget the shame of your youth, And will not remember the reproach of your widowhood anymore. For your Maker is your husband, The Lord of hosts is His name; And your Redeemer is the Holy One of Israel; He is called the God of the whole earth. For the Lord has called you Like a woman forsaken and grieved in spirit, Like a youthful wife when you were refused, Says your God.*

God did deliver me from the shame and guilt I felt because this was my third failure, I felt like a three time loser. But God wouldn't let me stay there. His love and compassion are overwhelming.

Too often we can't receive because of the problems that seem to overwhelm and bring us into crisis. We feel broken under the weight of it all. This thing that has us bowed together is bringing us into idolatry. Our problem is heavier on our hearts than the One Most High God.

When we give in to it, we are focusing on it above God. We are lifting It up higher in our thoughts than the God Who can do the impossible [Lk 1:37]. When this happens our expectations become a dread. We become very negative. Disappointment sets in because we can't receive from God. But our God is gracious - renounce this idolatry. [Ps 97:9]. We can make our problem like a god and pay too much attention to it.

Thou shalt have no other gods before my face.
Exalt the Lord high above the earth,
He is exalted far above all gods

Ask for and receive forgiveness, then exalt our rightful King. Worship Him. Bow down before Him only. Now you are in position to receive from God the healing and deliverance needed to overcome the enemy. He gives grace to receive.

2Peter 1:3-9 reminds again of our incorruptible inheritance. It is by our Father's abundant mercy we can walk in a living hope. Folks, it's alive, not something we store in a closet and take out when we get desperate. It's a live hope. If it's alive it needs to be nourished.

For we are saved by hope. But hope that is seen is not hope; for what a man sees, why does he yet hope for? But if we hope for that which we see not, then do we have patience to wait for it.[38]

We do that by walking in it, letting hope be our daily companion. As we walk in this live hope, our faith gets stronger and more firmly established within, to trust in God.

Then when - not if - we are grieved by various trials, that faith will be found genuine; not a facade we try to put on to get us past the hard places. Here's the secret. Proverbs 24:13-14.

My son, eat honey, because it is good and the drippings of the honeycomb are sweet to your taste. So shall you know skillful and godly wisdom to be thus to your life; if you find it, then shall there be a future and a reward,
and your expectation shall not be cut off.
Thy words were found and I did eat them.[39]

The honey and the honeycomb are the 'Word and the revelation of the knowledge of God'. They are sweet to our taste and will cause a solid foundation of faith and hope on which to grow in skillful and godly wisdom.

For surely there is a latter end [a future and a reward]
and your hope and expectation shall not be cut off.[40]

This faith becomes established through many trials and yes, failures. It's okey to fail in the Kingdom of God. In the world people sometimes laugh and mock when we fail. In the Kingdom of God we can let our failures be stepping stones toward total dependence on God. And God does not laugh at our mistakes. He is pleased when,

Whom having not seen, you love[41] *[and trust!]. In whom, though now you see him not, yet believing, ye rejoice with joy unspeakable and full of glory.*

David had this faith, trust and hope in God.

He put a tent on Mount Zion, placed within it the Ark of the Covenant and went in and worshiped so many times. David was so ready to repent of all his failures and outrageous sins, that he knew he was in right standing with God. He had the most devoted priests of God praising God and continuously sacrificing lambs before the tent of His Holiness. [1Chronicles Chs. 15-16].

I will build again the tabernacle of David.

WITH BOLDNESS - ENTER IN!
Free to Worship the Lord of Glory.

The Tabernacle of David was built on such heart-felt worship that it is given as the highest example as David wrote His psalms of praise to His God and Lord. He speaks often of meeting with God there in His holy presence, face to face. David adored his God.

I was writing chapters of what and how God did and still was delivering me from things that tried to destroy me.

The word *suffered* in 1Peter 5:10 means to experience attacks and accusations from the enemy and come out the other side in victory. Because we are alive and satan only wants to destroy us, he will come after us. But 1John 5:4 is our assurance.

Seek first the Kingdom of God and all these things will be added to you. For whatever is born of God overcomes the world; and this is the victory that overcomes the world, even our faith.

Hook up to Hope - The Anchor of Your Soul
Attached Within the Veil, Sure and Steadfast.

1 Peter 5:10-11 But may the God of all grace, who called us to His eternal glory by Christ Jesus, after you have suffered a while, perfect, establish, strengthen, and settle you. To Him be the glory and the dominion forever and ever. Amen.

Ps 118:19-20 *Open to me the gates of righteousness; I will go through them, And I will praise the Lord. This is the gate of the Lord, Through which the righteous shall enter.*

My hope and expectations are now in God and there will never be any disappointments.

Enter in, Ye King of Glory
I've opened the door to my heart
Oh, hallelujah, My Lord of Hosts -
The gates of my mind
Are open to Your truth.
Your gracious mercy
Has fed my soul And my spirit
Rejoices in Your beauty ❤

STUDY GUIDE

1. Do you keep a list of past disappointments, even in your head?
2. Do they tend to keep you in depression for several days?
3. Do they keep you from pursuing new goals?
4. Is there a list of names attached to these disappointments?
5. The first step toward healing is forgiveness.

God will move in your behalf.

7. You can now make some new decisions. You can determine to let the *God of hope fill you with all joy and peace in believing; that ye may abound in hope, through the power of the Holy Spirit*

If you have felt alienated from God because of fear to trust Him, there is reconciliation. Turn to 1John 1:9 and do what it says. Then you tell fear to go from you in the name of Jesus. Ask God to heal the pain of past failures and regrets. Forgive all who betrayed you. And now, forgive yourself for failing. Put all these things in God's hand. Read 1Peter 5:7-10.

8. Cast all your mistrust and old habit pattern cares on God because He cares for you. After you have suffered a little while, [that is, died to King Self in all these matters; that is stop trying to make it happen], the God of all grace will Himself complete; make you what you ought to be.

9. So what happens after we start believing what God has said in His Word? How is it actually applied to our life? We speak to God about it, remind Him of His promises [Isaiah 43:26], and tell Him that's what we want. We are coming into agreement with His Word for our lives. That is His intention. Pray the Scriptures. Thank God for His joy and peace and that He is bringing you into His rest. Speak it. Receive it.

10. Agreement is coming into harmony and unity with His will for us [Amos 3:3, Mt 18:19]. When we are a member of the family of God we have a right to everything in the Kingdom of God, just as we should have partaken of our earthly family. If it was dysfunctional, God will heal. Trust Him. James tells us if we want wisdom, ask for it. When we know God's will in our matters, we speak it out as though it belongs to us [Ro 4:17] We receive it for ourselves. [Mt 11:23-24 and see Mal 3]].

11. We can believe that the Bible was given to us to show us what is our inheritance. That's also how we receive from God, that which is contained in His Word. But He will still accomplish these things in His way and in His time. And in the end God will gather all His belongings [that's us] into His glorious Kingdom for ever.

12. An independent spirit is a misguided attempt to solve our own problems or meet our needs without regard to God's solution. If you want to make God Laugh? Tell him all about your plans. This is mostly an attempt to fill the empty space of unmet love. This is a legitimate need - but only God can fill that emptiness - not some way the human heart can come up with.

13. Jer 17.5-10 We must trust in God alone.
Ps 118:19-20 Then the gate of righteousness will open for us.

Addicted to an independent spirit - addictions are a counterfeit intimacy. True intimacy is found through forgiveness, self acceptance, and love - only found in God. The solution is to switch my focus - my attention to what God's Word says and how I can appropriate His promises; and most of all to bring God into the center of my life.

14. I cannot strive to gain His approval, I already have it by accepting God's salvation through the Blood of Jesus. Ep 2.1-10. If my mind is feeding on fear and anxiety of losing control; the solution is faith and trust in God. Defeat comes from feeding on lies. I have believed many lies that have become truth to me. I will trust in God - He will reveal the lies and show me His truth.

15. Victory comes from feeding on Jesus. He is the Way, the Truth and the Life. He is my Bread of Life. My greatest weapon is to trust in God's love. He will never fail or betray me

Hebrews 13.5 *For He has said,*
I will never leave you nor forsake you.

All of the good changes in my life so far have not been of my own striving. These changes have only been the result of God working in me, His love, His faithfulness, His caring, because He is indeed my real Father. I am a child of the Most High God, and my inheritance is the fullness of the Kingdom of God. 2Co 6.16-

All our changes are for us to becoming....
PRAYER: Father, I come to You boldly - confess discouragement and giving in to hopelessness and despair.

Make necessary changes that I may take hold of the hope set before me; to learn to look for the reward of trust. Do a deep work here. Plant hope deep in my soul that I may draw from it continually as I walk in covenant with You. Thank You Jesus ♥

Please know His gracious care for me
has continued all these 50 years.

SCRIPTURES

1. Ps 62:5-8
2. Re 22:5
3. 1Jn 5:11-13
4. Ep 2:19-22
5. Ps 16:11
6. Jn 1:13
7. 2Pe 1:4
8. Ps 32:8
9. Heb 13
10. Ps 94:12-15
11. Rom 4:13
12. 1Pe 2:9
13. Heb 5:14
14. Rom 12:3
15. Rom 14:23
16. Ep 1:11-14
17. Heb 11:6
18. 1Jn 5:4
19. Rom 15:13
20. 1Jn 3:20
21. 1Jn 3:21
22. Ep 1:5-6
23. Mt 17:20
24. Heb 10:19-20
25. Rom 5:5
26. Heb 10:23
27. Ge 15:2
28. Rom 4:18
29. Heb 12:2
30. Rom 3:3-4
31. Heb 6:13
32. Heb 9:14-15
33. Heb 11:6
34. Heb 6:18-19
35. Ep 5:19
36. Co 3:16
37. 2Ti 1:12
38. Ro 8:24-25
39. Jer 17
40. Pr 23:18 Amp
41. 1Pe 1:8
42. Ep 2:21-22

I traverse the circle of the earth
I sail the seas of the world
I wander the deserts
And climb the mountains
And yet - where am I
Who am I?
Behold the image of God
Created by His loving hand
Born to carry His love abroad
To those lost in darkness and shame
Behold the image of God
Created with His loving hand
All I can say
And confess with my heart
Here am I Lord - Here I am.

Broken bread and poured out wine
Is what made the Savior mine
You alone would draw me near
With Your sweet song of redemption
As I cast my cares upon You
Bring me into Your embrace
That my soul shall be renewed
By Your sweet song of grace
Broken bread and poured out wine
Take me and make me, Thy will be done.

One day I was experiencing a lot of regrets that seemed to fill my heart with so much guilt and condemnation. But God is so merciful He spoke to my heart and gave me peace.

Don't go back there honey
To that dark and dismal place
I've made a way for you
To walk in My grace
Every tear you shed
Was for guilt and shame
But I've taken over your life
You're not the same
The Blood I shed
on the cross for you
Has banished your
shame and guilt
Remember when at
prayer one night
I told My Father -
'whatsoever You wilt'.
I died so you could walk
free of regret
So you don't have to
go back there
Walk by My Spirit,
die to your flesh
And never have any fear
So let Me dry your tears,
And stay with Me a while
I know how you are hurting,
You've been defiled
If you will trust Me,
I'll show you how
You may become
all you were created to be
And we can start right now!

❤

THE DECEITFULNESS OF THE HEART.

*The heart is deceitful above all things,
and desperately wicked; who can know it?
I the Lord, search the heart and test the conscience,
to give every man according to his ways,
and according to the fruit of his doings.*[1]

The power of deception is based on the fact that we don't know we are being deceived. Once we realize what's happening we have the power in the name of Jesus to overcome, and receive truth in that place.

*Behold, you desire truth in the inward parts,
and in the hidden part thou
shalt make me know wisdom.*[2]

A person's will that is bound by rebellion
cannot receive truth.

The inward parts - the hidden parts where God wants truth and wisdom established, could be our decision maker. The choices that become the motives of our heart are herein resolved. This is our will; our free will to do as we please. God wants us to love Him and worship Him because this is our motivation for our life.

I heard a story about a father trying to make his little son sit down in Church. After several attempts, he finally sat him down forcibly. But the boy declared, I may be sitting down on the outside but on the inside, I'm still standing up.

The intentions of our heart are decided and declared by decisions we have already made and our natural determination carries them out. First of all, the information on any issue must be brought into our mind, sorted out and consideration made on each. It takes longer to write about it and read, than we spend actually doing. But know that in our decisions, lie our commitments.

Very often, because of circumstances we are forced into instant decisions. If we have not already chosen to establish truth and wisdom in our inner parts, our heart; then we are controlled by our emotions, by double mindedness, the fear of making a mistake, and peer pressure. Now deception has a foothold in the door.

Col 2:2-3 says He gives us the,
*Riches of the full assurance of understanding...
For in Christ are hidden all the treasures
of wisdom and knowledge.*

The next verse tells us we can be beguiled by enticing words. But we still have a free will and can make new decisions depending on new information. The new information I saw and heard caused me to decide to want to know Jesus and to follow Him.

The Church at Smyrna sees the Alpha and Omega, the Author and Finisher of their faith; the first and the last, the beginning and the end. In between A and Z there is a time of walking in faith, waiting on God. Here is a time of humbling - soul searching - repentance, that we may receive from Him the true victory over sin the Word promises. Hebrews twelve tells us of, *The sin that doth so easily beset us*.
The Amplified Bible says, *The one that so readily [deftly and cleverly] clings to and entangles us*.

This is the sin that competes with us [see Strong's Concordance N.T.#2139]. When we are in competition, we are determined to win. This besetting sin will compete for our total focus to have priority and pre-eminence in our life. Here is all the references to this word. Paul knew what he was talking about.

2139: competition to be established. refers to ...
2095: well done
4012: through, all over, around

2476: continue, covenant,
4008: to pierce [the soul].
All this is the fruit of a 'besetting' sin.

That's why it's so hard to overcome. It dominates our thought life and heart attitudes. It controls us. We believe this is a part of who we are, and so we are convinced we cannot overcome it; we just act it out in our daily life. It's NOT who we are, it's an alien stronghold that hides in our personality. It permeates all our decisions though we are not aware.

For example: if we have a deep seething anger that has been with us from childhood, we are really not aware of it; but it comes out in criticism, sarcasm, an abusive attitude, remarks that put others down. All these words that come out of our mouth that cut. And it really seems that we have no control over it.

We can be set free by the Blood of Jesus if we confess it as sin. Only God can set us free, but we have to want to be free. *He gives grace to the humble*. This alien comes with an assignment meant to destroy you and others he aims at - But God.........→

> He delivers us from our pests, not our pets.

As I said before I had a lot of anger and could not overcome it. I asked God why; He said,

'You don't have anger,
you are an angry person'.

I was undone. How do we change our personality and character traits? This was a 'besetting sin'. But God! His mercy and grace toward me is the most awesome thing in my life. I cannot survive without His love. But please note that I never took this anger out on another person; the anger within me caused a spastic colon. I thank God for His mercy, forgiveness and deliverance. His love for me is overwhelming.

Paul speaks to this competition as something that drives us. It is a strongman that Jesus reveals in Mt 12.29. In the name of Jesus and with the power Jesus gave you in Lk 10.19 *I give you power over all the power of the enemy*. I confessed it as sin and was delivered from its power.

Jesus has given us power of attorney to use His name, so use it and be free. Declare that this strongman's assignment on you is over, cancelled! But first confess whatever it is, as sin, receive forgiveness, forgive all involved, and forgive yourself. Then comes freedom!

The tribulation comes when we try to put down the flesh. It does not want to die. We have to kill it! The competition between flesh/soul and spirit, is a battlefield of blood and guts. It cost us everything for our flesh to die - but only through the gates of death will we find resurrection. Death to SELF.

And now, with patience and hope in God, He brings us through it all. We are to endure with patience the thing set before us. As in Ro 5:3-4; tribulation brings patience, patience brings experience, experience brings hope.

2 Cor 2:14 *But thanks be to God, Who in Christ always leads us in triumph [as trophies of Christ's victory] and through us spreads and makes evident the fragrance of the knowledge of God everywhere,*

Please understand that we will be tested again and again in the place that brings the most excruciating pain. God doesn't do this to punish us; He does this in order to give us the deepest and most everlasting victory over those things that rule our life. Some have been with us for our lifetime;

but it's time for them to go. He would make of us, overcomers! Thank You Jesus.

He will deliver us from our deepest fears and insecurities, so that we will be in charge of our decisions; so that we may impose our own will, [in subjection to the Truth,] over our decisions. God will see to it that we be free to serve Him in the utmost capacity. For this also, Jesus died. Verse 3,

Heb 10:35-36 *Therefore do not cast away your confidence, which has great reward. For you have need of endurance, so that after you have done the will of God, you may receive the promise:* And the power that comes through death to Self, is patience to trust and rest in God. This brings experience, which comes from the words [in Strong's Concordance #1381] to test, approve, try, allow, discern, examine, prove. All these words apply to trusting in God. Hoping and trusting in God only comes through the experience of relationship with God.

This experience speaks of a deeper more intimate knowledge of God which brings the hope that Romans speaks of, and of which hope we will never be ashamed - because it releases the love of God to work in us a greater weight of glory.

What Romans verse 5 reveals is awesome.
Such hope never disappoints or deludes or shames us,
for God's love has been poured out in our hearts
through the Holy Spirit Who has been given to us.

Eight times in 1John, he speaks to the sin of lying, and tells us what happens when we don't practice truth. Chapter 5:6 tells us of the sin that leads to death and reveals what it is in verse 1:8.

The person that is so deceived that he believes he has no sin, therefore he does not need a Savior. Revelation 22:15 tells us who may not inherit eternal life,

Whosoever loves and practices a lie.
Romans 12:1-2 declares we must be transformed [metamorphosed like a butterfly] by the renewing of our mind.

I beseech you therefore, brethren, by the mercies of God, that you present your bodies a living sacrifice, holy, acceptable to God, which is your reasonable service. And do not be conformed to this world, but be transformed by the renewing of your mind, that you may prove what is that good

and acceptable and perfect will of God. We need to radically change our way of thinking. Jeremiah 17:10 continues to say,
I Jehovah search the heart, I try the reins.
Strong's Concordance translates the word reins, #3629 to mean figuratively; the mind [as the inner self] and relates to #3627 - something already established in us. We've already decided how we will respond; it is our attitude.

The Word tells us our mind must be renewed. I interpret that to mean we must periodically go through our file cabinet and re-evaluate our doctrines, decisions, ideas; what we think God is saying, and what we've received from other people. One of the most important decisions we must make, as silly as it may seem, is to not get our spiritual doctrine from television or movies that we've seen....

The food we needed as babies with no teeth will not sufficiently nourish us as adults. We come into the Kingdom with all our ideas of what, when, where and who - we think God is all about. We are directed to capture our thoughts and bring them into captivity to the Word.[3] ....➔

> And to renounce those things in the light of the Word of Truth.

I like to immediately do [Phil 4:8], *Whatsoever things are pure, lovely, of good report, if it has virtue and is praiseworthy, Think on these things...* , as a follow up to re-condition and renew. Replace the old with the new and don't leave any blank spaces. Continue to seek God's will.

[Lk 11:24] When you choose to do this The Holy Spirit will fill your mind with the things of the Kingdom as He brings back to your memory, Scripture you are already familiar with; or lead you to truth in the Word of God, to counteract misunderstandings.

It is vital to our spiritual health that we continue in the Word. It was with the Word that Jesus overcame the devil in the wilderness at the beginning of His ministry [Lk 4]
All scripture is given by inspiration of God and is profitable for doctrine, for reproof, for correction, for instruction in righteousness, that a man [or woman] of God may be complete, thoroughly equipped for every good work.[4]

Have you learned yet, how to pray the Scriptures. It's not there to just spend time reading it although that is a good thing;

BUT DO YOU GET IT!!!

<u>We have to pray it.</u> God only wants our sincerity. We can pray the Word, receive it and it becomes a part of who we are.

Example... Gal 6.7 tells us, *Be not deceived*... So we can pray: 'Father, in the name of Jesus please show me every place I am deceived and help me to renounce it and replace it with Your truth, that I may walk in Your wisdom. Thank You Lord'.

Now do you get it? It's that simple. Do this all through Scripture for all the verses you want to work in your life.

Does the Word of God inspire or incarnate? The key to the written Word of God is being able to relate personally to what it is saying. A relationship between you and the written Word brings about relationship between you and the Living Word. There is under- standing the Word with your whole being - drawn into experiencing what it is saying. Relationship is experienced in your spirit, soul and body. It becomes flesh in you.

This is what He meant when He said '*eat my body, drink my blood*'. That's how the Word of God ministers to the believer. And that's why studying and meditating on the Word; and even reading it aloud, is of utmost importance to know what God is saying. If a verse or passage stands out, ask God what it means to you, then ask God to make it a part of your life.

One day, Mt 11.28-30 stood out to me. God said I was carrying responsibilities that I had no business doing. I gave them all to the Lord and was released. Thank You Jesus. You can ask God about this. He will tell you if this is for you.

Be an archeologist - dig deep into the Word of God.

Jesus is the Word of God, the language of God [John 1.1].

We should probably learn to speak His language.

Do James 1.5. Praise God, He does not want us ignorant. Because of this chapter's opening verse, it behooves us to ask God to search out the hidden depths and be sure to bring all into His light. His desire is that we be *conformed into His image*.

He corrects each one according to what we're all about and He'll bring us the easiest way we'll go. If we will to see His hand of mercy in those things that seem to backfire in our life; perhaps we can more quickly yield to His correction. It's His work. Rom 2:4 *He's the author and finisher of our faith.*

In Hebrews Chapter 12, we are exhorted to endure the chastening of the Lord that the peaceable fruit of righteousness may come forth. Our character is being changed and we are maturing. As God brings our self life to a place of brokenness, the Lord may use this empty vessel to show forth His glory.

The fruit of righteousness is not borne by striving to be Christ like. An apple tree bears apples because it is an apple tree. That's its nature. When the nature of Christ is brought forth in us, it is because we are being invested with His holiness and righteousness; the characterizations of the Son of God; as His nature is being manifested through us. The fruit of the Spirit will grow because we are becoming, day by day, Christ-like..........................➔

> Only with this real truth available, can we ever make the decision to change.

Eph 2:10 *For we are His workmanship, created in Christ Jesus for good works, which God prepared beforehand that we should walk in them.*

This deep work of grace in our lives is God's intention to make of us His 'workmanship'.

The Passion Translation says this...
We have become His poetry, a recreated people that will fulfill the destiny He has given each of us.

God is well aware of the thoughts and intents of our heart. That is, what we think about doing, and our motives for doing it. God has revealed in His Word how we deceive ourselves.

Let no person deceive himself. If anyone among you supposes that he is wise in this age let him become a fool [let him discard his worldly discernment and recognize himself as dull, stupid, and foolish, without true learning and scholarship] that he may become [really wise]. For this world's wisdom is foolishness [absurdity and stupidity] with God.[6]

Please read the rest in context for God declares our thoughts and reasoning - futile. 1John 1:8 tells us, *If we say we have no sin [refusing to admit that we are sinners] we delude {deceive} and lead ourselves astray, and the Truth [which the Gospel presents] is not in us [does not dwell In our hearts]....*

The Amplified Bible tells it like it is, though we may not want to hear it. God doesn't pull any punches because He knows how vital it is we recognize ourselves for what we are. He made it all possible, so we could follow in His footsteps because...

All things are naked and opened unto the eyes of him with whom we have to do.[5]

God knows what's going on in our lives, that's why He is so able to know how to help us. So it us that has to relinquish our own agenda for His. Please know that it is the most marvelous thing that can happen to us. Please read Lamentations 3.22-26.

If we think we're doing okey, we'll dig a rut walking back and forth in the same mind set. A rut is only an open ended grave, and there we are at a standstill. Change comes by yielding to God because our most precious, merciful Savior has cleared away all the obstacles.

My little children, I write you these things so that you may not violate God's law and sin. But if anyone should sin, we have an advocate [One Who will intercede for us] with the Father - [it is] Jesus Christ [the all] righteous [upright, just, Who conforms to the Father's will In every purpose, thought and action]. And He [that same Jesus Himself] Is the propitiation [the atoning sacrifice] for our sins. Whoever says, I know Him [I perceive, recognize, understand, and am acquainted with Him] but fails to keep and obey His commandments [teachings] is a liar, and the Truth [of the Gospel] is not in him.[7]

Here is self-deception, a walking in one's own wisdom. Oftentimes as we read the Word we superimpose on each verse or passage, our pre-conditions and presumptions, until we have before us a god we can serve. I would like to encourage all in the Kingdom of God to ask continuously,

Search me oh God, and know my heart; try me and know my thoughts; and see if there be any wicked way in me, and lead me in the way everlasting.[8]

Psalm 139 reveals how intimate God is with all our doings. He created us for Himself and this is the last verse. He understands us as no one else ever could. His mercy and grace are everlasting. He sees our pain and is really the only One Who can help us. He asks us to choose His ways.

We should understand the necessity and importance of bringing our imaginations into captivity to Christ by using 2Co 10.5 and Phil 4:8. Having the Word captive in our heart [our mind], holding fast to the Word of life; brings the life of God into the place where the devil wants to bring death and destruction. We must not leave our minds blank; an open door for slewfoot activity. We are to bring our will into submission to God's will, asking God to bring our wants, desires and needs, etc., in line with His plan and goal for our life [2Pet 1:3-11].

All the wisdom we need for this age is contained in God's Word. He prepared a simple guideline for us to follow. Even a child can understand how to trust God and believe His Word.[9]

Hebrews chapter four is interesting in that God has a place of rest for us, called the Sabbath. It was always His plan to bring His people into a place of rest. It tells us those of the Old Testament never gained this blessing and so He saved it for us.

That place of rest is discovered in verses 9-16. When we allow the Word of God to pass that sword between our soul [the old nature] and our spirit [the new man created to do only good works], we discover that we don't have to perform any mighty deeds to be acceptable in His sight.

We don't have to be a man-pleaser, nor strive any longer to change or to hide our failures, or stay in denial of taking responsibility for our own sin. The work of God is for us to be centered on the person of Jesus. We are growing in Him day by day.

He is our High Priest standing before the throne of God presenting the Blood He shed on the cross for us. The very moment we humble ourselves and acknowledge our sin, it is thrown into the deepest ocean, never to arise. Remember 1John 1.9:

If we confess our sin, He is faithful and just
to forgive us our sin and to cleanse us
from all unrighteousness.

Believing and trusting in God that He has forgiven and wiped the slate clean [Isa 1:18], brings the power of the Blood to bear, and our evil conscience is cleansed that we may continue to draw near to Him with a true heart in full assurance.[10]

For He that has entered into his rest has himself also ceased from his works as God did from his.

God rested on the seventh day from all his works. It's pretty clear that we cannot come into His rest until we lay down the works of our flesh. Added to this is verse 12 explaining that we must use the Word of God to help us discern between the soul and the spirit.

A person's will that is bound by rebellion cannot receive truth.

The soul nature always wants to do something for gain. But God is saying as in Gal 3,

Received ye the Spirit by the works of the law, or by the hearing of faith. Are you so foolish? Having begun in the Spirit, are ye now made perfect by the flesh?

We began in the Spirit when we realized we could not save ourselves. If God didn't do something we were lost for eternity. In our helplessness, we believed God and trusted Him cause we knew only God could do it.

Too often we then fall into unbelief when it comes to God being able to take of our stuff. We have to maintain charge and control or it will all fall apart............➜

> The next verse tells us to not harden our hearts.

The children of Israel could not enter into God's rest because of unbelief [Heb 4:6]. Remember only two of all who came out of Egypt believed God, and they went into the Promised Land. The others didn't think God capable of taking care of the giants in the land; or continuing to take care of them.

They were fed every day for 40 years and their clothes did not wear out.

Back in 1Corinthians 3, we are told that we deceive ourselves when we are trusting in our own wisdom and power to direct our lives. It is so easy to fall into the trap of thinking we can make it, we just need a push and then we can take off ourselves.

It boils down to not wanting to give up the control of our lives. We can become prideful and hard-hearted and refuse to hear God, nor receive His correction. But the truth of the matter is we are never in control. Outside of God's grace and mercy is the power of darkness to deceive us into thinking everything is going great.

Read how disobedience leads to deception.

Jer 25:3 *Do not go after other gods to serve them and worship them.* And Jer 43:2 *Do not go to Egypt to dwell there.*

But they did it anyway.

Jer 42:19 *The Lord has said concerning you, O remnant of Judah, 'Do not go to Egypt!' Know certainly that I have admonished you this day. For you were hypocrites in your hearts when you sent me to the Lord your God, saying, 'Pray for us to the Lord our God, and according to all that the Lord your God says, so declare to us and we will do it.' And I have this day declared it to you, but you have not obeyed the voice of the Lord your God, or anything which He has sent you by me. Now therefore, know certainly that you shall die by the sword, by famine, and by pestilence in the place where you desire to go to dwell.*

There was much deception going on in Jeremiah 44. Judah fell into brazen idolatry. Please read all of chapter 44.

Jer 44:16 *As for the word that you have spoken to us in the name of the Lord, we will not listen to you! But we will certainly do whatever has gone out of our own mouth, to burn incense to the queen of heaven and pour out drink offerings to her,*

Vs.17 *But since we stopped burning incense to the queen of heaven and pouring out drink offerings to her, we have lacked everything and have been consumed by the sword and by famine. Did we make cakes for her, to worship her, and pour out drink offerings to her without our husbands' permission?*

Now they are given great warning - but did they listen?

26 *Therefore hear the word of the Lord, all Judah who dwell in the land of Egypt: 'Behold, I have sworn by My great name,' says the Lord, 'that My name shall no more be named in the mouth of any man of Judah'. [and you will be consumed by the sword and famine].*

Pr 3.7 *The wisdom of this world is foolishness with God, for it is written He takes the wise in their own craftiness.* So...

Do not be wise in your own eyes .

Back in Genesis 3, when Adam ate of the fruit of the tree of knowledge of good and evil, God says something astounding;

Behold the man has become as one of us,
to know good and evil.

God did not create evil. Lucifer; created to worship God and lead the heavens into praising the holiness of God, wanted that praise for himself.

There can never be any one higher than the Most High God. And so, rebellion cannot live in God's presence - he was thrown out of heaven; could never again occupy his former place.

Ezek 28:12-13 *You were the seal of perfection, Full of wisdom and perfect in beauty. You were in Eden, the garden of God; Every precious stone was your covering: The sardius, topaz, and diamond, Beryl, onyx, and jasper, Sapphire, turquoise, and emerald with gold. The workmanship of your timbrels and pipes Was prepared for you on the day you were created.*

He was a musical instrument and wore these precious stones as a cloak.

And in Ezek 28:14-15 *You were the anointed cherub who covers; I established you; You were on the holy mountain of God; You walked back and forth in the midst of fiery stones. You were perfect in your ways from the day you were created, Till iniquity was found in you. You defiled your sanctuaries By the multitude of your iniquities,*

Isaiah 14:12-15 *How you are fallen from heaven, O Lucifer, son of the morning! How you are cut down to the ground, You who weakened the nations! For you have said in your heart:'I will ascend into heaven, I will exalt my throne above the stars of God; I will also sit on the mount of the congregation On the farthest sides of the north; I will ascend above the heights of the clouds, I will be like the Most High.' Yet you shall be brought down to Sheol, To the lowest depths of the Pit.*

I asked God where did this iniquity come from, that was found in him - He said *'He had a free will and that was his choice'.* I can see that all have a free will because God wants us to choose to serve Him. He will not force any one to do anything.

To 'know' is to experience it. God did not want His wonderful creation to always be fighting evil; and perhaps, at last be drawn into living in that lifestyle. He created Adam to be pure and holy as He is; to walk in God's grace, heart to heart and always want to be in His presence. But now, this is impossible. God cannot fellowship with evil. And so Adam could not have access to the tree of life.

Deceitfulness has already entered the heart of Adam.

So lucifer already had access to Eden; that's why he was there. The snake and the tree gave that liar access. It was a fig tree. They were standing next to it and that's why they covered their nakedness with its leaves, and that's why Jesus cursed the fig tree.

It was the birth of the sin-nature of which we are all born with; because we are now born of the image of Adam. The image of God was buried under the sin-nature of Adam. Mark 11:20-21 *Now in the morning, as they passed by, they saw the fig tree dried up from the roots. And Peter, remembering, said to Him, Rabbi, look! The fig tree which You cursed has withered away.* So - to get back to Adam...

Gen 3:22 *Then the Lord God said, Behold, the man has become like one of Us, to know good and evil. And now, lest he put out his hand and take also of the tree of life, and eat, and live forever* [Live forever, becoming more evil as the years went by, yet never finding peace in death].

It was imperative that he be cut off from the other tree in the garden; the Tree of Life; rather than live forever in his carnal state. Unable to make decisions in the wisdom of the Lord, he would have produced chaos with no way out; eternally lost in his own absurd impotence. Sad to say, though Adam did not live forever, his rebellion was passed down to his son Cain. And whose jealousy was it that took part? And all that was passed down until the flood. But how did it get going again - through Ham who produced Nimrod.

God says to have the knowledge of good and evil makes us like Him. But the Creator of the universe is all omnipotent, omniscient, omnipresent, the only wise God [1Tim 1:17]. Along with knowing all things, God is also all wisdom. So we think we have all the answers. We become our own god. That's exactly what has happened; but without God's wisdom, life is futile.

For us to know everything about good and evil doesn't give any reward. In our carnal mind we still are ignorant of the power of good and evil to benefit or destroy. We don't have the Godly wisdom to let it prosper us. The only answer to this crisis is to get under the umbrella God has provided. The covering of the Blood of Jesus brings us into a place where the wisdom of God is available for us [James 1:2-8].

When we isolate ourselves from the body of Christ and the corporate anointing He has provided for His people, then satan has the opportunity to deceive us into thinking we are doing okey as long as we love the Lord. We fall back into relying on our own wisdom and understanding, and essentially cut ourselves off from the Tree of Life.

All our plans will backfire

John chapter 6 tells us we need to continually feed on the Body and Blood of Jesus, Who IS the 'Tree of Life'. In order for this to happen we must find a Church body of believers to fellowship with, have our faith built up, be encouraged, join in with prayer, share in the Word and the communion of saints. Our faith and trust in God grows, and this is the whole point.

Psalm 133 is an allegory of the body of Christ. When we come together in unity we receive the corporate anointing pouring down from the Head

Christ, the Anointed One.

We manifest the priesthood of believers coming into maturity as the whole body is consecrated and set apart for God.

They that wait upon the Lord shall renew their strength,
They shall mount up with wings as eagles. They shall run
and not be weary, they shall walk and not faint.[12]

The word wait means to be entangled with Him! It's amazing how free we can be of worry and fear when we lay our burdens on the Lord. The stress of working to find solutions for our many dilemmas is a burden we were never meant to bear. That's why Jesus says,

Come unto me all ye who labor and are heavy laden,
and I will give you rest. Take my yoke upon you and
learn of me, for I am meek and lowly of heart
and ye shall find rest unto your souls..

How desperately we need to come into His rest. This is His good pleasure. His yoke is easy, His burden is light. We must be of the same mind if we are to be yoked to the Lord. Amos 3:3 asks us..

Can two walk together, accept they be agreed?

Lord, My heart is not haughty, nor mine eyes lofty;
neither do I exercise myself in great matters, nor in things
too high for me. Surely I have behaved and quieted myself,
as a child that is weaned of his mother;
my soul is even as a weaned child[13].

A weaned child looks no longer at the provision but to the provider. This is the essence of the rest of God. It is not just for one day of the week, a day we designate as Church Day. Coming into the rest of God is coming into total trust in His ability to take care of all that concerns you, seven days a week, 52 weeks of the year [1Pet 5:7].

It is humbling yourself, putting all your life into His trust worthy hands and resting in His love; and trusting that His Word is truth. Read Numbers Chapter 14 to see why that generation of Israel did not receive His covenant Promises.

David was to be king of Israel. There were men in his command. He had life and death situations and decisions to make. He had lain down his pride and knew He could not rule over the people without Jehovah, truly his God.

1Samuel 30 records that David's wives and the families of his men were kidnaped by the Amalekites at Ziklag, as he was off fighting elsewhere. When they got back their families were gone. His men wanted to stone David. Ziklag means overwhelming despair. He was greatly distressed but he did not run off to handle this himself. David could have declared, I'm ruler here. I'll do it my way. But David was not deceived,

He knew his wisdom came from the Lord.

David encouraged himself and sought God. He cast this care on his Lord. What seems a crises in our life is indeed a small matter for the eternal God Who knows the end from the beginning. In reading the account we find that God said,

pursue, overtake, and recover!

He was not concerned with the details of how or where to go. God said!! That's all David had to know. God took care of the rest. God actually led them directly to the enemy camp. He could have been chasing all over the countryside to find them. God knew where they were. None escaped the sword of David and his men except those of whom he let go. Everything that was stolen from them was recovered. As we trust in God to be in charge and show us the way, He gives us wisdom and grace to walk through any issue. David quieted his soul, and did what he knew best to do.

Remember the word unto thy servant,
upon which thou hast caused me to hope.[14]

I'd say that he was praising God as he pursued; praised God when they found the slave in the desert, and continued to praise God as they came upon the enemy camp. David was a worshiper, and so he just naturally worshiped God. He had taught his soul to rest in the Lord.

Unless the Lord build the house, they labor in vain.
Allow the Lord to lay the foundation, and let Him place every brick in its proper place. It's okey if we do it through tears. God will cleanse our soul as He delivers us from our enemy, and fills us with His love. Ask Him to do this for you.

I counsel you to buy of me gold tried in the fire, that you may be rich; and white raiment that you may be clothed, and that the shame of your nakedness does not appear; and anoint your eyes with salve that you may see. As many as I love, I rebuke and chasten; be zealous, therefore, and repent.[15]

Remember - grace is the enabler.

God resists the proud and gives grace to the humble.[16]

God knows how hard it was before He so graciously came into our lives; keep control or be run over! But now, there is a place of quiet rest deep in the heart of God. Are you willing to pursue this place of intimacy where darkness and deception dare not enter. Read and apply Jeremiah 17:14,

Heal me, O LORD, and I shall be healed;
save me and I shall be saved; for thou art my praise.
Only in Christ is there safety to renew our ways; to learn to trust and rely on God. He is the Way, the Truth, and the Life. He is trustworthy and faithful. If we will yield our lives to Him we will finally experience that word;

By this I know that you favor me, because my enemy does not triumph over me.

STUDY GUIDE

1. What does God's Word say about our own devices?
2. What does 1Peter tell us about the roaring lion?
3. 2 Corinthians 4:2 gives us a clue how to control the temptation to devise our own schemes. Renounce it.
4. This is a battle in the spirit realm. How Does God help us?
5. Allow God to search your heart - to reveal the ways you can let go and let God. And ask Him to reveal your true motives and attitudes. No matter how bizarre this sounds, take this for an instance; do you attend a prayer group so that others will think you are a devout pray-er, when you are

not? Do you volunteer for things so others will think highly of you? Now prayer and volunteering are wonderful, and we should keep doing them. But ask God to purify your motives so that you can do those things for God's glory.

6. If you've made any errors in judgement, do you believe God can help you change any of it?

7. David was a man who knew God. Did he do everything right, or was he human like us? Did God help him work through his failures?

8. What do you suppose our Father God is looking for in His kids? [honesty, integrity, righteousness]

9. Where is the place of rest and peace our Father has saved for us? [Ps 91]

PRAYER: Father, I pray in the name of Jesus and with the help of the Holy Spirit, that I will renew my mind through Your Word, and that I will use that Word-mirror for what it was meant. Help me Lord to not have a divided heart. Show me where ever you see that I've given in to deception, that I may walk in Truth. I ask for and receive your help to discover and dump all the trash I've accumulated throughout my lifetime.

Oh, Hallelujah
Give God All the Glory
For He Does All Things Well.

SCRIPTURE

1. Jer 17:9-10
2. Ps 51:63.
3. 2Co 10:4-5
4. 2Ti 3:16-17
5. Heb 4:13
6. 1Co 3:18-19 Ampl
7. 1Jn 2 Ampl
8. Ps 139
9. Mk 10:1
10. Heb 10:22
11. Pr 3:7
12. Isa 40:31
13. Ps 131
14. Ps 119:49
15. Rev 3:17-19
16. 1Pe 5:5
17. Ps 41:11-13

OFFENSES

*Great peace have they who love thy law,
and nothing shall offend them.[1]*

Luke 4:43 tells us Jesus came to preach the Kingdom of God. Jesus came to seek and to save that which was lost. What was lost? Adam lost his authority over the Kingdom of God. Satan stole it by deceiving them into believing lies about God. They believed He was holding back something they needed. Jesus came to reveal the truth and give it back to us. So what is the Kingdom of God?

The government of God ruling on the earth, through His creation. So wherever God is honored, His presence rules.

Just as a side note: satan does not walk around the earth in his own authority. He stole Adam's. Romans 13 tells us, *There is no power or authority but of God - so whoever resists that authority resists the ordinances of God.*

We are told to resist the devil; so now we know the authority or power the devil tries to take over us, is illegitimate. He's a liar and has no rights in our life. Jesus came to destroy the works of the devil [1John 3:8]. You see, God has other plans for us. This is for what we were created; to fellowship with God and walk in His authority over His creation. Adam reneged. Suddenly God could no longer hold His treasure. Although the pain in His heart must have been great, I praise God and thank Him that He was not offended by Adam's blatant rebellion, walk away in a huff, and not speak to His creation, ever again!

Please understand that God was the first to be offended. When His beautiful creation of praise and worship to The Most High God, wanted to be higher [Isa 14.13-14] - And when His image and likeness wanted to be his own god...
LOL - 'Just move God out of the way and let us do our own thing'.

Well, how's that workin' for ya??

No matter - He would already have a plan to upset their applecart.

God's love is so powerful, it caused Him to make preparations even before He spoke us into existence [Rev 13.8]. Isn't it likely He was speaking life and love into that mud pie, carefully patting out the features of this marvelous thing He called man. He made covenant for life that day;

It could not be broken!
He is also a God of hope [Rom 15:13]. Perhaps He hoped man would not turn from Him, but when or if he did, God would already have all the solutions worked out. His response to our terrible dilemma of separation from God was to come Himself and repair the breach [Rom 5:17].

That Covenant for Life Would Never be Forfeited.
For by one man's offense death reigned by one, much more they who receive abundance of grace and of the gift of righteousness shall reign in life by one, Jesus Christ.

Adam was given authority over the earth when he was created. He relinquished it when he turned his back on God and yielded to satan. He became the god of this world.

Jesus came to the earth, to give all authority back to His people and teach them how to hold on to it and to manifest the Kingdom of God on the earth. As we yield to God and release ourselves to Him, the more He will manifest His true nature; Who He is and who we are in Him [Jn 14:17]. Dear John, chosen from the womb to, *Make straight the paths of the Lord*,[2] He was the first to receive the revelation of the,

Lamb of God who taketh away the sin of the world. [3]

Can we possibly imagine John's amazement, that as he looked at his cousin; the Spirit of God revealed to his heart............................➔

> This is the One you've been waiting for.

At Jesus' birth there were prophesies about Him - and it is recorded in the gospels for us, some 30 years after His resurrection. John did not have all these words in a notebook to refer to as the events occurred.

John may have grown up with the knowledge of his father's prophecy at the time of his own birth. But it is most probable John the Baptist had no understanding of how it would be implemented; or that his own cousin would be the One.

I knew him not.[4]

Until that moment John knew Jesus after the flesh. Now he would know Him after the Spirit, as Savior and Lord. He saw the Spirit as a dove descending on Jesus and declared that Jesus would baptize with the Holy Spirit and with fire [Something before unheard. John 3:30].

I saw and bore witness that this is the Son of God;[5] and made that remarkable statement,

He must increase, I must decrease.
Yet in prison John wrestles with his own expectation of what the Messiah of his vision would really be like. Do you think Jesus was offended by John's honest questions? Did John fail in his calling because he had doubts? God will always bless a seeking heart.

If you seek me and search for me with all your heart,
then I will be found by you.[6]

From a gracious and compassionate heart Jesus said, *Go and show John again...*[7] Reassure him. Whatever are our expectations, we can lay them down; that we may be reassured again and again, as we put our trust in God.

There is a difference between the disrespect and even mocking remarks heard from challengers of the gospel message. Though sometimes I wonder if even these come from an offended heart asking why, why? May I ask dear Readers, whosoever has been offended in Jesus because He did not do what was thought of Him. Did He not heal or answer prayer when it was expected, or the way it was anticipated.

We have many misconceptions and false images of God carried over from our unregenerate days. It is impossible to really know God in an unredeemed, unrenewed mind. Understand that B.C., before Christ came into our lives we all had an unredeemed, unrenewed mind that was set on things of the world [Col 3:2].

We had our own ideas of who God and Jesus were. Most of them were wrong, or so corrupted by man's traditions as to miss the point of why Jesus came into the world. These misconceptions & misrepresentations are often based on false expectations and assumptions. Jesus said the men of that generation were like children playing their little games. They sat in the marketplace awaiting the clowns.

We have piped unto you and ye have not danced;
we have mourned to you and ye have not wept.

John came fasting and he has a demon.[8] Jesus came eating and drinking and he has a demon.[9] They all had their narrow minded notions of how God was going to bring His Messiah, and what He would do when He arrived. The Jews were offended when He claimed He had come down from heaven.

Many arrogantly shouted, Who do you think you are! Others thought perhaps He is the promised One. Some said, *Shall the Christ come out of Galilee?*

Who do you say is Jesus?
Of Himself He declared,
I am the light of the world; he that follows me shall not walk in darkness, but have the light of life.[11]
Don't let offenses keep you from the joy of your salvation; that is fellowship with Jesus and the Father and the Holy Spirit Who wants to bring you into God's peace and rest.

The Pharisees were irate when He rode through the gate of Jerusalem on a donkey and the whole city exalted Him as King of Israel. The prophetic word in Zechariah of which the Pharisees were familiar, was being fulfilled before their eyes, yet their heart was hardened. They demanded He shut them up! The men of that generation were prideful and self-righteous. Indeed, were they even looking for Messiah. It seems the status quo suited them just fine. Why change things now of all times.

Is God messing with your status quo?
What is your response?

The Pharisees knew Jesus came not to just give the people a few pointers but to actually change their way of life. Jesus said, Do what they teach, don't do what they do.[12] They taught God's Word, and looked good on the outside, but their heart was full of hypocrisy [Mt 23:13]. The office of priesthood had become prestigious; influential to say the least. They had the full attention of all the people and power though limited under Roman rule, held sway over the daily life of Israel.

They did not want anyone to upset their apple cart. And indeed were they outraged to the point of murdering Him - for daring to confront their pious fraud. Their fury at His interference revealed the nature of their heart; and so the Kingdom was torn from them. The hungry ones on the other hand, were open to correction. Myths and disappointments were dispersed before their eyes and in Luke 7:23 Jesus declares,
Blessed is he, whosoever shall not be offended in me.
Offend: cause to stumble, to trip up.
Many new Christians have stumbled and been offended by another Christian using the Bible to slam dunk them; and because of it have turned away from God. They don't understand that this is not God's way, but only the emotions

of an immature Christian that has not learned to wait on God [Rom 2:4].

There are some who have been offended by circumstances and/or people so as to be scandalized. Webster's Dictionary tells us this means; to shock the feelings of; to subject to disgrace; malign; bring reproach; misrepresent willfully the conduct or character of...

If this happened to you, you know it! Sometimes it seems the situation was set up beforehand. Because of the circumstances or people involved, it could not be avoided. You could not stop the process. Your expectations had become a comic/disaster in the light of reality.

But why is it our nature to consistently blame God for what people do? What we're looking at is flesh flaunting itself, sometimes on both sides of the fence. If we are vulnerable to hurt feelings we will be offended - often

This portion of flesh along with all the rest must be quickly put to death. How to do that? You yield it to God. Ask for and receive forgiveness for the resentments and judgments you've had for others that arose because of offenses; Forgiving those who offended you does not turn them loose to keep wounding you, it turns you loose from a broken heart, and from the anger that is doing a job with your headaches and stomach pains.

Now you are free to ask God to heal your emotions in all the past experiences that brought offenses. Then turn away from self-pity. If there is a deep root of bitterness, ask God to help you take the axe to this root and drive it out by the power of the Blood and the name of Jesus. Please know the foregoing instructions come with a condition and a warranty.

> The condition: Choose to forgive and humble yourself before God.
>
> The warranty: The life of God flowing through your life.

Searching the Word we find many references to being offended.

> 1. offenses will come.
> 2. the penalty for offending His little ones.
> 3. offended because of being a disciple.
> 4. we are not to offend our brother.
> 5. offended by Jesus. etc.
>> Look at this one! [Mt 17:27],

Notwithstanding, lest we should offend them [cause the tax collectors to stumble] Peter, go fishing, get the money, and pay our taxes.[13] Jesus Himself would not offend those offensive tax collectors.

As Matthew recorded this puzzling event, he must have pondered in his own heart; remembering quite vividly what he thought at the time. *Just who is this man?* Perhaps that's what drew Matthew to Him, hungering and thirsting for more; finally abandoning his own treasure chest to follow Jesus.

If we continue to walk in our own ideas of what to expect from God we may never walk in His grace. Mt 13:21 tells us some are offended because of the Word.

Ephesians chapter 2 tells us what God did to bring us to Himself. We must have the Word engraved in our heart and know who we are in Christ. It is imperative we know what is our inheritance so we may partake.

One in leadership who is predisposed to offenses will be constantly defending position and credibility. Of the characteristics incidental to being offended, murmuring and complaining lead the list. Little realized synonyms mentioned in a previous chapter, are found in any Thesaurus.

Here we find in continuation - whine, grumble, self pity, sob, blubber, snivel, gnash one's teeth, scowl, faultfinder, discontent, unrest, disappointment, malcontent, complainer, ungrateful, quarrelsome, dissatisfied, down in the mouth gossiper. Did I leave any out? We are easily offended as these things and more are embraced in our heart. Whether expressed or not, it matters not. We will reap what we sow. How do we get offended:

#1. When someone does not meet our criteria!
#2. When our own thing is denied.
#3. If someone throws a spear.
  [Remember what David did?]
#4. When we arrive at Church and someone is sitting in our seat. If we are slave to offenses this will cause what is known as the snitty attitude. We will be subject to its control all through the sermon. The fruit of walking in the posture of offenses is found in Matthew 7.

Judge not that ye be not judged. For with what judgment ye judge, ye shall be judged; and with what measure ye measure it shall be measured to you again.

Carrying offenses always leads one to judge and criticize the offender. Then Matthew 7 is carried out to its full measure. We may become offensive, and obnoxious! This vicious circle can only be broken as we humble ourselves before the cross and allow forgiveness to complete its own circle of healing.

Far too often the offended becomes the offender. The ground of pride gives root to offenses and the fruit will poison many lives if allowed to continue.

Bitterness and contempt are thorns for this tree. The sharp edge of criticism will wound many hearts. And please understand that the attitudes of the heart can be far more dangerous than our verbal accusations because it is hidden and we think it is not important. We can't imagine how far this stone of offense thrown into the waters of relationships will continue to ripple. And so we need massive surgery to cut into and remove this cancer from the soul. Remember the Word says,

Keep your heart with all diligence
for out of it springs the issues of life.

There are other means of greater dimension that attempt to sear our heart, and disengage us from society and from God.
- If we lose control or it is taken from us by physical or emotional trauma.
- If our defenses have been broken down by the insensitive.

There is also an offense that comes when we have gone through an excruciating experience and perhaps the one person we share it with does not believe us. Or may not attach to it, the same measure of importance. The emotional shock that our pain has been degraded may lead to more pain and offenses. A good example is sharing the trauma of date rape, only to have one snidely put it off as perhaps it was our fault. This can cause deep rage and outrage.

Without diminishing our reality we can lift this up to the Lord. He is the One that will understand. Why didn't He stop it from happening? We have a free will and what happens to us many times is a consequence of our choices, although not always. Asking God's wisdom will bring the right answer. And if He gives none - we can still deposit this into His hands.

We can be sure that as we go to the Lord with these things He will bring healing and restoration. Prayer and seeking God before we make decisions will also bring wisdom.. And, although we do not understand everything, God can and will give us peace and deliver us from the trauma and pain.

It is vital you understand that the enemy of your soul will try to isolate you at this time; try to make you pull back into self-pity. Even though your heart is grieving, if you will make the choice to turn to the Lord, He will meet you where you are. Psalm 62 tells us we can,

Pour out your heart before him, God is a refuge for us.
Let this be a continuous attitude because offenses will come. Every time they come, we can pull on God's grace-ability.

There are many experiences that bring such agony and pain to us that we think we will never be able to get on with life, and no one else will ever understand. The burdens of life can bring such stress, the heaviness of our soul translates into our body and soon we are experiencing constant illness.

Isaiah 53 tells us when Jesus died on the cross. He bore our griefs and carried our sorrows; wounded for our transgressions and bruised for our iniquities; beaten that we might have peace.......................�→

> By His stripes we are healed.

Jesus came into our world at a time when execution of criminals was at the apex of brutality. He knew life can be brutal. He did it deliberately. He was innocent. He chose to do this for us so that we might receive His life. But we must ask for it. Like a bank account, one must withdraw the funds in order to use them. When the law of the Spirit of life in Christ Jesus abides, we are delivered from the law of sin and death. Now we may benefit from the gifts and provisions God has already brought forth.

In our old man' we did not have to strive to do the works of the flesh. In our new man created to do good works - we don't have to strive; only yield. Then when sin shows its ugly face, grace abounds [Rom 5:20].

Remember offenses will come. We can ask God to purge us from our defense mechanisms that can develop into resentment, bitterness and anger. We can walk in the footsteps of Jesus, the only example on which to depend. Our adversary is ever out to rip off our inheritance. Examine your heart. God only responds to the humble, not the proud.[15]

Child of God, you may be set free as you turn to Jesus. He was scandalized on the cross for you. As you forgive those of whom offended you, this pain and anger can be placed under the Blood. We must begin with forgiveness, for all the people involved.

Proverbs 25:21-22 tells us, *If your enemy be hungry. give him bread to eat; and if he be thirsty, give him water to drink; for thou shalt heap coals of fire upon his head, and the Lord shall reward thee.*
What happens here is actually taking this offensive person to the altar of incense in intercessory prayer where the burning coals of fire will bring the sweet odor of your humble yielding and forgiveness, right before the throne of God [Ps 141:2].

The reward is God's grace and peace surrounding your broken heart to heal. And instead of berating our soul for being such a failure, and getting into this trouble, we can forgive ourselves. Now the restoration will begin.

The destructive force of the enemy will be broken as you draw nigh unto God. His peace will dispel the outrage. God is restoring our souls [Ps 23]. His love will calm the storm and we may come into a place of trusting God and putting our expectations in Him without fear of betrayal.

- Ro 4:25 He was delivered for our offenses.
- Ro 5:15-21 He took our offenses to the cross.
- Ro 9:33 calls Jesus a stumbling stone, a rock of offense. He became an offense so we could go free; so we could rest in the Lord and cease from anger. Jesus knew the hearts of men.

He allowed no person or thing to offend Him.[16] He deposited His expectations and His hopes in His Father.
He kept His focus on what He was sent to accomplish. He came to reveal the Father.

I have glorified thee on the earth. I have finished the work which you gave me to do.[17]
God is pleased for us to finish the work which He gives us to do.[18]

When we lived in the world most of us became well trained in self-righteousness. We learned to defend and protect our rights against any and all who would dare to question our motives. That battle runs rampant in the world. [Jn 17:16]. But we are not of this world if we have been born of the Spirit. Sometimes born-again Christians still respond in this manner, though not fully aware of what we are doing or how it is effecting us.

Many years ago, God showed me something that changed my life. Someone had said something to me that offended me very deeply. I was reacting with anger and hurt inside myself. The next day as I was praying I began to read Ephesians. I was being blessed by seeing what was my rich inheritance in Christ, even though I didn't have a good understanding of it all. As I came to the sixth chapter I was feeling very vulnerable, and so I began to put on the armor of God.

I'd had a habit of starting at the top and working down so that I would be consciously aware of His protection. As we mature in Christ we realize we don't have to take it off, but acknowledge that it is there. The helmet of salvation felt very comfortable. I was praising God that I knew I was His child and saved by the Blood of Jesus.

My next piece of armor was the breastplate of righteousness. As I began to say the words, they would not form in my mouth! I knew it had to be an attack of satan's bag of tricks, so I rebuked, renounced and broke his power.

But down deep inside my spirit, that still small voice spoke and said, It's Me, Dory. After I got up off the floor, [ha,ha] I was really concerned. Why could I not use the Word of God that I had fed from and relied on since I'd been saved?

Then I remembered, the same thing happened to me once before. I was in a beautiful praise and worship service and suddenly I could not sing praise to God. It was just cut off! In praying and asking God for the answer, I knew. In my inordinate attitudes towards my circumstances at the time, I had cut myself off from God.

It occurred to me, the reality of God inhabiting the praises of His people. God did not want to fellowship with me in my rebellion. NO! He did not leave me. I am a born again child of God and His Spirit dwells within me. He will never leave me nor forsake me.[19] If I am truly His, He must correct me [Heb 12:8]. And His Word always gives us instructions. Jesus left us an example that we can follow in His steps.

He who did no sin neither was guile found in His mouth;
when he was reviled he reviled not again;
when he suffered he threatened not, but committed himself
to him that judges righteously.[20]

He taught me the breastplate of righteousness cannot work in its power if I am going to protect my own rights. He said when I was offended the other day I responded in anger and hurt feelings and I was holding onto the hurt and not letting it go and forgiving.

The only way I can be forever free from this is to give up my right, not to be offended and hurt. Oh, how we have learned to protect our rights!. Eccl 10:4 tells us,

If the spirit of the ruler rise up against thee,
leave not thy place, [don't stomp out of the room]
for yielding pacifies great offenses.

Living in this world we have mastered worldly concepts. If we don't defend ourselves no one else will. Beloved we are not of this world.[21] All through scripture it tells us what God will do for us if we trust in Him. *He is our Shield, our Refuge.*

The Lord is our Defender, our Keeper, our Provider, our Helper: Trust in the Lord it says.

Seek only the Kingdom of God.

Is God really all these things in your life, or are they just some nice sounding words that we sing about? If God is really your Rock and Fortress, then He must be capable of protecting you. See, the truth of the matter is when we are protecting our own rights it's because we believe we are right. Now that translates into self-righteousness. We are right in our own eyes................→

> A self-righteousness perhaps buried in pride. Defense mechanisms can be deeply ingrained in our emotions.

But the Word says there is none. All our righteousness is like filthy rags with which we cover and protect ourselves.[22] If we are going about defending our rights then we are going about in self-righteousness.

Jesus said all who would follow Him must take up his cross daily.[23] We need the strength of our self-life crippled, as also did Jacob at the Ford Jabbok.[24] FORD: to pass over; JABBOK: pouring forth, to pour out, to empty. Ask God to help you empty your self-life. Who did it first - Jesus!

We are to live/walk in His righteousness [2Cor 5.21]. As he wrestles with the angel of God, Jacob asks, 'Tell me your name', and the answer was, 'Why are you asking? You know who I Am. You've heard of me all your life and I met you at Bethel, running from Esau. Now you are still running from the consequences of your sin. Stop - and look at where you're going, or you'll be on this treadmill for the rest of your life'. By the time God got through with Jacob, he knew he'd been touched by the Most High.

When He touched Jacob's thigh, He crippled him for the rest of his life. A reminder to Jacob that he has no strength of his own; a reminder of how vulnerable and puny is his manhood, without God. You are invited to Peniel and see God face to face, to see how fragile you are. Without God we are helpless and hopeless.

And thus saith the Lord, but to this man will I look,
even to him that is poor and of a contrite spirit,
and trembles at my word.[25]

Contrite means crushed, maimed, crippled. Jacob wrestled with God. Would his self-will win out or would he yield to the One he called his God. The hollow of Jacob's thigh was put out of joint and he was lame for the rest of his life. The Interlinear Bible says;

The power of his strength was broken.

Jacob knew exactly what this meant! Here then is that to which the strength of Jesus' self-life may be compared. He depended totally on His Father, and our self-life must also, if we are to be metamorphosed into the image of the Son.

How can God protect us with His breastplate of righteousness as long as we are walking in our own? Needless to say, the only answer for our dilemma is to lay our rights and our righteousness on the altar of sacrifice to be burned up; so that we might manifest more and more, the righteousness of God in Christ.

Many of our fiercest battles come from the root of what we think is our deepest need;

To be justified in the sight of men.

Jesus left us an example that we can follow in His steps.

When he was reviled he reviled not again.[26]

Most of us have read John 15 - the vine and branches verses. Jesus was abiding in the Father, therefore He experienced Verse 10. He kept His Father's commandments and the Father's love was abiding in Jesus. But remember this is not just any kind of love. It is the Father's love. The Father's love is unique in that it transcends all barriers.

It could be for us; so extravagant as to pour out on
others even as they are offending us.

Jesus took on humanity. He walked the earth as our perfect example. He talked it - He walked it. So in the same way that Jesus did verse 10, He's telling us we can do it. Keep His commandments and the Father's love will abide in us. What is His commandment here? Forgive those past and present offenses. And plan on saying no to any future offenses trying to gain place.

*If we revile not again, the Father's love may
find an opening into that unguarded moment
that could possibly change lives.
When he suffered he threatened not,
but committed himself to him that judges righteously.*

When we are offended and respond in anger and hurt feelings, holding onto the hurt and not letting go and forgiving; we are defending our rights. The only way we can be forever free from this is to give up our right, not to be hurt. Much of what offends us is petty in comparison to Jesus' life.

Isaiah 58 tells us we have been given the ministry of repairing breaches. We must practice what we preach and repair the breaches between ourselves and others before we can share this wonderful news with hurting people.

Our broken and offended heart can be placed under the Blood, because for this also, Jesus died.

So the question is - will you die to these things? If you seek after demanding your rights, you will lose your life. If you yield to God, you will gain the glory.[27] Beloved, we can be free from offenses and hurtful attitudes............................➜

> Renewal begins with 1 John 1:9.

Our Father is already waiting for us to come to Him. As we confess our sin, we can receive His forgiveness and forgive those by whom we were offended. And then we can speak forgiveness over our own lives. We can shed guilt and condemnation and receive the life of the Spirit to flow through us. Ask God to help you sort things out.

- Am I offended because this particular person does not meet my expectations?
- Or because they are doing something I don't like?
- Or have they said something offensive to me or about me?

Self-righteousness can be a form of self protection; a mechanism that we use if we have been repeatedly abased and degraded. It may be an unconscious reaction we are not aware of. But if someone punctures this balloon, we may react in fury; offense or defense. As a result, we may become offensive.

It could be, we have been greatly abused. These offenses will keep us in a prison of unforgiveness, bitterness and fear. Satan loves to bring these memories to our attention, often. However we have a mighty Redeemer Who has won for us the victory over this pain. As we let go of all these things, God will set us free and heal our broken heart [Lk 4:18]. The Amplified version of the Bible tells us in Matthew 6:15,

Forgive others their reckless and willful sins,
letting them go, and giving up resentments.

We were not created to scrutinize nor judge others. We are though, called to search the Word and allow it to mirror our behavior. We can ask God to bring correction. The more we line up with the Word we become more like Jesus.

Then, because we are able to extend God's hand of love, mercy and grace into any situation, we are not offended by what happens. There are many sources of offenses, we can be healed from all this pain.

And this commandment have we from him,
that he who loves God loves his brother also,[28] *Because*
love is ever ready to take no account of evil done.

Offenses will continue as long as we are in the world. We don't have to receive offenses nor even respond to them. Remember to pray for your enemies and do it with Gods love.

This attitude will change your life; it did mine. I carried offenses in my pocket all the time. But now, I try to be a quick learner. So now I was learning to live another way.

Now I had more peace in my heart than I ever had before I found this treasure in God's Word.

Matt 5:43-48 *You have heard that it was said, 'You shall love your neighbor and hate your enemy.' But I say to you, love your enemies, bless those who curse you, do good to those who hate you, and pray for those who spitefully use you and persecute you, that you may be sons of your Father in heaven; for He makes His sun rise on the evil and on the good, and sends rain on the just and on the unjust. For if you love those who love you, what reward have you? Do not even* the tax collectors do the same? And if you greet your brethren only, what do you do more than others? Do not even the tax collectors do so? Therefore you shall be perfect, just as your Father in heaven is perfect.

> They drew a circle
> and shut me out,
> I didn't know what
> it was all about.
> But God's love
> forgave my sin;
> We drew a circle
> and pulled them in.

> For in many things we all stumble. If any man offend not in word, the same is a perfect man, and able to bridle the whole body.[29]

The forgiveness cross:
1. Ask God to forgive you
2. Forgive others.
3. Forgive yourself.

The place of resurrection is called Jehovah Jireh [Gen 22.14], *the Lord Who Sees* [our need and will provide]. When the Law of the Spirit in Christ Jesus abides in us, we may benefit from the gifts and provisions God has already brought forth.

Remember Jer 33.3 Run to Him - He loves you so much.

And one of my first promises from my Jesus ...

Jer 15:16 *Your words were found, and I ate them, And Your word was to me the joy and rejoicing of my heart; For I am called by Your name, O Lord God of hosts.* Thank You Jesus

In our old man we did not have to strive to do the works of the flesh. In our new man created specifically to do good works; we don't have strive either, just yield [Phil 4.24].

As I live by the Father, even so shall You live by Me.

What makes all this possible is described in 1Co 6.17.

He that is joined to the Lord is one spirit.

There was a time when our spirit was dead. Our inheritance derived of the Adamic race is to be born with a dead spirit and a carnal mind [Gen 5.3]. On the day Adam sinned his spirit died and he could no longer fellowship with God Who is Spirit.

There was created the 'sin-nature', of which all human beings are born with; born in the image of Adam. This is what Jesus took to the cross so we could become again, sons and daughters of the Most High God.

Adam was created so perfect that it took 930 years for his body to wear out and die. But the most significant and totally devastating demise was accounted to his spirit. Remember God warned him,

On the day you eat of this tree, you will surely die.

This brought separation from the Source of Life Himself. But God could not leave us in this position. He had already made these decisions before He created man. And so, in the fullness of time, our fate was altered.

From the beginning to the end, Jesus worked out and finished all things pertaining to His creation who would become His family. Even as He was forming that mud pie, and gave his laws to His people; He knew He would eventually write His laws on our heart. Prophesied in

Jer 31:31-34 *Behold, the days are coming, says the Lord, when I will make a new covenant with the house of Israel and with the house of Judah — not according to the covenant that I made with their fathers in the day that I took them by the hand to lead them out of the land of Egypt, My covenant which they broke, though I was a husband to them, says the Lord.*

But this is the covenant that I will make with the house of Israel after those days, says the Lord: I will put My law in their minds, and write it on their hearts; and I will be their God, and they shall be My people. No more shall every man teach his neighbor, and every man his brother, saying, 'Know the Lord,' for they all shall know Me, from the least of them to the greatest of them, says the Lord. For I will forgive their iniquity, and their sin I will remember no more.

And substantiated in ...

Heb 8:7-13 *For if that first covenant had been faultless, then no place would have been sought for a second. Because finding fault with them, He says: Behold, the days are coming, says the Lord, when I will make a new covenant with the house of Israel and with the house of Judah — not according to the covenant that I made with their fathers in the day when I took them by the hand to lead them out of the land of Egypt; because they did not continue in My covenant, and I disregarded them, says the Lord. For this is the covenant that I will make with the house of Israel after those days, says the Lord: I will put My laws in their mind and write them on their hearts; and I will be their God, and they shall be My people. None of them shall teach his neighbor, and none his brother, saying, 'Know the Lord,' for all shall know Me, from the least of them to the greatest of them. For I will be merciful to their unrighteousness, and their sins and their lawless deeds I will remember no more. In that He says, A new covenant, He has made the first obsolete.*

Now what is becoming obsolete and growing old is ready to vanish away.

STUDY GUIDE

1. If these things apply to you, Jesus understands. Talk to Him. Pour out your heart before Him [Ps 62].
2. No one ever said it would be easy. Jesus tells us to count the cost. I would exhort you to not allow this to cost your inheritance; to just get into heaven by the skin of your teeth, when you can be a victorious overcomer.
3. At what level of maturity does a Christian stop responding to offenses? We are all growing - let's take some giant steps here. God is faithful.
4. He can help us sort out our priorities.
5. Don't let the devil have the last word in these issues. Ask God to reveal all the lies you have believed and replace them with His truth.

PRAYER: I hurt so bad sometimes I feel like I'm being smooshed. Your Word says I can walk in liberty. If You will show me the door I'll walk through it. I'll trust You to guide and teach me and heal me. I put this in Your capable hands. I will begin by asking forgiveness and forgiving - and forgiving myself for all my mistakes that got me into trouble; and most of all, learn to love those of whom have offended me.

There's a new song in my heart Holy Spirit fragrance flows
With the joy of His redemption As His life within me grows
So cause me to come to Thy river, Oh Lord,
Cause me to drink fully of Thy love and grace
Cause me to humble myself before You
To enter into Thy Holy Place.

SCRIPTURES

1. Ps 119:165
2. Mt 3:3
3. Jn 1:29
4. Jn 1:31
5. Jn 1:34
6. Je 29:13
7. Mt 11:2-4
8. Mt 11:16-18
9. Jn 8:48 and Jn 7:20
10. Jn 6:41
11. Jn 8:12
12. Mt. 23:3
13. Mt 17:27
14. Mt 11:28-30
15. 1Pe 5:5
16. Ps 63:5-8
17. He 4:15
18. Jn 17:4
19. Jn 6:29
20. He 13:5
21. 1Pe 2:22-23
22. Jn 17:16
23. Is 64:6
24. Mt 10:38-39
25. Ge 32:22-30
26. Is 66:2
27. 1Pe 2:23
28. Is 60:1-2
29. 1Jn 4:21
30. James 3:2

* From their point of view, they did murder Him - and think they got away with it. They did not know God had a plan!

There's no condemnation
To those in Christ
He's set us free from sin
When He came He brought His Kingdom,
Now He invites us to come in.
There's treasures and blessings
We know nothing about
Mysteries, secrets, darkness and light
And He calls us to search them out
We live in Christ, He lives in us
Such joy we have never known
But revelation comes to us
From the seeds we have sown.

♥

THE SPIRIT AND THE SOUL.

*And the very God of peace sanctify you wholly;
and I pray God your whole spirit, soul and body
be preserved blameless unto the coming
of the Lord Jesus Christ.*[1]

To be sanctified means to be set apart for a specific intent. Scripture declares that God created us for a purpose - to have a people of His own; to have relationship and fellowship; a family.

If you're alive, you have purpose!

The first Adam, and every Adam after him, intentionally rebelled against God because of that sin nature. But God has even extended so graciously as to create a New Man that we can put on...[Col 3.9-10]............➜

> Put off the old man, put on the new man.

This new man was created to be like God in true righteousness and holiness.[2]

*For we are his workmanship...
created for good works.*[3]

So, this new man was specifically created to be righteous and holy and to manifest the fruits of the Spirit which is the character of God. That's why He can tell us to be holy, because He knows He gave us the right equipment to carry out the command. His holiness dwells in us. Allow it to manifest!

Even after we made such a mess of what we were given in the first place; it's like a Mom dressing her 2 year old in the most elegant finery to attend the party of the year. Soon as her back is turned the kid heads for the nearest mud puddle. With love and compassion we are bathed and clothed anew. Psalm 139 tells us that our Creator saw us as we were being formed in the womb.

For thou has possessed my inward parts. ♡

Possessed means: manufactured for the purpose of owning. The inward parts are the reins - or the innermost substance: figuratively speaking, the mind.

Boy, if that's not something satan wants to rule over, I don't know what is! That's why it is imperative that we renew our mind as instructed in Romans Chapter 12. May we ask ourselves,

What is my mind stayed on?[4]

Again God's Word has the answer.

Isaiah 26:1-4 *We have a strong city; God will appoint salvation for walls and bulwarks. Open the gates, that the righteous nation which keeps the truth may enter in. You will keep him in perfect peace whose mind is stayed on You, because he trusts You. Trust in the Lord forever, for in YAH, the Lord, is everlasting strength.*

    If we are in blood covenant with the God of Jacob, then we may apply this to our personal life. This Scripture almost encompasses the whole of the Good News of God's Word. It is not surprising that we can find this message recorded many times, in many ways, throughout the Bible.

    Now I said all that to say this; It never ceases to amaze me that of billions of people on the earth today, there are not two of us exactly alike. Even identical twins are different somewhere in the make-up of their personality or character; their heart of hearts.

    Each of us individually was created for a specific purpose and given in the womb, the traits and resources to gravitate toward that purpose.

*Train up a child in the way he should go,
and when he is grown he will not depart from it.*[5] God's Word tells us to Train Strong's #2596 - to be narrow - like a tunnel with walls all around. You have to go in the direction of the path - you can't veer off to a 90 degree angle. Train - discipline,

The child in the way he should go.

    The tendencies a child has to go in a certain direction, can become apparent as he grows in your home, through prayer and guiding his interests and behavior patterns.

The way he should go is translated,

The mouth of his way ....→

| He will not depart from it. |

in the Interlinear Bible. The Concordance refers to Breath. God wants to direct the force of this life in a certain manner. If the child is disciplined, trained, directed - on his own individual path - created expressly for him while being formed in the womb - of course, *He will not depart from it.*

    Even to be left handed may have been designed for this child. And I have found that children who seem to be destructive in tearing things apart; well perhaps it is a curiosity to see how things are made and maybe this child will be creative to find better ways.

As he is in training, he is following the road God prepared for him before the foundation of the world and it will lead him into the Kingdom. Sad enough to recount how many lives are destroyed because these gifts from our heavenly Father have been perverted.

There are certain musicians in the world today that have an awesome charisma to lead others into their own brand of destruction. At many concerts, young people are duped into giving their lives over to satan.

I don't doubt at all, this leadership ability was the gift God gave them in the womb to evangelize for the Kingdom of God; their musical talents given to worship the Lord of Life, perverted to worship the god of sheol.

There are many of us who have chosen to walk on God's path of righteousness. Perhaps our route got sidetracked because there was no early understanding, but now we've turned into that tunnel that leads us in the direction we were meant to go. The 23rd Psalm tells us,

The Lord is my Shepherd,
I shall not want. He leads me...

and goes on to show us how God can restore us from the destruction in our souls. The word lead means to run with a sparkle! There are no conditions set up or expected for our salvation. We just need to receive His gift of eternal life.

For by grace are ye saved through
faith, not of yourselves, it is a gift of God.[6]

You can't earn it lest you become prideful. God's love is unconditional.

God commended his love toward us in that, while we were yet sinners, Christ died for us.[7]

We were dead, and we were darkness,[8] when God poured out His love on us for the purpose of intimate relationship............➔

| It is His good pleasure |

God does not love us any more when we are obedient to His Word than He did when we were darkness. That's what unconditional means. No matter what you do or don't do, God's love never changes. What will you do with His love? Will you respond to it?

But going back to the Shepherd Who is leading us on the path of righteousness - there is a condition here mentioned very clearly [Ph 2:13]
I shall not want.
This condition could be that,
I shall not have any wants of my own!
If we have our own agenda,
where does God fit - in His will for our life?
*For it is God who works in you to will
and to do of His good pleasure.*
He loves us and salvation is free. But if we want to partake of His Kingdom, we shall have to do it His way. God's ways are so far above ours, His thoughts are so much higher. Saints, as long as we have personal plans and goals, how can God carry out His ways. [Ps 119:15 Ampl]
I will meditate on Your precepts and have respect to Your ways [the paths of life marked out by Your law].
When we do turn to God, He begins to develop the gifts planted inherently within. Some of us were so buried under - that what God had intended for us was totally obliterated. For example, after I gave my life to Jesus, He began to develop in me the gift of painting. I'd never known I was bent that way, but some [not only friends] tell me my paintings are quite good. I did not take art lessons; God just began to bring to fruition the seed of creativity He planted in the womb.

I did attend some art classes but I was already selling some of my work. It was a gift of God to me. I did not earn it, although I spent some years refining it with prayer and supplication, with thanksgiving. It has been such a blessing to me and a time of allowing the Creator to be creative in me.

Yes! God is giving back what was stolen from us; restoring our souls. Now when the Holy Spirit comes to dwell within, God wants to prepare us for use in His Kingdom through the gifts of the Holy Spirit. And God does bestow gifts on and in His children, but it is vital to remember the most important reason why God brought us into His Kingdom. That is simply because He loves us. His top priority is that we know Him on a personal intimate basis. It matters not If you come in last. You still win the crown.

John 17:3 *And this is life eternal, that they might know thee, the only true God, and Jesus Christ, whom thou hast sent.*

This must be our top priority. We must keep Jesus as our first love. Without this relationship, all that we do is in vain because we will not have His love to flow through us, and without His unconditional love we cannot minister His life to others, which is the whole point. And where did we get the power to love Him. Look at 1John 4.19:

We love Him because He first loved us.

So when Rev 2.4-5 says 'we have left our first love; remember from where we have fallen...' What is our first love. It was receiving God's love. Acknowledging His love that enabled us to be born-again into His Kingdom. We get so busy thinking we are doing stuff for God, that we allow the awareness of His incredible love to drift onto the back burner of our lives.

Our spirit and soul are two different things [organs]. Within our soul lies our identity, character, personality. We make our choices from the experiences that are already established in our soul. [Like the 3 young men that were thrown into the fiery furnace. They'd already chosen to worship the one true God and could not be dissuaded].

Our choices can be resolved and changed according to God's Word which we should know is truth. Let truth reign in your heart. God's love is powerful to turn our life around. Please let Him do it. Let His love penetrate your soul and your heart.

Our heart and soul are connected, in agreement. When our heart finds the reality of God's Word, it will become established in our soul so that we will never deny Him. Our mind comes into agreement, and we can live by the Word of God. Holy Spirit lives in our spirit to lead and guide and teach - [John 14.26].

Sometimes we think because we still acknowledge Him then we're OK. We think the strife that comes back into our lives is just because we're Christians, and we can learn to handle it. Of course that's only until we realize we are bent over by the burden of trying to handle life by our own resources. Then comes depression, etc. We think God has left us. No...Repent of trying to live for God out of your own ability, to love or to do anything else for the Kingdom.

Let the sword of the Spirit slice between your soul and spirit and get back to knowing you can do nothing without God's love dwelling in the innermost part of you; and being every moment aware of that love. When was the last time you thanked God for His precious gift of love for you? You can start now, and continue to do so every day, as you fully acknowledge His presence and love in your life. Don't ever again let go of it.

What we think of as natural abilities are really gifts from God and they must be refined, cleansed, sanctified, be tied to the altar and purged by fire of any human effort, before they are of any use to the Kingdom of God.

We can rampage through the Kingdom using our gifts to justify our actions. Which is why we must have the flesh, the works of our soul power separated from these gifts, and destroyed. Our soul power is a mighty force in our lives. In The Latent Power of the Soul, by Watchman Nee, Christian Fellowship Publishers, Inc. New York, tells us in His Preface,

> Many well disposed brethren thought of it as merely a dispute over words having no great significance. Our conflict is not with words but with what lies behind. The spirit and the soul are two totally different organs; one belongs to God, while the other belongs to man...completely distinct in substance. Confusion with these may lead to deception. Satan is behind all parapsychology, using the latent power of our soul to accomplish his goals. For this reason all who develop their soul power cannot avoid being contacted and used by an evil spirit.

So we must renew our minds, bring our soul nature under submission to the Holy Spirit, and allow God to develop the fruit of the Spirit beginning with His unconditional kind of love. The Word says if you have not love, you are like a roaring sound - one that turns people off.

He must first develop the fruit of the Spirit, that we may minister in love, joy, peace, patience, gentleness, goodness and faith, meekness and self control. The fruit of the Spirit does not function through our flesh nature.

No matter how loving we may think we are, only God's unconditional love empowered by His Spirit, will set prisoners free. Only God's unconditional love will minister to the broken heart and wounded spirit for those of whom need to see this mercy and grace poured out on them. And understand that the fruit is love...all else pours out from that place.

God indeed wants to involve us in the work of the Kingdom and we also need to allow Him to develop the gifts and train us to use them properly. I've observed for quite some time, in myself and others, how God allows us to move out in certain ministry and then it seems to fade away for a season. [This happens more in our early years than in the latter].

We wonder what we did to make God angry at us and guilt and condemnation come pouring in at an alarming rate as we scramble to carry out our mission although it no longer seems to be bearing much fruit. We begin to think He has left us. But no, we have left the acknowledgment of His great unconditional love on the back burner. [Rev 2.4]

I would like to suggest this season of coming apart is for the restoration of our souls. The God of peace wants to sanctify us wholly; spirit, soul and body. God pulls us back so that we might be refreshed and restored, and we may grow in Him. Remember, this is a process - God's timing, our yielding.

Sometimes it is of enormous dimensions, to heal and deliver and transform us in order that the God kind of character and integrity can become part and parcel of our life, our identity. Paul says,
I bring my body under subjection [to my spirit] lest by any means when I preach to others, I myself should be a castaway.[9]

In the preceding verses he speaks of the race we are in to gain that incorruptible crown, pressing toward the mark for the prize of the high calling of God in Christ Jesus.

What Paul emphasizes in Philippians 3 is that all the accomplishments of his flesh counted for nothing. They all had to be laid on the altar and consumed. He had to get his priorities in order, and had to deal with his flesh as Romans 6&7 aptly describes.

Nothing came automatically to Paul, any more than it comes to us. Paul spent many years in the desert as God revealed to him the law of the Spirit of life in Christ Jesus Rom 8:2. The world, the flesh and the devil are deceitful opponents. We don't know of what our hearts are capable. God knows and gave us an appropriate prayer.
Search my heart oh God, try me and know my thoughts; and see if there be any wicked way in me, and lead me in the way everlasting.[10]

Before we are saved we are ruled by our carnal nature inherent in our soul, emotions, unrenewed mind and our self-will. We are captive to the law. In making Jesus Savior and Lord, the Holy Spirit takes up residence in our spirit.

Now we can be led by the Spirit of God, not by our own imaginations. We must be sure to know it is our choice which way we go. God does not force us to do anything. It is because of His awesome love, that we choose to do those things that please Him [1Jn 4:19].

It is in our character, personality, and identity that His divine nature will come forth. The gifts of the Spirit are for this earthly ministry only. We will not need them in eternity. They are for ministry to the Body.

But the fruits of the Spirit; these will be continuously developed within us along with having the -

Spirit of our mind renewed.[11]

Look it up. It means renovate [down to bare bones] the vital principles of our understanding.

As God restores our soul and we learn to walk in trusting God, developing that intimate relationship with Him, we find ourselves coming into His rest more and more, as we cease from our own works.[12]

As we quit doing our own thing we can trust God to do His thing through us. God is looking for empty [of self] yielded vessels. Our self-life in the grave with the old man,[13] allows the New Man to walk in the works for which he was created. God is bringing us into balance, adjusting our nature [Jn 6:28-29].

What must we do, that we might work the works of God?: ....→

> This is the work of God,.. that ye believe on whom he hath sent.

When we first come into the Kingdom there is a lot of unbelief in our heart. But we can humble ourselves and come to Jesus as the father of the deaf and dumb child in Mk 9 and cry out,

Lord I believe, help thou my unbelief.

Thank God for his mercy and grace.

What makes all this possible is described in 1 Corinthians 6:17. There was a time when our spirit was dead. On the day Adam sinned his spirit died and he could no longer communicate with God Who is Spirit. Our inheritance derived of the Adamic race is to be born with a sin-nature and a dead spirit, incapable of communicating with God Who is Spirit. Not to say God does not hear us. He heard the cry of my heart and gave me this Word.

Ps 116:1-2 *I love the Lord, because He has heard My voice and my supplications. Because He has inclined His ear to me, Therefore I will call upon Him as long as I live.*

The Great 'I Am' saw my lost soul and had mercy on me when I didn't even know He knew I existed!

Adam was created so perfect that it took more than 900 years for his body to wear out and die. But the most significant and totally devastating demise was accounted to his spirit. On that day, came a veil of separation from the Source of Life Himself; a veil that could only be torn asunder by the coming of the Lord. Now the way is opened for us to come into His presence, and here, with God's grace, go His people to conquer and tread underfoot the enemy of their soul. In our soul, our emotions; satan has access to us through our mind. Our mind must be renewed to not accept his lies. This is one reason why we must know the Word; know the Truth.

Satan cannot touch our spirit.

Our spirit can only be joined to the Lord. It was vital that God bring our spirit back to life. In the world, our soul is ruler of our life. The power of our soul must come into subjection to our spirit, in submission to the Holy Spirit that dwells within us. We are to be led by the Spirit of God through our spirit.

Our soul housed the old man. Let the new man take over the lease. When we are led by our soul, we cannot receive from God. God saw our need - the empty progression of futility lived out with no hope. But the God of the universe had already made provision for Whosoever will. Within the arena of God's grace there is power and strength to overcome. That's what grace is for, to walk in the perfect law of liberty.

Grace was created especially for the spirit man; to empower the spirit man. Jesus did it first. He walked in God's grace, He died in God's grace. And because of the resurrection we also may walk in the fullness of His grace.

But we see Jesus who was made a little lower than the angels for the suffering of death, crowned with glory and honor, that he, by the grace of God, should taste death for every man.[20]

God's grace brought Jesus through the cross -
For in that he himself hath suffered being tempted, he is able to help

them that are tempted.[21] ....→

What a gracious Redeemer has given us all precious promises to bring us through safely into His presence [2Pe 1:4]. We are on a journey into a far country. We know not which direction to go. There will be many stop signs. There will be many yield signs. There will be many Y's in the road. Which way shall we choose?

> God's grace will always be sufficient for us.

There is a map, of course. It was carefully designed and written out plain, to show each stumbling block and each well of refreshing. It points to the Way. And on our journey we are given the ability - the graceability to overcome. Jesus tells us,

My grace is enough. For my strength is made perfect,
it is brought to its fullness, through your weakness.

Jesus was innocent. He chose to do this for us so that we might receive His life. But we must ask for it. Like a bank account, one must withdraw the funds in order to use them. The Word reveals what we need. When Jesus went back to the Father, He sent His Holy Spirit to lead, guide and teach. It is the same Holy Spirit that brooded over the genesis of our universe. The same One Whose glory invaded the realms of death and broke loose that One of Whom it gripped most severely.

The same Holy Spirit that dwells in us, Who draws us into His Kingdom, reveals to us the deep things of God, that we might know the things that are freely given to us of God [1Co 2:10-12]. This Holy Spirit asks, *Does any lack wisdom,*
let him ask of God who gives liberally.
This same Holy Spirit heals our broken heart and will evict the trespasser. Trust Him, He'll do it!

The Word tells us the Old Testament was written to teach us examples of the principles of the Kingdom of God. The Lord is good to us to show how the rubber meets the road. I need a working model. That's where I'm at, how about you? Exodus 17 tells us,

Then came Amalek,
and fought with Israel in Rephidim.

This encounter with the enemy goes on to reveal that Joshua led the armies against Amalek. Moses, Aaron and Hur went up the hill to pray. As long as Moses held up his hands, Israel prevailed. When he let down his hands, Amalek prevailed. We can gain much insight as we research and seek to know God's ways.

The Word of God is a deep realm of hidden treasure.
Amalek comes from the root word meaning toiling, laborer; or the works that come from our flesh. Rephidim means: to spread a bed, make comfortable. Hur comes from the root word meaning white linen, or righteousness. Aaron represents the priesthood. Moses represents the anointing of God.

Then comes Amalek. Every time we purpose to serve God, here comes the flesh, looking to remind us how comfortable we had been in doing our own familiar thing. It cost something to walk in obedience to God, and the price is our flesh, our self-life.

The spirit and soul of man will not die, only the flesh of his body [1Kings 17:21-22]. It tells us in Eccl 12:7 that when our bodies die, our spirit returns to God who gave it. In the creation of man, [Ps 146:4].

God breathed into his nostrils the breathe of life
and man became a living soul ❤

Within our soul resides our personality, emotions, our will; who we are, our identity. The breathe of life, our portion of spirit, is given in order that we may communicate and fellowship with God Who is Spirit.

In Mt 10:28 it tells us to fear the One that is able to destroy both soul and body in hell. Obviously this tells us if a person is not born again, the breathe of God - the gift of spirit, separates from the soul and goes back into the presence of God. His soul descends into the place of the dead, sheol [Ez 18:4].

The unbeliever is now and forever void of the presence of God and can never again have the opportunity to communicate with Him.. Soon, at the resurrection of the dead, his body will join his soul [his personality, emotions, will and identity] into everlasting torment, the lake of fire [Re 20:10, 15.

Luke 16 tells us the dead are very much aware of who they are and where they are. We know Lazarus and this rich man had their bodies buried in the ground. It was their soul and spirit that went to these places. Cognizance resides in our identity of memories and who we are [Isa 66:24; Rev 20:15].

The worm refers to the lust that drove them in their lifetime, that they were not willing to turn to the Savior. This lust will never be satiated, not for eternity and everlasting.

On the other hand, if a person gives his life to God, his soul becomes bonded and united with God.

Here is a few Scriptures you can refer to. There are many more in the Word you can look up for more understanding. Pr 13.2; 23.14; Ps.16.10; Mt 10.28; Especially Ezek 18.4, *The soul that sins shall die* [because you never asked for forgiveness]. The Holy Spirit dwells in our human spirit; life ever-lasting [1Co 6:17]. Romans 8 asks, *Who can separate us from the love of God?* Then it tells us nothing can!......→

And so, our spirit and our soul, forever in union with the living God, returns to God to await that glorious resurrection morning when our mortal bodies will be given the gift of immortality [1Co 15:53-54]. *And so shall we ever be with the Lord* [1Pet 2:25; Ps 104:29]. Some other Scriptures to consider; Jesus commended His spirit to the Father before He died.

| He that is joined to the Lord is one spirit. |

Into Your hands I commit my spirit.
His spirit did not go into the place of the dead with Him. Job 27:3; 32:8; Eccl 12:7; Ps 146:4. James 2:26, without the spirit the body is dead. God breathed [spirit] into the man and he became a living soul. The breath of God goes back to God. Nothing of God can go into hell [1Th 5:23].
Numbers 16:22; 27:16; Ezek 18:4; 1Pe 4:19. Ps 104:29.

He takes away their breath, they die and return to their dust. Only man's body is made of the dust of the earth [Job 34:14-15].

BREATH: [Strongs Concordance]
#7307 ruwach - wind, spirit   #7308   mind, spirit, wind.

This is not a doctrine to depend on for salvation. It is a comfort to know that we will be with the Lord when we are finished with this earth life. 2Co 5:8 tells us, *to be absent from the body is to be present with the Lord.*

No flesh shall glory in God's presence. So If we want God's help, we must choose to leave our comfort zone. It will be a battle. Amalek, the flesh, always wars with the Spirit, the anointing [Gal 5:17]. Going back to Exodus 17, Let's consider the three men on the hill. Ecclesiastes 4:12 tells us,
And if one prevail against him, two shall withstand him;
and a threefold cord is not quickly broken.

Cord means to sew together, be attached. The Father, Son and Holy Spirit are of one accord - working together to bring us into victory over our enemy. Our armor has been provided [Eph 6:10-18]. Put it on, walk around in it.

Aaron was the high priest. Moses was the anointing. Hur stands for the righteousness of God in Christ. These three stand together to overcome the enemy. Righteousness and holiness were joined to the anointing; another triple braided cord the enemy cannot prevail against.

We are priests of the Most High God. As we pray and worship, God gives us victory to walk in His Spirit...............➜

> The armies of the Lord are on our side.

But ye are come to Mount Zion,
the city of the living God,
the heavenly Jerusalem,
to an innumerable company of angels.[22]

And Joshua - Yashua, - Jahvahshua or Jehovah - how ever you want to pronounce the magnificent Name of Jesus, Lord and King; our Captain victorious stands with us. And so in victory,

Moses built an altar

Jehovah Nissi; the Lord our Banner.

His banner over us is love.

Isa 140.7 *Thou hast covered my head in the day of battle* ❤

Yes! He's got our back!

With this kind of help how can we possibly lose? He is worthy of our praise and worship. Paul recognized how stinted was our arena of set standards. Laws and demands, spoken or silent, have shaped our personalities and character from infancy and yet beyond because of generational conformance. We have the authority and anointing to release ourselves from generational sins and curses that have been handed down to us by our forefathers.

We do things in a certain way because it has been saved in our hard drive. We believe in certain things because when the question arises, the answer has already been established. Perhaps until now, these limitations have not been tested for Spirit strength. God cried out through Isaiah,

Enlarge the place of thy tent and let them stretch forth

the curtains of thy habitations; spare not, lengthen thy cords, and strengthen thy stakes.[25]

Paul tells us in Ephesians 4, the walk of a believer in Christ is to grow up in Him in all things;

Unto a perfect man, unto the measure of the stature of Christ.

If this is ever to happen we shall have to begin to question and examine our beliefs and standards; to plumb line each and all against the only true standard, the Living Word and His written Word.

As Paul lay in blind darkness for three days his mind must have been overrun with questions, just as ours does. God doesn't perform a disectomy on us to remove our past history. We are who we are, and God saves us where we are.

We are still the same person, the day after we are saved. Yet now we have other options. Only our destination has been changed and our spirit is now alive to communicate with God. Our journey to that destination is the path of change.

Explained in Romans 7 is that we were once married to, or bound by the law. We had to obey it. Now we are married to another that we should bring forth fruit unto God. We were held in that bondage to law - but now delivered to serve life in the Spirit. 2Co 1:9-10 tells us this is a process; delivered, doth deliver, and He will yet deliver. The word deliver means to grab by force. When we yield our life to God, He forcibly removes us from the bondage of satan who does not want to let us go; but he has no other choice!!

The Spirit Himself bears witness that we are the children of God.[26]

Our big brother Jesus, comes to set us free from the bully. Anything that is alive must grow. We see in a mirror what kind of man we are, and then compare it with the Word. Wherever we see the discrepancies, this is what God wants to pinpoint with the,

The perfect law of liberty, which is:

The Law of the Spirit of Life in Christ Jesus.[27]

Then James sites Abraham, who lived before the law was given; that by faith he was called a friend of God. I want to be called, A friend of God.

Yield yourselves unto God, as those that are alive from the dead, and your members as instruments of righteousness unto God.[28]

STUDY GUIDE

1. Romans and Galatians are good resources for studying the soul verses the spirit.
2. Know that Paul had to work through these truths. With prayer and trusting in God it does not have to be a struggle, either to understand or to have it become heart knowledge and workable in your life. Trust in the Holy Spirit to lead and guide you.
3. God worked it all out for us, He only wants us to enter in. How can this begin to happen?
4. Are you more sure now that God loves you, than when you began? Getting strong in the Word and in fellowship with God will give assurance.
5. And don't forsake the assembling of yourself with others. It is imperative we remain under God's protective grace, mercy, peace and rest. These are some of the things the Blood of Jesus bought for us.

PRAYER: Father, help me. I can do nothing without You. I want to receive all You have for me. Please move forcibly in my life to bring about the changes needed to grow in You.

SCRIPTURES

1. 1Th 5:23	2. Ep 4:23	3. Ep 2:10
4. Is 26:3-4	5. Pr 22:6	7. Ro 5:8
8. Ep 5:8	9. 1Co 10:9	10. Ps 139
11. Ep 4:23	12. He 4	13. Co 3:9
14. Ac 3:21	15. 1Pe 1:12	16. Jn 20:10
17. Ro 8:11	18. Jn 6:57	19. 1Co 6:17
20. He 2:9	21. He 2:18	22. He 12:22
23. S.S.2:4	24. Ps 140:7	25. Is 54:2
26. Ro 8:16	27. Ro 8:2	28. Ro 6:13

You Sent down Your Love
In the Form of a Man
Two Arms That Reached Out,
Two Feet That Walked My Path,
A Heart That Was Broken
And Tears That Were Shed,
With the Love
That You Sent down to Man ❤

LAW TO GRACE

But he said to me, my grace [my favor and loving-kindness and mercy] is enough for you [sufficient against any danger and enables you to bear the trouble manfully]; for my strength and power are made perfect [fulfilled and completed] and show themselves most effective in [your] weakness. Therefore I will all the more gladly glory in my weakness and infirmities, that the strength and power of Christ [the Messiah] may rest [yes, may pitch a tent over me and dwell] upon me [Co 12:9 Amplified Version.]

In looking up 'grace' in Strong's Concordance # 5485, it says *The divine influence upon the heart and its reflection in the life.*

In 2Cor 12:9 God told Paul...*My grace is sufficient.*
In Phil 4:13 Paul says, *I can do all things through Christ who strengthens me.*

Grace must be an impartation of strength from God to live the life God has for us.

Ps 27:1 tells us, *The Lord is the strength of my life.*
Paul begins all his letters with,
Grace be unto you, and peace from God our Father, and the Lord Jesus Christ.

Grace-charis: a kindness granted, a favor done without expectations absolute free loving kindness of God to men; joy, pleasure, liberality of spirit. This grace is given to the humble [for God resists the proud], to enable us to walk in the Spirit.

John G. Lake, an early century missionary and Apostle of God's healing power, casts light on what God told Paul about his thorn.

Paul prayed three times. The first and second time he was not conscious of the answer. He prayed again, bless God. This time God met his faith and said to him, Paul, my grace is sufficient for you. Apply it, Paul. Dive in Paul and take all you want of the grace of God. It will fix your thorn in the flesh, and everything else that is troubling you [John G. Lake, Kenneth Copeland Publications, Fort Worth, Texas].

Paul had that working knowledge of what God's grace was about. May God give to us the same deep understanding.

To Timothy, Paul adds mercy which concerns itself not with sin, but with God's compassion on the consequence of that sin. God is in the business of restoration.

God's creation passing from law to grace was a finished work on the cross of Jesus. The new Covenant was written in Blood and sealed by the death of the testator[1].

Yahvahshua - The LORD is salvation.

Paul wrote letters to the Galatians and Romans between 52 and 58 A.D., about 20 years after the resurrection of Jesus.[2] He worked out the matters of law and grace in his own life, then shared it with us. These letters record the struggle one man came to terms with as he tried to get real.

Soon after his conversion, Paul went to Arabia.[3] He didn't go back to Jerusalem to learn from the disciples - he closed his closet door and sat at the feet of Jesus.[4] He shares with us what God taught him.

This man was a strict Pharisee, the son of a Pharisee, separated unto the law and very religious. His zeal for defending the law carried over to torture and murder. He truly believed he was doing God a favor. The works of the law were ingrained into his personality and character. Any one thought to be an enemy of God was fair game for his judgment. He believed these Jewish converts were mocking the law............................➔

> He was its ferocious protector.

Those followers of Jesus were blasphemers, and he considered Gentiles the scum of the earth, to be compared with the unclean animals forbidden on the Jewish menu; yet he calls himself the worst of sinners. Letters Paul wrote were to Gentile believers and every letter begins with -

*Grace and peace from the Father
and our Lord Jesus Christ.*

Where did that come from! Acts 9.10 - Paul was 3 days blind and crazy from what happened to him on the road of his madness ready to search out these Jews who would renounce the law and jump into freedom in Christ. This man stern as the law, could not allow this.

But God had a different plan. He sent Annanias whose name means 'grace', to confront the law with God's grace. As Paul opened his eyes, the grace of God went deep into Paul's soul and a man truly after the heart of God, was born again.

Now baptized into Christ, He humbled himself and went into solitude to learn from God and
> *'To reveal His Son in me.*
Now God has a work to do in Paul as well as me and you.
Gal 2:19-21 *For I through the law died to the law that I might live to God. I have been crucified with Christ; it is no longer I who live, but Christ lives in me; and the life which I now live in the flesh I live by faith in the Son of God, who loved me and gave Himself for me. I do not set aside the grace of God; for if righteousness comes through the law, then Christ died in vain."*

> Ah! Truth pervades the heart and soul and we are as ready as Paul to allow God to invade our prejudices and the lies we've believed. To bring truth and reality, ready to live there - AND...

We must move into grace or there will be no joy.

Those things that offend us are the very issues God will keep before us until His work of love and grace permeates the very root of pride and self-righteousness, and cleanses us from our filth.

Now God could walk Paul through religiosity, law and ritual; his flesh, his prejudices, and finally his worldly inheritance - out into grace and love. Everything that could be shaken in Paul - was! Even though much of Paul's letters are given over to Church issues at hand, there is woven throughout, the graphic auto-biography of a man sold out to God.

There is revealed in each of the books of the Bible, the person that carries the anointing. From Genesis to Revelation there is the disclosure of Life Himself. There is also the human author and his humanity, as each truth was developed in the heart and established in the spirit.

We see Abraham, Isaac, Jacob, Moses, Jeremiah, Elijah. Many more; the men and their lives. God is not raising up zombies. We are individuals with an acquired personal social history that will respond to the viable relationship of another person and more vitally, to God Himself.........→

It helps to understand the writers of the Book were just like us. They were ordinary people who allowed God to change them and use

> It certainly helps to realize that I too, can walk in victory.

them to transmit His will, the glorious Gospel, the Good News - to the next generations.

I'm so glad to find these people were not somewhere up in the ozone, unreachable and obscure; so religious as to be unapproachable. Paul wanted God's will more than his own. I'm so glad to see that he and others overcame some of the same struggles I have.

Ah, but the grace to walk in
and live by that faith, must be received.

The works of the law contains what you do to satisfy a criteria. *Now faith is the substance of*; the tangible stuff we can base our hopes on. That is, passionately consumed and digested by our spirit until it becomes character and identity. [Just as the food we eat becomes us]. Faith must be executed every day, moment by moment as we battle the frustrations of our life. As we walk by that faith, grace; that is the power to live the Word, is imparted to us by our gracious Lord.

We are finely honed by society to work out our own salvation by taking charge of every detail. I saw and experienced in the terror of a nightmare, the paralyzing fear that kept me bound in anxiety every time I attempted to go deeper into trusting God. I tried to work things out so I could go around the problem and not have to actually face it.

Like a revolving door, fear was my limiting tread. I rationalized to myself why I couldn't do certain things; always having an excuse or reason. But I yielded the whole issue to God. He is faithful, and by His magnificent love, God delivered me into His Law of Liberty.[4]

The next day there was a renewed joy in my heart. I didn't have to do anything to receive this deliverance. I yielded the whole issue to God, and I praise the Lord for it. I only want to serve God with all that is within me, with fear and trembling before Him; and so I look to Him to work out the details.[5]

The realm of the Spirit is supernatural and must be revealed to us. Our natural mind sometimes screams too loud. That's why God wants us to come into His rest. That place of rest is found in the faith, trust and grace of God.

Soon after my graphic deliverance from that fear, the old thoughts were trying to gain entrance once more. God flashed in my mind a picture of Jesus in the middle of that storm, asleep on His pillow in the stern of the boat. Isn't God funny?

When we are in a place concerning a specific issue, it is just like our gracious loving Father to bless us with surprises, as we are waiting for Him to take care of our cares.

If there is grumbling and complaining[6] our compassionate Lord may still work out His plan for us, but we will probably miss out on the wonderful joy of fellowship with our God. The reason for our hope may never be shared with fellow sojourners.[7]

God is a lot more interested in what is going on within us than what we are doing on the outside. He knows from the heart pours forth the issues of life. As James so aptly recognized, faith without works is dead. But faith cannot function in the atmosphere of Law. Only by grace can we stand in faith.

James was the brother of Jesus; a natural son of Joseph and Mary.[8] [His real name was Jacob]. John 7:4-5 shares his concern for what Jesus was suddenly doing. James, as His brother in the flesh, could not believe the claims of Jesus to be the Son of God; nor in His divine mission.[9] After all, they grew up in the same house.

Mark 6 records Jesus going back home to Nazareth. These people knew Him in the flesh also. They knew His family. They were astonished [to strike, or shock, or disturb] at His claims. He went back to bless His friends. They greeted Him with unbelief. He could do no mighty works there.

Interaction between God and His people happens moment by moment. It happens as we acknowledge Who is our God.

Many of us have difficulty witnessing to family or friends who know us after the flesh. The law of natural expectations is graphically in place. They are shocked and astonished because we want to come out of the old wine skin. We need to go ahead and do it anyway. Follow your heart, don't offend.

1Corinthians 15:7 reveals James' personal encounter with the risen Lord. Did James look in that mirror and see his natural man? Was that the turning point of his life? It is only God's grace that produces a bondslave. It is only grace that keeps you there [James 1:23]. It could only be grace that engulfed his troubled heart and led him to lay down flesh ties and write Verse One of his letter to the twelve tribes.

James, a servant of God and of the Lord Jesus Christ...

His confession; he was a servant of his Lord, a bondslave. He no longer knew Jesus after the flesh, or from a human viewpoint.

Even though Paul wrote 2Corinthians 5:16 he did not know Jesus after the flesh. He did not follow Jesus and hated all who did. Could this have been written as a result of meeting with James,[10] who knew Jesus after the flesh more than any other, yet now, His servant by the Spirit.

Peter writes of the fiery trials we must walk through because our faith is more precious than gold. Like gold, it must be refined and purified. [1Peter 1:7]. Faith...

Though it is tested by fire,
may be found to praise, honor and glory
at the revelation of Jesus Christ

Luke 22 reveals the breaking of a proud man. His agony of heart at seeing himself mirrored in the courtyard of Pilate's palace, could have destroyed him. What fiery trials did he walk through in that furnace? Peter carried the sorrow and pain that he too had betrayed his Lord. Yet grace covered Peter and brought him through the sifting process [V.31-32]. Peter was healed and restored as Jesus spoke, *Do you love me, Peter*?

Three times He denied Jesus; three times God's grace and love washed over him. 'Then, Feed my sheep Peter, take care of my lambs'. What release and freedom to know His Master again entrusted in his care, the people God loved.

Needless to say the ropes were burned away, and what was left, was to the Lord of glory, a sweet aroma. His soul set free from condemnation and guilt, Peter never looked back. It only made him more determined to serve his Lord and Master.

Perhaps all this is speculation, but we must remember these were real people used of God to transmit His purposes to the world. I have noticed that all these men share in their writings, a specific work God did in each of them, because of and through His grace. I believe their lives were changed because of what God did in and through them.

There is much overlapping. We have to hear something 20 times before we believe. But there is such a personal flavor to each of these Bible books. If God is setting forth His standard of righteousness to guide His people safely home, He must have the standard on the earth to work with.

Don't all builders use a standard measure? If not we would have some pretty awful structural disasters. The Word of God is not just a collection of nice sayings or things to do to keep us busy.

The Scriptures are eternal truths; life changing, character building, glorious plans the Lord has for His people. God is building His dwelling place [Eph 2:22]. As Isaiah 60 declares, the nations will be drawn to the light shining forth from His people. It is His standard; holiness and righteousness that is being established in us which they will see.

It is the love imparted by His grace that enables us to overlook what other people are all about. The most incredible work we can do on the earth is to love the unlovable. Whatever it is we do, will be the result of the attitude of our heart.

We are no longer restrained by the law
to do good works - or else!

Only the grace of God will allow His unconditional love to pour out on the lost. The peace that God's grace produced in my life [at a time when I should have been stressed out], directly witnessed to a person as such that she gave her heart to the Lord. That's the witness - what God is doing IN us.

Jesus called the Pharisees hypocrites. They were doing things on their outside that had no meaning on their inside. They were frauds. They obeyed the law to perfection and institutionalized every jot and tittle until it squeaked. They were bound by law and would not let grace do its work.

And so, in their bondage, there was no grace for their fellow man. Oftentimes their own family fell victim to their elaborate schemes to emulate holiness [Mk 7:6-13]. God wants us to be real and will change our character and personality into His plumb line standard - His image. God's Word declares that

His love is shed abroad in our hearts
by the Holy Spirit. [11]

The Greek translation of this word shed is: to gush, run out greedily - and is the Perfect Indicative Passive Tense meaning: it stands written, asserted as fact, a verb to be, continuous action, living water! This passage reveals that His love is also poured out on us even while we are yet sinners. This love of God is so strong as to transcend all barriers [Rom 5.1-11].

Not a one time occurrence. God's love is poured into our aching, troubled hearts spontaneously by the Holy Spirit Who dwells within us. It reaches us even in our lowest pit of despair. It is by His mercy that we are capable of receiving His love and by His grace we are able to walk on the path He has for us created.....................➜

> Is your receiver turned on?

The creating of a new heart in Christ; a new mind in Christ; this is what is needed. Saints - Jesus IS the Creator. Only through this process can we see and walk in the Kingdom of God, our inheritance. The law calls for total righteousness. None of us can fulfill that. Only by the righteousness imputed to us in Christ can we have any hope of fulfilling the law. We look to the great exchange of 2 Cor 5:21. *He became sin for us, that we might be made the righteousness of God in Christ*. We are subjected to fulfill the law of the flesh in our minds as we seek to satisfy our frustrations and needs by focusing on them, more than on the things of the Spirit.

It is the law - the fear of the law that often has us bound. There's either grace or law. If you're not walking in the *liberty with which Christ has made you free* [Gal 5:1] then you are bound by law. The law makes you feel condemned if you're not perfectly lined up. People who have not yet experienced the grace of God have a habit of believing Christians should be perfect and accuse them of hypocrisy if they don't toe the mark.

Just remember this. In order for an apple to become perfect, it had to go through the growing process from a seed to maturity. And so God is asking us; if we will yield to the love and grace of God, we will slowly but surely grow and mature in His Kingdom.

And brand new believers fall prey to satan's lies that they are hypocrites because they are supposed to be perfect, and there they go again falling into that same sin as they did before. But Galatians 3:21 should be mandatory meditation for every believer, young and old. *I do not make void the grace of God, for if righteousness came by the law [or our own merit], then Christ is dead in vain*.

The law of perfection brings the fear of man. We must do everything perfect or we will be judged and criticized, This brings on more stress and fear; anxiety and the fear of rejection torment us constantly.

We are individuals with an acquired personal history. Everything that has happened to us is etched into our nature; into our soul. We learn a lot of negatives. We have established a formidable defense system around our city. In the face of any size threat we arm our cannons and line up our sites. Somewhere in here God would like a word with you. If you will disarm and open the gates [to your heart] his peace will cover you as a warm blanket and His grace will bring you into rest as your enemies are disbanded [Ps 24:7-

It is a done deal. Nothing we do can change the facts, but we can negate it in our lives by striving to live the life in Christ that only God can cause to happen. Read and study what Paul discovered and shared with us in Gal 2:20 & Ph 2.13. Jesus fulfilled the law in us by His death on the cross.

In the Sermon on the Mount Jesus gave us the keys to fulfilling the law. Every time someone said, the law says [so and so], He came back with the spiritual principles for fulfilling it; attitude! Romans 13:8&10 declares... and -
Gal 5:13-14 agrees with this. *If love fulfills the law then, Love is the fulfilling of the law.*

Love is the key to perfection.

Mt 5:43-48 has Jesus explaining how important it is to love others, no matter who they are or what they've done. Love operating through the law is selfish and demanding. That's why we need God's unconditional love working through grace. Grace only comes because the law has been fulfilled by Jesus' sacrifice on the cross, in the shedding of His Blood [Heb 9:11-15]. Then He tells us,

Be ye therefore perfect, even as your Father,
who is in heaven is perfect.

So friends, love is the key to perfection. Perfection comes as we grow in His love. Nothing done by the law counts for anything, [Gal 5:6 Ampl].

Only faith activated and energized
and expressed and working through love

The character of God is being established within us. Galatians 5 reveals the fruit of the Spirit. It begins with love, and all else flows together. Not by law but by grace they are manifested as we yield to God.

Judas saw what he had caused to happen immediately after the encounter in the Garden of Gethsemane. He became despondent but it is not recorded that Judas repented. After being with Jesus all that time, and hearing of God's grace and love - and being a witness of personal ministry from the heart of God; he never applied it to himself.

David knew God was the only shelter from the storm. The Old Testament reveals a God of compassion and grace. David knew the source of grace even though he lived in the middle of the law. King Saul chose not to touch this fountain of life. He instead, reaped what he sowed - the law of sin and death.

Do you touch it? Are you drinking from this well of salvation? Do you know God's grace? We have permission to swim in it, and to share with others. The law was given as a, *Schoolmaster, to bring us unto Christ, that we may be justified by faith...Christ is become of no effect unto you*, whosoever of you are justified by the law; ye are fallen from grace.[14] *God resists the proud and gives grace to the humble.* [15]

because it is pride that says I can do it myself.
Until the grace of God sets us free, we may be bound by the laws of our humanity. Those things we inherited from our generations will effect our lives as any other law, positive or negative.

Christianity is not ritual and regulations. It is not an exercise in gymnastics. The Kingdom of God is reality. All else will be judged by the principles of the Kingdom. This is who we are; our way of life. If we have a heart to overcome, God is right there to deliver us from what hinders; to encourage and build up. He is in the business of restoration.

Except the Lord build the house, they labor in vain.[16]
A house is built one brick at a time. We learn to trust in God one day at a time. When we repent [turn around] grace gives the ability to walk in newness of life.

Where sin abounded, grace much more.[17]

His grace enables us to overcome even in the fiercest of battles, mostly because we have to submit to God to receive grace; and when we humble ourselves before God we can hear clear direction for the battle [1Sam 30:6-8].

We can reckon the old man dead, and the curse of the law may no longer apply. Romans chapters 5-8 tells the story. Allow the truth of the Word to blanket your soul and comfort your heart.

God recreated us a new man specifically to walk in good works, by grace through faith, and this passage ends with an incredible revelation; the magnificent truth that nothing can separate us from the love of God. Read also Ephesians 2;

For we are his workmanship.
This word means a specific product, fabric, something made. The substance of this new man was created with a direct purpose. The purpose of this new man was that he would walk in God's grace. He was ordained, decreed to walk in this grace.

Col 3:9-10 *Since you have put off the old man with his deeds, and have put on the new man who is renewed in knowledge...* Ps 139:13 agrees with this as God tells us,
For thou hast possessed my inward parts

The word possessed means to create for a specific purpose.

The word workmanship means a specific product made for a specific purpose. This new man was created in righteousness and true holiness. This new man functions only by grace. He knows nothing of the letter of the law. That's why it is imperative that we put on this new man. As we allow God to adjust our focus and correct our image we will naturally walk in newness of life.

The old man received the verdict of guilty. The law demands that it must die. The death sentence was carried out to the full penalty of the law. It was nailed to the cross and went into the grave with Jesus. [Romans 6:6].

But Resurrection Morning Cometh.
Knowing this, that our old man is crucified with him, that the body of sin might be destroyed, that henceforth we should not serve sin. The last jot and tittle to pass away;
Death where is your sting; grave where is your victory.[18]

When Jesus came back from the place of the dead, He left the old man there. It's still there after 2,000 years.

[It's pretty shriveled up by now].

Likewise, reckon yourselves to be dead indeed unto sin, but alive unto God through Jesus Christ, our Lord. Here we have a new life in Christ to live; made alive in Christ, set free by the knowledge of the Truth...........→
For sin shall not have dominion over you,

This is the transfer from law to grace.

for you are not under the law but under grace
The deceiver continues to try pulling us back into that old man stance; with guilt and condemnation, striving to prove we are good enough, trying to force us to live by the law. But we know the truth!
*Stand fast therefore, in the liberty
with which Christ hath made us free,
and be not entangled again in the yoke of bondage.*[19]
In <u>The Silence of God</u>, by Sir Robert Anderson, [Kregel Publ. Grand Rapids, Michigan] He explains that judgment is being withheld for a season and has been replaced by grace.
It is by grace ye are saved.
God has graciously stepped back and is allowing His creation to choose life or death. We wonder why God's hand of judgment does not stop the atrocities of the world as He did in the Old Testament. If He did that, none of us would live long. The judgment for my sin was death. I should have been dead a long time ago. By God's mercy, compassion and grace, I survived until someone could tell me about Jesus.

And I thank God for it.
Romans 2:4 tells us it is *The goodness of God that leads us to repentance*. This is a time set aside of the law, because of the blood. Too often our desires of God and man are unrealistic. Without being aware and because of frustration and anxiety we many times demand our needs be met regardless of the consequences. What it does through control and manipulation is keep others under the law - ours!

They must comply with our standards or we criticize and judge them. Even if there were no universal laws nor the law of the Creator, we would be obliged to obey by the law of expectations: other's and our own. A sense of failure and condemnation tells the story. But the Word says,
*If our heart condemn us, God is greater
than our heart, and knows all things.*
2Co 5:16-17 tells us we are to know no man after the flesh. *Old things have passed away, behold, all things are become new*. We are not bound by catch 22.

There is grace, looking into that perfect law of liberty.
Grace allows us to be who and what God has ordained. It is obvious this must be applied to others as well as ourselves. God speaks to self-centeredness through Psalm 119:36-40. I'll give it to you as He gave it to me.

Incline mine heart unto THY testimonies [word] and not to MY covetousness [self-centeredness] which is idolatry. Turn away mine eyes from beholding vanity, [the world revolving around ME] and revive thou me in THY way. Establish thy word unto thy servant who is devoted to thy fear. Turn away my reproach which I fear, for thine ordinances are good. Behold, I have longed after thy precepts; give me life in THY righteousness [Not seeking my own rights].

When as a born-again believer, you commit your life to God - He commits Himself to you. This is called Covenant. It is of unique importance that we become fully aware of God's great love for His creation - for YOU.

If there seems no other revelation for us, this we must have. God's love is the basis for everything we become in Him.

His great love caused Jesus to lay aside His rights as Deity,[20] To clothe Himself with humanity.

So completely did Jesus yield Himself to the Father's plan of salvation for mankind, that the graphic meaning of Jn 17:5 is asking His Father to give back to Him what Paul records in Phil 2:6-8; the glory He *had with the Father before the world was.* [Amplified Version] *And now Father, glorify Me along with Yourself and restore Me to such majesty and honor in Your presence as I had with You before the world existed....*

Did He so totally give up the glory He had with His Father; so totally give Himself up to the Father's plan, that He cut Himself off from ever taking it back for Himself..→

| Could Jesus not take it back HImself? |

His separation became so graphic on Golgotha.

My Friend, My dearest Friend, have You also abandoned Me?

While on the earth, Jesus had an open heaven with His Father. He declared, *What I see My Father do, I do also; and what I hear My Father say, that I also say.* He was in constant, face to face communication and fellowship with His Father.

But when Jesus was on the cross, He became our sin; and here, the Father could no longer remain in fellowship with His Son. The heavens were closed to Him.

Jesus took on Himself the dreadful separation from God that mankind was cursed with because of sin. Was it that stress of separation that caused Him to sweat blood in the garden. I am so grateful to Jesus that He was willing to experience my judgment, so that I could spend eternity with My Father ♥♥♥

In John 17:22 we can see that God gave Him another kind of glory, that of a Son of God. This is the glory, reputation and character, that He passes on to us, the sons of God [Jn 17].

And the glory which you gave me I have given them, that they may be one, even as we are one.

Because of His total submission to the Father's will, Jesus also walked in God's grace. Remember He became fully human even though He was also totally God. He never stopped being God.

Col 2.9   *All the fullness of the Godhead dwelt in Him.*

Philippians 2.5-8 reveals that He laid down all His rights of divinity in order to carry out God's plan. So Jesus had to have grace in this humanity; the ability to do what God ordained for Him. Because of His absolute submission to the Father, Jesus was now able to transfer the glory of a son, on to us, [2Cor 4.17 & Jn 17.24 Amp].

For our light, momentary affliction [this slight distress of the passing hour] is ever more and more abundantly preparing and producing and achieving for us an everlasting weight of glory [beyond all measure, excessively surpassing all comparisons and all calculations, a vast and transcendent glory and blessedness never to cease].

That they may be with me where I am, to behold the glory which you have given [back] to me.

Jesus counted it all done even before the cross, because he understood the will of God. We can also count it all done when we know the Father and yield to His perfect will for us.

When we are born again of incorruptible seed [1Pet 1:23], we are now in position to receive the nature, reputation, character, and glory of a son of God. He so identifies with His creation, that He has remained in His resurrection body as all who will; having answered His call and He has come back to receive us unto Himself.

1Corinthians 15:23-28 tells us, *Christ the first fruits; afterward they that are Christ's at his coming, Then cometh the end, when he shall have delivered up the Kingdom to*

God, even the Father, when he shall have put down all rule and all authority and power. For He must reign till he hath put all enemies under his feet.

The full meaning of this passage is one of the mysteries of the Kingdom. Jesus was given all authority in heaven and earth [Mt 28:18]. There comes a time when it is given up to the Father. If we want to come into our inheritance; which is in reality, God's inheritance in us, then we must give up all our expectations and rely on God to show us the full meaning of Psalm 62. *My soul, wait thou only upon God; for my expectation is from him* - and what this means to us, because [2Cor 2.9]
Eye hath not seen, nor ear hath heard what God has in store for those who love him.

There are many mysteries of which we will receive understanding when we see Him face to face.

'I go to prepare a place for you'.[2] ❤

a deeper, higher walk in the realm of the Spirit of which is hidden because of the veil of our flesh - but will be revealed.

These are basic principles of the Kingdom of God. He longs to reveal Himself to us. We cannot truly understand the fullness of why the mighty Creator desires to dwell in His puny creatures; but He has purpose and a destiny for His Church, His bride. He has obligated Himself to her. He can never revoke His Word. [Rom 11:29] He will never take back what He has given.

Isaiah 60 reveals His plan to fill us with His glory and allow others to actually see it. He will arise to fulfill His final solution to hardened hearts. He will implement this through His covenant people [Ps 149].

What God is depositing in His Church in these days will become a river of life to the nations. God wants to use us to show forth the love of God, the mercy of God, the grace and loving kindness of the Creator reaching out to draw those for whom He died; back into His heart. He is waiting for us to yield to Him, to give Him absolute priority in our life [Eph 3:10] because of this............................➜

> It is His good pleasure to give us His Kingdom.

The more we search the Word, the hidden manna[22] will be revealed to us. Psalm 119 reveals the vitality of the Word,

His testimonies and statutes. Such is the word of John 14:23; abode means staying place and it comes from the same Greek word as mansions in John 14:2. Are we His many mansions - that place where the Father has chosen as His resting place, His abode [2Co 6:16; John 14.23].

Jesus came to reveal the Father, that we may know Him as we are known. We have many carnal ideas and imaginations about who is this God the Father, and His Son Jesus. 1Jn 2:3-6.

Until our mind is renewed we cannot know Him.
Jesus desires an intimacy with His bride that of which our understanding as yet, is so limited. He wants to open our hearts, extend the tent pegs of our tabernacle. We were created specifically to bear His glory. We do this only with His grace.

We've read the last chapter and can see the end results. Wherefore then, shall we place our trust and expectations. How do we make the transition from law to grace?

Faith comes to us through hearing, and hearing the Word of Truth. We receive His grace by walking in this truth through faith, believing God [see James 4:5; 1Pet 1:7 and Ex 34:14 Amp].

The Spirit Whom He has caused to dwell in us yearns over us with a jealous love and He yearns for the Spirit [to be welcome] for our God is a jealous God. But He gives us more and more grace; that is the power of the Holy Spirit, to meet every adverse condition. That is why He says, God sets Himself against the proud and haughty, but gives grace continually to the lowly. *But God - so rich is He in His mercy...*[Eph 2.4]

Because of and in order to satisfy the great and wonderful love with which He loved us, even when we were dead [slain] by [our own] shortcomings and trespasses, He made us alive together in fellowship and union with Christ; [He gave us the very life of Christ Himself, the same new life with which you are saved]

For it is by free grace [God's unmerited favor] that you are saved [delivered from judgment and made partakers of Christ's salvation] through [your] faith. And this [salvation] is not of yourselves [of your own doing, it came not through your own striving] but it is the gift of God. I have been crucified with Christ [in Him I have shared His crucifixion]; it

is no longer I who live, but Christ [the Messiah] lives in me; and the life I now live in the body I live by faith in [by adherence to and reliance on and complete trust in] the Son of God, who loved me and gave Himself up for me
[Eph 2:5-8; Ga 2:20] All from the Amp Bible.
Simon Peter, a servant and apostle of Jesus Christ, to those who have obtained like precious faith with us by the righteousness of our God and Savior Jesus Christ: Grace and peace be multiplied to you in the knowledge of God and Jesus our Lord, as His divine power has given to us all things that pertain to life and godliness.[23]

Please read the rest of God's purposes...
*And greater works than these
shall he do, because I go to my Father.*
[John 14:12].

*The glory of this latter house
shall be greater than of the former,
saith the Lord of Hosts*
[Hag 2:9].

You left Your glorious throne for me
And came to be a man
To seek and save this long lost one
To make me be all I can
Oh my Lord, my God, my King
I only ask this one thing
Restore my soul, restore my soul
That I may bring an offering.

♥

Life is like a waterfall
It thunders deep in our soul
As it rambles on toward the sea
It conquers all in all
The rocks and debris are carried along
For a space and then let go
It settles down to be forgotten
As the river continues to flow
So all the sorrows of time gone by
Can be taken into God's arms
Carried along by His sweet love
That they shall no longer harm
So the waters of life flows over me
And the love of God prevails
They were hammered into
His hands and feet By those old rusty nails
To conquer every sin and shame
In the glory of His name

♥

STUDY GUIDE

1. What is the only thing that enables us to live in Christ?
2. Where is the grace of God being established?
3. How can we know God?
4. Why are we so special to God? Do you think God loves any one else any more than He loves you?
5. What does the Word say about living by the law? [Gal 3:10-
6. What can our expectations be as we walk in the Kingdom?
7. How can we get a better understanding of covenant love?
8. Jesus paid a high price for this covenant. What are you willing to do?
9. Although we can't earn it - how can we respond? [Psalm 1.16].
10. God is our refuge and our strength, a very present help in time of trouble. Can He help you through the storm you're in right now? Don't just ride it out. There is a gushing river of grace awaiting the expectant heart. Ask God to show you the issues concerning this. He wants to heal and restore. And He gives grace to the humble....

Gal 5.16-18 *As you yield freely and fully to the dynamic life and power of the Holy Spirit, you will abandon the cravings of your self-life. For your self-life craves the things that offend the Holy Spirit and hinder Him from living free within you. And the Holy Spirit's intense cravings hinder your old-self life from dominating you! So then, the two incompatible and conflicting forces within you are your self-life of the flesh and the new creation of life in the Spirit. But when you are brought into the full freedom of the Spirit of grace, you will no longer be living under the domination of the law, but souring above it!* [The Passion Translation].

PRAYER: Lord Jesus, there are so many things to deal with, but I put my trust in You that You will help me sort them out. Not only that, but You will also help me to deal with them one at a time. Your Word says You care for me and You are willing to bear my burdens. I want to learn to live by Your grace. I lay down all those things that have me wanting the things of the world, and receive Your forgiveness. I release my life and all this 'craving of my flesh', and yield myself to Your Holy Spirit for the changes He arranges; to bring us into His Holy Place. It began with the Tabernacle and the Altar of Sacrifice - Salt poured on it was for the grace and mercy From the *God of all grace* - 1Peter 5.10.

Thank You Lord, for Your Grace ❤

SCRIPTURES

1. He 9:16-17 and 70-72
2. 1Co 15:18
3. Ga 1:12
4. Ga 5:1
5. Ep 2:8-10
6. Ph 2:14
7. 1Pe 3:15-17 and Ph 2:12-13
8. Mt 13:55
9. Mt 13:57
10. Ac 21:18
11. Ro 5:5-8
12. Ps 78:52-53,
13. Ps 51
14. Ga 3:24;5:4
15. 1Pe 5:6
16. Ps 127:1
17. Ro 5:20
18. 1Co 15:55
19. Ga 5:1
20. Ph 2:6-7
21. Jn 14:2
22. Re 2:17
23. 1Pe 1:2

OBEDIENCE AND THE WILL OF GOD.

Beloved, now are we the children of God, and it does not yet appear what we shall be, but we know that, when he shall appear, we shall be like him, for we shall see him as he is.[1] *God is love, and he that dwells in love dwells in God, and God in him. Herein is our love made perfect, that we may have boldness in the day of judgment because as he is, so are we in this world.*[2]

1John 3:2 signifies character change; while 4:16-17 indicates our position, seated in heavenly places with Christ Jesus.[3] To suppose that our soul is transformed into His image on being born again into the Kingdom, is to presume that all things come into being immediately upon being decreed. From God's perspective, yes it does. Revelation 13:8 says Jesus was

slain from the foundation of the world,
but we know He had to bring that into the physical realm to be fulfilled, and then declare,

It is finished ✟

We must acknowledge that Kingdom realities have been stated hundreds and sometimes thousands of years before they come to completion. And know this; none of us would be where we are if not for Jesus being obedient to the will of God.

God's truth never changes. As He sends forth His Word to be accomplished; it will be, in His time, in His way. This accounts for the working out of our own salvation with fear and trembling. Philippians chapter Two declares how to do this...............................➜

> Have the same mind in you which was also in Christ Jesus.

It means we die to self - not my will - but Thine! There is a vast chasm as deep and wide as a grave, that separates us from the image of Christ. Only the Cross spans this breach and we must overcome much to reach His resurrection likeness. The Scriptures write of something more than receiving Christ as Savior! Mt 10:38-
He that takes not his cross and follows after me, is not worthy of me. He that finds his life shall lose it; and he that loses his life for my sake shall find it.

And note what Paul has discovered,   [Ph 3:10-14]

That I may know him
and the power of his resurrection.
Obviously Paul knew he was saved; so what could this possibly mean? There really is a working out of our salvation [Phil 2:12]. Romans 12:1-2 gives us another clue.

The central point of working out our salvation is not - trying to do things ourselves through our own fleshly works. What it is - is response and submission to all God says. And He speaks to us through many different avenues, not only the Word but in music, other printed matter, in nature, in other people, and of course that wonderful still small voice. We can learn to have trustful acceptance of all He gives. This is dying to self.

It helps to note the cross does not hold its victim forever, but a person on a cross can't look back, can't come down, and has no plans for the future. When the flesh dies, then comes resurrection - new life!

And be found in him not having mine own righteousness which is of the law, but that which is through the faith of Christ, the righteousness which is of God by faith;
that I may know him and the power of his resurrection and the fellowship of his suffering, being made conformable [adjusting our nature] unto his death, If by any means I might attain unto the resurrection of the dead,
not as though I had already attained, either were already perfect, but I follow after, if that I may apprehend that for which also I am apprehended of Christ Jesus. Brethren, I count not myself to have apprehended, but this one thing I do, forgetting those things which are behind [all our failures and accomplishments] and reaching forth unto those things which are before, I press toward the mark for the prize of the high calling of God in Christ Jesus.[4]

The work of the cross is to put to death our self life. The Word gives the example. First the natural then the spiritual. What Isaiah saw before his eyes, was a graphic picture of Spirit truth. I've read that king Uzziah was possibly Isaiah's uncle. If that's true the significance of flesh/spirit was inscribed perhaps deeper into Isaiah's heart.

In the year King Uzziah died I saw the Lord high and lifted up and his train filled the temple.[5]

As he was worshiping, Isaiah saw the Lord-Master-Adonai. As His glory filled the temple, Isaiah saw the Sovereign Ruler of the universe in His throne room - at the altar of incense, as angels ministered and worshiped [Rev 5:11-14]

Mine eyes have seen the King, the Lord of Hosts,
but only after king Uzziah died.

2Chronicles 26 gives the history of king Uzziah. He was just 16 years old when he began to rule over Judah. He did right in the sight of God and as long as he sought the Lord, God made him to prosper. His name and fame spread far abroad for he was marvelously helped [by God]; until he was strong. His name Uzziah means strength in the Lord.

But when he was strong his heart [his flesh] was lifted up to his destruction for he transgressed against the Lord.

Pride first of all. Then what he did was impose himself on an office of authority in the temple that only God can give. He was not a Levite.

Moses' brother Aaron and sister Miriam transgressed the Lord's will when they also came against God's appointed authority and leadership. They both wanted to exalt themselves in the matters of the Kingdom of God; on their own, in their flesh, not delegated by God. She paid the price; so did he.

She was stricken with leprosy - but Aaron knew that he had gravely offended his God. Only because he was high priest did God not afflict him also, because he carried the priestly anointing. They both had to die to their flesh.

Uzziah was king over Judah, but he was not permitted to go in and out of the temple as a priest. His rulership was for one position only. He had the honor to rule on his throne with the authority given to him by God. He did not have the honor or covering of the Lord to tend to matters in the temple.

One day he decided he would barge right into the presence of God. He went past the blood without applying it. He went past the laver without washing. He went past the bread without eating and past the light without acknowledgment.

Uzziah stood with censer in his hand ready to burn the incense. The altar of incense was in the Holy Place just before the entrance into the Holy of Holies; the presence of the Shekinah Glory!............................➜

> The place where priests could be slain in their shoes.

See Lev 16 and Num 18 for God's purposes for burning incense. Ezekiel 44 explains the import of the priest and their charge of temple duties. They were there to protect, defend, cover, safeguard, keep with all diligence, the treasuries and holy things of the temple.

Only certain priests could offer incense. The father of John the Baptist was one who could burn incense. Other families in the tribe of Levi were appointed to specific duties. And remember Aaron's sons. Even though they could offer sacrifices, they did it in the manner they chose, not according to God's instructions. It was called strange fire. God rained His brand of fire down on them and consumed them. Our God will not be mocked, then or now.

Uzziah so offended the anointed consecrated priesthood that eighty-one of them confronted him in the temple. He was furious when they withstood him. He demanded he be left alone to pursue his goal. And even as his rage was at its peak to impose his right to do as he pleased in the Temple of the Most High God, leprosy rose up on his forehead. His self-will was such an abomination to the Lord that his pride of life became manifested first in the place it was spawned; his head, his mind, his will. The priests began to thrust him out of the temple. By this time the fear of God had come upon him and verse 20 declares,

Yea, he himself hastened also to go out
because the Lord had smitten him.

He lost his crown to his son, authority in the Kingdom was no longer his to command, and he was cut off from his own family. King Uzziah died a leper. The Word tells us no flesh will glory in God's presence. Self-will is joined with self-righteousness. It has little if any regard to authority and strives to stand in its own power; without accountability. No price to pay. Uzziah was the greatest example of 'stinky flesh' and he paid a dear price for wanting what could never be his.

But, Paul tells us in Philippians 3 what is the price.
Having no confidence in the flesh...
what things were gain I count loss.
Everything I have done, is as dung!
2Co 10:13-15 tells us how God feels about reaching [encroaching] beyond the scope of our anointing. Does King Uzziah have a place in your heart?

Are you jealous of another's anointing?

Have you been given a ministry but strive to function in this capacity without marching orders from the Master? Have you been strengthened by the Lord only to move ahead into areas in which you were not called? There is also another point here to look at. Keeping in mind that reality follows shadow, 1Cor 15:46 tells us first the natural then the spiritual. Example...

Jesus is Prophet, Priest and King. He is the fulfillment of these three Old Testament offices of ministration to the people of His Kingdom. When He died and was resurrected, there was no more need for the priesthood in the temple or for animal sacrifices; for we now have the written Word.

He is our great High Priest, He is the Word of prophecy. There is no earthly king over His nation; Jesus is our King of kings and He has given us 'communion, the bread and wine' to remember what He did to set us free from our sin nature [Heb 1:1-2].

Eph 4:8 tells us, *But to each one of us grace was given according to the measure of Christ's gift. Therefore He says: When He ascended on high, He gave gifts to men*

1Peter 2.9 *But you are a chosen generation, a royal priesthood, a holy nation*, and -

Rev 1:5-6 *To Him who loved us and washed us from our sins in His own blood, and has made us kings and priests to His God and Father, to Him be glory and dominion forever and ever. Amen.*

These gifts are for the Church, the body of Christ, to use for the maturing of the saints [see vs 11-16] There will be no more need for men to fill these functions in a temple. Remember, there are signs and wonders following every believer.

The Old Testament unfolds the coming of our Redeemer. Threaded throughout these ancient writings we will find types and shadows that point to His ministry to the fallen creation of God. Abraham's sacrifice of his son - God's sacrifice of His Son.

The shadow and the reality.

Hundreds of prophecies concerning Him were spoken centuries before His birth; indeed He was revealed there in Eden for Adam and Eve [Gen 3:15]. Many prophecies were fulfilled in Him during His life on the earth.

The only natural Old Testament type and shadow of the Messiah that God would permit was David, the man after God's own heart [Acts 13:22]; the shepherd that snatched his lambs out of the mouth of the lion and the bear [1Sam 17:36]. David was the only figure and type of Christ that God allowed in the Old Testament, to show the three offices of authority Christ the anointed One, would manifest as Savior and Redeemer.

In the Psalms, David is prophet. In 1Chr 15:27, 2Sam 6:14-18, he is shown to be in the office of priest, for only a priest could eat the temple bread, wear the ephod, and offer sacrifices. David had privilege that no other, outside the priesthood could ever walk in. A man after God's own heart - from a boy to a man to a king - David was a worshiper before anything else. In 1Chr 11:3 here he is anointed king.

And because David was the appointed figure of Christ, it is said of Jesus that He will sit on David's throne and reign over His people [Lk 1:33]. Saul was king and prophesied [1Sam 10]. When he tried to enter the office of priest [1Sam 3:6-14 & 15:12-30] to exalt himself and look as though he really was in charge and had it all together in the eyes of his men; he was sacrificing animals that God told him to annihilate along with the Amalekites. He saved the animals and the king.

His rebellion was as witchcraft which led him into pride and deception. He begged the prophet Samuel to pray to his [Samuel's] God for him. King Saul no longer recognized Jehovah as his God. His god was self-will.

The prophetic voice of the Word will not be submitted to man's foolishness. *To obey is better than sacrifice.*

God tore the Kingdom from him.

King Uzziah tried to impose on the priestly office. David only, was permitted; accepted as a type and shadow of Jesus. All others were rejected. Numbers 16:40 tells us,

No outsider, who is not a descendent of Aaron, should come near to offer incense before the Lord.

Ps 141:1-2 *Lord, I cry out to You; Make haste to me! Give ear to my voice when I cry out to You. Let my prayer be set before You as incense, The lifting up of my hands as the evening sacrifice.*

God will choose His own vessels of honor.
The flesh will profit nothing.

Korah was a Levite, but he and his companion rebels would have burst into an office not assigned to them.[6]

Remember the tribe of Levi was chosen by God to minister, or take charge of His tabernacle.

It was only the descendants of Kohath who was a son of Levi, that God chose to minister in the temple proper. [Moses and Aaron were grandsons of Kohath]. See Num 7:9. Only Aaron's sons were the High Priests; they tended in the holiest place, the sanctuary; and when Israel went to move in the desert, they covered the holy furniture before the others picked it up. No one but Aaron's descendants could look on the holy things!

These Levites sons of Kohath, were separated into families and given specific duties. Uzziel was another son of Kohath, and this family carried the Ark, the Lampstand, etc. The other Levite families tended to the different ministries necessary to temple functions and they carried the curtains, poles, etc. Read Numbers 3,4,16,18 and it will be more clear.

Korah was Moses' cousin. Korah means, ice, depilate, make [self] bald. Figuratively speaking he wanted no God appointed authority over him. He wanted a higher position than was allotted him. He was jealous of Moses and Aaron. God opened the ground and swallowed him and his followers.

It is astounding to me what occurred the next morning. Even after seeing the terrible judgment of the Lord, there were even more rebels to be dealt with as they came against and questioned even Aaron's right to the priesthood. God took a dead piece of wood and gave it life to show that His anointing was on Aaron only. All other would-be infiltrators need not apply.

Nevertheless the children of Korah did not die.
Remember Korah was cousin to Moses and Aaron. We can certainly choose to be in rebellion or not. If not, we had better separate ourselves from those of whom will to rebel; even if they are family.

It is vital to understand that we as God's anointed, impact much more than we see with our natural eyes. In these last days it is imperative we listen and follow God's orders for our own life. The master of deception is out to pulverize us. And don't even be concerned about what God is doing in your neighbor's life. Remember what Jesus told Peter, [Jn 21:22]

What is that to you?

This is why we've been given spiritual discernment. This is why we seek God's will and obey what He says. The

New Covenant has made His people to be priests and kings unto Him. We may approach Him because of the Blood. Only Jesus made this possible. We will never come into His presence through our self-aggrandizement.

These Old Testament references were given as graphic illustrations for us to come into a knowledge of God's ways. He wants us to understand. As we mature in the Lord, God is looking for a more mature obedience, and indeed expecting it. Leaving the milk of the Word and getting into the meat is what Paul reveals in Heb 5:11-14.

Please note that it is only through His mercy are we able to live in this grace as God has dealt a measure of faith to walk in the gifts and callings of God; each in his own office of ministry as God enables. Whatever that ministry may be; Pastor of a large church or changing diapers in the nursery,

God's grace is sufficient [more than enough]

In Romans 12:2 concerning knowing what is the will of God, we can see a progression of proving or testing His will for us as we mature in Christ. God declares in Isaiah 55 that His thoughts and ways are so much higher than ours. But 1Cor 2:16 makes an awesome statement.

We have the mind of Christ.

If we continue on into Chapter 12 of Romans, we are beseeched to present our bodies a living sacrifice, holy and acceptable to God, our reasonable service. Then we are commanded to have our minds renewed so we can know the mind or will of God as that possibility is revealed in this portion of the Word. We are not to think more highly of ourselves, but to think soberly [or be of sound mind]. Verse 16 tells us,

Be not wise in your own conceits.
[or your own opinion]

As we dissect 12:1 with a Greek dictionary we can know what God is really asking. For those who are hungry for the meat of the Word, stand before God as His bond slave - offer your life as a sacrificial victim. [Who does that sound like?] Uzziah was certainly not there in a posture of humility.

It goes on to say we are not to set ourselves above any other, we are equal though diverse and must move only in love. If we are willing to die to self, God will show us great and mighty things which we know not of.[7]

Since the Old Testament was given to us as an example, we can compare some corresponding scripture from the Old Testament to New Testament. We can look at Isaiah 66:2 where God declares,

> But I will look toward this one,
> to the afflicted [humble, lowly, needy, poor,
> contrite, maimed, crippled, lame]
> and the contrite of spirit, even trembling at my Word.

What the passage in Romans may be saying to us is that as we die to all our plans and goals, desires and self-will, we can have access to the unsearchable riches of His wisdom and knowledge.

If Moses could know His ways,[8] then so can we. God's ways are past finding because of superficial consideration. His ways are unsearchable or untraceable, but who knows what revelation God has for the hungry heart.[9] [see Jeremiah 33.3].

This one will seek and search, not satisfied with the abridged version. To this one will be proven,

> What is that good and acceptable
> and perfect will of God,

and know the mind of the Lord. May we press toward the mark of His highest calling, to know the Father.[10] Psalm 91 declares a blessing on those

> Who hath known my name;

The word known implies familiar intimate friends. Those who would be transformed into His image have committed to the bottom line. Not my will but thine, for You Lord must increase and I must decrease. John the Baptist never pulled any punches. He told it like it was, as truth of the Kingdom burned in his soul. He knew all must be tested by fire.

> What did you come to see, a reed shaken by the wind?

John was a Kingdom trumpet! His boldness to declare truth had not been witnessed in centuries. Perhaps they believed God's hand of judgment had been withdrawn.

But he was paving the way for the One called 'The Way'. John the Baptist was to inherit the priesthood from his father Zechariah, but he gave up this prestige and honor to follow his heart in what God had planned for him; that is to introduce [Heb 4.14] The Great High Priest Jesus, to the world He came to save. Actually John the Baptist was the last high priest of the Old Testament. This inheritance was from his father, Zechariah. He chose to minister in a different way.

This Kingdom that cannot be shaken was proclaimed abroad as in the days of Noah. Both John and Noah were calling forth the Ark of safety, for they both saw the coming judgment.

One comes who is greater than I, he shall baptize you with the Holy Spirit and with fire. He will thoroughly purge his floor and will gather the wheat into the granary, but the chaff he will burn with fire unquenchable.[11]

The Greek word for floor [Strong's #257] refers figuratively to the grain itself. The floor is not purged, the grain is; and the grain is us. God wants to purge us of all that defiles.

You be holy for I am holy.[12]
Only those things which cannot be shaken may remain..➜
Wherefore receiving a Kingdom which cannot be moved, let us have grace, by which we may serve God acceptably with reverence and godly fear, for our God is a consuming fire.[13] *And he that overcometh shall inherit all things, and I will be his God, and he shall be my son.*[14]

| Who has an ear to hear? |

The Scriptures will always uncover a prerequisite for New Testament theology. Paul's Bible was the Old Testament. God added the icing, the grace; and even this was also part and parcel to David's relationship with God, as revealed in his Psalms.

Old Testament justice was more often swift, but here in the New Covenant there is a place for the repentant heart to receive forgiveness and cleansing. Reading Isaiah 33:14-17 we can see that playing with fire sometimes pays off.

Who among us shall dwell with the devouring fire?
Who among us shall dwell with everlasting burnings?
He that walketh righteously.
Thine eyes shall see the King in his beauty.

The Spirit Filled Life Bible has the notation for these verses, *Who will endure the devouring fire of testing? The righteous who will also see the King in His beauty.*
God would have us welcome that fire, to yield the chaff in our lives to be consumed as we are changed from glory to glory.

There's a song the Body of Christ sings, All consuming fire, You're my hearts desire.... It's interesting to note that when something is burned up there is no life left in it. This brings about two results:
1. The enemy of our soul can no longer pull those strings.
2. Jesus can bring His resurrection life into that arena.

So let's invite that fire!

With every glorious encounter between God and man there is an impartation of His nature. God's dealings with us enables a revelation of His holiness to impregnate our nature with His. He does not do this against our will. As we yield to God He draws us ever closer to His heart.

From God's prospective we have been in that place before the foundation of the world. From our point of reference, it is a walk, a changing, a maturing. God wants us to dwell in His presence not just visit once in a while.

2Samuel 15 records how Zadok the priest remained faithful to David the anointed of God, the appointed authority. He put his own life in jeopardy to protect the things of God and left a mighty heritage established for his sons. Ezekiel 44 tells us about the sons of Zadok [sons of righteousness] who remained faithful to their anointing during a time they were in captivity, in a foreign land.

They only, of all the priests who returned from exile at that time, were given access to the Holy of Holies, the very manifest presence of God.

And they shall keep my charge.
To guard His holiness is what it means. Remember what the priests did when Uzziah went behind the veil? And God?

Is the holiness of God precious to you?

Ask God to show you what that means between you and Him.. I asked God to tell me what it means to come unto Him. He said,

Come to Me with reverence for My holiness,
reverence with awesome respect that is due a holy God.

We don't really know how to relate to a Being that is so far out of our league, so far above us, so much greater. We must learn, and He is so willing to teach us and help us. Without Him we can do nothing. God is calling us into His Kingdom; 1Thes 2:12 for 2Thes 1:11-12 to be fulfilled.

Only as we draw near to God in the Holy of Holies can we minister to Him. Because at the death of Jesus, the veil that separated us from God was split open; He has given us permission to approach. But we must stand still before Him until He makes His will known to us.

Watchman Nee in Twelve Baskets Full, says about standing: Stand and await orders; Stand and minister to Me!

A servant should await his master's orders before seeking to serve him. Nee lists two types of sin before God.
#1.Rebelling against His commands.
#2.Going ahead when the Lord has not issued orders.
One is rebellion, the other is presumption. Let us seek grace of God that He may reveal to us what it really means to minister to Him.

With ever increasing knowledge of Him, do we become partakers of the divine nature. We get to know Him by coming into His presence.

Having therefore, brethren, boldness to enter into the holiest by the Blood of Jesus, by a new and living way which he hath consecrated for us through the veil, that is to say, his flesh, and having a high priest over the house of God, let us draw near with a true heart In full assurance of faith, having our hearts sprinkled from an evil conscience [fear, guilt, shame, condemnation] and our bodies washed with pure water.[15]

The word sprinkled comes from a Greek word meaning aspersion. The dictionary tells us this means [as in casting aspersion] something that effects our very character and credibility in a negative sense. This is why Jesus took our carnal [sin] nature to the cross. It was worthy of death. [Rom 6.23] It is our sin conscience that keeps us bound in fear, separated from God. See Heb 9.11-15; Heb 10. 19-23; 1John 3.19-22 - Read until you get it and can walk in it.

Actually the essence of our carnal nature has been declared worthless.

BUT...The Word has made provision. That's why Jesus shed His blood for us. And the Word of God is most thorough to explain to us what God has done for us. [Heb 10:19-22 Ampl].

Since we have full freedom and confidence to enter into the [Holy of] holies [by the power and virtue] in the Blood of Jesus, by this fresh [new] and living way which He initiated and dedicated and opened for us through the separating curtain [veil of the Holy of Holies], that is through His flesh, And since we have [such] a great and wonderful and noble Priest [Who rules] over the house of God, let us all come forward and draw near with true [honest and sincere] hearts In unqualified assurance and absolute conviction engendered by faith [by that leaning of

the entire human personality on God in absolute trust and confidence in His power, wisdom and goodness],
Hold a sleeping infant in your arms and you will understand the truth about leaning. Think about this. Do you want your inheritance in the Kingdom of God? Do you hunger and thirst after it?

It is the Father's good pleasure to cleanse our heart from the guilt and condemnation of our past. The devil loves to remind us of what terrible things we've done; and all our failures. Well, we failed! Agree! Repent! [Mt 5:25]. As we draw near to God confessing our guilt - We can stand on 1John 1:9,

If we confess our sin,
then we claim the last part; *cleansed from all unrighteousness* - that is the evil conscience - the guilt and condemnation, and all our negative imaginations that deny the Truth of Who Jesus really is.

Our self-sufficiency puts a stop sign in God's path. Remember it's the Blood of Jesus whereby we are forgiven and so we must forgive ourselves. And - only in our failures does God have permission to intervene. God calls it an evil conscience because it is in total opposition of what God calls us to be; a Chosen Generation, a Royal Priesthood, a People of His own. He has called us out of darkness into His glorious light to show forth His praises [1Jn 3.21]

*If our heart condemn us not
then we have confidence towards God.*
Now we may come with boldness before the throne of our Most High God to worship with a pure heart.

Grace and peace be multiplied unto you through the knowledge of God, and of Jesus, our Lord, according as his divine power hath given unto us exceedingly great and precious promises, that by these ye might be partakers of the divine nature...through the knowledge of Him.[16] Ps 24:1 declares, *The earth is the Lord's and the fullness thereof.*

This fact will never change. Jesus is the Creator and has always maintained ownership.

Genesis 1:28 records God giving dominion of the earth over to the man He had just breathed His life into. God made man to be steward over God's domain. Adam was overseer and had the authority of God's government standing behind him.

But Adam was also give a free will. We all are born with a free will. God will never take away our free will. But the truth is we get into more trouble because of this free will. And the exercise of this free will, led Adam down the path of rebellion and separation from God.

So completely and without reservation was this dominion given to Adam, that when he rebelled against God and lost it, the identity of its new administrator was never questioned [Lk 4:6].

2Corinthians 4:4 calls satan the god of this world, and Jesus calls him the prince of this world. From this and other scripture, it is assumed that Adam yielded his dominion of the earth over to satan.

But please note that all authority comes from God [Ro 13:1], so though satan may have stolen dominion, Jesus took it back and now he has no authority on the earth... [Luke 10.17 -20]. Only what he can deceive us into accepting

Man was given stewardship, but was not found faithful. God did not give satan the authority to rule in the world, man did! When Jesus died on the cross, you remember He went down to hell and He took the keys of death and hell, and took dominion back - for us.

Rev 1:17-19 *"Do not be afraid; I am the First and the Last. I am He who lives, and was dead, and behold, I am alive forevermore. Amen. And I have the keys of Hades and of Death.*

He destroyed the works of the devil and took it all back. So we have to learn to walk in it again. We do this through the authority Jesus gave us.

Back to Psalm 8:6 we see dominion being given to Jesus and transferred to His creation. This was carried out before Jesus returned to His Father. Remember Mt 28:18-20.

Now will we be found faithful?

Compare Genesis 1:28-29 blessings with Genesis 3:17-19 curses. Satan told Eve that if they ate of the tree of the knowledge of good and evil they would be as God. [Strong's Concordance #430 Elohim]. The Word declares man already was created

In the image of God after His likeness, only lacking a little, [because we will never BE God], that we may live in dependent relationship/fellowship in submission to His government ruling within us.

Satan deceived Eve into thinking he could give them access to the wisdom and knowledge of God; something they already had. The only way we can receive and maintain true authority on the earth is to be in submission to the government of God. Adam said, NO, and bit off much more than he could chew. He lost the Kingdom!

Immanuel, God in the flesh, became a man[17] - the last Adam came to retrieve what the first Adam had lost. Adam gave up his authority in the Kingdom of God on the earth. Jesus came to restore His Kingdom on the earth and in His people. Jesus came to...[Lk 19:9-11; Mk 1:14-15].

Seek and to save that which was lost; [the Kingdom!]
As they heard these things...
they thought the Kingdom of God would
appear immediately.

But I'm sure they not yet had the vision of what this really meant. On the Mount of Transfiguration they were again assuming Jesus was now bringing in the Kingdom [Let's make booths]. The Feast of Booths, or Tabernacles is the only feast that has not yet been fulfilled; God is saving it for His return. Research it for yourselves and realize the significance.......................................➔

Yes, Jesus came to save whosoever [Jn 3:16], but when He comes back He will not be looking for ones of whom managed to control their behavior. He'll be looking for His mirror image. For comparison, please study and implement Mt 5-7. See Luke 18.8 If we are raptured out before He comes back, why would He be looking for faith? In the unredeemed?

| When Jesus comes back He'll be looking for His friends. |

He'll be looking for the standard of the Kingdom that has been deposited; the rulership and government of God established in the heart because, Rev 12:11 *They overcame by the blood of the lamb, and by the word of their testimony, because they loved not their lives to the death.*

Abraham so totally submitted to God's rulership that he was called a friend of God, and was made heir of the world. As a believer, this is passed on to us.

Rom 4:13-17   *Clearly, God's promise to give the whole earth to Abraham and his descendants was based not on his obedience to God's law, but on a right relationship with God that comes by faith. If God's promise is only for those* who obey the law, then faith is not necessary and the promise is pointless. For the law always brings punishment on those who try to obey it. [The only way to avoid breaking the law is to have no law to break!] So the promise is received by faith. It is given as a free gift. And we are all certain to receive it, whether or not we live according to the law of Moses, if we have faith like Abraham's. For Abraham is the father of all who believe. That is what the Scriptures mean when God told him, I have made you the father of many nations. This happened because Abraham believed in the God who brings the dead back to life and who creates new things out of nothing* [NLT].

Jesus tells us, *Ye are my friends if ye do whatever I command you.*[18] We each have a unique calling on our lives. It was deposited within us as we were formed in the womb, as were all the gifts to implement such a calling, that we may fulfill our Godly destiny. Romans 11:29 tells us it will not be rescinded.

We are to abide in the same calling in which we were called [1Cor 7:20]. God has given each of us a free will, so this calling is an invitation, a bidding to yield to God's will for our lives. The anointing for our lives is found in the call on our life. Everything we need to function in the anointing is found in this calling; clarity, discernment, power, vision. grace. Stay within the borders of your calling and the anointing is there for you; wisdom - fire for God, etc. And God's Holy Spirit is the power to enable.

HE IS FAITHFUL WHO CALLS US.
This is your inheritance.

Your calling is birthed in God for a specific purpose. Your anointing is in your calling. It will stir you up to fulfill your calling. Like anointings will stir you up and this confirms your calling and will cause you to love what you do. But nobody does your calling like you.

What Adam did was a legal transaction, and it must be countered by another legal transaction. Adam was an earthborn man. The law demanded another earthborn man had to enter litigation; had to pay the penalty to the full extent of the law of sin and death.

I thank God Jesus fulfilled His calling. ♥

Since our Creator planned that man should have this dominion, He had to take it back legally. And He did just that, because He became a man [Heb 2.16-17; especially Phil 2.5-8].

All authority [all power of rulership] in heaven
and on earth has been given unto me.

Then He tells us to go in His name and in His authority.[19] We have been given power of attorney to do the works of the Kingdom of God, in Jesus name [Lk 10.19]. We were born and born-again to walk in the will of God. Our earnest prayer should be as Mary spoke,

Behold the [servant] of the Lord.
Be it done unto me according to thy word.

Walking in the Spirit humbly submitted to God, walking in the light because He is the light, living by faith, being led by the Spirit because we are the sons of God; we shall come before our King of kings and Lord of lords and see Him enthroned in all His glory. **This is our inheritance.**

It is a comfort to know that God has provided all the wisdom and knowledge we need to fulfill His will here on the earth. He gave us a graphic example in living color of how to serve God and do His will. He will not pull any surprises out of His hat, there at the judgment throne. The perfect Son of God came to show us how to be a son of God. He fulfilled His destiny. He lived it out every day of His life, and showed us that it works. Then He gave us the ability to follow Him....→

> Grace is the ability to do what God has called us to do.

He humbled Himself before His Father, and yielded to His will. If we are to fulfill our destiny, all we have to do is see how Jesus did it. God has given us the tools; faith, grace, hope, His love, His compassion for our blunders, forgiveness and renewal, and restoration. And so much more that we may not even be aware of. So read the bottom line of Jesus' success with the Father:

I am able to do nothing from Myself [independently, of my own accord, but only as I am taught by God and as I get His orders]. Even as I hear, I judge {I decide as I am bidden to decide. As the voice comes to me, so I give a decision], and My judgement is right. [just, righteousness], because I do not seek or consult My own will. [I have no desire to do what is pleasing to Myself, My own aim, My own purpose] but only the will and pleasure of the Father Who sent Me. [John 5:30 Amplified Bible]

Remember John 10, we will know His voice;
and with His wisdom we are able to make wise decisions.
Setting our immigrants aside -
There Will One Day Be
A Foreign Invasion - a Welcome Invasion
Of God's Glory to Cover the Earth.

The will of God is all I need
And to His call I will ever heed
His glory is what He shares with me
My faith is that He cares for me
His love sets my heart on fire
He will always be my one desire
God wrapped me in His love and grace
One day I'll see Him face to face
I've been stamped and sealed,
I belong to Him
Cause He has set me free from sin
With Glory He has covered me
In Christ I will always be
I am His true inheritance.

And thou hast made us unto our God
kings and priests,
and we shall
reign on the earth.[20]
And it shall come to pass that all flesh
shall come to worship before me,
saith the Lord.[21]

♫ Cover Me Lord with Your Fatherhood,
Cover Me over with Righteousness,
Heal Me Now in the Depths of My Soul,
♫ and Cover Me over with Love

♥

STUDY GUIDE

1. How important do you think obedience to God really is? 1Sam 15:22-23.
2. Listen to what the very Son of God said.
   > *I came down from heaven, not to do my own will but the will of him that sent me.*
3. Do you know what God's will is for you? Have you asked Him to reveal what your calling is, that you may walk in it and receive the anointing to fulfill your destiny in Christ?
4. Read what instructions Jesus left with us just before He returned to the Father in Jn 14:15-27, and see the awesome reward.

PRAYER: Only by Your strength can I fulfill Your will - only by Your grace. So Lord, I present myself a living sacrifice, holy and acceptable to You. [Romans 12]

SCRIPTURES

1. 1Jn 3:2
2. 1Jn 4:16-17
3. Ep 2:6
4. Ph 3:9-14
5. Is 6:1
6. Nu 16
7. Je 33:3
8. Ps 103:7
9. Mt 5:6
10. Jn 17:3
11. Mt 3:11-12
12. 1Pe 1:16
13. He 12:28-29
14. Rev 21:7
15. He 10:19-22 [Ampl]
17. Jn 1:14
18. Jn 15:14
19. Mt 28:18
20. Re 5:10
21. Is 66:23

HALLELUJAH
OUR GOD REIGNS

THE PERFECT LAW OF LIBERTY

In August 2010-
Because the prince of Persia [from Daniel] was on my mind, I asked the Lord 'what spirit did You assign to America when it was founded'? He told me...The Spirit of Liberty.

'Because the Jews were being kicked out of Spain', and many other countries, He was opening a safe place for them, a new America, and for the many who would come because of religious persecution. The Spirit of Liberty covered the United States - but after some time - a libertine spirit [no restraint] has compromised us. They say 'we can do as we please...we don't need God'.

I remembered what was happening at the same time... Spain was kicking the Jews out of their country; and they were desperately trying to get out. They were buying all the available ships, so Columbus wound up with 3 decrepit ones. Columbus was looking for ships to sail to the West Indies, when he actually discovered America. I do believe that God purposefully led Columbus to exactly where he was supposed to go].

In April, 2012- During the time of intensive worship at church, God showed me the Spirit of Liberty being given again - He said, *"The Spirit of Liberty will once again cover this nation. It will begin as I cover the Churches"*. I had a sense God was speaking of the Churches that would "Say what the Father is saying And do what the Father is doing". That's what Jesus did. Can we do any less? [All these meanings are taken from Strong's Concordance].

THERE ARE TWO KEYS TO LIVING
IN THE PERFECT LAW OF LIBERTY.

#1 KEY. OBEDIENCE TO HIS WORD.
James 1:22-25 *But he who looks into the perfect law of liberty and continues in it, and is not a forgetful hearer but a doer of the work, this one will be blessed in what he does.*
#2 KEY. LOVE FULFILLS THE ROYAL LAW [OF LIBERTY].
James 2:8-13 *If you fulfill the royal law according to the Scripture, you shall love your neighbor as yourself, you do well;*

ROYAL: from a foundation of ruling power to walk in this liberty.

James 2:9-13. *But if you show partiality, you commit sin, and are convicted by the law as transgressors. So speak and so do as those who will be judged by the law of liberty. For judgment is without mercy to the one who has shown no mercy.*

MERCY TRIUMPHS OVER JUDGMENT.
Gal 5:13-14 *For you, brethren, have been called to liberty; only do not use liberty as an opportunity for the flesh, but through love serve one another. For all the law is fulfilled in one word, even in this: "You shall love your neighbor as yourself."*

2 Cor 3:17 *Now the Lord is that Spirit; and where the Spirit of the Lord is, there is liberty.*
Rom 8:2 *For the law of the Spirit of life in Christ Jesus has made me free from the spirit of death.*

Where do we get the power and grace to live and walk in the Perfect Law of Liberty? Only from the Spirit of God. But we must choose to yield our own agendas and prefer this higher calling.

Rom 13:10 *Love does no harm to a neighbor; therefore love is the fulfillment of the law.*
Col 3:14-15 *But above all these things put on love, which is the bond of perfection.*
Gal 5:1 *Stand fast therefore in the liberty by which Christ has made us free, and do not be entangled again with a yoke of bondage.*
Bondage to what? God has set us free from having to function out of our old nature; to the way the "Old Man" lived.

LIBERTY - WHAT IS IT REALLY? WHAT DOES IT MEAN?
Unrestrained, legitimate freedom. Exempt from obligation or liability, deliver, make free. No longer obligated to follow our sin nature. There are several different meanings to the word "Liberty".
Rom 8:21-22 *Because the creation itself also will be delivered from the bondage of corruption into the glorious liberty of the children of God.* LEGITIMATE FREEDOM

Gal 5.13 *Stand fast therefore in the liberty by which Christ has made us free, and do not be entangled again with a yoke of bondage.*
LEGITIMATE FREEDOM again

1 Cor 8:9-10 *But beware lest somehow this liberty of yours become a stumbling block to those who are weak.*
SENSE OF ABILITY, PRIVILEGE, COMPETENCY, TO MASTER [Get good at it; but Who are we to trust in it, on Whom can we depend?]

James 1:25 *But he who looks into the perfect law of liberty and continues in it...*
LEGITIMATE FREEDOM and again?
James 2.12 *We will be judged by the law of liberty.* Are we willing to allow others to live in their legitimate freedom or do we judge them? REMEMBER *Mercy triumphs over judgment.*
LEGITIMATE FREEDOM [Oh Yes]
2 Cor 3:17 *Now the Lord is that Spirit; and where the Spirit of the Lord is, there is liberty.*
Again...LEGITIMATE FREEDOM How many time must He say this before we will begin to live so free from the ties that have bound us to the world of darkness and come live in His Kingdom of Light.

1 Peter 2:15-17 *For this is the will of God, that by doing good you may put to silence the ignorance of foolish men — as free, yet not using liberty as a cloak for vice, but as bond servants of God.*
TO REPAIR OR ADJUST [your nature]
    Is this liberty to do as you please or...
1 Cor 8.9 *Take heed lest by any means this liberty of yours become a stumbling block to them that are weak.*
PRIVILEGE [with humility]

Luke 4.18 Jesus came to set at liberty them that are bruised. [Bruised: to crush, to break, crack, shatter, lacerate... A wounded soul].
FORGIVENESS, REMISSION, FREEDOM, DELIVERANCE, SEPARATION, COMPLETENESS.
Isaiah 61 "*The Spirit of the Lord is upon me, because The Lord has anointed me to preach good tidings unto the meek; he has sent me to bind up the brokenhearted, to proclaim*

liberty to the captives, and open the prison to those who are bound".
TO MOVE RAPIDLY TO FREEDOM,
SPONTANEITY OF OUTFLOW.

NOW - PERFECTION - WHAT IS IT REALLY?
The Hebrew and Greek meanings of the word "perfection" include "uprightness, having neither spot nor blemish, being totally obedient." It means to finish what has been started, to make a complete performance. John Wesley called this concept of perfection "constant obedience". [grace!!!!]

The word 'Perfect' is noted 6 times in James.
42 times in the N.T. Over 100 times in the Bible.

Did you get what 'perfect' means. It is - complete, full maturity.

And 'liberty' is noted 27 times in the Bible ❤

Just remember that to gain perfection is a process. Watch an apple reach perfection on its "home tree". It starts out as a blossom. Then it passes through stages before it is an apple in the true sense of the word. This is us. We begin to blossom when Jesus comes into our life. Every day, as we allow the Sunshine to penetrate our heart we are changed from glory to glory.

All it means is 'grow up'.

2 Sam 22:31 *As for God, His way is perfect;*
2 Sam 22:33 *God is my strength and power, and He makes my way perfect.*
INTEGRITY & TRUTH
1 Kings 8:61 *Let your heart therefore be perfect with the Lord our God, to walk in his statutes, and to keep his commandments,*
SAFE, COMPLETE, FRIENDLY
Heb 6:1 *Therefore, leaving the discussion of the elementary principles of Christ, let us go on to perfection,*
COMPLETED, CONSUMMATED

Heb 7:19 *For the law made nothing perfect; on the other hand, there is the bringing in of a better hope, through which we draw near to God.*
TO ACCOMPLISH
Heb 13:21 *Our Lord Jesus...Make you perfect in every good work to do his will, working in you that which is well pleasing in his sight, through Jesus Christ; to whom be glory for ever and ever. Amen.*
COMPLETE THOROUGHLY

1 Peter 5:10-11 *But may the God of all grace, who called us to His eternal glory by Christ Jesus, after you have suffered a while, perfect, establish, strengthen, and settle you. To Him be the glory and the dominion forever and ever. Amen.*
COMPLETE THOROUGHLY His goal for us, He'll finish it.

1 John 4:17 *Herein is our love made perfect, that we may have boldness in the day of judgment: because as he is, so are we in this world.*
MENTAL, MORAL CHARACTER

1 John 4:19 *There is no fear in love; but perfect love casts out fear: because fear hath torment. He that fears is not made perfect in love. We love him, because he first loved us....I am persuaded that He is able to keep that which I have committed to Him against th at day.*
COMPLETION, FINISHED   [1Timothy 1]

Acts 24.22 Perfect knowledge of that way. The straightest answer you can get, knowledge of the Kingdom of God.
PRECISE, MORE EXACTLY
Heb 6.1 *"Let us go on to perfection".*
COMPLETION
"If God will permit".
LIBERTY, LICENSE, GIVEN DIRECTION.

He will never let us get lost.
"I will never leave you nor forsake you." Jesus Said it Was Finished. The Law of Sin and Death Has No More Power over Us. Are We Convinced That the Blood of Jesus Has Really Set Us Free to Walk in His Glory and Light; In His Perfect Law of Liberty?

Or Do We Have to Earn It?
No - It was paid for - by the precious
Blood of our Redeemer, Jesus Christ.
He alone can save us. There is no one else.
And He doesn't need help from any one else.

SO WHERE DO WE GO FROM HERE?
THE CHOICE IS ALWAYS OURS.

Col 3:12-17   *"Therefore, as the elect of God, holy and beloved, put on tender mercies, kindness, humility, meekness, longsuffering; bearing with one another, and forgiving one another, if anyone has a complaint against another; even as Christ forgave you, so you also must do. But above all these things put on love, which is the bond of perfection. And let the peace of God rule in your hearts, to which also you were called in one body; and be thankful. Let the word of Christ dwell in you richly in all wisdom, teaching and admonishing one another in psalms and hymns and spiritual songs, singing with grace in your hearts to the Lord. And whatever you do in word or deed, do all in the name of the Lord Jesus, giving thanks to God the Father through Him".*

2 Cor 10:7   Do you look at things according to the outward appearance?

2 Cor 10:3-5   *For though we walk in the flesh, we do not war according to the flesh. For the weapons of our warfare are not carnal but mighty in God for pulling down strongholds.*

Now we may walk in the Perfect Law of
Liberty because Christ has set us free.
The Perfect Law of Liberty

My All, My All - That's my call
To follow Your path
Just as You ask
To be like You That's my desire
That You would set my heart on fire
I say yes - yes to all Your will
That even my soul
Would have its fill   ❤

WHAT OF THE CRUCIFIXION

Our God is so wonderful and good to us. Many throughout history have shared their dreams and visions the Lord has given; revealing His nature and His works among men. I too had a dream; this one of the cross.

In this dream of many years ago, I was sitting behind the crossbar which held fast those arms that once hugged a leper. I was more fascinated with what I saw, than the fact I was present; for God opened to me what Jesus was looking at as He hung there dying for the sin of the world.

At His feet were the Roman soldiers gambling for the garment they would not divide. Besides fulfilling Scripture, it was Hebrew custom to rend the clothes as a sign of mourning. These soldiers were not Hebrew, nor mourning Jesus' death.

And there were the women - and John. Farther back were the chief priests, scribes and elders; then the scoffers, the mockers, the mob; jeering and shaking the fist of victory over this divinely obstinate conqueror of hearts. Far enough away as not to call attention, was Peter and the other disciples, for fear they too would be hauled to the cross.

Peter little knew at that time, his life would end there also, but in total victory - hung upside down on his own cross. Because Peter would die to his own life now to follow after Christ, this future cross could hold no terror.

We are all mostly familiar with the scene on Golgotha, the place of the skull. But now through what some call the corridors of time there was much more to be seen. The mist and darkness were lifted but for a moment as it revealed what the King of Glory was beholding.

There amid explosions and violence were the vehicles of future wars and murder; cruel and sadistic, vicious acts of torture. The rebellion, the abandonment of responsibilities to family and mankind. The pain and loneliness, the wounded spirit of those for whom no one seemingly cared.

In the heart of God for all eternity has been the goal and fulfillment of the purpose for creation. Our Lord Jesus has had His eye on His glorious Bride. One brought forth and made in His image, brought through horrendous trials and difficulties out into victory.

John the Revelator accompanied our exalted Bridegroom through the midst of His Church, seeking and searching for overcomers. These will rule and reign with Him.

These will share His throne.[32] The bride of Adam was the graphic illustration of the Bride of Christ. Eve - made pure and holy, covered with His glorious light, walking in majestic innocence and love. As He was forming her of a portion taken from Adam's side, there came forth an indescribable gleam in His eye as He saw into the distant future, His own Bride.

Now here on the cross, the work would be finished. It was time. Out of His side would come the endowment for His beloved.

By the Water and the Blood would the ransom be paid.
Hebrews 12:2 tells us,
Who for the joy that was set before him, endured the cross.

As He and I searched the horizon there appeared a pinpoint of light, and at the same time, there in the corner of His eye was caught a tiny flicker of joy that she would soon be His! This was the very central purpose of our creation; to bring forth the Bride of Christ. The purpose of our redemption was to heal and restore -
in order to make this possible.

To him that overcomes will I grant to sit with me in my throne, even as I also overcame, and am set down with my Father in His throne. [Revelation 3:21]

What a magnificent inheritance is in store for God's people. The love He has for us is beyond our understanding at this time - but soon we will know. The angels were amazed at creation - they saw the glory covering the man. They were amazed that the man cast off that covering to seek his own way. They were amazed at Jesus - to see the glory covered by flesh. They were amazed at Pentecost to see again the flesh covered by the glory...

The glory in and around earthen vessels.

Oh what love the Father has for His own. Let us be glad and rejoice, and give honor to him; for the marriage of the Lamb is come, and his wife hath made herself ready. And to her was granted that she should be arrayed in fine linen, clean and white, for the fine linen is the righteousness of saints. blessed are they who are called to the marriage supper of the Lamb.[33]

And the Spirit and the bride say come.
And let him that hears say come.[34]

♥

That we may have the richest measure of the divine presence and become a body wholly filled and flooded with God Himself. [35]

When Jesus died on the cross His side was opened and the Spirit of the Bride was sent forth into the earth - to beckon all who would receive the invitation; the consummation of our union with our glorious Bridegroom

STUDY GUIDE

1. Why was man originally formed in the image of his Creator?
2. If any think they can blame Adam or Eve for man's troubles, please consider and evaluate those times of rebellion to authority that may be listed to your own account.
3. But God has made a way. Man has been reconciled with God by the Blood of Jesus. Ephesians chapter 2 tells the story of what God has set before us. Which portion do you need to ask your Father about?
4. We cannot change our image into His. What are some of the ways God accomplishes His purposes in us?
5. As God deals with our flesh, 1John 1:9 can be implemented time and again as the Word of God brings forth His objective. Pray the Scriptures and remind God of His Word. No, He hasn't forgotten - we are in essence, agreeing with Him that He alone is our answer. He loves you.
6. And the God of peace will soon crush satan under your feet [Romans 16:20].
7. What shall I render to the Lord for all his benefits toward me?   Read Psalm 116.
8. Can anyone see Christ in us? We may be the only Bible some people ever read. Has our hope of glory spilled out on anyone else lately?

Maranatha - *Come, Lord Jesus!*

♥

No law against the fruit of love
No law that says we can't
No law that binds our heart from it
So take it, it can be ours
It's ours if we search for it
It's ours if we dare
It's ours cause He says it is
No rhyme or reason to declare
Because...
His Blood was shed for our healing
The cross brings an end to all strife
Jesus took captivity captive
Bound in His love, set free by His truth
Brought into His grace and His life

Father God Is a Second Chance to Have a Dad,
When Many of Us Were Ripped Off.
My Abba Father.

♥

SCRIPTURES

1. Ge 2:18-24 [Amp]
2. Ro 5:5-11
3. Ro 8:29
5. Ma 3:17
6. Col.2.9
7. Jn 17:21-2
8. 1Co 6:17
9. 2Co 3:18
10. Ep 3:19
11. 1Pe 1:15-16
12. Heb 12:5-15
13. Ro 11:25
14. 1Co 13:12
15. Co 1:27
16. Jn 17:22
17. 1Co 15:49
18. Am 7:7-8
19. 1Co 6:2-3
20. Ph 2:13-15
21. 1Ti 1:16
22. Jn 17:14-15 [Amp]
23. Ga 5:22
24. Ro 8:18
25. 2Co 4:17
26. Mt 11:6
27. 2Co 4:7
28. Co 1:27
29. Ep 3:19
30. Jn 14:17&23
31. 1Ki 6:7
32. Re 5:10
33. Re 19:7-9
34. Re 22:17
35. Ep 3:19b [Amp]

You Were So Aware of Me
Of a Heart
E're Longed to Love
You Knew How Lonely
and Lost I Was
You Chose Me from
Millions of 'Are Nots'
You Put Your Arms
Around Me,
You Made Me Your Child
You Took Me as a Baby,
And Brought Me Day by Day
You Gave Me
the Courage to Pursue
Those Things
I Never Knew Existed.
Now I Know
It Is You I Am Seeking
Cause You Are All
I Will Ever Want
or Need - And
You Will Always
Be Enough.

Thank You Lord For loving me
For letting us hang You
On that tree
The Blood You shed
Broke every curse
But separated from You -
That was worse
So thank You Lord
For the Blood You shed
It brought us back
Cause that's what You said
So long ago in Covenant
Your promise came to pass
You revealed the Father,
We're home at last.

♥

AND NOW THE MOST HORRENDOUS OFFENSE IN ALL OF CREATION - IS ABOUT TO COME ON STAGE.

We were in a prison of our own making, of which we were not even aware. The decree of death had already been pronounced, et Jesus was prepared to pay the price, to buy us back. He confronted death, and walked away!

How the heart of God must have yearned over the man whom He had created for Himself. As that fallen nature became more depraved down through the centuries, God's love was held captive in the heavenlies, awaiting the appointed time.

The most colossal injustice was about to be played out in dramatic sequence that could not be halted. The performers took their place and the greatest offense of all time disclosed its grisly itinerary.

The rocks indeed cried out. The heavens wept. The sun hid its glory. Even death trembled. All creation watched in horror as their Master was made repugnant before their eyes. The angels desired to look into how their Creator would ever reverse man's unwitting fury to annihilate his race. Perhaps it was the angels that inquired,

What is man, that you are mindful of him?
Through the ages they watched as the plan of man's redemption painstakingly unfolded. Was their angelic understanding opened to them as one after another prophecy was announced and inscribed? Each utterance pointed in the same direction but surely they knew not how the plan would be engineered [1Pet 1:12].

Was it known they would soon be spectator to unfathomable love expressed through ignominious sacrifice; yet bound from releasing their glorious King as the vicious mob jeered at His pain.

Could they have wept in frustration at not being able to come to His rescue, though they numbered ten thousands of ten thousands? For unmentioned time the host of heaven was fine tuned to obedience. Here and now they hung suspended; searching for one tiny sign that would give permission. They watched and waited - yet no signal came forth. Their ears only heard the Savior's words of unrelenting love and forgiveness.

No attention paid to His own desperate state, only to the great wall of separation between the Father and the man created in His image. Their eyes only saw the lifeless body being tenderly lowered from the cross into the bowels of the earth.

Were they caught in malaise as they looked down at the tomb? Perhaps in shock, they wondered-how can this be? They had worshiped and served Him, for how long; eons of eons? - since they first gazed upon their Creator and caught the glory and light of His majesty.

How can a spirit being that will never die, understand death; especially the death of One they knew to be their Creator. This is quite impossible! This cannot be! Perhaps they above all could bond with the Eleven as they also would try to deal with their shattered vision. The men would express physically to that which those glorious spirits were responding.

Perhaps here in this place was created a communion of men and angels that birthed the care and compassion these messengers from the heavenlies now have for their charges. These holy ones could not bring themselves to leave their post and so became privy to the most spectacular display of God's glory on the earth as His presence attended resurrection morning.

The Prince of Life victoriously arose to conquer death,

hell and the grave - for us, His inheritance -

The seed went into the ground and bear much fruit. His grave became the cradle of a new race of man. This life giving Spirit, sent forth His life into our dead spirit. For what purpose?

The tombstone set in place, The agony was over
The cross was now laid bare, A shroud was His cover
Death now had a grip, He thought he'd won the prize
He mastered over this man Of Whom he'd spread the lies
The people He loved so much Had ranted, raved at Him
They wanted Him be gone So they could hide their sin
So finished, here we are His grave had hid His love
Until the greatest glory Was sent from above
The Spirit entered there And life began to stir
The stone was rolled away The New Man came to birth
Now the glory resides in us His chosen, His bride
Eternity will have its way - Forever at His side.

As I live by the Father...even so shall [you] live by me.
He that is joined unto the Lord is one spirit ♥

JESUS - THE SON OF GOD - SON OF MAN

John the Apostle was on the Isle of Patmos. He saw Jesus, the embodiment of the entire promise of God in the plan of our redemption. He is revealing to John - His Character, His Personality, His Nature. From Revelation 1, John walked with our glorious Savior, Lord and King, as High Priest and Bridegroom, searching for the overcomer, His priest/bride, in the midst of His church body (Revelation 2&3). Jesus will speak to His people through these seven churches. Many are called but who will answer?

Jesus Is Searching for His Bride.

1. Seven golden lampstands - the Church, His body. He is the Head. AND HE IS STANDING IN HER MIDST.

2. He is the Alpha and Omega - the First and the Last - the Beginning and the End. There is no other God but Him. HE HAS THE FINAL WORD FOR ALL WHO EVER LIVED.

3. In His Holiness and Glory; Hair white as snow [wisdom], Eyes a flame of fire [discernment], Feet like bronze burned in a furnace [judgment]. He has come to judge His people. HE IS SEARCHING FOR HIS BRIDE!

4. His voice is like many waters; He speaks to every kindred and tongue - people and nation. NO ONE IS OVERLOOKED.

5. Seven Stars - He will judge especially, the leadership. Are they in that position FOR HIS GLORY - OR FOR THEIRS.

6. With His manifested power, He sends forth His two-edged sword to divide soul and spirit. HIS WORD - HIS TRUTH!

7. And He holds the keys of hell and death!

SEVEN JUDGMENTS - GOD'S PERFECT WILL.
Fear not; I am the first and the last; I am he that lives, and was dead; and, behold, I am alive for evermore, Amen, and have the keys of hell and death. And, behold, I come quickly, and my reward is with me, to give every man according as his work shall be. Blessing, and glory, and wisdom, and

thanksgiving, and honor, and power, and might, be unto our God forever and ever. Amen.

Now He who is alive forevermore, is searching for His bride throughout all His churches [Revelation 1-3].
Seven Golden Lampstands - His Church - Has the Attention Of the One Who Died for Her.
Captain victorious - The First and The Last
There is no other God.
He stands in golden attire
With predestination,
His heart on fire
Eager to gather His saints to Himself
He calls to His valiant ones
These are ready to hear His voice
These are ready to rejoice
As they join with Him in one accord
Forever with their Lord.

Worthy is He Who shed His Blood, to redeem His creation, that we might worship Him only. Chapter five reveals the Lion of Judah opening the scrolls to release God's final will. And He only is worthy to take the scroll and begin to shake the world of its very foundation. His purpose...to set His people free from bondage, free to worship the One True God; to raise up a body of believers and lovers of God who would separate themselves from worldly things, to desire eternal life with their Savior,

Gone from Visitation to Habitation.

John 3:16-17 *For God so loved the world that He gave His only begotten Son, that whoever believes in Him should not perish but have everlasting life. For God did not send His Son into the world to condemn the world, but that the world through Him might be saved.*

John 3:18-21 *"There is no judgment against anyone who believes in him. But anyone who does not believe in him has already been judged for not believing in God's one and only Son. And the judgment is based on this fact: God's light came into the world, but people loved the darkness more than the light, for their actions were evil. All who do evil hate the light and refuse to go near it for fear their sins will be exposed. But those who do what is right come to the light so others can see that they are doing what God wants.*
New Living Translation.

His glory contained, at last was shed forth
In resurrection power
No longer hidden from our eyes
His life is now ours
Covered by His presence With peace at last
Overshadowed by His glory, our past is past
He became our sin, the bounty was paid
We became His love, My God - what a trade!
Light for darkness, life for death
The grave holds no terror
For our last breath
Our glory contained In resurrection power
His presence will be there In our last hour.

Then from the throne there came a voice saying,
Praise our God, all you servants of His,
you who reverence Him, Both small and great!
After that I heard what sounded
like the shout of a vast throng,
Like the boom of many pounding waves,
And like the roar of terrific and mighty peals of thunder,
Exclaiming hallelujah, praise the Lord!
For now the Lord our God
The Omnipotent, the all ruler, reigns.
Let us rejoice and shout for joy, exulting and triumphant!
Let us celebrate and ascribe to Him glory and honor,
For the marriage of the lamb at last has come,
And His bride has prepared herself.
She has been permitted to dress in fine radiant linen,
Dazzling and white - for the fine linen is -
signifies- represents the righteousness,
the upright, just and godly living,
Deeds and conduct, and right standing with God,
Of the saints, God's holy people.
The angel said to me, Write this down;
Blessed, happy, to be envied, are those who are
summoned, Invited, called,
to the marriage supper of the Lamb
[Revelation 19: 5-9 Amplified]

♥

THE BRIDE OF CHRIST

Now the Lord God said, It is not good [sufficient, satisfactory] that the man should be alone; I will make him a helper meet [adaptable, complimentary] for him. And the Lord God caused a deep sleep to fall upon Adam; and while he slept, he took one of his ribs or a part of his side and closed up the place with flesh. And he built up and made a woman and brought her to the man.

And Adam said, [WOW!] *This creature is now bone of my bones and flesh of my flesh. She shall be called woman because she was taken out of man. They shall become united and cleave and shall become one flesh.[1] For you have made him lack a little from God and have crowned him with glory and honor.*

[Interlinear Bible, Hebrew and Greek with literal translation. Hendrickson Publishers, Peabody, Mass]

In Psalm eight David was given a revelation of what really transpired on that magnificent Day of Creation as he declares, [The Amplified Bible translates v 4,]

What is man that you are mindful of him, and the son of [earthborn] man that you care for him.
Yet you have made him a little lower than God.
Some translations use the words,
lower than the angels.

Strong's Concordance Hebrew reference is #430 - Elohim, the same Word used for God in Genesis 2:7. In verse four the son of man is not referring to Jesus. The King James Version says in verse four,

What is man, that you visit him?

meaning to visit with friendly or hostile intent. Jesus came that the world through Him might be saved. That sounds pretty friendly. Psalm 144:3 repeats the question,

Lord, what is man that you take knowledge of him?

The word knowledge means, by seeing, recognition, observation, care, acquainted with and finally, have understanding. This sounds like intimate relationship with the man that God is mindful of;

Or the son of man
that thou makest account of him.

The word account means, to plait as to braid hair together, intertwine, or to penetrate, to weave. Man has been entwined with his Creator by the cords of love. God is ever mindful of us for - **We Are the Focus of His Attention.**

The Bride of Christ and the Marriage of the Lamb are not just concepts that sound good or religious. The whole matter was birthed in the heart of God before the creation of anything. Then He formed the man and the woman and brought them together in the physical realm to be the shadow of God's reality. See Ephesians 5:3-4 for the comparison.

As God created Adam all that mankind was going to encompass, Adam was made male and female. God did not create Eve. He took her out of Adam. Woman is simply saying, man with a womb, capable of pro-creation, giving birth to the seed.

When all the animals passed by Adam and he named them, he saw they each had their mate. Adam looked for a being comparable to his likeness and image. He did not find one because his counterpart was hidden within himself. God put him into a deep sleep and the woman was brought forth from his rib. They had the same DNA! But the breathe of God created a new soul [Gen 2:7].

When God created the first Adam everything of human attributes was deposited in him, so that God could bring forth and separate the male and female and yet there was provided a way to make them one again.

Man was created in God's image but then we were separated from Him; our image greatly marred by sin. He made the way for us to be reconciled again with Him. Jesus is called the,

First born among many brethren.[3]

Just as Adam was the first born of his race - Jesus is the first one of a kind - out from among the dead, the *New Creation*. This does not mean He has ceased to be God. He was God in eternity past. He Will Always Be God.

Col 2:9-10 *For in Him dwells all the fullness of the Godhead bodily; and you are complete in Him, who is the head of all principality and power.*

He became man when He was born on the Earth; Fully God and Fully Man. He became this New Creation/New Man, for us to follow Him into God's plan for us; to be born-again of His incorruptible seed [1Peter 1:23]. This New Man

Is renewed in knowledge after the image of him that created him.

This NEW MAN never before in existence came forth from the grave. Our birth into this new creation comes forth only through death. When we choose to die to our old life to live in Christ, we become a new creation. The fulness of what God has for us is still shrouded in mystery for He tells us,

*Eye hath not seen, nor ear heard,
neither have entered into the heart of man,
the things which God hath
prepared for them that love him.*

The fire of His love sees our pain. His care for us is beyond comprehension. His eyes see our heart so hungry for love, and for truth. The compassion that flows from Him to us, enables us to receive more of Him; with the God kind of faith of which absolutely nothing is impossible; a servant's heart, and faithfulness, all of which will be measured in the crucible of suffering. [1P 5:10; Rom 8:17-18;1Pet 4:12-19].

We have been brought into the Kingdom to pursue holiness. Paul bared his soul to the Philippians in Chapter three - everything his life counted for - was dung. Whatever it took - Paul would pursue holiness. Well it takes death, the denial of all our so-called rights. Die to being noticed; die to being thanked; die to being included. Die to our exalted self for the prize of the high calling of God in Christ Jesus.

This Kingdom will not tolerate hypocrisy or compromise. The heart is what God is interested in. His goodness leads us to repentance. Actually Jesus was the first to break the sound barrier. He invaded our world and spoke His love to our hearts; His unconditional love.

We are so precious to Him, we are His treasure; His purpose for all of creation. He wants to saturate us in His love that His love may pour forth through us unto others.

The Christian life is often compared to the eagle. No other creature soars as high nor has the acute vision of an eagle. Their eyes are protected from the glaring sun by a membrane. They do not blink. They become single minded to scan the earth for the slightest unnatural movement.

The eagle saint may ascend as high in the spirit realm as he chooses to die to self. We may come into His glorious presence protected by the blood. We can see clearly the future that God has in store for us.

*He hath begotten us again unto a living hope by the
resurrection of Jesus Christ from the dead, to an
inheritance incorruptible*

and undefiled, reserved in heaven for you, who are kept by the power of God through faith unto salvation ready to be revealed in the last time...Whom having not seen, ye love; in whom, though now ye see him not, yet believing, ye rejoice with joy unspeakable and full of glory .

We may become single minded as we press in with all our heart toward the prize of the high calling of God in Christ Jesus. Search me oh God...Let Your feet of bronze stand in judgment of my enemies; the evil intents and purposes of my heart, and cleanse me.[4] Satan has tried to drag the Bride through the mud, but Jesus has come with His bulldozer and plowed up that field. He found every pearl for we are of great price to Him and - He was willing to pay,

And they shall be mine in the day when I make up my jewels.[5]

During a wonderful worship service as the Body of Christ was being anointed with His manifest presence, I saw a vault being opened and within, it contained a most beautiful radiant jewel that shone with a heavenly green light. The color green depicts new life.

The vision faded and I began to ask the Lord where is the wall that holds this wonderful compartment. I saw the Lord standing before me, and as He opened up a place in Himself, He revealed this vault again, containing this beautiful jewel, and He said -

This is my Bride, I carry her within me wherever I go.

Green Is the Color of Life, and the Bride Derives Her Life From Our Glorious Savior, Lord and Bridegroom,

Jesus Christ. *His body, the fulness of Him that fills all in all.*

Paul's letter to the Ephesians declares that we were chosen in Christ before the foundation of the world. At least a dozen times throughout this letter, the Holy Spirit proclaims that all things were done in Christ - and then...

GOD PUT US IN CHRIST.

Chapter 1:3,7,11,13 are example verses to find a small portion of our inheritance.

All the fullness of the Godhead bodily dwells in Christ - and we are complete in Him.[6]

The results of this uniting and cleaving to Christ is,

As thou Father art in me, and I in thee, that they also may be one in us, I in them and thou in me.[7]

2Cor 1:21 By the power of the Holy Spirit we are established in Christ. I can't help but wonder how or to what degree was Adam's relationship with his wife fragmented. Since healthy relationships are built on trust - did satan also begin his destruction of the family unit there in the garden. It didn't take very long for his seduction to erode the meaning of,
Two shall become one,
for just six generations from Adam, Lamech took two wives. Discord and disunity is now planted between man and wife. Now comes confusion of roles and identity crises.

Genesis 4 gives a brief outline of Lamech, the seed of Cain. Rebellion to this [two shall become one] led to strife and murder. Lamech gloated to his wives, I fixed his wagon,
I have slain a man for wounding me,
and a young man for hurting me.
The pride of life ran rampant. Researching the word wounding, we find the word split. Did Lamech murder a man for trying to break up this unnatural triangle. Was it satan's way of first - mocking the Trinity - and then also perverting the true meaning of marriage and God's purposes for the family? And more important the union between God and man.

We become one with the Lord when we are joined to Him by the Spirit [1Co 6:17]. But we have to know it is a 'one on One' relationship. Each of us have to make that choice.

I don't believe satan understood at that time, any of what were God's intentions. Now, he knows what the Bible says maybe more than we do, and he uses it. He knows it but He doesn't understand it. He perverts the Word and its meaning and purposes. I do believe he often shotguns situations to bring about his vicious plans to deceive, confuse and destroy. But there was no written Word at this time of creation.

His rage at being thrown out of heaven could now be dumped on the man. Jealous of the relationship between the man and God, his fury would have no equal. His own rebellion bore no fruit, but now he would get even. His attack was on the credibility of God's word. He called God a liar.
You shall not surely die.
Satan had no idea what it meant to die. After all, he and the other angels had been alive for how long - there was no time frame. He'd never seen anything or anyone die. Death had never before been manifested in the universe. How could he know? He does not have the attributes of God!

So when he told Eve she would not surely die, he was not deliberately lying. But in the end, he had no idea what would really happen - that man's spirit would die! Man's spirit was a gift to the man, to enable fellowship with God Who is Spirit.

Satan's intention was for this wonderfully made, pure and innocent man and woman to serve him and not Elohim. But more profound - they would serve him with the holiness and covering of glory they were manifesting in the garden.

After all, that's what satan was after - the glory! So his purpose was to bring God's credibility under suspicion; bring Adam to distrust God. In distrust there is unbelief. In unbelief there is no relationship with God.

Satan did not realize the glory would depart in the presence of sin; that a wall of spiritual darkness would come between God and His creation! He thought God would leave and he and Adam would turn the garden into his Kingdom. Wasn't he surprised when they were all thrown out?

Wasn't he surprised as he watched down through the centuries, our merciful Creator working to restore the relationship which had been broken. He was furious when he saw the glory again being poured out on the man, on the day of Pentecost. He realized he had lost his chance.

No more separation by the veil of flesh -

now again, one with our Eternal

loving Creator God [1Jn 3:2].

For man though, it was a chance renewed. Poured out on His people was restoration. A taste of glory - but the promise of fullness. The marriage supper of the Lamb - perfect union with our Bridegroom.

God has a plan. The world revolves around God's plan. He has not fit His plan into the world. His Church, His Bride is the focus of His plan. Everything in the universe revolves around this one point of being. Praise God! *Without me You can do nothing.* God please help us to understand how much we really need You.

The universe was created specifically to house God's people; to prove them, to test their loyalty. To grow them up and bring them to Himself. It is God's design to bring His people into unity with Himself through the principle of absolute obedience and submission to a one Spirit judgment. Again, two shall become one.

He that is joined to the Lord is one spirit.[8]

God has purposely designed for each interlude of our journey through the earth, there would be an authority over us. He knows our rebel heart. For my own sake I have found safety under this umbrella. If we can't submit to another of whom we can see, how can we truly submit to One we can't see. Only through submission to Christ and conforming to His will can we all with,

Unveiled face beholding as in a mirror the glory of the Lord [and] are changed [transfigured, metamorphosis] into the same image from glory to glory, even as by the Spirit of the Lord.[9]

We may try to exclaim His majesty but we can never explain it. Our flesh cannot understand nor experience the awesome depths of His love any more than these eyes can see His true Glory. That's why we need a new body, able to function in the presence of His holiness, and receive our full inheritance.[10]

We become a mirror reflecting the character and attributes of Christ. We are commanded to '*Be holy, for He is holy*'.[11] It is the presence of the Holy Spirit within that brings us to holiness, as we yield ourselves to be brought under the Spirit's correction.[12] We accomplish nothing of ourselves [Jn 15.5] How does this happen? Character is not received by osmosis. It is developed by continuing to choose God's ways over our own. Integrity is developed by walking in truth.

The Word 'beholding' means to mirror oneself, to see reflected the same image. God is waiting for the fullness of the Gentiles.[13] Now part of that can mean when the last, 'Yes Lord, be my Savior', is echoed through the universe. But Scripture is ever revealing the deeper and wider range of His glorious purposes for His beloved creation.

We will know Him as we are known.[14] Taking into consideration Psalm 139 and the intimate knowledge the Creator has of us - will we have this knowledge of Him? Who knows?

Perhaps in a million years!

The union of man with God that is disclosed in John 17 is of awesome relevance. Verse 22 says,

The glory you have given me, I have given them.

He has given us the glory of a son of God, such as He carried while on the earth. Because of this union with Jesus, we may behold His glory. Then Jesus asks His Father to return the glory He had with the Father before the world was, to which He has now returned. We will soon be joined completely with Him in the end.

Then, we shall see Him no longer in part but in fullness; no longer in reflection or vision but then face to face. Glory Himself dwells in us.[15] The anointed One anoints His Bride that she may bear His glory.[16] *We shall bear the image of the heavenly.*[17] To bear means wear as clothing. Image means likeness, representation. Because of 1Co 2:9-16 we are enabled more and more to perceive the gravity of comparing spiritual things with spiritual.

When God sees His government - His absolute rule and reign - being lived out on the earth in His people; when God sees His holiness, righteousness, and glory being reflected back to Him; then He will have the plumb line;[18] His standard with which to compare and judge the world.

Thy Kingdom come, thy will be done,
on earth as it is in heaven.

When we come to realize the true import of this, perhaps we will understand more what Paul tells us,

Don't you know the saints will judge the world - and angels?

Isaiah 28:17 tells us,

I will make justice the measuring line,
and righteousness the plummet.

Rev 21 tells us of whom He speaks; the Bride of Christ, adorned with love, righteousness, holiness and purity.

He is waiting for His Bride -
without spot or wrinkle.

God is a righteous Judge. The world will be judged by His standards. There will not be one fraction of a point of criticism before His judgment Throne. God is a present help in time of need.

He has provided the atonement, that we need not stand before Him guilty. The Blood of His cross has washed us clean and made us worthy to receive His forgiveness and unconditional love.

Acts 3:21 tells us Jesus is waiting in the heavenlies until the times of restoration [or completion]. Jeremiah 35 gives us an Old Testament example of the standard of obedience that permits God to bring judgment on disobedience [the plumb line]. What else should He expect from a people that will judge the world and angels!

Zechariah 4 also speaks of a plummet, which basically means to divide and separate. Zechariah 2 declares,

For I, saith the Lord, will be unto [My people]
a wall of fire round about, and will be
the glory in the midst of it.

Are we ready to separate ourselves from Babylon [the world] totally and finally so that God can be that wall of fire around us. God declares, Zech 2.7 *Deliver thyself, O Zion.*
Phil 2.13 *It is God who works in you, both to will and to do of His good pleasure. Do all things without murmurings and disputings. That ye may be blameless and harmless sons of God, without rebuke in the midst of a crooked and perverse nation, among whom ye shine as lights in the world.*[20]

    We are made a pattern for others to follow. But He doesn't leave us to our own devices, we have none of any Kingdom value. He is our pattern.[21] God has separated His people from the world, yet He has left us here for His glory. Jesus actually disengages His people from the world and sanctifies them - [set apart for God] - and deposits them into the Father's hand.

> *They do not belong to the world*
> *as I am not of the world.*
> *I do not ask that you will take them*
> *out of the world, but that you will keep*
> *and protect them from the evil one,*
> *consecrate and separate them for yourself.*[22]

His secret place, His pavilion, His inner chamber is total surrender to His majesty, Lord and King, Jesus Messiah. [Ps 27:5; 31:20].

    Romans 12 gives a good example of the life style He's looking for in His holy nation. He's not coming back for a puny wimp. God is looking for His victorious warrior. One that is yielded, obedient, meek. For a good example, look unto Jesus. He was strength under control and clothed with humility.

    The fruit of the Spirit,[23] portrays the nature of God, for God is love. The attributes of the fruit listed in Galatians 5 begins with love. The characteristics of love are found in 1Co 13.

> *If I have not love I am as [clanging] brass,*

and nothing else will ever seem to come together for us.

    God cannot lie. He is faithful. He is just. His character and integrity are being established within us to become an inherent part of who we are as we allow the Holy Spirit to lead and guide and direct us.

    The Bride of Christ will have every aspect of her personality and character passed through death and resurrection. The personality and character - the image of Christ - must pervade her very being. The wife of the Lamb must be metamorphosed until she is perfect as He is perfect and it all begins with love.

When God made Adam a help-meet for him, He made a counterpart. Eve, formed of the substance of Adam - bone of his bone, flesh of his flesh.

Will Jesus settle for anything less?

The Bride of Christ will be His counterpart. Roget's Thesaurus #21 has counterpart as copy, facsimile, as a result of imitation [2Co 3:18].

Beholding as in a mirror the glory of the Lord,
we are changed into the same image
from glory to glory

These take residence in our nature out of which pours excellency in life and in ministry. To manifest excellence is to glorify God. Holiness will line us up with God's will and bring us into unity with Him. It is a natural product of yielding self - for Him.

God has chosen to reveal and make available to us, His character and nature; that we may yield ourselves to be changed into His image.................➜

Then we shall see Him as He is,
because we will be like Him.

| Holiness - Integrity - Character. |

Genesis 2:24 tells us the man shall cleave [or be joined] to his wife and they shall be one flesh. This is a type and shadow of what God has in store for those of whom love Him. Again we see in 1Co 6:17,

He who is joined unto the Lord is one spirit.

This is such a profound statement!

The context of Eph 5:22-32, captures the relationship between the physical facsimile and the spiritual proto-type. When the Creator brought forth a Bride for Adam He foresaw His own Bride; Eve - the type and shadow of the Bride of Christ.

As Eve was formed from the very substance of Adam, so the Bride of Christ is being created and formed of the very substance [DNA] and image, character and personality, holiness and purity of that glorious Lord and Savior; our heavenly Bridegroom.

Her destiny is bound up with Jesus, Her Bridegroom.

The Bride is formed from the continuous process of death and resurrection; dying to self, alive to Christ. We decrease, He increases. And He does it all. We can't accomplish this. We yield - He works it out. Death to self happens when we cry out for the presence of God.

Our direction will be walking in the Spirit, obedience to God, the baptism of fire, purging, chastening and correction. Living in His supernatural grace and favor gives you the ability to be who God has ordained you to be, and to do what God has anointed you to do. His Bride will have:
1. No personal plans or goals.
2. No hidden agendas.
3. No will except His be done.
4. No independent decisions.
5. No focus except Him.

Perhaps this means not having any wants of our own, so that we may experience what God has for us.
Ephesians 1:2 brings us grace and peace from our Father and our Lord Jesus. Peace would be hard to come by unless you were walking in grace and how can you receive grace except by faith. So these three must be linked together. See Eph 2:8. Salvation means to be made whole. Oh, how we all need that.

He's growing us up guys! He's fixin' us. Our nuts and bolts have been scattered, but He's kept track of us since we were in the womb. Rest in your faith and peace will come.

God is trying to bring us into His rest. Some of us are kicking and screaming every step of the way, because it means we have to give Him the steering wheel of our life.

The Lord is my Shepherd I shall not want.
Anxiety and frustration rules over not getting what and when we want it [Ph 2:13].

The sufferings of this present time are not worthy
to be compared with the glory
which shall be revealed in us. [24]

Maybe it's when one has lost everything that one learns of values and priorities, and can place things in their proper perspective. To have Jesus is to have everything. All things are lawful, but not all things are expedient [1Co 6:12].

For our light affliction, which is but for a moment, works
for us a far more exceeding and eternal weight of glory. [25]

Of the letters to the seven churches in Revelation, Ephesians is the first. The only charge against this church is that, *You have abandoned the love you had at first. You have deserted Me, your first love.* We get too busy with doing - and forget

We love Him [only] because He first loved us.
Too often we put His love for us on the 'back burner' as we become engrossed with doing for the Kingdom. Would that be like a woman wanting the security a marital relationship has to offer, but having no desire for intimacy. Can this be translated over into Kingdom language?

Even the world knows you are what you eat.
Except ye eat the flesh of the Son of Man,
and drink his blood, ye have no life in you.
It is Spirit and it is life. Jesus declares,
There are some of you that believe not...
Blessed is he who is not offended by me.[26]

Resurrection life comes only after the cross. The Bride is being formed for the purpose of being the fullness of Christ. John 17:22 declares,

And the glory which You gave me, I have given them.
[the glory of being a son]. Remember the glory that was given Adam, that clothed him so he wouldn't be naked? It was lifted because of sin, and given back to us because of Jesus. God told Isaiah [46:13],[New Living Translation]

I am ready to save Jerusalem and give Israel my glory
But in 42:8 He says,

My glory I will not give to another,
neither my praise to graven images.

This is not a contradiction. The context tells us this is speaking of another spirit entity, speaking of their idolatry. He would not allow other gods before Him, [Ex 20:3] to share in offerings and sacrifices. But He was especially jealous when they expended their God-given glory on those demon idols.

Anything that takes our attention away from God may become an idol, even if it is negative and destructive. God is to be, not only our focus, but the very center of our being. All our life emanating from Him as He leads and guides us every day.

So, invite Jesus to live in the very center of your being.

Because our God - Yes! He is a jealous God. We are not another! We are being formed of His substance. We have His Spirit. Yet we must remember the highest place of glory is kneeling at the feet of our Lord and Master. Our submission to God brings us into His presence [James 5:8]. And do as Jesus did when He received glory - He passed it on to His Father [Jn 17:1].

Hebrews 11 speaks of those men of faith who knew there was something more worthy in the future. Something already prepared for them. *They desired a better country, for he hath prepared for them a city.*
The Greek word for country has its root in the word Father. There was deposited in our humanity the hunger to discover from where we came, and to whom we belong. Our eternal home is not so much a place - but a person!

OUR GLORIOUS CREATOR GOD!

Proverbs 8 is a portion of Manna we need as a steady diet. The nourishment of the Bread of Life is given to the hungry ones who will devour each parcel; to hunger and thirst after more. God speaks in these verses, of wisdom that will be sought after and preferred rather than silver and gold. Then He tells us:

I [Wisdom] lead in the way of righteousness, in the midst of the paths of judgments, that I may cause those who love me to inherit substance; and I will fill their treasuries.

Right in the middle of trials and testing God moves in our life in power, to heal and restore.

Every other use in the Bible, of this word 'substance', relates to wealth or prosperity. This one is different. The Word used in this verse means: entity - to exist; to be who we are! It goes back to the root word: to breathe, to be, in the sense of existence.

The word substance is used here to refer to the existing materials a person is made of; the very life and fabric of their being. If we allow God's wisdom to lead us [in prudence, discretion, consideration, and understanding] on the path He has chosen for us; and seek His righteousness; then we will find the treasures of our identity in Him;

For we have this treasure in earthen vessels.[27]
We will inherit the fullness of, Christ in you,
the hope of glory.[28]
And we will, know the love of Christ
which passes knowledge,
that ye might be filled
with all the fullness of God.[29]

❤

Your love comes down
Like a fire in my soul
It draws me into Your presence
Your will be done against my will
To consume my all in all
Cause I surrender to Your holiness
To yield and be still
So speak to me, Father
Hold me close to Your heart
Your greatness unimagined
I want to be a part
Never would I walk alone
I need Your love and grace
To know You as You know me
Together - forever In Your embrace.

♥

OUR HOUSE - OUR HOME

Christ loves His Church [His people] so much *that He will,*
Sanctify and cleanse it with the washing of water
by the word; that he might present it to himself
a glorious church, not having spot, or wrinkle,
or any such thing; but that it should be holy
and without blemish.
The mighty God of creation has drawn up His plans. He has chosen to build His dwelling place within His people.[30] The architecture must be perfect with no spot or wrinkle; cleansed unto holiness; sound unto righteousness; yet no hammering will be heard in this temple.

Neither hammer nor axe nor any tool of iron
heard in the house, while it is in building.[31]
We have a building of God, a house not made with hands,
eternal in the heavens, desiring to be clothed upon
with our house which is from heaven,
if so be that, being clothed, we shall not be found naked.
We are built upon the foundation
of the apostles and prophets,
Jesus Christ himself being the chief corner stone,
in whom all the building fitly framed together
grows into a holy temple in the Lord;

*in whom you also are built together
for a habitation of God through the Spirit* [2Cor 5.3]

Each brick will be laid with tears of repentance. Each column is held fast on the humble knees of prayer. The ceiling will be constructed of praise and worship, and the foundation is built upon no less than the Rock, the Redeemer, our glorious Lord and King,
JESUS MESSIAH - Our Chief Cornerstone.
But remember,
*For it is God who works in you both to will
and to do of his good pleasure [Ph 2:13]
Trust in the Lord with all your heart and lean not
unto your own understanding.
In all your ways acknowledge him
and he will direct your paths* [Pr 3:5-6].

❤❤❤

HAVE YOU DONE THIS RESEARCH?

Because Jesus Gave His Life, He Gave His Body of Believers To Inherit the Kingdom of God; and Here Is a Small Portion of That Inheritance.

So, in order to partake of what this offers, here is an advance notice of what we can expect from the God Who loves us.

He Has Given Us His Word.

Does the Word of God inspire or incarnate? The key to the Word of God is being able to relate personally to what it is saying. A relationship between you and the written Word brings about relationship between you and the Living Word. There is understanding the Word with your whole being - drawn into experiencing what it is saying. God wants relationship, Spirit to spirit. Relationship with others and with the Word comes through the body and soul. We hear it and believe it and then live in it.

Relationship is experienced in your soul and body. It becomes flesh in you. That's how the Word of God ministers to the believer. And that's why studying and meditating on the Word, is of utmost importance; to hear what God is saying. I will let the Word of God speak for itself...

Thy kingdom come, thy will be done...
Do You Just Want it - or Do You Intend to Have It?
He Has Brought Us out of Darkness into His Glorious Light.

God planned from before the foundation of the world, that we would have an inheritance in Him. This is one of the mysteries of the kingdom. We have become so attached to our God through the Blood sacrifice of His only begotten Son Jesus, that He is our inheritance [we are his heirs], and nothing can take this away from those of whom have given their life to Jesus. See Rom 8.17; Gal 3.29; Titus 3.7; James 2.5 We are heirs of the Kingdom of God.

Ezekiel 44:28 *It shall be, in regard to their inheritance, that I [God] am their inheritance.*

When we have come out from the unclean things and have separated ourselves unto God, He has received us;
2 Cor 6. 17-18 *And I will be a Father to you, and you shall be my sons and daughters, says the Lord Almighty.*
Genesis 15:7 *Then He said to him, I am the LORD, who brought you out of Ur of the Chaldeans, to give you this land to inherit it.*
Ur, a flame - the Chaldeans were astrologers. So God brought Abram out of the fire of idolatry, and gave him an inheritance in the Kingdom of God. He has also brought us out of the fire that was consuming our soul; and into His glorious presence Col 1.14 *in whom we have redemption through His blood, the forgiveness of sins.*

Genesis 28:4 And gave us the blessing of Abraham.
Hebrews 4.17- He promised Abram the nations of those who *would believe through the righteousness of faith.*

Against hope we believe in hope - We are not weak in faith We stagger not at the promises of God.

We are strong in faith - And we are fully persuaded. All this favor has been imputed to us because,

We believe on Him Who raised up Jesus our Lord, from the dead.

Psalm 37:9-11 *But those who wait on the LORD, They shall inherit the earth... the meek shall inherit the earth, And shall delight themselves in the abundance of peace.*
Proverbs 8:20-21 *I traverse the way of righteousness, In the midst of the paths of justice, That I may cause those who love me to inherit wealth, That I may fill their treasuries.*

Matthew 25:34-35 *Then the King will say to those on is right hand, 'Come, you blessed of My Father, inherit the Kingdom prepared for you from the foundation of the world:*

Acts 20:32-33 *So now, brethren, I commend you to God and to the word of His grace, which is able to build you up and give you an inheritance among all those who are sanctified.*

Ephesians 1:11-14 *In Him also we have obtained an inheritance, being predestined according to the purpose of Him who works all things according to the counsel of His will, that we who first trusted in Christ should be to the praise of His glory. In Him you also trusted, after you heard the word of truth, the gospel of your salvation; in whom also, having believed, you were sealed with the Holy Spirit of promise, who is the guarantee of our inheritance until the redemption of the purchased possession, to the praise of His glory.*

Ephesians 1:17-18 *That the God of our Lord Jesus Christ, the Father of glory, may give to you the spirit of wisdom and revelation in the knowledge of Him, the eyes of your understanding being enlightened; that you may know what is the hope of His calling, what are the riches of the glory of His inheritance in the saints,*

Col 1:12-13 *Giving thanks to the Father who has qualified us to be partakers of the inheritance of the saints in the light.*

Hebrews 9:15 *And for this reason He is the Mediator of the new Covenant, by means of death, for the redemption of the transgressions under the first Covenant, that those who are called may receive the promise of the eternal inheritance.*

DO YOU BELIEVE ALL THIS?
THEN HONOR HIM AS YOUR LORD GOD AND SAVIOR.

His love is faithful, His love is pure
Of this one thing we can be sure
His love is steadfast, His love is alive
His love will always be my guide
How great is our God,
How great is our God.

❤

WORDS OF KNOWLEDGE

One night in 1985, the Lord got me up out of bed to write these things down. As fast as I was able to write, He gave me the paraphrased version of the Word, the Scripture reference, and then on to the next verse.

All told, I found I had written down 88 verses of God's wonderful plan for our lives as told in story form, one verse after another compiled in little more than one hour.

It had to be the Lord, for even though most of these Scriptures were familiar to me, I could never have produced all these, in this sequence, in less than several days, with many hours of research in the process. Since I know it was Spirit led, I am including these in the book.

FOR THOSE WHO ARE IN CHRIST
He that is joined to the Lord is one spirit. [1]
Your body is the temple of the Holy Spirit who is in you. [2]
If any man be in Christ, he is a new creation, old things are passed away, all things become new. [3]
For in Christ Jesus neither circumcision availeth anything nor uncircumcision but a new creation. [4]
So put on the new man which after God is created in righteousness and true holiness. [5]
Put off the old man - put on the new man that is renewed in knowledge. [6]
And we have the mind of Christ. [7]
For God reveals the things of the Spirit to us by His Spirit. [8]
The same Spirit that raised Jesus from the dead dwells in you. [9]

If you are led by the Spirit of God you are a son of God. [10]
If a son of God then an heir of God, joint heirs with Christ. [11]
Because we are called to His purposes. [12]
It is God who works in you to will and to do of His good pleasure. [13]
For Jesus is the author and finisher of our faith. [14]
And He makes us perfect in every good work to be pleasing in His sight. [15]
Therefore let us continually offer the sacrifice of praise unto our God. [16]
For He hath said, I will never leave thee, nor forsake thee. [17]

For the Kingdom of God is righteousness, peace and joy in the Holy Spirit. [18]
The Kingdom of God is not in word, but power. [19]
It is the Father's good pleasure to give you the Kingdom. [20]
That we might be conformed to the image of His Son. [21]
For He is the first born. [22]
From the dead so that He might have the pre-eminence. [23]
That he might bring many sons to glory. [24]
That He might bring us to God. [25]

For in Him dwells all the fullness of the Godhead bodily. [26]
And we are complete in Him. [27]
The Father gives us the Spirit of wisdom and revelation in the knowledge of Him - the eyes of our understanding being enlightened. [28]
To understand the power working in us. [29]
The resurrection power that raised Christ from the dead. [30]
For once we were dead in trespasses and sins. [31]
And He's made us alive together with Jesus and forgave all our trespasses. [32]
Buried with Him in baptism and risen with Him, through faith that all things are possible with God. [33]
If we confess our sins He is faithful and just to forgive us our sins and to cleanse us from all unrighteousness. [34]

For He that knew no sin became sin for us, that we might become the righteousness of God in Christ. [35]
And we are the temple of the living God, as God hath said, I will dwell in them and walk in them and I will be their God and they shall be my people. [36]
Be ye holy in all manner of life, Be ye holy for I am holy. [37]
For we shall bear the image of the heavenly. [38]
We continue to reflect the glory of the Lord as we are changed into His image more and more every day by the Spirit of the Lord living in us. [39]
As the inward man is renewed day by day. [40]
We shall all be changed. [41]
With Christ in us the hope of glory. [42]
For we are a chosen generation, a royal priesthood, a holy nation, a people of His own. [43]
He has made us kings and priests unto God. [44]
So that we can show forth the praises of Him who called us out of darkness into His marvelous light. [45]

Through the shed Blood of Jesus, we have our consciences purged from dead works to serve the living God. [46]
Because we are all as an unclean thing and all our righteousness is as filthy rags. [47]
But even when we were dead in our sin. [48]
God who is rich in mercy, with His great love for us. [49]
Made us alive in Christ. [50]
And by His grace saves us through faith. [51]
It is His gift to us. [52]
Not of works lest any man should boast. [53]

He gathers us into His household. [54]
And frames us together with each other, to be His holy temple. [55] To be the habitation of God through the Spirit. [56]
That we might be strengthened with might by His Spirit in the inner man. [57]
That is renewed day by day. [58]
That we might experience the love of Christ which is so far beyond anything we might imagine - and be filled with all the fullness of God. [59]
And be partakers:
  Of Christ [60]
  Of the heavenly calling [61]
  Of grace [62]
  Of the Holy Spirit [63]
  Of the gospel [64]
  Of His holiness [65]
  Of His inheritance [66]
  Of His promise in Christ [67]
  And of Christ's suffering [68]

For the glory of the Son has been given to us. [69]
As Jesus prayed for us who were yet to believe on Him. [70]
So that we might be made perfect in one. [71]
So the world might believe and know that Jesus has come. [72]
And all that come to Jesus He will in no wise cast out. [73]
That we might have everlasting life and be raised on that last day. [74]
And all that receive Him, He gives the power to become children of God. [75]
That we might eat of the tree of life which is in the midst of the paradise of God. [76]
We will not be hurt of the second death which is the lake of fire. [77]

*And we will eat of the hidden manna and receive
a new name in Christ.*[78]
We will walk with Jesus in robes of righteousness, for He has made us worthy.[79]
We will be pillars in the temple of God and never leave His presence.[80]
We will sit on the throne with Jesus.[81]
And receive power to rule over the nations.[82]
And we will reign on the earth with Him.[83]
And have the privilege, with billions of other ransomed believers, of falling down before our precious Lord and Savior and worshiping Him for eternity.[84]

*And the King shall say unto us, Come ye blessed of My Father,
Inherit the Kingdom prepared for you from the foundation of the world.*[85]
And we shall inherit all things, and He will be our God and we shall be His sons.[86]

*For me to live is Christ
and to die is gain.*[87]
*Surely I come quickly. Amen.
Even so, come, Lord Jesus.*[88]

♥♥♥

THOSE IN CHRIST SCRIPTURES.

1. 1Co 6:17	2. 1Co 6:19	3. 2Co 5:17
4. Ga 6:15	5. Ep 4:24	6. Co 3:10
7. 1Co 2:16	8. 1Co 2:1	9. Ro 8:11
10. Ro 8:14	11. Ro 8:17	12. Ro 8:18
13. Ph 2:13	14. He 12:2	15. He 13:21
16. He 13:15	17. He 13:5	18. Ro 14:17
19. 1Co 4:20	20. Lk 12:32	21. Ro 8:29
22. Co 1:15	23. Co 1:18	24. He 2:10
25. 1Pe. 3:18	26. Co 2:9	27. Co 2:10
28. Ep 1:17	29. Ep 1:19	30. Ep 1:20
31. Ep 2:1	32. Co 2:13	33. Co 2:12
34. 1Jn 1:9	35. 2Co 5:21	36. 2Co 6:16
37. 1Pe 1:15	38. 1Co 15:49	39. 2Co 3:18
40. 2Co 4:16	41. Co 15:51	42. Co 1:27
43. 1Pe 2:9	44. Re 1:6	45. 1Pe 2:9
46. He 9:14	47. Is 64:6	48. Ep 2:5
49. Ep 2:4	50. Ep 2:5	51. Ep 2:8
52. Ep 2:8	53. Ep 2:9	54. Ep 2:19
55. Ep 2:21	56. Ep 2:22	57. Ep 3:16
58. 1Co 4:16	59. Ep 3:19	60. He 3:14
61. He 3:1	62. Ph 1:7	63. He 6:4
64. 1Co 9:23	65. He 12:10	66. Co 1:12
67. Ep 3:6	68. 1Pe 4:13	69. Jn 17:22
70. Jn 17:20	71. Jn 17:23	72. Jn 17:21
73. Jn 6:37	74. Jn 6:40	75. Jn 1:12
76. Re 2:7	77. Re 20:6,14	78. Re 2:17; 3:4
79. Re 2.17; 3.12	80. Re 3:12	81. Re 3:21
82. Re 2:26	83. Re 5:4	84. Re 5:13
85. Mt 25:34	86. Re 21:7	87. Ph 1:21
88. Re 22:20		

Dedicated to the Bride;
The mirror image of our gracious Lord
Who shed His blood
That she might come forth pure and holy
Clothed in righteousness, grace and love
To rule and reign at His side forever.

❤❤❤

EPILOGUE

It is so wonderful to know we may continue to grow into wholeness. We in this world have not hardly scratched the surface of God's abounding wisdom and knowledge. Even on into eternity. A billion years from now, we will still be expanding our understanding of universal truths.

Our knowledge of the Kingdom begins at zero on our born-again day, because we cannot know God through an unredeemed, unrenewed mind. So this world is sustained by God as a school of training for His children. Where else would we get the hard lessons that make us come out like pure gold.

In order to purify gold the metal is heated to extremely high degrees and the impurities come to the top. They are then scooped off. The metal is again subjected to impossibly hot temperatures, and again the impurities come to the top to be scooped off; much like boiling jelly is prepared.

The temperature must not be allowed to get too high or the gold will be destroyed. Too low a temperature and the purpose will not be accomplished. So the process must be watched over carefully by One who is totally involved [1Pet 1:7].

That the trial of your faith, being much more precious
than of gold that perishes, though it be tried by fire,
might be found unto praise and honor and glory
at the appearing of Jesus Christ

Who is more involved with our lives than the God Who created us for Himself? And so the process continues until the quality control officer declares it finished. We all know Who is our Quality Control Officer; The Holy Spirit. He lives within us and knows us better than we know ourselves. Only He can say when our fiery trial is over. [James 1:12]

Blessed is the man that endureth temptation;
for when he is tried, he shall receive the crown of life,
which the Lord hath promised to them that love him

We may murmur and complain but He may turn the heat up. If we've learned to escape from a situation in which God wants to teach us something, well, God may allow another just like it. Hebrews 12 tells us God so loves His sons that He must chastise us. We must be corrected, or we are not His sons [Mal 3:16-17]. He is committed to bringing His sons to glory.

If we fight to maintain our status quo, all we are doing is showing our stubbornness and rebellion and we will be robbed of our inheritance. The terrible truth is exposed in Isaiah 50:11 in the Amplified Bible.

Behold, all you [enemies of your own selves]
who attempt to kindle your own fires
[and work out your own plans of salvation]...

Paul said he had not already attained what God had for him, but he kept going for it. Our life in Christ is an ongoing experience. We have not arrived simply because we have gained a victory. There are many facets to our personality and character. We cannot see ourselves until the Spirit of God reveals to us the true motivations of our heart in any given matter.

Our soul is desperately in need of healing and restoration.

The key is to continuously acknowledge the Lordship of Jesus and praise Him and thank Him for what He is doing. He will, day by day, correct our course and lead us toward that mark of the high calling of God. It is His work in us. He must do it so that no flesh can glory in His presence. We can only yield and obey [Ph 2.13].

Going back to the verses in the first pages of this book, there is a Scripture many of us have not tested. 2 Chronicles 20:15&17 tells us, *We shall not need to fight this battle. Stand still and see the salvation of the Lord with you. The battle is not yours but God's.* Psalms 35:10 tells us,

All my bones shall say, Lord, Who is like You,
delivering the poor from him who is too strong for him.
Yes, the poor and needy, from him who plunders him.

There are many battles we fight, and the Word and the Spirit teach us spiritual warfare. Ephesians 6 gives us our armor to protect us against the evil one. Yet, even though we constantly bombard it with our faith and the Word, too many of us have a battle in our lives that never seems to budge. Perhaps God is saying, will you still serve Me and stay faithful even through this hard thing.

The Scripture in 2 Chronicles is a great example of the principle of the protection of God that is woven throughout God's Word. Please read the whole chapter. Find out what He did for Jehoshaphat.

His name means 'God is judge'.

Our Lord of Armies will judge between His heir of the Kingdom, and the enemy that He defeated on the cross.

When we find the enemy is too strong for us, we have a God that will fight our battle. *He will bring perfect peace to whose mind is stayed on Him* and [Ps 35:10

Understand that we have to lean ourselves wholly on Him, come into a place of rest; and believe that His incredible love can bring us through to victory. The part we can do - we do. The part we can't do - God does. This was new to me when the Lord first put these thoughts in my heart.

I'd been battling an infirmity from surgery for many years, but no matter what I did or said, I was constantly brought down by fear and defeat. I was constantly battling with my mind, where the enemy spoke lies about God's goodness and love.

Sure He can heal, but not you!

As the years went by, the symptoms got worse and the evidence became harder and harder to overcome. But God! In His mercy and grace, His Word pierced my heart, and my back was healed. [See Isaiah 53:5, it all happened at the same time!!]

Now, every time I become aware of the symptoms, I also become aware that my Jesus is the Lord of Hosts - The Lord of armies. The battle is not mine, but the Lord's. He is delivering me from him who is too strong for me. Reading Romans 16:20, we can see God's final solution.

The God of peace will soon crush satan under our feet. Faith in God. Faith in Who He is; the tangible reality of casting our cares on Him because He cares for us. The strength that comes from knowing God. These are the things in which we must grow.

He also showed me that when we allow our problems - whatever they are; sickness, emotional need, financial, whatever - to outweigh our faith in Him, cause frustration, worry, anxiety, etc, to bow us down under the weight of it, giving it too much attention, making this thing an idol and are, in reality, bowing down to worship. However perverted it may sound, it is reality.

We have such an inadequate revelation of the holiness and glory and majesty of the God Who created us for His pleasure. Only as we go deeper into trust and faith in the Way, the Truth, and the Life, will we receive further revelation of *the exceeding greatness of His power toward us who believe*. We are familiar with Scriptures that convey the message of being led by the Spirit. Let's see how this one applies to our life.

He leads me beside still waters.
This word lead means, to run with a sparkle. It also means, to flow, hence to conduct [and by inference] to protect, sustain, carry, feed, guide, lead [gently on]. Reading John 17:15 we find that Jesus prayed to the Father in our behalf that,
I do not ask that You take them out of the world, but that You will keep and protect them from the evil one.
To nurture and protect His children is our Father's plan.
In His love and compassion He gives us joy
as we follow Him.
The Father reached down through Jesus to reconcile us to Him; to call His prodigal son home. He clothes us with His righteousness, shods our feet with the Good News, and feeds us with his glorious manna, the Word of Life.

Through our life on the earth God will train us to be victorious overcomers, that we may fully partake of His divine nature; that we may live in His presence for eternity, to be at home with His glory and holiness. If we've been wounded and torn by our earthly father - God wants to heal and restore. Satan has perverted the family system so that many of us would not look to a Father God, and never even want to be reconciled, because our concept of Father has been despoiled and pillaged.

I'm here to take a stand against that deception. My Father God has shown me His true colors. He is faithful and just, compassionate and kind - ever reaching out to me to draw me to His side. He's never too busy to listen and help me in my troubles. His grace and mercy are constant companions as they follow me on the path God has chosen for me. Of all the songs written until now; this following one continues to bless me as no other.

♪ Great is Thy faithfulness, Oh God my Father.
There is no shadow of turning with Thee.
Thou changest not, Thy compassions they fail not.
As Thou hast been Thou forever will be.
Great is Thy faithfulness, - Great is Thy faithfulness.
Morning by morning new mercies I see.
All I have needed Thy hand hath provided.
Great is Thy faithfulness, Lord unto me. ♪
[Christian hymn written by Thomas Chisholm with the music composed by William M. Runyan - 1923].

Some of what I've shared in these writings has been

repeated several times. Faith comes by hearing over and over again until the truth gets buried in our soul and becomes a living part of us.

But never take my word or anyone else's for that matter. Check every thing you hear or read, with the Word of God. It is the only standard of righteousness. It is the only Source of Truth. Our concept of Who is God, must go through some drastic changes that,

Eph 1:17-19 *He may give us the spirit of wisdom and revelation in the knowledge of Him, to open the eyes of our understanding that we might know the hope of His calling, and what is the riches of the glory of His inheritance in the saints, and what is the exceeding greatness of His power toward us who believe.*

When we cut off the craving of our flesh, and desire only those things which are from above - then,

Christ, who is our life, shall appear,
then shall ye also appear with him in glory
And when I come before my Lord,
I want to hear Him say,
Well done, thou good and faithful servant.
Enter thou into the joy of the Lord.

But please know and be assured that all this is not accomplished overnight, in a week or even a year. We have much flesh to die to, God is patient. His goal is make us like Jesus. It's His job to do that, it's our job to say OK and yield to his work in us.

Philippians 2. 12-15, read it until you understand what it is saying.

I am now 90 years old and God is still restoring.

Thank You Jesus for 50 years with You.

Our glorious inheritance is to receive His glory! None of us can possibly imagine what that really means; but as we fellowship with God, He reveals to us His wonderful treasures [Isaiah 45:3].

There is now going forth, a move of God such as never before witnessed. Past revivals will pale in the light of God's end-time harvesting. He is coming for His Bride! Her blood has smeared the earth since the beginning of time and her Lord is about to take vengeance [Isaiah 60:1-2].

Arise, shine; for thy light is come,
and the glory of the Lord
shall be seen upon you.

This Is Our Inheritance, The Father's Good Pleasure.
So now we ask, how do we get there from here?
Having therefore, brethren,
boldness to enter into the holiest
by the Blood of Jesus, by a new and living way,
which he has consecrated for us,
through the veil, that is to say, his flesh,
and having a high priest over the house of God,
let us draw near with a true heart
in full assurance of faith...

These Verses Repeated - Cause this Really is Our Inheritance:
To enlighten all men and make plain to them what is the plan of the mystery kept hidden through the ages and concealed until now in the mind of God Who created all things...The purpose is that through the church the complicated, many sided wisdom of God in all its infinite variety and innumerable aspects might now be made known...His eternal and timeless purpose...carried into effect in the person of Christ Jesus our Lord. [That] He grant you out of the rich treasury of His glory to be strengthened and reinforced with mighty power in the inner man by the Holy Spirit, Himself indwelling your innermost being and personality. May Christ through your faith actually dwell, settle down, abide, make His home in your hearts!

May you be rooted deep in [His] love and founded securely on [His] love. That you may have the power and be strong to apprehend and grasp with all the saints, God's devoted people, the experience of that love, what is the breadth and length and height and depth of it. That you may really come to know practically, through experience for yourself, the love of Christ which far surpasses mere knowledge, without experience; that you may be filled through all your being unto all the fullness of God; and may have the richest measure of the divine Presence, and become a body wholly filled and flooded with God Himself. [Ephesians 3 Amplified Bible]

This Is Your Destiny. Do You Believe It!!
Do you receive it???

Into the throne room of Jesus
Into Your presence I come
Mercy and grace surrounds me now
As before You I humbly bow
Your wraparound love
I hug to my heart
To keep me here on earth
For the joy You have given me
Ever since my re-birth.
Into the throne room of JesusInto
Your presence I come
Mercy and grace surrounds me now
As before You I humbly bow.

❤

The legacy we leave behind
Will have the world to know
What God accomplished in our life
And the seeds we have sown
Did we learn to love
Not just our own kind
But people from another place
And bring them to mind
They have needs same as us
But the greatest of them all
Is to know the Father
To answer His call
So we can spread the Word
To touch the deepest part
As they come to know the Lord
And give Him their heart.

For our God is absolutely good
and there is no other
like Him.

❤❤❤

OTHER BOOKS BY AUTHOR: Dory Robertson..
You may order any of these books from:
doryptl7@hotmail.com

THESE ARE ALL $10.00, plus $4.00 postage
The Temple of God Restored - The Ark of Our Covenant
A Word on Wisdom and Knowledge
　　　Keys of the Kingdom
The Enemies of Our Land - A Manual for Warfare
The Love of Jesus - Journey Into Reality
Home Away From Home - We're Just Passing Through
He Never Came Back - Recovery From Divorce
Hope and the Will of God - Our Inheritance
The Gift of Life - His Hand Is Reaching out to You
Songs of My Life - Poetry and Prose
　　　From the Heart of God.
Freedom From the Spirit of Fear - The Law of Liberty
The Seven Churches of Revelation -
　　　Jesus is looking for His Bride
The Manifested Bride of Christ - Who is She?
Knowing Abba Father - Finding Our Real Father
The Tabernacle of God - Journal of Redemption
Notes From a Newborn - Memoirs of a Baby Christian
　　　Longing for Maturity.
Arbitraries - Unreasonable, Unconditional,
　　　Irrational, Incidents.
Habitation of God - We celebrate His Presence.
Transition - Renewing Old Concepts.
Who is Jesus - Reality Check
Do You Know The Word of God - Is it Truth or Fiction
Songs of Redemption - Can We Really Know?
AND
Our Inheritance - Father's Good Pleasure $15.00

　　　　　　MARANATHA - COME Lord Jesus.

❤❤❤

Made in the USA
Columbia, SC
16 February 2023